MILLER'S

GODDEN'S NEW GUIDE TO

ENGLISH PORCELAIN

MILLER'S

GODDEN'S NEW GUIDE TO

ENGLISH PORCELAIN

GEOFFREY A. GODDEN

GODDEN'S NEW GUIDE TO

ENGLISH PORCELAIN

GEOFFREY A. GODDEN

First published in Great Britain in 2004 by Miller's, an imprint of Octopus Publishing Group Ltd,2–4 Heron Quays, London, E14 4JP

Miller's is a registered trademark of Octopus Publishing Group Ltd

Senior Executive Editor: Anna Sanderson
Executive Art Editor: Rhonda Fisher
Copy Editor: Claire Musters
Editor: Catherine Emslie
Designer: Peter Gerrish
Proofreader: Clare Hacking
Indexer: Geoffrey Godden
Production: Sarah Rogers

Values should be used as a guide only, as prices vary according to geographical location and demand. US prices have been calculated at a rate of 1.5. Please note that unfortunately it is not possible for the author or Miller's Publications to provide valuations for any personal items.

ISBN 1 84000 987 X

A CIP record for this book is available from the British Library

Set in Sabon and Trade Gothic
Produced by Toppan Printing Co., (HK) Ltd.
Printed and bound in China

Jacket 107 A graceful Derby dancing group, model number 16. Typical rococo base and pale colouring. Incised number "16", three pad-marks, 19cm (7½in) high, c.1790, Godden of Worthing, (see p.92).

Half Title A very finely decorated Daniel porcelain fruit cooler or ice-pail from a large Royal service, which included three-tier cake stands, c.1825–30, formerly in the Godden collection. (see p.63)

Title Page A 19th-century Continental hard-paste porcelain copy of an 18th-century Derby soft-paste figure of Falstaff. Decorative but not period. Impressed model numbers, 22cm (83/4in) high, Godden collection.

Contents A typical well-modelled and colourful Chamberlain-Worcester poodle model – one of a pair. This and other factories produced similar animal models. Printed Royal Arms and name and address mark, 10cm (4in) long, c.1820–30, Godden of Worthing, (see p.188).

Contents

Preface

This "New" guide to English porcelain supersedes my well-received and popular *Godden's Guide to English Porcelain*, which was published in 1978 and revised in 1992.

The original book was written for our son Jonathan, then aged nine. It was intended as a simple guide written in a relaxed manner – father talking to his son. It explained the basic points about the manufacture of porcelain in the 18th century and went on to discuss the later developments in the industry. It also covered how the wares were made, how they were decorated, and why everyday old wares are often collectable.

I started writing this new version in June 2001, not for the further education of Jonathan but for his daughter, Hannah, then all of six months old! Already, Hannah was showing clear signs of becoming a great collector. She reached out for pretty things, she was inquisitive and interested in her surroundings. She liked to feel the texture and even the taste of objects as most were taken to her mouth – as if to test the type of porcelain – bone ash or a soapstone body!

In a very short time she will, hopefully, start asking questions, later she will be reaching deeper, reading books, or carrying out her own researches. I, now in my 70s, will not be around to rejoice in some of these later natural developments. Perhaps this book will serve as a primer, leading on to deeper reading or research.

I was born on 2 February 1929 while Jonathan was born on 1 August 1969 – at the time of the first human landing on the moon. Young Hannah arrived on 10 December 2000. I have spent most of my life in the Antique Trade, specializing in ceramics, but retired in December 1996 – to give more time over to research, lecturing, writing, and to my hobby, which is bowling.

In the 20 plus years since the first edition of this work was published, much new information has come to light. New, revised, attributions have been made, the story has changed to a surprising degree – as has the format of this book. Many new instructive illustrations have been added here, and there are now over 270 colour pictures.

Even with all the changes over the years the second of my original two-paragraph "Preface" is, I trust, as apt now as it was when written:

I hope to steer the reader clear of the many pitfalls that lie in the path of the collector, to cover many points not mentioned in other books on British ceramics, and to open the reader's eyes to the pleasures that await an inquisitive new collector or to broaden the interests of those who have already tasted the delights of owning and using pleasing porcelain, be it antique or modern.

I have often been told that this is various collectors' favourite book because of the helpful, personal manner in which it is written. In fact, only last week a former Chairman of the Northern Ceramic Society told me that it was the first edition of this book that started him on a happy, and continuing, hobby and interest. I have endeavoured to make this new, enlarged edition even more helpful, to the experienced as well as the new or would-be collector of English porcelains.

Good luck Hannah.

Have fun – enjoy life and, hopefully, your collecting.

Grandad Godden
Findon, West Sussex

Right One of a pair of Derby bulb pots with a central panel in the manner of George Complin, crowned crossed batons and "D" standard mark, 25cm (10in) long, *c*.1805, formerly in the Vera Browne collection, (*see* p.55).

Other books by Geoffrey A. Godden

Victorian Porcelain
Encyclopaedia of British Pottery and Porcelain Marks
An Illustrated Encyclopaedia of British Pottery
and Porcelain
The Handbook of British Pottery and Porcelain Marks
Minton Pottery and Porcelain of the First Period
Caughley and Worcester Porcelains 1775–1800
Coalport and Coalbrookdale Porcelains
The Illustrated Guide to Lowestoft Porcelains
The Illustrated Guide to Ridgway Porcelains
Jewitt's Ceramic Art of Great Britain, 1800–1900
British Porcelain, an Illustrated Guide
British Pottery, an Illustrated Guide
Godden's Guide to English Porcelain
Oriental Export Market Porcelain and its Influence on
European Wares
Godden's Guide to Mason's China and the
Ironstone Wares
Chamberlain-Worcester Porcelain, 1788–1852
Staffordshire Porcelain
English China
Lowestoft Porcelain
Ridgway Porcelain

Eighteenth Century English Porcelain – a Selection
from the Godden Reference Collection
Encyclopaedia of British Porcelain Manufacturers
Davenport China, Earthenware and Glass 1794–1887
(with T.A. Lockett)
Collecting Lustreware (with Michael Gibson)
The Concise Guide to British Pottery and Porcelain
Godden's Guide to European Porcelain
Collecting Picture Postcards
The Concise Guide to European Porcelain
Godden's Guide to Ironstone, Stone and
Granite Wares
New Handbook of British Pottery and
Porcelain Marks
New Hall Porcelains
Godden's Guide to English Blue and White Porcelain

Unfortunately, most of these titles are now out of print, but copies should be available in most major public libraries. New and many out-of-print books can however be obtained from "Reference Works", 12 Commercial Road, Swanage, Dorset BH19 1DF, United Kingdom. Tel: 01929 424423.

1
Forming a collection

When I started collecting in the 1940s, while still at school, I used my modest pocket money to purchase broken specimens of attractive 18th-century porcelain in the same way that others of my age might have spent their pocket money saving for a new bike or model train. This is, I must admit, not easy to emulate today, as even damaged pieces may command high prices. There were, then, two basic types of collector: the man or woman who purchased, as opportunity and purse permitted, anything that attracted his or her eye without any overall plan, and the studious collector who tended to specialize in order to build up a worthwhile collection showing the whole range of his or her chosen subject and its development. Both types of collecting can give a lifetime of pleasure, with the second providing the bonus of adding to our general fund of knowledge.

There is, however, today a third class of collector: the investor. This includes those who start with no great love of the subject but buy only because they seek a hedge against inflation and the lowering of the value of money and savings. I am not singling out the pound sterling here, as almost every form of modern currency seems to have suffered from the same loss of confidence, and far-seeing collectors of most nationalities seek articles of beauty and rarity in which to invest their paper currency.

In my previous books I have steered well clear of the investment angle and I have refrained from discussing price but, in seeking to give guidance now, I must offer some words on this tantalizing topic.

Investing in porcelain

Porcelains and most "collectable" articles have tended over the years to increase in value at a faster rate than inflation has eroded the value of money, and certainly their "performance" has been better than many stocks and shares. A Minton *pâte-sur-pâte* vase by Solon (*see* p.208), which I sold in the 1950s for £172, in June 1975 fetched at auction £1,750. Today's price would be very much higher, perhaps reaching as much as £10,000 ($15,000).

Nobody can guarantee that this state of affairs will continue, however. There are fashions in collecting as

well as in everything else. Besides, diamonds, pictures, coins, or porcelains do not pay interest or dividend. Any financial profit results only from the long-term capital gain. Do not expect to enter the market as a novice, buying in the wrong places at the top of the market, and show a profit at the end of the year!

You can, however, enter the market with great success if you have taken certain precautions, such as researching your subject and learning more about your speciality than the average dealer. You should also bide your time and buy with discretion, from the right sources. Also do not be afraid to take advice – or even to seek it. Leave others to follow fashion and trust your own taste, not that of others. Above all, try to form a collector's collection!

The last piece of advice may take some explaining, but it brings us back to what collecting should be about – whether we are talking about collecting purely for pleasure or for profit, or for any combination of the two. Surely there can be few, if any, collectors who have not over the years seen their collection multiply greatly in value, although this would not have been the reason why they started it. It is not all that long ago, in 1966 to be precise, since I wrote a popular little book entitled *Antique China and Glass under £5*. How times change! You would be hard pressed to keep within that limit today and this must be why the publishers allowed this little book to go out of print after a brief life.

There are collectors who seek to amass a great bulk of objects, perhaps a thousand teapots, then there are those who endeavour to form a "collector's collection" of teapots. In the latter case each item will have been chosen for its purity of design, for the beauty of its decoration, and because it helps to tell the story of the evolution of the vessel and its development in England. The changing basic shapes, styles, and sizes should be illustrated with good, perfect pots. Such a collection, of perhaps 100 teapots, will be far more valuable than those 1,000 pots gathered without thought or real interest in the subject. On the other hand there are those – Philip Miller in particular – who have formed vast collections, of over 2,000 teapots (now housed in the Castle Museum at Norwich), which could be called research collections. With such collections the aim would have been to amass as many specimens of an item as possible in order to link different shapes or patterns to the rightful factory by means of exactly matching handle forms, knobs, or similar common denominations. Here the more specimens there are available the easier the task should be. Unfortunately it often seems to become more difficult! Such a research collection can be very rewarding and may well lead to exciting discoveries and the publication of a book such as *An Anthology of British Teapots* by Philip Miller and Michael Berthoud.

If research is the main ideal you do not have to worry about condition, as a badly cracked pot will be just as helpful as a mint one. The damaged specimen can have the advantage of being very inexpensive, but the danger is that a collection of hundreds of cracked, stained, or lidless pots can become very depressing and is unlikely to increase in value, at least not as much as would ten well-chosen near mint specimens.

I have singled out teapots to make these basic points, but they can obviously be applied to all other collecting subjects. Not only in single objects, jugs, sugar-basins, animal models, figures, miniature cups and saucers, or thimbles, but also in the wares of one factory or region. Only a collector with more money than sense would buy every example of Chelsea, Worcester, or New Hall that came his or her way. Such a mass of objects would lack personality. You must use discretion, filling in gaps to show the whole picture, weeding out inferior pieces as you find (or can afford) the better specimens.

Very little has been written about "weeding out" a collection, but this can be an extremely important exercise. Just as a shrub or tree will benefit from careful pruning to improve its shape and vigour, so too will your collection. Even if your taste does not change over the years, your collection may have grown too large or become out of balance. Damaged or surplus pieces can in effect be traded-in for a superior example.

On this subject I will quote the views of the late Perceval D. Griffiths, writing in the 1930s:

No collection can ever be perfect. The collector who knows this, and has the heart to part with one possession in order to acquire another, and does so deliberately and with discrimination is still collecting, and is exercising his taste.

Mr Griffiths was writing of furniture collecting, but his views are equally sound for stamp collecting, for coins, for porcelain, or indeed for any other form of collection. A collection is, or should be, quite different from an accumulation!

The choice of what is collected often arises from a chance acquaintance: perhaps you have been given a trinket, maybe a model cat in porcelain, or you simply take a fancy to a cottage night-light holder in a shop window or museum. You may, alternatively, read a magazine article or book or, more likely today, watch a TV programme such as the *Antiques Roadshow* and see an interesting object brought in and discussed. The countless seeds of collecting are floating in the wind and they settle as fate decrees. Most find a very fertile place to grow and to give years of pleasure.

Of course, there are many limitations, those of the purse and of space being perhaps the greatest hurdles. A young school teacher should not start to collect yellow-ground Dr Wall Worcester porcelains, nor should anyone that is living in a bedsit seek to collect exhibition *tours de force*! However, just as much pleasure can be derived from collecting less expensive small objects and often the restriction of space can be a distinct advantage – if only because it forces the collector to be selective. Also, do not select a class of object that is almost impossible to find. The ideal might be to collect a line that, with a little trouble, you can find, say, 30 objects a year in your price range, so that from that number of "sightings" you could pick out perhaps ten to add to your collection.

Having chosen an object or factory, how would you expect to start collecting? The main sources of supply have always been dealers and auction sales.

Starting your collection

There are, of course, many different types of dealer and antique shop. Indeed, many establishments that boldly display the description "antiques" appear not to stock a single item over 50 years old let alone the statutory 100.* But we need not worry about this for "age in itself is not a virtue", and you can find a shop that does stock the type of object you are seeking. You will have acquired local knowledge of likely shops in your own district and if you hunt further afield there are now helpful directories (such as *Miller's Guide to Antiques Shops, Fairs & Auctions*), which should be available at bookshops and many antiques dealers. You can also study the advertisements in the various collectors' magazines to seek out people who advertise items in which you are interested. Some trade associations, such

---

* It is generally accepted that an "Antique" is at least 100 years old. But mere age does not make a bad object good!

as the British Antique Dealers Association and LAPADA (The Association of Art and Antique Dealers), publish lists of their members (*see* my chapter on General Advice, p.226, and the Bibliography on p.266 for details of these and other organizations).

A good way of discovering dealers who stock the type of article that you are seeking, who cater for your price range, or appeal to you as helpful friends, is to attend some of the several antiques fairs that are now held – and that are not only limited to cities and large centres. The organizers usually advertise their shows in the collectors' magazines and, once contact is made, they should be happy to keep you informed of future events.

Once you have found a dealer's shop do not be afraid of entering even the grandest-looking premises – many of my most exciting finds have come from such establishments. An item that is out of this world to you may be only an average specimen to a specialist and he or she could be glad to take a modest profit on cost and at the same time make a new customer. Dealers usually realize that it is in their own interest to foster new collectors. Many believe, as I did, that the best form of publicity is to give the collector a bargain as he or she will (hopefully!) always remember such a kindness and return again and again to that dealer. At the other end of the scale do not forget the "junk shops". Great finds have been made in such places – and at jumble sales and car-boot sales! Here, however, you may need to be on your guard as many fakes and reproductions exist.

Now let's look at the plentiful, small, so-called "Antiques Fairs" or "Collectors' Fairs" as they might be more correctly termed. While enjoying a country break I hopefully followed the roadside signs to an antiques fair. Having arrived and paid an entrance fee (!), I looked in vain for a single antique. Indeed, I seemed to be older than any of the exhibits! Yet just a short walk away I found a traditional antiques shop. Here, without paying any charge to enter, I found a clean, well-described stock. I made some happy purchases and was, of course, supplied with a detailed receipt. Nevertheless, while I favour such traditional buying (and selling) the shop was empty of other customers, while the "Fair" was crowded. Most of the items in the fair may not have been more than 50 years old, but they were of varied types and they gave amusement and interest to young and old alike. Hopefully those people will be great collectors of the future.

Probably the most important first step for any collector is to make friends with a knowledgeable dealer or collector who is prepared to guide and advise them and help them avoid the many traps that await the unwary, the over-confident, and, especially, the greedy! On your part you must remember that the dealer has to make a living, so do not expect, as a right, free valuations, nor credit on articles that could have been sold ten times over for cash. If you want to see the cream of a dealer's new stock, see that you pay at once and do not haggle when you both know the price is reasonable.

Buying at auction

Purchase at auction can present problems. You have only to read the conditions of sale printed in catalogues to learn that most auctioneers claim only to be an agent and therefore consequently disclaim responsibility for an incorrect description or for any faults. This is not to say that all lots are miscatalogued or that every article is sprayed over to hide the cracks, repairs, or even replacement part! Most lots are genuine and reasonably described, depending on the knowledge of the auctioneer, or rather the cataloguer, but you do not get the full guaranteed invoice that most dealers will give and you will not have an opportunity to change your mind. If you do buy at auction, make sure that you carefully view the goods on the appointed view day and if you attend the sale in person make sure that you are not carried away into giving more than your predetermined limit, and that you do not start bidding for lots that you have not personally examined just because they seem cheap – there is usually a very good reason for the low price!

If you cannot attend an auction sale yourself, you may leave commissions with a porter (who will expect to be tipped if an item is purchased), or direct with the auctioneer (who will not require any extra payment as commission payment is provided by the seller). Alternatively you can discuss the sale with your dealer friend who may well be able to give you valuable advice and be prepared to act for you. A dealer may well rightly expect payment for such professional services so make sure you discuss this beforehand.

Although I have just said that an auctioneer should not accept commission from both the buyer and the seller, most auctioneers do now charge the buyer a so-called "premium". This varies from firm to firm, but can be 15 per cent, or even more. You will also have to pay VAT on that premium as it is (wrongly) regarded as a service. These additions can add quite an amount to your bill if you are bidding in hundreds of pounds. You should also bear in mind that you may have to make an additional journey to collect your purchase, or at least

1 A selection of Samuel Alcock cups and saucers, *c.*1835–45. Cups and saucers are relatively inexpensive and show a range of forms and added patterns.

wait until the end of the sale. You may also experience difficulty in paying by acceptable means unless you have previously "registered" with the auctioneer. (*see* the footnote on VAT on p.242).

Do always remember when buying at auction to read the conditions of sale very carefully – they are usually printed in the firm's catalogue. Such conditions can vary greatly from one firm to another. I repeat, you should also view the sale. This usually has to be done on the preceding day, or days, not on the sale day – again read your catalogue to check such points.

As you view each lot, circle or otherwise mark the lots in which you are interested, make any relevant notes as to the condition, and fix your top price for each*. Do not leave this decision to the heat of the moment, unless you have an ample bank balance! It is so easy to get carried away or get nudged into giving imprudent extra bids when the lot is about to be "knocked down" to a rival bidder.

Some private buyers believe that if they top a dealer's bid they are bound to have a cheap purchase. The theory behind this is that the dealer will have to ask a profit and so the auction price will be below the dealer's shop price. The trouble can be that the dealer may be acting for an extremely rich customer who has set his or her sights on that one piece and is determined to buy it well over the odds! More likely the dealer knows and has *entré* to the top buyer or collector of such a piece, say in the United States or in Australia. You are up against not one dealer, but the cream of the world's buyers!

I may in these warnings have over darkened the picture. You certainly need not worry about buying a lot by the action of blowing your nose or rubbing your eyes – the difficulty may be in catching the auctioneer's attention when you do wish to bid. Indeed in some auction rooms you need to "Register" first and once details are recorded you will be given a numbered "paddle" to wave at the auctioneer. Bargains can still be had at auctions, even at the grandest, but not all the items can be so described, for often a similar object can be found at a more modest price sitting in a nearby dealer's shop, without an additional premium being added to the bill. I, of course, write as a former dealer as well as a collector, but I have been engaged in the trade for over 50 years, and have bought and sold in all the possible traditional ways.

My readers in the 21st century will have means open to them that were never dreamed of in my day. Currently, I refer to the Internet. I have no knowledge of this, but I do understand that a lot of buying and selling is carried out on the Internet, saving much time, trouble, and travelling. Convenient as these modern aids may be, you do not have the advantage of seeing or handling the items or discussing the piece with the seller, who may or may not be a dealer, eye to eye. Can you tell from a screen image if the piece is restored, or even genuine? You also have to arrange payment and await delivery – hopefully in a sound condition. I, a traditionalist (some would say a stick-in-the-mud), prefer to see and handle the pieces I might consider purchasing. I wish to support the Trade in a personal manner, and I like unhurried contemplation and discussion. I would hate to see trade characters replaced by impersonal screens! The current collectors' magazines do carry advice on such Internet trading, which is perhaps more popular in America than in Great Britain (yes, I am a traditionalist – I prefer the full description *Great* Britain!), and is probably more suited to some collectables than to antique porcelains. Here some knowledge is required and the ability to distinguish the wheat from the chaff – both in regard to the object being viewed and the person attempting to dispose of it! If you are interested in buying and selling on the Internet you should make sure you acquaint yourself thoroughly with how it works and what the pitfalls are (you may well find *Miller's Antiques, Art & Collectables on the Web* a useful guide here).

What shall I collect?

You may ask how you can acquire the knowledge that will help you know the good from the bad. The trouble with such a question is who is to say that one thing is good, the other bad? Different people, at different times, have different standards. Some types of Victorian or Edwardian (see p.230 for the reigns of kings and queens that led to the use of these period terms), or later, porcelain are today commanding very high prices and there are many serious collectors of such wares, but some 40 years ago these objects would have been scorned. Our tastes change; time hides faults or helps to reveal assets. It is also important to bear in mind that as fashionable 18th-century porcelains become harder to find and more expensive to purchase so collectors will tend to seek other less fashionable and inexpensive wares. Certainly the 19th century produced a bewildering range of collectable items. I cannot claim all were good pots but then a collection does not have

---

* It is a good idea to use a personal code to mark your catalogue, using letters rather than figures. This avoids roving eyes seeing that you have marked a lot at a particular price.

to comprise only perfectly conceived and produced items. Witness the great collections of pot lids, of fairings, of mass-produced Staffordshire figures. Few of these can be termed good from a potter's or artist's point of view, but what pleasure they have given collectors and what service and satisfaction they gave to the original purchasers of these humble wares.

To appreciate a good form you probably need some experience. It may help to have had some training in the craft of potting, to have coaxed a shapeless lump of clay into a graceful, balanced shape on the potter's wheel. Viewing a large museum collection such as that housed in the Victoria and Albert Museum, The Potteries Museum in Hanley, Derby, or Worcester can perhaps help you divide the bad from the good in some way. It will certainly enable you to tell which pieces or types you admire and which you dislike.

If it is really impossible to teach what is good and what is bad, then at least you can learn to appreciate quality. To do this, and learn more about the varying styles or types of porcelain, you can make good use of not only museums but also auction galleries. Here, particularly in London auction rooms, you can see and handle, on the advertised view days before the sale, a large quantity of very varied objects. These are not always displayed to advantage but they are available, which is the important thing.

I may well be prejudiced, but I cannot but think that the most helpful source of learning is a dealer's shop – not any dealer but a specialist in the subject of your choice. In such an establishment you would expect to find a select group of articles that not only can you handle at leisure, but the dealer should be able to discuss the pieces intelligently and also give valuable guidance should you wish for it.

Well, would-be collectors, I think that is enough for my first, introductory, chapter. We can now proceed to learn about the porcelain bodies (there are various types), about how those materials are turned into useful and beautiful objects, and how they can be decorated. We will then look at the main makers of English porcelain and how all the different types of porcelain made between 1745 and 1900 can be identified. I then provide more helpful advice within Chapter 11 and proceed to discuss values and changing times. A helpful bibliography also lists other specialist books that will take your study even further than I am able to do in this introductory work.

2
Porcelain – the material

Here let us briefly discuss the variable ceramic materials. The word "porcelain" is used to describe a unique, quite beautiful ceramic derived from materials that vitrify under great heat and become non-porous and translucent. As well as being beautiful, porcelain is both a workable and durable material. It was introduced in China in about AD 700 (the exact date is not known), which is about 1,000 years before a similar ware was produced in Europe. The English name porcelain, the French *porcelaine*, and the German *Porzellan* are believed to have been derived from the Portuguese *porcella*, which means cowrie shell. The white shiny inner surface of this seashell is similar to the Chinese porcelains that were first imported into Europe by the Portuguese in the 16th century.

The difference between porcelain and pottery lies in the fact that porcelain is translucent whereas pottery is opaque. This property is best shown if you pass your hand between a light source and the piece of porcelain. You will see the shadow of your hand like a cloud rolling across the sky. Many people place a lot of importance on the degree of translucency in a given porcelain but at this early stage in the story it is best to remember that the degree of transmitted light is very variable according to the body mix. Much depends also on the thickness of the piece, a thin cup for example showing better translucency than a thickly potted dish. Less obvious is the fact that slight differences in the firing temperature will actually affect the translucency of the porcelain to a remarkable degree – overfired pieces are more translucent, while underfired examples show less light. Different light sources will also give different readings and added decoration can mask out the transmitted light. The difference is also noticeable in the sound of porcelain if struck – the Chinese tended to respect the clear "ring" of their vitrified porcelain body, contrasting with the duller sound of lower-fired earthenwares.

White-surfaced earthenwares

While the main attribute of porcelain is now believed to lie in its translucency, its initial impact on a world accustomed to clay-coloured pottery must have been the clean, smooth white body. Potters thought that the easiest way to emulate this white Oriental porcelain was to coat a relatively coarse and clay-coloured earthenware body with a thin surface of whitened clay, or more often with a glaze made opaque and white usually by the addition of tin oxide. Such wares were widely made in the Near East and in southern Europe, where the term "maiolica" was used from the 15th century; further north in France the description "faience" was adopted; while with similar Dutch types of tin-glazed earthenware we use the term "Delft", after the geographical centre of that Dutch trade. In the British Isles there was a tendency to use the term "delft-ware" (with a small "d"). The simple descriptive term "tin-glazed earthenwares" is now more favoured. All these earthenwares are discussed in Alan Caiger-Smith's excellent book, *Tin Glaze Pottery in Europe and the Islamic World* (Faber, 1973) and in other such specialist works.

The Italian maiolica wares of the 16th and 17th centuries were, in their way, far more decorative than the Chinese porcelains of the same period, for the lower firing temperature needed for pottery permitted the use of overglaze enamel colours. In objects like large circular dishes the Italian potters, or rather their painters, treated the tin-glazed pottery as a canvas and some wonderful decorative work was produced.

In Holland and Great Britain these delft-type tin-glazed earthenwares were more subdued and were very often decorated only with cobalt blue. They usually show a distinct Chinese air in the decoration. The potters were no doubt producing a poor man's version of the fashionable imported Oriental porcelain; the European products, however, had many defects in use. The underlying clay body was friable, weak, and porous, while the covering white tin glaze tended to crack and flake away from the body, particularly at the edges, so exposing the porous clay-coloured body. The delftwares now seem to have a great charm and indeed they are highly decorative and collectable, but to the housewife of the 18th century they must have caused much concern. In practice the wares could not be trimly potted, or rather the thick white glaze blunted the potting. The body and tin glaze did not seem very

suitable for the manufacture of teawares (the staple article of the porcelain trade): at least, very few delft examples have survived. One can almost hear the housewife craving for clean, trim porcelain on her table, not earthenware dressed up in a white coat.*

Chinese porcelains

The earliest Chinese porcelains were not necessarily as delicate, light, and thin as later examples are. Indeed they were often quite heavy and rather similar to stonewares. Nevertheless by the Ming dynasty (1368–1644) the Chinese porcelains had been so refined and the manufacturing processes so perfected that the resulting porcelains are similar to, or surpass, our present-day conception of this exceptionally fine material.

The often superb Ming porcelains were frequently painted with a rich cobalt blue – a pigment painted on the raw unglazed and unfired body – and these wares are the prototype of a vast and interesting range of Oriental and European porcelain that we refer to as "blue and white" (*see* p.54 in Chapter 5). Although we tend to think of the Chinese as the originators of blue-and-white porcelain it is believed that this wonderful colour (cobalt) was imported into China from Persia, where the basic materials erythrite and cobaltite were found and used by the Persian potters on their glazed pottery. Later, in the middle of the 15th century, the

2 A superbly potted, neatly painted Chinese (hard-paste) teabowl from a tea service made for the European market. Such porcelains were our inspiration – and our despair!

Chinese began to make use of their newly discovered native cobalt-asbolite, a mixture of the oxides of cobalt and manganese.

Just as the first cobalt used by the Chinese potters was imported, so too were some of the designs or shapes. There is evidence, for example, of the influence of Near Eastern wares as well as Mongol designs. Nevertheless, from the 15th to the mid-18th century these mainly blue-painted Chinese porcelains represent the only true porcelains known to man. They were widely exported and everywhere held in high repute, rare objects worthy of royal gifts and articles deemed suitable for mounting in precious metals. Countless chemists and others sought to win untold riches by trying to learn the mystery of porcelain manufacture and to introduce porcelain manufacture into Europe.

Japanese porcelains

Before turning from the East to the Western efforts to produce porcelain, I must mention Japanese porcelains. These wares are little understood in Great Britain but they had a very real influence on English manufacturers and when the companies started to produce porcelain in the mid-1740s and 1750s it would seem that they

---

* John Black's *British Tin-Glazed Earthenware* (Shire Publications Ltd, 2001) is a good basic guide to such wares.

usually chose to copy Japanese designs rather than Chinese. It is often thought that the Dutch were the main importers of Japanese porcelains into Europe and some authorities have even stated that the Dutch East India Company held a monopoly in the trade. In practice this was clearly not so and tens of thousands of pieces were imported in the early 18th century by the English East India Company and sold in their London auction sales; in fact it would seem that some homecoming East India Company vessels carried to London more Japanese porcelain than Chinese, and all this at a period some 50 years before porcelain was made in England. The standard book on these fine pre-1750 Japanese wares is Soame Jenyns' *Japanese Porcelain* (Faber, 1965), although my book on Chinese porcelains contains helpful information on the related Japanese pieces – *Oriental Export Market Porcelain* (Granada, London, 1979), Chapter 10. A good study of the Dutch trade in Japanese ceramics is *Porcelain and the Dutch East India Company*, by T. Volker (Leiden, 1954 and 1971).

The early European porcelains

There were one or two isolated attempts to make a type of porcelain in Europe before 1700, but these can be considered to be little more than trials and, while examples such as the extremely rare Italian Medici porcelain of approximately 1575–87 command very high prices on account of their extreme rarity, they had no discernible influence on the introduction of porcelain into England.

There were also some efforts to produce a type of porcelain in France in the 17th century but the first real success was achieved in Germany c.1707–10. The place this occurred at was the famous castle of Albrechtsburg near Meissen in Saxony and the persons were the imprisoned alchemist Johann Friedrich Böttger and his protector, the physicist Ehrenfried Walther, Count von Tschirnhaus. In about 1707 they produced a very fine and hard stoneware, which was cut and polished as a precious stone would be. In about 1708 they discovered a fine white body that was very similar in appearance to Chinese porcelain, and in 1710 the Meissen porcelain manufactory was established. (This is normally referred to as "Dresden" in Britain.) Before long the various Courts of Europe were striving to set up rival porcelain factories. In general terms, only the products of Meissen and the French National factory at Sèvres were to influence the English manufacturers in any great way, and the dominant influence remained with the Eastern Chinese and Japanese porcelains.

Hard- and soft-paste porcelain

There are two basic types of porcelain – hard- and soft-paste. The Chinese and the Japanese were of the type that we now call true or hard-paste porcelain, and the Meissen (Dresden) and most European porcelains were also of this type. On the other hand the early Vincennes or Sèvres French porcelain of the period 1745–72 is of the artificial or soft-paste type, as was most 18th-century English porcelain. Visually the true porcelains, or rather their surfaces, appear white and glittery and they can also feel cold and unfriendly in comparison to soft-paste. These hard-paste porcelains are also rather brittle and tend to chip at the edges; such a chip or body fracture should appear conchoidal with flakes or facets like a chip on glass. The body is indeed physically hard and in the old days collectors were encouraged to take a file to their porcelain. It is said that the metal file will not cut the body if it is of hard-paste, whereas a soft-paste body can be quite easily cut on the edge of a foot-rim or similar spot. One can often see a little nick cut into English porcelain where some unsure person has been ill-treating his or her treasures! Such a person will, however, still be unsure, for a good-quality file in reasonable condition will in fact cut most so-called hard-paste porcelain. The old test is at best unreliable and is an affront to the porcelain. It should be possible for the novice, with a little practice, to be able to differentiate by eye and touch between hard-paste and soft-paste porcelain. To do this you need to have available reference pieces that you can handle frequently. These pieces need not be expensive, perfect examples; damaged objects (or factory "wasters" – *see* p.25) are fine for this purpose.

Some people get very worried about the fact that there are two types of porcelain and wonder how they can learn to tell one from the other. Let me say at once that you can form a superb collection and obtain a lifetime's pleasure from it without having the slightest clue about the difference between hard- and soft-paste. However, if you can tell the difference this may well save you from making a costly error in buying a French 19th-century hard-paste copy instead of the original English 18th-century soft-paste figure or group. Have another look at the figure shown on page 2 – do you know which it is?

The 18th-century English soft-paste porcelains, especially those of Bow, Chelsea, and Derby, while not feeling exactly soft do have an almost warm and friendly feel (at least the related covering glaze does). While a hard-paste porcelain has a hard glittery glaze, a soft-paste body has a relatively soft glaze. This soft

3 A Worcester (soft-paste) moulded salad bowl, left, with its slightly cream-coloured body, shown with a Chinese hard-paste copy, right. This is whiter and has a more glossy (glass-like) glaze. Usually the English copied Chinese porcelains, but in the 1780s the Chinese copied some English forms – to undersell the English manufacturers.

glaze is found on many plates and dishes, and often shows knife cuts or staining. It is said that the enamel colours tend to sink into the soft-paste glazes and that they stand or lie on top of a hard-paste glaze. In practice, however, this is a dangerous rule to apply when trying to discern between hard- and soft-pastes as much depends on the amount of flux that is added to the enamels and to the firing temperature. Also in some English glazes, such as those used at Worcester and Caughley, the colours do in fact tend to remain on the surface because the glaze is relatively hard. If the underlying soft-paste body is exposed by a break or chip it should appear granular like a lump of sugar, not conchoidal like glass or flint. The soft-paste body,

when exposed by an old chip, can also appear slightly stained and coloured, not a pure white.

I have described hard- and soft-pastes as having these relative characteristics but there is a school of thought that suggests that these terms only relate to the firing temperature, the hard-paste wares being fired at a high or "hard" firing of some 1,300–1,400°C (2,372–2,552°F) and the soft or artificial English wares being matured in a "soft" fire of about 1,200°C (2,192°F). Certainly, whatever the body mixture, hard-paste porcelains must be fired at a higher temperature than the soft type.

The object of knowing if you are handling true hard-paste or the soft-paste variety is to narrow down the possible source of origin of the example and also, in some cases, to tell if a piece is a fake or reproduction. If the porcelain you are holding is hard-paste then it can be Oriental, Continental, or, if English, it could be from the Plymouth or Bristol factories. Continental fakes and reproductions of Chelsea, Bow, Derby, and

Worcester porcelains will be hard-paste whereas the original would have been soft-paste or one of the several subdivisions that will be discussed later. The piece on page 2 poses such a problem!

The chemical make-up of porcelain

True or hard-paste porcelain comprises china-clay or "kaolin" (that is, silicate of alumina) and china-stone or "petuntse" (silicate of alumina, potash, and soda) fused at or above 1,300°C (2,372°F); the related glaze comprises petuntse, lime, and potash. The normal method of firing Continental hard-paste porcelain is to set and dry the unglazed object with a low initial "biscuit" (unglazed) firing, then to glaze the object and to fire again at a high temperature in the 1,300–1,400°C (2,372–2,552°F) range, so that the body and the glaze mature and bond together. The Chinese method was reputedly to glaze the raw ware and then to have just the one high-temperature firing with the glaze.

Although the Chinese method was known in Europe and in England through the writings of Father d'Entrecolles (he was a Jesuit missionary at the Chinese ceramic centre of Ching-te-Chen*), as spread in various 18th-century books such as Du Halde's *Description de l'empire de la Chine*, with English translations published in 1738 and 1741, the earliest English porcelains and the methods employed in its manufacture differed widely from the Chinese.

The great difficulty was that the essential raw materials, kaolin, and petuntse, were not available in England – or at least they had not yet been discovered in Cornwall – and while the would-be porcelain manufacturers had presented before them the imported Chinese porcelain and they had no doubt heard of the riches that could be earned from such porcelain or "chinaware", they had to discover new ways of making similar material.

It was fortunate that the British had not discovered the raw materials needed to make true porcelain, for if an abundant supply of kaolin and petuntse had been available in the 1740s ordinary, dull, straightforward copies of export-quality Chinese wares or of Meissen porcelain might have been produced. As it was, the objects that were made in Britain suited the available materials. These pieces may not be as technically slick as the Meissen porcelains or as large as some Chinese pieces but they possess a friendly warm feeling and an air that is so English. I say that they are very English, which is correct, but we must not lose sight of the fact that Chelsea and other early English porcelains are remarkably similar in body to some of the early French soft-paste porcelains.

In an effort to find a body that had at least some translucency, glass was added to various mixes. This gave rise to the need to find a material to bond the body together, so that the glassy mix would not melt and distort out of shape at too low a temperature. What was needed were the bones to add strength to the glassy flesh – indeed at some factories, most notably at Bow, Lowestoft, Isleworth, and Derby (*see* Chapter 6, pp.71, 107, 97, and 87) calcined (burned) and ground-up bones were added to the mix for this purpose and they proved to be very successful. Many other materials were used; silica in the form of ground, calcined, flint or sand; chalk (lime); various clays, such as pipe-clay, were helpful and special clay was even imported from North America; but, most importantly, some experimenters added steatite or soapstone (silicate of alumina and magnesia) from Cornwall.

The above allows us to create certain subdivisions of 18th-century English soft-paste porcelain: glassy bodies, such as those produced at Chelsea, early Derby, and Longton Hall; bone-ash bodies, such as Bow, Isleworth, Lowestoft, Derby (after *c*.1770), and some Chelsea porcelains; and soapstone bodies, such as early Bristol, Vauxhall, Worcester, Caughley, and some Liverpool porcelains.

Some of these English soft-paste wares are referred to as "frit porcelains" because part of the glassy mix was first "fritted", that is baked, or fused together then ground to a powder and added to the basic clays.

From about 1790 into the 1810s several factories produced a type of hybrid hard-paste porcelain. These little-understood wares are discussed in Chapter 7 (*see* p.132), and from about 1800 there was the introduction of bone china, a white workable body that was to become the standard British porcelain superseding all others. This "English Bone China" is discussed in Chapter 8 (*see* p.170).

Analysis

The attribution of English porcelain by means of an analysis of the mix is not an exact science, certainly not for the amateur, although in many cases such analysis can be very helpful. For example, if on testing a white cup we find no bone ash in the form of phosphoric acid then this cup will not have been made at Bow or at one of the other factories that are known to have used a

*This continuing porcelain centre has been renamed Jingdezhen. Another important area, Canton, is now Guangzhow.

significant amount of bone ash (even 40–50 per cent) in its porcelain. Similarly, if we test a blue-and-white leaf dish and find present 30–45 per cent soapstone in the form of magnesia then we can consider that such a piece was made at Bristol (prior to 1751), Worcester, Caughley, or some of the Liverpool potteries. However, it must be remembered that any one factory was apt to change its recipe from time to time, either in an effort to improve the porcelain visually or, more often, in an endeavour to make it more workable and more stable in the kiln. Also, the supply of raw materials may have been unreliable, necessitating a change if the factory was to remain in operation during times of shortage. Remember also that the ingredients would not have been so pure as modern manufacturers would expect. It must also be borne in mind that many, if not all, factories used some ground-up fired porcelains from other sources in their mix to add strength. Certainly the area around the Caughley grinding mill contained a huge range of Chinese as well as English porcelain, fragments of which would or could have varied the Caughley "standard" mix to some extent. There are also contemporary accounts of mills around London grinding Oriental porcelain for reuse by the potters, and the closing "lots" in each East India Company chinaware sale comprised cases of damaged porcelain, some of which seems to have found its way into English porcelain bodies. Any one factory during its working life used several differing bodies – there is no one Chelsea paste, no one Derby mix.

While I have introduced the idea of analysing the chemical make-up of porcelains, I should make it clear that no collector lacking chemical knowledge and equipment can carry out a complete analysis. There is a fairly simple standard method of testing for bone ash or phosphoric acid (see *Burlington Magazine*, Vol. 51, September 1927, pp.142–4), but apart from this the porcelain has to be professionally tested and a small section of the example is required, or at least a hole has to be drilled to provide a "specimen". In recent times porcelains have been submitted to spectrographic analysis. Normally the result is not complete, although in years to come, when we have been able to build up a reference collection of master character-patterns for various makes of porcelain, this system may well prove very helpful, but again the necessary equipment is unlikely to be available to most collectors.*

In the 1950s much importance was placed on the reaction of ultra-violet light on porcelains, for by the use of such special "lamps" different fluorescence could be discerned. Personally, I find these lamps unhelpful for, as I have already explained, the mix could, and often did, vary from month to month within any given factory. Moreover, one has to be accustomed to using such a lamp in order to be able to discern the differences in fluorescence. It also seems that the rays react on the rather soft English lead glaze, rather than on the underlying body.

Be not dismayed, there are many other reasonably reliable ways of identifying English porcelains. It is also often forgotten that we should collect the object for its own grace and beauty rather than because it was made at factory A or at factory B.

It is regrettable that some collectors purchase a poor example simply because it was made at their favourite factory and pay no heed to a gem from another manufactory.

---

*As I write in the early 21st century research is still being carried out on the analysis of different ceramic bodies and some regrouping or linking of factories is being suggested. Previous and current research is available in the *Transactions of the English Ceramic Circle* (*see* Bibliography).

3
Basic manufacturing processes

Having found a mix that would produce a white translucent body when correctly fired, the would-be porcelain manufacturer had relatively few other difficulties to surmount – given that the funds were available to establish a factory, buy equipment and raw materials, and pay a workforce – for the basic methods of manufacture differ little from those traditionally employed to produce pottery, stoneware, or delft-type wares. The manufacturing "know-how" was largely available in the mid-1740s when the English porcelain story was unfolding, although the all-important firing of the new material presented great problems. It is the traditional methods of production that we will discuss here.

Throwing

There are two basic methods of turning a shapeless lump or mass of clay into an object of beauty and use (apart from the primitive non-commercial method of forming it by hand). A potter seeking to produce a set of identical objects has to fall back on some form of mechanical aid. For objects having a circular plan, such as cups and saucers, plates, bowls, and simple vases or pots, the potter's wheel is invaluable. This device has been aptly described as the only machine made by man that has done nothing but good! The wheels are worked by the potter's hand or foot*, which turns, by various gears or pedals, a heavy circular wheel on which the potter "centres" a lump of clay. Once exactly centred the wet spinning clay can be pressed and coaxed upward or outward using fingers or hands into the desired form. By means of fixed gauges or pointers a series of objects of similar size and shape can be produced by the skilled operator. It is fascinating to see a good "thrower" at work, deftly producing vase after vase or bowl after bowl from the lumps of clay.

Such thrown wares, if they are intended for use and for subsequent decoration, are normally dried to a leather or cheese hardness, to use apt descriptions, and are then trimmed on a wheel or lathe with the aid of a sharp chisel-like turning tool. The purpose behind this is to pare away surplus clay, to reduce the walls of the object to a visual daintiness and a true shape, as well as to obliterate the marks or ridges formed by the fingers during throwing. In some modern pottery, produced by studio potters, these throwing marks are left to give a robust lively appearance, but for the more delicate porcelain wares trimming is necessary. Also at this "cheese-hard" stage the foot or base of the object can be formed by gouging out surplus clay from the thick base. There are some exceptions but objects formed by hand on the potter's wheel will be of circular outline. To such a circular outline a handle can be added to form a cup, or a spout and a handle added to form a teapot or jug. The potter's wheel was much used in the porcelain industry up to about 1800 but to a lesser extent after this, as the then fashionable oval or Rococo forms and relief ornamentation did not lend themselves to being thrown on the wheel (see, for example, picture 235 on p.189).

There is no great virtue in throwing porcelain objects on the traditional wheel; indeed for large-scale factory production other methods have advantages and impart less stress on the clay. There is, however, a spontaneous fitness of purpose to hand-thrown wares. A good thrown bowl, for example, will, or should, have a natural line and "life" – an individuality.

Moulding

Moulding is necessary for most non-circular objects and is also often employed for convenience in the manufacture of wares that could be thrown. Moulding is ideal for long runs of objects that have to be identical in form and size or for intricate shapes, figures, or groups. For some wares the important method known as "jollying" is employed. This is, simply, the marriage of throwing and moulding. Thrown objects have a plain surface (unless they are separately embellished with added, or "sprigged", relief designs) so objects with a recessed or embossed design such as fluting (see picture 4), ribbing, or a floral pattern have to be jollied or moulded. To create such a piece, first someone

---

* In a traditional factory the thrower was more likely to have a boy turning a large wheel, which was connected by a belt to the potter's wheel.

4 A superb early Worcester moulded milk jug of rare but typical form. Enamelled Oriental-style decoration, 9.5cm (3¾in) high, *c.*1755, Jonathan Godden collection.

5 A plaster of Paris mould for a small leaf-shaped dish, along with an unglazed factory waster and a finished example of its reduced fired size, ex-Caughley factory site, *c.*1785, in the Ironbridge Gorge Museum.

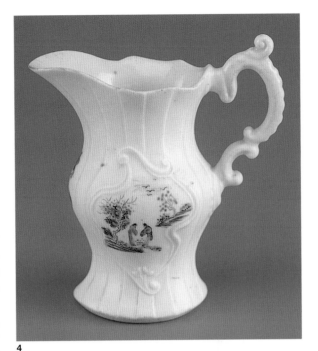

4

5

whom we would now call an art director or designer has to think up a basic shape or design. The designer, or a modeller, then prepares a positive master model (larger than the finished article) and from this many working moulds can be prepared. These working moulds were traditionally usually made out of plaster of Paris but some factories, such as Worcester, favoured "pitcher" moulds, i.e. fired clay. Moulds may also have been made of wood or of metal but these were suitable only for the press-moulding technique (*see* below).

The jolly-mould is then affixed to the wheel-head, and the thrower then prepares a "liner" or bat of clay and presses this into the low revolving mould. The clay takes up the recessed or embossed design from the mould to form the exterior design, while the potter, using his or her hands or with a "profile", forms and smoothes the inside surface, turning the walls to the correct thickness, and, in so doing, compressing the malleable clay well into the patterned mould. The charged mould is then set aside, the clay starts to dry and, as it does so, the body will slightly contract away from the mould and the object can be withdrawn when capable of being handled in the leather-hard state. The foot is then formed by turning. This description relates to an object such as a bowl or cup that has the moulded decoration on the exterior, but a similar process can transfer a relief or impressed design to the inside of an object – to a saucer or plate for example. The process is simply reversed so that the patterned mould of the approximate size and design has a bat of clay laid upon it; this is then pressed down upon the mould in order to take up the design. The top of the clay-bat, the reverse of the plate or saucer, is then shaped with the help of a profile.

Apart from the jollying method, employing as it does a patterned mould and the turning wheel, there are two basic methods of moulding – mainly employed for non-circular or intricate objects.

The first method is the traditional form of press-moulding, where thin bats of prepared clay, or rather the porcelain body, are pressed into and against a mould. The moulds are normally in two or more pieces or units that are linked together by means of male and female locating notches. Articles made from such two- or three-piece moulds will normally show a slight seam mark where clay has pressed into the joint between the different parts of the mould, although these seam marks should at least have been reduced and made less apparent by "fettling" (the piece, once hard enough to handle safely, should have been wiped over with a fettling tool, rag, or brush to remove such blemishes before the biscuit [unglazed] firing and subsequent glazing).

Some small objects, such as leaf dishes for example, were traditionally formed from one-piece moulds such as that shown in picture 5. This open mould from the Caughley factory site is shown with its matching unglazed "waster", which is the spoilt and discarded piece, and a finished example. It is easy to see how a thin bat of clay was prepared and pressed into this mould, the clay pressed against the mould and the top or inside smoothed relatively flat with a damp cloth. This is rather similar to the method employed when forming the pastry case of a tart by pressing the thin bat of rolled pastry into the tart pan. When semi-dried on contact with the plaster of Paris mould, the clay image will shrink away from it so that the dish can be extracted and the mould reused, after drying.

Units such as solid, but shaped and relief-patterned handles and knobs for example, are formed by pressing a roll or ball of clay into a two-piece mould, the two parts of which are then squeezed together to shape the whole. Such units are affixed to the main object – a vase for example – by means of a thin coat of "slip", which is simply a bit of the clay body diluted to the consistency of thick milk or cream. The added parts are then affixed before firing.

Some, mainly irregularly shaped objects, such as trays and teapot stands, can be formed by a subdivision of press-moulding, using a process rather similar to jollying, but without the wheel. Here a prepared shape mould or "hump" forms the inside of the tray or stand when a bat of clay is laid over it and pressed down to take its shape. The surplus material at the edge is then simply cut away, just as the pastry overflowing the edge of a pie dish is trimmed off.

Slip-casting

Some 18th-century factories favoured the press-moulded technique while many others preferred the alternative method of slip-casting. With this method, an absorbent mould of plaster of Paris has to be made from the permanent and hard block or master mould. The two or more component pieces of the working mould are then assembled and tied, or otherwise fixed together, while an open top or bottom is left. Into this opening liquid slip is poured until the mould is full. (It may require topping up with extra slip as the mould absorbs the liquid.) Some additives may be employed to speed up or slow down the setting of the mix, depending on the size or other characteristics of the piece or moulds.

The plaster of Paris mould will take up the surplus water from the slip nearest to it, so forming a skin. The longer the slip is left in the mould the more water will be absorbed and the thicker the outside skin will

6 Lowestoft porcelain tea canister (and cover) with part of the plaster of Paris mould from the factory site. The canister is painted in underglaze blue with a Continental-style pattern and there is a crossed-swords device on the flat, glazed base, 9.5cm (3¾in) high, c.1780–85, Godden collection.

become, until it has formed a wall. After a period gauged by experience (depending on the size of the mould, its condition, etc) and by the degree that the slip has sunk down from the top of the mould, the surplus slip will be poured out and the mould left to dry and set the coating of hardening porcelain within. On drying, this porcelain slip will slightly shrink away from the mould, which can be taken apart to leave a perfect but slightly smaller and reversed replica of the mould's interior form. As I have previously explained, the slight projection or seam where the different parts of the mould join are later trimmed away or fettled, and any other units such as handles can be added or the foot turned on the wheel or lathe before the piece receives its first firing.

One side of a plaster mould used for a Lowestoft porcelain tea canister is shown in picture 6. You can see a male, or protruding, locking notch on the side and when the four sides were assembled the outline of the object would be complete. A glazed and decorated tea canister (used to hold tea leaves) from such a mould is also shown; it is smaller in size because on drying and firing ceramic bodies shrink up to 10–30 per cent, depending on the mix.

The cover to this tea canister (a unit that is so often missing now) would have been moulded separately as would have been the flower knob and the leaves. These last two embellishments would have been formed in a simple press-mould used for sprigging. (Flowers can also be formed by hand.)

A characteristic of slip-moulded ware is that the relief or indented design will appear in a blunted form on the inside of the object, for the walls are of equal thickness. If we look at the Lowestoft tea canister, a convex rib on the exterior will reappear as a slight concave indentation inside. If the Caughley leaf dish shown in picture 5 (*see* p.21) had been slip-cast the leaf-like feet under the base would show a mirror image inside the dish.

Plaster moulds

Plaster of Paris is a relatively soft material (powdered calcined gypsum mixed with water, a mixture that sets rapidly) and the moulds tend to wear with use. The relief or other pattern will lose its sharpness, the edges wear, and the joints tend to open, resulting in more prominent seams appearing on the moulded object. Two sauceboats, for example, from the same mould but made at different times in the life of a mould would appear very different to the discriminating collector. One would have a sharp, clear moulded pattern, while

7 A typically attractive, well-designed, and moulded early Worcester milk jug of small size. It has simple Chinese-style enamelled decoration, 9.5cm (3¾in) high, c.1755, Jonathan Godden collection.

the other would be flat and dull in comparison. The manufacturers employed several methods of preserving the moulds, they were normally painted with soft-soap or a similar preparation before use, but the fact remains that they had to be renewed or recut from time to time. They were also prone to handling, rather mishandling, damage and were troublesome and bulky to store. Yet moulds were, and still are, essential to the running of any porcelain factory and some of the 18th-century porcelains that issued from these plaster cases are delightful, especially the thin Worcester pieces such as the milk jugs shown in pictures 4 and 7 (*see* p.21 and above). Most of the credit for such minor masterpieces must go to the designer and/or the block maker cum mould maker, but in most cases we now have no idea of the names of such important people. In practice, when using moulds many are required because a factory will not make one teapot or other object at a time. A series of, say, 40 will be made, which requires many moulds. Such pieces will be glazed and fired then stored in an undecorated state until orders for such enamelled, decorated, articles are received. At this point the blanks will be taken out of the store and decorated over the glaze in the manner the orders requested. The mould-making department of a large factory was, traditionally, a very important one. Without a constant supply of plaster moulds the factory would have come to a standstill. In modern times new materials have tended to replace plaster of Paris. For example, pliable rubber-like moulds assist production and do not wear out as quickly as the former soft-plaster moulds.

Figure moulding

I have explained that handles, knobs, spouts, and other, similar appendages are formed separately and fixed to the main unfired body with slip. Ornate objects, such as figure models, are built up from many components, each moulded individually; for example, with a figure of a woman, the head, a hat, the arms, feet, and body are made separately, as is the base. The reason for this is that there can be no undercutting in a completed moulded shape for the hardening clay could not be extracted from the mould if the design included undercut portions. The various moulds would have been made traditionally by cutting up the original clay or wax figure that had been sculptured by a modeller or designer employed at the factory into appropriate sections. Not so many units are required today as the mould is more pliable, so the item can be made in almost one piece.

The skilled workman who assembled the separate pieces with slip was called a repairer. He had to ensure that the completed figure looked natural with arms, legs, etc. positioned in a lifelike posture. It is all too easy to make the parts of a shepherd look like a scarecrow! The repairer or assistant would also make small embellishments, such as bows on the shoes or on the dress, by hand or with the aid of sprig-moulds, and they would also usually ornament the base with leaves and flowers (*see* picture 9). A sprig-mould is normally small in size and the design is cut in reverse in the plaster or other material. A squeeze of clay is then pressed into the prepared mould and lifted ready to be placed on the figure or base with slip. The relief motifs on traditional Wedgwood jasper wares were formed in this way. A sprig-mould is rather like a miniature edition of the press-mould shown in picture 5, except that the indentation would not be so deep and the formed sprigged ornament would be solid, not hollow.

Biscuit firing

Having formed a soft-paste object by throwing on the wheel, by jollying, or by moulding, and having trimmed away any seam marks, made a foot or base (and in the case of thrown wares turned the object on a lathe), and added any required handle or spout, the piece is left to dry. After as much water as a warm, dry atmosphere will take up has been extracted, the object is checked for any imperfections and, if perfect (or nearly so!), it will then find its way to be biscuit fired. (If the object was hard-paste it would probably be glazed before the body receives one firing.)

With soft-paste porcelains the first, or biscuit, firing is the most extreme, as all subsequent firings are at progressively lower temperatures. The English biscuit-firing temperature is 1,050–1,250°C (1,922–2,282°F) and here the drying, shrinking porcelain, experiencing its highest temperature as it matures, is most prone to damage. It can explode, if not previously dried adequately, distort, or simply melt into a shapeless mass if the temperature is too high (underfiring will cause troubles at later stages), or it can become stained by smoke or fumes within the kiln.

Saggers

To obviate such fire damage the wares were placed or packed in circular protective cases called "saggers" (or safe guards) that, once filled, were placed in the kiln, affixed one on top of the other, in great piles, each cemented to the one above with clay (*see* picture 8). The traditional kiln fuel was wood or coal, both of which give off smoke, and the object of the saggers used then was to enable the wares to reach the very

8 A small sagger from the Caughley factory site, with a totally collapsed item (possibly a bowl, but it is impossible to tell) in the base. A three-armed stilt or separator is on the rim. The diameter of the sagger is 10.75cm (4¼in), but such objects vary according to the object to be placed inside, Ironbridge Gorge Museum.

high firing temperature without the contents coming into direct contact with the flames, fumes, and smoke. The thick, clay, protective saggers also helped to average out the heat and the wares would be heated and cooled more gradually than would otherwise have been the case.

In this biscuit firing, before the wares were glazed, there was no great need to separate the objects. Bowls or saucers, for example, could be stood one inside the other in safety, although some factories used a thin parting layer of alumina-powder or ground flint to ensure that the wares did not flux together at the normal firing temperature. However, to help the wares retain their shape during the stresses of firing, rings or specially shaped strengtheners of a like body were made and placed in the rims of teabowls, cups, etc. Factory sites are often littered with such placing-rings. Unglazed teapot lids or jug covers were often fired on their pots, again to help preserve the shape.

I have already explained that the saggers helped to distribute the heat evenly and that they tended to take up the initial heat shock. It is most important that wares are heated and cooled gradually, so the firing of a potter's kiln in the 18th century was a very lengthy business, taking days rather than hours, and the kiln would not be opened to the cold air until the saggers and their contents had all but cooled. Once taken from the kiln wares are again checked for condition, perfect pieces sorted and put on one side for decoration in blue and for glazing. The badly damaged pieces are then discarded, after the cause of the failure has been properly investigated. For example, the teapots might have collapsed because they were thrown or turned to too thin a gauge. Some managements paid throwers and moulders on a piece-rate basis and then only on items "good from the oven"! However, some slightly faulty pieces, would have been accepted, especially in the early days, and subsequently finished and sold as "seconds", at a low price to recoup some funds.

Wasters

Discarded pieces were originally waste and so were known as "wasters". Whole, faulty pieces were in most cases broken to ensure workmen did not sell damaged pieces off cheaply on their own account, and to save space when tipped on convenient spare land within, or sometimes outside, the pottery site. To present-day researchers these wasters are of the greatest interest, for when a site is available for excavation (many are now built over and inaccessible) they show the range of objects made on that site and in many cases their half-finished state reveals to us the factory's various modes of production. In several cases spoilt, unfinished examples from a site provide the only evidence relating to shapes, for many wasters are as yet unmatched by completed pieces in known collections. The Caughley site in Shropshire was particularly rich in such surprises.

Most factory sites have been disturbed at one time or another or have been inhabited at later periods, so only unfinished or fire-damaged pieces should be accepted as coming from the factory (that is, only pieces that were damaged during the manufacturing process, so were dumped on site). Moreover, several managements dealt in wares from other factories or countries and several purchased broken china in bulk to be ground up and incorporated into their own mix. For example, much Chinese porcelain was found on the Caughley site in the heart of English countryside. Therefore accept as firm evidence only unglazed or obviously unfinished spoilt factory wasters. An extreme failure is shown in picture 8, collapsed within the sagger.

Such waster evidence can be very important; in the late 1980s relatively small finds of shards and kiln furniture at Limehouse and Vauxhall in London enabled two important groups of mid 18th-century porcelain to be reattributed to their true London source (*see* pp.100 and 116). In the 1990s finds at or near Isleworth evidenced the true source of some wares formerly attributed to Derby and other factories (*see* pp.97).

Underglaze blue

Our story, charting the process of manufacturing porcelain, has progressed to the point where the unglazed, fired porcelain has cooled and has been taken from the biscuit oven, checked for condition, and sorted. Traditionally, pieces that were to be decorated in cobalt blue under the glaze were then put on one side and, as required, passed to the blue painters who would paint a stock pattern freehand, straight onto the unglazed porcelain. A fuller account of underglaze blue decoration and printing is given in Chapter 5 (*see* p.54), but, briefly, the blue pigment (cobalt oxide) has to be hardened on by firing, to drive out the oils that would make the subsequent glazing difficult, and also to fix the blue so that it is not rubbed off by handling.

Glazing

The blue-painted (or blue-printed) wares, together with the white porcelains that are to have overglaze enamel decoration, are glazed next. Traditionally, most

9 A pair of Derby porcelain figures that have open baskets to hold various goodies, and which were for ornamental use on the table or mantle. The upturned example shows typical pad-marks on the base – the remains of separating pads of clay, 22cm (8¾in) high, c.1765, Godden of Worthing Ltd.

pieces were dipped in a large vat of liquid glaze, and the surplus shaken off – none of today's spray guns! The glaze, which looks white, rather like thick milk, settles on the ware and is partly taken into the semi-absorbent body. Fingermarks can be touched in with a brush and, when dry or nearly so, the glaze can be wiped away from the bottom of the foot-rim or other parts where it is not wanted. This is an important task, for in the next process, when the now opaque powder-like glaze is fired and becomes translucent, it is made at least semi-liquid before cooling and acts like a glue, fixing objects to the sagger or to the supports and kiln furniture. Some 18th-century manufacturers had the inside of foot-rims wiped or "pegged" clear of glaze so that the surplus glaze would not run down the foot and fix it to the sagger. In forming this fire-break-like gap the tool very often also cleared an area on the inside of the base within the foot-rim. This process used to be called glaze-shrinkage but glaze does not shrink, it spreads! It was also thought to be a sure sign of a Worcester origin for a piece. This is not necessarily so for, while most Worcester porcelains of the 1760–90 period do show this glaze-free line, it is not normally present on earlier or later examples and, even more importantly, other factories used the same technique with the same result. For example, the Caughley porcelains nearly always show this so-called Worcester characteristic. The glaze-free line also appears on some Liverpool porcelains and even on some 19th-century bone-china pieces.

The flanges of Worcester and Chinese teapot covers were also wiped or trimmed clear of glaze, again so that it would not run down the flange and stick the cover to the sagger or kiln shelf, or more likely so that the covers could be sat on circular placing-rings to avoid distortion. Some other factories, notably Lowestoft, on the other hand, surmounted the difficulty in other ways and one finds glazed flanges on their teapot covers. Plates, dishes, and other objects could be arranged so that they rested on little triangular stilts rather than on their foot-rims or bases (*see* picture 8), on supports fixed in the sides of the saggers, or simply on roughly circular pads of clay under the base to lift it away from the kiln shelf or sagger base in order to stop the pools of surplus glaze acting as a glue between the figure and the kiln furniture. For a detailed account of "kiln furniture" read David Barker's English Ceramic Circle paper "Bits and Bobs. The Development of Kiln Furniture in the 18th Century Staffordshire Pottery Industry", published in the *Transactions of the English Ceramic Circle* [E.C.C.], Vol.16, Part 3, 1998.

Again, these differing methods of surmounting basic manufacturing problems can be very helpful when identifying pieces. For example, figures made in the 18th century at the Derby factory will often show under the base three pad-marks, which appear as slightly darker patches (*see* picture 9).

Plates and other flat objects made at the Chelsea factory were supported on three or more stilts, the points of which leave little pimple-like blemishes in the glaze (*see* picture 10) while Bow (and some other mainly earthenware) plates and dishes were supported on triangular arms that were affixed one above the other in the sagger walls. These left rough lines at three or more places around the rim on the underside. Such marks on the underside of the flange also occur on tin-glazed, and other types of earthenware, plates and dishes.

Porcelain is normally glazed because the unglazed body can be slightly porous, which means that it would take up staining liquids and be unhygienic in use. The glaze acts as a glass-like surface that, when uncrazed (*see* p.27), forms a watertight skin. Also, the unglazed porcelain is slightly rough to the touch and can have an unpleasant feel. The added glaze flows over the rough body and presents a flat, even, pleasant, clear surface. It forms a near perfect base for any added enamelled decoration or gilding and protects any underglaze decoration. In short, the glaze seals the body, gives a pleasing surface, and facilitates the decorating process.

On the other hand, the glaze does also tend to clog any moulded features and it is amazing to see from unglazed factory wasters how sharp the original

10 The reverse of a red-anchor marked Chelsea plate (*see* picture 99). Note the three spur marks (at the 12, 4, and 8 o'clock positions), the slight spots or blemishes, the ground foot-ring, and the small size of the anchor mark, painted red-anchor mark, *c.*1755. Private collection.

the right conditions. Overfired glaze will bubble, be rather matt, and appear uneven, having run in streams down the pot. Thickly applied glaze tends to bubble too, so that, like boiling water, it loses the all-important translucency. Underfired glaze tends to craze – that is, break up into a network of fine lines.

Glazed wares

By this point a soft-paste English porcelain object has been formed, biscuit fired, glazed, and fired again, at a somewhat lower temperature. It is now ready to be decorated, or possibly to have overglaze colours added if already decorated underglaze. A few pieces would have traditionally been sold in the white, completely devoid of decoration. Such white pieces would have fallen into two classes: those pieces sold to the public for use in this white state, presumably at a rather low price, and other pieces sold to non-factory decorators for them to add their own embellishments. Such independent decorators themselves fell into two classes: the amateur china painter – and there was quite a craze for this form of do-it-yourself painting, the amateur artists being so proud of their work that full signatures would be added, often with the date – and secondly, the many trained and talented ceramic artists who worked alone or in a studio-like establishment, decorating in a highly professional manner white "blank" purchased from the leading manufacturers (*see* Chapter 6, p.68).

Of the many books on the traditional methods of factory production, I find the Revd Malcolm Graham's old work *Cup and Saucer Land* the most informative. Importantly it was written and illustrated with a good range of "action" photographs taken at a period before the whole industry changed, after World War II, which is when high wages speeded up the introduction of automation within at least the major factories. This undated, but *c.*1918, book, published by Madgwick, Houlston & Co. Ltd of London, has the following subtitle: "Being a simple descriptive account of the present day methods of Earthenware production with sixty illustrations from photographs taken by the author when Vicar of a Pottery Parish in North Staffordshire." This book is of course long out of print, but is well worth seeking out.

There is also a very interesting series of Victorian photographs of factory interiors included in Chapter 23 of *Staffordshire Porcelain*, under my editorship (Granada, 1983), but this book is also out of print and therefore will unfortunately be difficult to obtain.

moulding was before the added glaze blunted the design. Glaze can also crack or "craze". This is normally due to an unbalanced coefficient of expansion between the body and the glaze, so the body contracts on cooling at a greater rate than the glaze, which tears it apart. Ideally the glaze should exactly match the body, expanding and contracting with it. Apart from manufacturing faults, sudden heat or too rapid cooling can craze a glaze when the piece is in domestic use.

Glost firing

Glazed objects were next carefully packed in saggers and the saggers placed in the glost kilns to refire the glazed wares. As with the biscuit firing, 18th-century manufacturers had to ensure that smoke and foreign bodies did not stain or otherwise disfigure the ware, but at this point each piece also has to be kept separate from its neighbour for, as I have explained, the melting glaze acts like a strong glue. After glost (or glaze) firing up to some 1,000°C (1,832°F) the wares are taken, after cooling, from the kiln and the saggers. They are examined again for condition and, if perfect or nearly so, the glazed object is passed on to the warehouse. Glaze has to be fired at the correct temperature and in

4
Basic ceramic forms

The proprietors and managers of the newly founded English porcelain factories in the mid-1740s and early 1750s should have acquired a good idea of what articles to produce, for they had, and made use of several sources of inspiration, such as:

(1) imported Chinese porcelains, which by this period almost entirely comprised shapes or objects made solely for the European trade, rather than porcelains made for the Chinese home market;
(2) contemporary European silver objects;
(3) contemporary European pewter wares;
(4) contemporary European porcelains;
(5) contemporary earthenwares;
(6) contemporary glasswares.

In practice these six categories are not really watertight compartments. For example, many of the Chinese porcelain forms had themselves been copied from European prototypes, mainly metal objects. As early as 1699 the English East India Company was matching pewter shapes to porcelain – "send 10,000 coarse and fine plates pewter-fashion", as one order says. In other orders these plates were referred to as "brim plates" to distinguish the European shape with a flat condiment rim from the Oriental, rimless saucer-like plate. On the other hand, early English silver teapots were probably copied from Chinese porcelain wine pots. Each of the European East India companies would have sent its own pattern pieces of silver, pewter, glass, or other materials to be copied in Chinese porcelain. But once the Chinese potters had received a new shape from, say, the French or Dutch traders then in subsequent seasons that shape would have been available in the port of Canton to the buyers of any nation!

Although the sources of inspiration for European porcelain were therefore extremely diverse, in one way and another the ceramic shapes by the 1750s were remarkably well established and international, at least for the standard tablewares that represented the daily production of any factory. Probably two thirds of any porcelain factory's production comprised such teawares. We will now take a closer look at some of these staple products.

Teawares

Any collection or gathering of English, or I suspect any other, porcelain will show a vast array of teawares – cups, saucers, creamers, waste bowls (*see* p.36), teapots, and similar items. Indeed teawares and tea services, or "tea equipages" as they were called, were simply the "bread-and-butter" products of all English porcelain factories.

A typical late 18th-century full tea equipage of good quality would have originally comprised a teapot and cover, a teapot stand, a tea canister (or tea vase) and cover, a milk or cream jug (these often, but not always, had a cover), a sugar bowl and cover, a slop or

11 Representative parts of a Lowestoft tea and coffee service, which have been decorated in underglaze blue and overglaze enamels in the Redgrave style. Coffee pots were not, however, usually supplied in such services, although they could be purchased separately, *c.*1775–80, coffee pot 24.75cm (9¾in) high. This service was formerly part of the Godden collection.

12 A rare form of Rockingham teapot – this was perhaps designed to be more of a cabinet piece to keep on display than a pot for everyday use, 17.75cm (7in) high, *c.*1830–35, formerly Godden of Worthing Ltd.

waste bowl, a spoon tray, 2 saucer-like plates or stands (these were normally of slightly different sizes), 12 teabowls (or handled teacups), 12 coffee cups (or often only six or eight coffee cups) and 12 saucers (*see* picture 11). In addition some services were completed with a coffee pot and cover (some of these pots had their own stand), but such pots were by no means a standard component of tea and coffee sets, which were actually both tea and coffee sets only due to the fact that handled coffee cups were included.

Not all porcelain buyers would have purchased a "full" service as listed. Very many would have needed only cups and saucers to go with their silver or Chinese porcelain tea or coffee pots, milk jugs, and other pieces. Other purchasers would have bought "short" sets that comprised only the main units plus six or eight cups and saucers. In fact then, as now, there was nothing to stop the cash customer (a rare bird!) from buying exactly what she or he wanted and no more. It would also seem likely that some pieces, mainly teapots, were

sold individually, for in several cases no matching teawares are known. In Worcester price lists from about 1760 all articles are listed and priced separately. When a fanciful teapot, such as that shown in picture 12, was purchased it probably didn't have matching cups and saucers, waste bowl, etc. Such a teapot served mainly as a talking point, a novelty, or gimmick, so the rest of the teawares were of a more orthodox nature, possibly not matching the teapot in any way. Even today some shops are full of such modern gimmick teapots, without matching cups and saucers.

Let us now consider each of the standard parts of a "full" tea service separately, for any collector of English porcelain is going to see, and, I hope, handle, an amazing selection of such units.

Teapots

See pictures 11–20, 74–75, 82, 88, 104, 118, 121, 131, 139, 142, 149, 155, 156, 161, 170, 176, 181, 192, 195–6, 198–200, 201, and 205

The general shape of 18th-century teapots was usually copied from the standard Chinese export-market examples, which were basically circular or globular (*see* picture 13). In a few cases English manufacturers divided the body into panels or facets so there are octagonal or hexagonal pots around. In some cases tasteful relief designs were produced by means of moulds, as seen in picture 14.

The delicate relief-moulded patterns seem unique to English porcelains and they can be most pleasing and elegant, especially the Worcester examples of the 1760s. The compact Worcester body permitted the production of crisply moulded relief designs, little spoilt by the near-perfect clear and craze-free glaze, but of course the main praise should be reserved for the unknown designer-modeller who worked the master model in the first place. These designs, while found on teapots, also appeared adapted for the related teawares such as milk jugs.

A very standard Worcester Chinese-type English globular teapot typical of the 1760–70 period is shown in picture 15. Other pots approached barrel shape (*see* picture 16 for an example) and many slight variations were made by various factories within this particular period, but in nearly all cases the circular plan was adhered to.

By the 1790s teapots with an approximately oval plan were introduced, and by 1800 these oval pots were almost universal in Great Britain. The basic shape, which can be called the oval Chamberlain-Worcester form (*see* picture 17), can be found in several versions – with a spiral flute to the body, with upright ribbing or flutes, or in a plain form. This is true of all approximately oval plan or indeed globular teapots. I have included in the description "approximately oval plan" pots those that are often called "silver-shape" (*see* picture 18), a form associated with the New Hall factory but by no means restricted to that manufactory. I call the New Hall-type specimens "turreted pots", as the covers sit within a raised turret-like projection; the time-honoured term silver-shape is unhelpful as practically any porcelain teapot shape can be matched to a silver example. The silver term "Commode shape" is sometimes employed for these forms as well as their many variations.

In the 1820s the teapots returned to the old circular plan but they had a rococo-type curved elevation and the majority of pots were mounted on low feet, again copying silver fashions (*see* picture 19). These moulded rococo-style teapots were capable of a great many variations and, as a general class, they remained in fashion throughout the majority of the Victorian era (*see* picture 20).

Apart from shapes, the main changeable feature over the years was the size of the pots. The early ones, made in the middle of the 18th century, were quite small, reflecting the high cost of tea. The standard teapots then became bigger until they were generally very large in the Victorian era. I have used the term "standard" because teapots, like most basic articles, were made in at least three sizes to suit individual requirements; for example a lone bachelor would not need a large family teapot.

The delicate porcelain teapots presented the English soft-paste manufacturers with many problems, for the shock of boiling water being poured into a cold pot often caused the body to crack. The 18th-century Derby teapots were particularly prone to this fault, while other manufacturers, such as the Worcester management, were able to make great play of the fact that their wares (like the Chinese) would withstand boiling water.

Teapots represent a wonderful field of study and large collections have been formed that focus purely on

13 A large-size Worcester globular teapot and cover. This was painted in underglaze blue with a rare, yet typical, mock-Chinese landscape design, painter's marks under base and inside the cover, 18.5cm (7¼in) high, *c*.1755–60, formerly in the Godden collection.

14 An attractive and well-potted Worcester eight-sided, relief-moulded teapot (missing its cover). Painted with mock-Oriental landscapes in a typical style, painter's mark, 9cm (3½in) high, *c*.1755–8, formerly in the Godden collection.

15 A typical Worcester globular teapot and cover decorated with underglaze blue "scale" ground. The reserved panels in this case are painted with flowers, blue square seal-type mark, 14cm (5½in) high, but sizes vary, *c*.1760–65, Godden of Worthing Ltd.

16 A so-called barrel-shaped Worcester teapot with its cover and stand – all with a moulded fluted body, neatly enamelled and gilt, 14cm (5½in) high, *c*.1775–80, Godden of Worthing Ltd.

17 An oval Chamberlain-Worcester moulded teapot and cover with spiral fluting. The same basic form occurs with vertical fluting, ribs, or simply plain. The neat enamelled and gilt pattern is typical of its period, inscribed, in gold, under the base with "Chamberlains Worcester – 1796 –" 24.75cm (9¾in) long, 1796, Godden collection.

18 A typical New Hall so-called "silver-shape" teapot and cover. Many versions occur and the basic form is not confined to any one factory. This example has a typical simple enamelled pattern, which was tasteful but inexpensive to produce. Raised on moulded feet, 22cm (8¾in) long (various sizes occur), *c*.1790, formerly in the Godden collection.

13

14

15

16

17

18

19

20

19 A superb-quality Minton bone-china "French"-shape moulded teapot and cover. Finely painted and intricately gilt in typical Minton style. Pattern number "763", 14cm (5½in) high, c.1830–35, formerly Godden of Worthing.

20 An early Victorian high, bone-china teapot and cover, with typical intricately moulded handle. It has printed royal motifs, overpainted with enamels, and has a lustre trim, 20cm (8in) high, c.1840–45, formerly Godden of Worthing.

this one article, for such a huge variety of shapes were made and so many different patterns employed to embellish the forms. A good range of early teapots are illustrated in Henry Sandon's *Coffee Pots and Teapots for the Collector* (John Bartholomew & Son, 1973), in Philip Miller and Michael Berthoud's joint book *An Anthology of British Teapots* (Micawber, 1985), and in *British Teapots & Tea Drinking 1700–1850* by Robin Emmerson (HMSO, 1992).

Many 19th-century examples and marked shapes are featured in general works, such as my *Illustrated Encyclopaedia of British Pottery and Porcelain* (Barrie & Jenkins, 1966) or *Staffordshire Porcelain* (Granada, 1983). Several books also feature details of later teapots and the tea-drinking habits of the various eras represented by them.

Teapot stands

| *See* pictures 11 and 16

Most 18th-century porcelain teapots originally had their own separate stand but today it is rare to find an antique teapot still complete with its stand. Today, a lone stand without its teapot represents a desirable find as such little trays are useful, decorative, and extremely collectable in their own right.

As early as 1710 the directors of the East India Company were ordering from China "5000 small deep plates for the teapots", and three years later they were sending a pattern shape formed in tin for the guidance of the Chinese potters: "2000 blue and white small dishes or patty pans to be deep and square according to the pattern in tin, for the teapots to stand on...". It is a matter of debate as to whether these dishes were to match the teapots in painted design but certainly the square shape was not a good match for the circular Oriental teapot forms, and with the later English stands there was also some divergence. A standard globular teapot with a circular plan would seldom, if ever, have a plain circular stand!

The basic teapot-stand shape at Worcester from about 1755 to the 1770s or 1780s had an irregular edge (*see* picture 16) and this form was standard at several other English factories too. On these forms stood a large range of teapots, both globular and barrel-shaped. The globular pots from the Lowestoft factory had a strange eight-sided stand (*see* picture 11), which is seemingly unique to that factory.

With the advent of the turreted teapot in the 1780–1805 period, larger stands were necessary and these were of a form that matched the shaped sides of the pot. Most factories of the 1790–1820 period produced oval stands for various forms of basically oval teapots, but with the introduction of the rococo teapot raised on feet in the 1830s the practice of producing a separate stand almost, but not entirely, ceased.

The object of the stand was to form an insulation between the hot teapot and the tabletop and also to catch any drips from the spout before they soiled a tablecloth. With these stands it is normal to find some rubbing of the overglaze enamels, which occurred due to the abrasive action of the teapot base. From the rarity of pre-1850 stands – they are far scarcer than the teapots – we may be able to assume that not all sets were sold with teapot stands; it may be that only the more expensive "full" sets were so equipped. Indeed, earthenware teapots are seldom found with matching stands. This may be due to the fact that earthenware sets were for the cheaper end of the market.

Tea canisters

| *See* pictures 6, 21, and 22

The "full" tea services of the 18th century, at least those from the major English factories, included an item called a tea jar, tea vase, or tea canister – this was a little covered pot – sometimes, and I believe erroneously, also called a tea caddy or even a tea poy, which are in fact wooden articles.

21

22

21 A uniquely inscribed Lowestoft tea canister (lacking its cover). It has typical enamelled decoration of the 1790s (*see also* picture 133) and monograms on each side, as well as being inscribed with "Joy guide her Footsteps" and dated under base with "1797", 10cm (4in) high, 1797, Godden collection.

22 Three late 18th-century Caughley tea canisters and covers decorated with overglaze enamelled and gilt patterns in very typical styles, 11.5cm (4½in) high, *c.*1785–90, formerly Godden of Worthing.

Britain was importing porcelain tea canisters from China in the 17th century and was ordering them by the thousand, both blue-and-white examples and those with enamelled patterns, in the early part of the 18th century, while the standard Chinese export-market tea services included this article. It would appear that porcelain tea vases were filled with Chinese tea, which was tipped or measured into the teapot on the table by the hostess. The (usually metal) tea urn held the hot water, not prepared tea. It has been stated that Worcester tea sets of the 1760s contained a pair of tea canisters, one for Bohea (or black) tea and one for green tea; although very few inscribed pairs are known as they were not part of standard sets (which contained only one covered canister).

These now rare and often delightful objects (alas so often missing their cover) seem to have gone out of favour by about 1800, and even before this at some factories. I do not remember seeing a Pinxton example, nor for that matter a Derby example after 1785 but at the Caughley (*see* picture 22) and Lowestoft works, at least, they were made into the 1790s. I cannot resist showing you a charming Lowestoft gem (*see* picture 21), which must surely represent a unique presentation piece. By the 1800s the lockable two-compartment wooden tea caddy seems to have come fully into fashion so porcelain examples were seldom produced.

In March 2002 the partners in Stockspring Antiques (in Kensington Church Street, London, W8) held a breathtaking loan exhibition of ceramic tea canisters. This was a wonderful, instructive array of Oriental, Continental, and British examples. The lasting value of this is to be seen in the excellent exhibition catalogue, entitled *Tea, Trade & Tea Canisters*, by Antonia Agnew, David Doxey, and Felicity Marno. This is a wonderful introduction to tea and ceramic tea canisters for any collector who is interested in learning more about this subject.

Milk jugs

| *See* pictures 4, 7, 23, 25, 58, 77, 79, 86, 98, 124, 150, 165, 167, 170, 194, 196, and 202

Milk jugs, or "milk pots", and the related creamers are among the most charming of 18th-century English porcelain objects. It is often difficult to know which is a milk jug and which is a creamer but it matters little. I regard upright jugs as being for milk and the low, long, ewers as creamers.

The simple sparrow-beak jugs (*see* pictures 11, 23, 76, and 77), so-called because of the resemblance of their neat, pointed lip to the beak of a garden bird, were

23

24

25

made at nearly every English factory before 1790. The early relief-moulded Worcester examples can be superb (*see* pictures 4 and 7) while the later, post-1790 milk jugs from all factories represent a wide field of study. I show in picture 25 a superb Neale porcelain covered example. From about 1820 the general tendency was for the milk jugs to be low, wide, and squat – typical examples are shown in pictures 220 and 221.

Cream ewers

| *See* pictures 24, 26, 84, 85, 98, 124, 144, and 146

It has been claimed that early tea sets of perhaps the 1760–70 period included both a milk jug and a cream ewer. I do not think this was the case and I cannot remember seeing any set with both these articles. It would also be difficult to find low cream ewers that match even the most common teaware patterns, although very many taller milk jugs are known of these standard designs.

Perhaps the best-known low shape is that which is known as the "Chelsea ewer", which is an 18th-century term for the basic form shown in picture 24. These are, strangely enough, very rarely found in Chelsea porcelain but are well known in Worcester and Caughley porcelain and they occur also in Lowestoft, Liverpool, New Hall, and Coalport wares. All these low cream ewers are attractive and collectable, and occur in some considerable variety. Cream ewers or milk jugs were made in hundreds of different shapes and were enhanced with thousands of patterns. (Pictures 4, 7, 23–26, 58, 77, 79, 86, 98, 124, and 150 show a small selection.)

23 Three "sparrow-beak" milk or cream jugs. Left to right: Bristol hard-paste with enamelled decoration, Worcester covered jug of soapstone body decorated in gilding, and Isleworth-type soft-paste jug with calcined bone added to the mix. Printed in underglaze blue with hand-painted border. Different styles of decoration and different basic porcelains, centre jug 12.75cm (5in) high with cover, c.1765–80, Godden Reference collection.

24 A New Hall "high Chelsea ewer" and Worcester "low Chelsea ewer" representing popular shapes made by most English porcelain factories in the 1770–1800 period. Various enamelled or printed patterns adorn such pieces, 9.5 and 7cm (3¾ and 2¾in) high (variations of size do occur), c.1780–85, Godden collection.

25 A very rare Neale porcelain Staffordshire milk jug and cover of superb quality. This was trimly potted and neatly painted by Fidelle Duvivier, 11.5cm (4½in) high, c.1790–95, Godden Reference collection.

26 Right, an unusually fine and ornate Chelsea milk or cream jug, complete with cover. Rare claret ground colour, neatly enamelled with tooled gilding – nearly the best that could be produced, representing an expensive tea service, perhaps originally costing 15–20 guineas, gold anchor mark, 12cm (4¾in) high, c.1760, Godden collection.

Sugar bowls

| *See* pictures 38–9

These bowls, variously called in the 18th century "sugar pots" or "sugar boxes", and, more recently, "sucriers", were in their various forms part of most tea services. They were intended, as the name suggests, to hold sugar and for this reason they originally had a cover, although some narrow boat-shaped sugar pots made at Worcester and Pinxton (and at a third unknown factory) in the 1795–1810 period were open, without a cover. In general sugar bowls were deeper but narrower than the open waste bowl (*see* below). Being standard articles sugar bowls were made at all factories and during all periods. In general they follow the basic shape of the teapot: for example, an oval teapot of the 1805 period would have an oval sugar box, while a rococo teapot, a rococo sugar bowl.

However, some low-priced 18th and early 19th-century tea services did not include a special, covered sugar bowl, but rather a small extra open bowl was included instead. This was simply a slightly scaled-down waste bowl.

Slop or waste bowls

| *See* pictures 11, 27, 97, 114, 115, 123, and 160

The low, open bowl or "bason" was a standard item of the tea service. Although made in various sizes such bowls seem rather large to us today and this may be because the silver tea-strainer was not in general use so each cup would have held more dregs than we are used to finding. We must also remember that the cut tea leaves were somewhat larger than we use nowadays.

27 A Minton bone-china slop bowl from a tea service. Each piece from the service was painted with different decorative views. The trellis – ground in gold – however, took longer than the enamelling to complete, pattern number 150, diameter 14.5cm (5¾in), c.1805–10, formerly Godden of Worthing.

Little can be said about these bowls; they follow the moulded or painted design on the teapot and can be decorative and desirable objects. It could well be that during the 1760–70 period some were sold with an underplate. A surprisingly large number of 18th-century slop bowls seem to have survived, perhaps because some were simply open sugar bowls, so tea sets started life with two bowls.

Spoon trays

See pictures 11, 28, and 29

These little narrow trays or "spoon boats" (to use a contemporary term), represent one of the rarest and most attractive items of 18th-century tea equipment. As the name suggests, these trays were to hold the wet teaspoons as, with the mode of drinking the tea from the teabowl on its saucer, if the spoon was left on the saucer it would either swing round to hit the drinker in the cheek or fall with a clatter onto the table or floor. Hence tea sets included one communal spoon tray that would have held six or so spoons; or perhaps the hostess, after pouring the cup, would sugar and stir it for her guests using one spoon only. This helped to keep the tea table neat and tidy.

Spoon trays are found in Chinese porcelain, in Staffordshire saltglaze stoneware, and in most other ceramic bodies, but no other has such attractive results as the porcelain examples. The fashion for these trays was changing in the 1790s and practically none were made after 1800. They are rare and desirable because they are so attractive but certainly not all tea services would have been sold with a spoon tray and English examples produced before about 1755 are particularly rare.

Bread and butter plates

Eighteenth-century English tea services did not include individual plates, which are now a standard part of modern sets. They did, however, include two saucer-shaped plates of slightly different sizes. The original uses of these two plates are open to some debate. They are often regarded as bread and butter or cake plates and indeed post-1800 services included two-handled plates or dishes for such usage. However some 18th-century records list these plates as being the slop basin stand and the sugar bowl stand and this may account for the slightly differing size of the 18th-century plates.

Even if the original use for these saucer-like plates was for stands, this would seem to have changed to the more normal use as bread and butter or cake plates by at least the mid-1780s and probably some time before

28

29

28 A rare Longton Hall spoon tray of characteristic shape, painted in underglaze blue with a design unique to this Staffordshire factory, 15.75 x 10.75cm (6¼ x 4¼in), *c*.1755, Godden and Dr Watney collections.

29 A rare Vauxhall porcelain spoon tray printed in outline in various colours. The special printed design would have been filled in or overpainted by hand, 12.75 x 9cm (5 x 3½in), *c*.1760, Dr Watney and Godden collections.

this. Certainly when the oval- or boat-shaped sugar bowl came into fashion the circular plates remained part of the standard service, although the oval sugar bowl would not sit evenly upon the circular plate!

Teabowls and saucers

See pictures 11, 30, 32, 141, 161, and 173

Early English tewares were adapted from Oriental wares and this is seen in the use, throughout most of

30 An attractive raised-anchor marked Chelsea teabowl and saucer, typically painted with landscapes and scattered flowers, raised anchor mark (on applied small oval pad), diameter of saucer 10.75cm (4¼in), c.1750, Godden collection, ex Uppark, West Sussex.

the 18th century, of handleless teabowls. Such a bowl can be trimly turned by a potter with little trouble, and the walls do not have to be thickened to take the weight and pull of an added handle in the firing process. Any potter would surely rather make a teabowl than produce a handled cup. It is little wonder then that the fashion for teabowls continued for so long: tea sets with handleless teabowls were cheaper than the better-class ones with handled teacups.

In use, however, the thin teabowl presents problems, especially when the bowl is small, as the early examples were. The bowl becomes very hot and can only be held by the finger and thumb grasping the top rim or the foot-ring, or with the thumb under the foot and the finger on the rim, but it cannot be picked up or set down using the latter approach. It can, of course, also be taken to the mouth on its saucer – if you have a steady hand and if you have previously placed the spoon on the spoon tray.

It is an over-simplification to state, as is so often done, that all early teacups were handleless; in fact some handled cups were made by leading firms such as the Worcester partnership and these, by their general low, wide bowl shape (in contrast to the tall, narrow coffee cups), are certainly teacups. These rather rare handled teacups were, as a rule, only supplied with the more expensive sets.

Teabowls were still made into the 19th century, especially for the cheaper range of teawares, but by about 1810 the handled and larger teacup was almost universal. Of all the porcelain teawares, teabowls and teacups are the most plentiful. Not only were 12 sold with each "full" set, as opposed to one waste bowl or milk jug, but also many sets of bowls and saucers were sold on their own. This is because a family with its own silver teapot, sugar bowl, and cream jug would still need china cups and saucers. Silver teabowls or cups are almost unknown for the simple reason that the hot liquid makes the silver too hot to hold. As early as 1681 we find remarks such as, "that which will turn us best to account are cups of all kinds, sizes and colours" in the instructions to the English buyers in China. To the present-day collector teabowls and saucers have great charm, especially the early relief-moulded teabowls of the 1750–60 period. The more mundane later examples, perhaps bearing an underglaze blue-printed design, represent the most inexpensive of Georgian ceramics. They can at the same time be typical pieces and also very attractive.

Coffee cups

| *See* pictures 11, 31, and 32

The pre-1790 English tea and coffee services were normally sold with twelve, eight, or six coffee cups. The exact number varied from factory to factory, or according to the purchaser's requirements, but separate saucers were not made as the coffee cups were used with the standard (teabowl) saucer. A coffee cup is normally tall and narrow, when compared with a teabowl or teacup, and has one handle (*see* pictures 31 and 32, right). In addition it can be found embellished with any of the standard relief-moulded designs or enhanced with any one of whole host of a blue-and-white or enamelled patterns.

31 An octagonal early Worcester coffee cup and saucer, typically painted in Oriental-style with semi-translucent enamel colours. The saucer is thinner in the potting than the Chelsea example shown in picture 30, diameter of saucer 10.75cm (4¼in), *c.*1755, private collection.

32 A Flight-period Worcester trio of teabowl, coffee cup, and saucer. Painted in underglaze blue, neatly completed in gold, small-size crescent marks, diameter of saucer 14cm (5½in), *c.*1785–90, Godden collection.

We call these taller cups "coffee cups" but there was nothing to stop them being used for tea, and they probably were. They are certainly more convenient to use than the handleless teabowl, and the smaller exposed surface area means the liquid retains its heat longer. While speaking of tea and coffee we must not lose sight of the fact that chocolate was a very popular drink in the 18th century and so many cups would have had a dual function; a 1710 buying instruction relating to Chinese porcelain makes this point: "8000 small cups with one handle, fit for coffee or chocolate", although by the 1760s the chocolate cups tended to be larger, sometimes with two handles and a cover. A teabowl (or cup) with a matching coffee cup (or can) with their saucer, is called a trio, *see* picture 32.

Coffee cans

| *See* pictures 33, 108, 134, 208, 218, and 220

A coffee "can" differs from a coffee cup in that the sides are cylindrical (*see* picture 33). Small cans or mugs were made at many porcelain factories in the 1750–60 period (at Bow and Worcester for example), but these rare early cans (or mugs) were never issued as part of a standard tea set. From about 1775 Bristol and other factories produced rather large straight-sided cans and saucers ornately decorated in the Sèvres style (*see* p.45) and these, like the fine Derby examples, were often individual pieces or pairs made for the cabinet rather than for everyday use.

By about 1800, however, the coffee can had almost superseded the shaped coffee cup at all the English factories, yet in the space of some 15 or 20 years the coffee can had, in turn, given way to more fanciful forms of coffee cup. It may be thought that apart from the different bodies and glazes, the straight-sided can offers little help to the inquiring collector. This is not so, for the different handles offer a very reliable guide to origin.

33 Left: a New Hall hybrid hard-paste coffee can. The scenic panel was printed by the bat-printing process, with gilt trim. On the right is a hand-painted and gift bone-china coffee can, from "Factory Z" (*see* p.166). 6.25cm (2½in) high, *c*.1805, Godden collection.

A good selection of coffee cups and cans as well as teacups are illustrated in Michael Berthoud's specialist book *An Anthology of British Cups* (Micawber, 1982) as well as in its two supplements *A Compendium of British Cups* (1990) and *Cups in Colour* by M. Berthoud and R. Maskell (Micawber Publications, 2003).

Coffee pots

| *See* pictures 11, 34–5, 96, 126, 143, 198, and 199

I have left till last the consideration of porcelain coffee pots for they were not part of the standard service, rather they were only part of special "long" services (services with extra units) or were supplied to the customer's express wish, since many families would have had their silver coffee pot.

Porcelain coffee pots are truly elegant pieces of traditional tall form; especially pleasing are the early Worcester examples (*see* picture 34*). It is strange but true that porcelain coffee pots of the 19th century are rarely found and yet hundreds of thousands of tea and coffee services were made and in constant use. The reason, as stated above, was probably that silver or silver-plated pots were used instead.

An interesting book that includes illustrations of various porcelain coffee pots is Henry Sandon's *Coffee Pots and Teapots for the Collector*.

Breakfast services

| *See* picture 36

As well as the standard tea services there was a far lesser number of breakfast services, which may loosely be regarded as enlarged tea sets. Such sets came into favour in about the 1790s. Apart from a rather large teacup (*see* picture 36), there were also the now rare egg cups (*see* picture 36), a pint-size milk jug, honey pots (these may be found in the form of a beehive), butter pots, covered muffin dishes, and sometimes small plates. An account for a Chamberlain-Worcester breakfast service** of the 1820 period lists:

12 teacups and saucers, 12 breakfast cups and saucers,
8 (3rd size) plates, 2 loaf (bread) plates,
1 sugar box, 1 square sugar basket,
1 pint jug (for milk), 1 cream jug,
1 slop basin,
2 muffins and covers,
2 butter tubs and stands,

34

35

34 A rare early Worcester coffee pot of small size, painted in underglaze blue with a one-off Oriental landscape design (reverse side shown), painter's tally mark, 14cm (5½in) high, *c*.1752–5, Godden collection.

35 An elegant and neatly potted Neale porcelain coffee pot in the classical style. Impressed mark saying "Neale & Co", 26cm (10¼in) high, *c*.1790, Godden collection.

* See *Godden's Guide to English Blue and White Porcelain* (Antique Collectors' Club, 2004), Plate 146, for the front of this small coffee pot.
** This make-up is by no means universal. Different firms at different times issued their own idea of a breakfast service.

36

37

36 Part of a richly decorated breakfast service from Chamberlain-Worcester. Note on the right the large-sized breakfast cup and saucer and the egg cup. Diameter of plate 23cm (9in), *c*.1830, Godden of Worthing.

37 A rare Caughley porcelain cabaret or déjeuné set, painted in underglaze blue and finished in gold. The set has underglaze blue "S" marks, tray 35.5 x 26cm (14 x 10¼in), *c*.1785, Godden collection.

38 Part of a Derby cabaret or déjeuné set with its tray, typically neatly and well-painted in puce monochrome. This set was probably painted by Zachariah Boreman, puce Derby crowned crossed-baton mark, tray 27.25cm (10¾in) long, *c*.1790, Sothebys.

39 A Minton ribbed bridal déjeuné or early morning tea set with its large tray. The company registered the basic shapes on 13 April 1850. This set has neatly enamelled and gilt decoration, a registration mark and Minton year mark, tray 44.5 x 31.75cm (17½ x 12½in), *c*.1850–51, formerly in the Godden collection.

1 teapot and stand, 12 coffees,
2 egg stands (three egg cups each).

While discussing the rare items such as muffins and butter tubs we can also add unusual objects such as covered custard cups. These rare little pieces were often sold in sets on a tray or stand. There are also covered "ice cups" or ice-cream cups, spoons, ladles, salts, and even, from about 1820, porcelain toast racks.

Cabaret or déjeuné services

| *See* pictures 37–9

These delightful tea equipages were set on a shaped tray and comprised a small teapot, a milk or cream pot, a sugar box, and one or two cups and saucers. This sounds simple enough but these services are little treasures, not only because the items are delicate and small, of forms not normally seen, but because they are usually decorated in rich styles.

One such set in the leading auctioneer Mr Christie's sale of Chelsea and Derby porcelains held in April 1771 was catalogued as, "a large déjeuné, consisting of a teapot, milk-pot, sugar-box, two cups and saucers, the stand for ditto most curiously painted in cupids, with a musical trophy, with a fine blue celeste ground round the compartment, curiously chased with bull-rushes and ornamented with burnished gold".

Typical if rather early examples are shown in Plates 150, 218 and 219 of my *Illustrated Encyclopaedia of British Pottery and Porcelain*. Other, later ones were made in the 1800–20 period and again in the second half of the 19th century by firms such as Mintons (*see* picture 39) and Royal Worcester. Pre-1820 examples are very rarely found complete and when they are you will have to be prepared to reach deep into your pocket if you want one!

Cabinet cups

| *See* picture 40

The superb, richly decorated cabaret services lead us on to a class of ornamental, often large, cups and saucers, with the cup often having a can shape with straight sides. These cups may be single or double handled and some of them originally had covers. The objects can be so fine that it is difficult to believe that they were made for use – hence the term "cabinet cup". This was a contemporary classification and yet they actually served a dual purpose for, to quote Mr Christie's 1783 catalogue of Chelsea and Derby or "Chelsea-Derby" porcelain, we find such pieces described in the following

38

39

way, "A pair of very beautiful caudle or cabinet cups, covers and stands, enamelled in compartments with rose coloured cupids and richly finished with burnished gold stripes." (This was knocked down to Mrs Christie at £2/19/0d.) or a "pair of very elegant caudle or cabinet cups, covers and stands, peacock pattern, enamelled fine blue and gold". (Caudle was a hot gruel-like drink spiced and laced with wine much drunk by invalids or nursing mothers.)

Others were described only as cabinet cups without covers, "a superb and elegant cabinet cup and saucer enamelled in compartments with landscapes, fine ultramarine blue ground richly furnished with chased and burnished gold." A further description acknowledges the rather obvious origin of these magnificent articles, the Sèvres factory, "One pair superbly elegant French-shape cups and saucers enamelled in compartments with figures, fine ultramarine blue ground richly finished with chased and burnished gold." The saucers that went with richly decorated Derby coffee cans (*see* picture 108) were originally described as "stands", perhaps suggesting they were display items. They were also individual pieces, not sold as part of a service.

The tradition for these fine cabinet cups, so suitable as presents, continued up to about 1820, with the Derby, Chamberlain-Worcester, and the Barr, Flight & Barr (and Flight, Barr & Barr) Worcester factories all specializing in such objects.

40 A fine-quality Chamberlain-Worcester cabinet cup and saucer, painted with named views in Scotland and Hertfordshire, written "Chamberlain-Worcester" mark with descriptions, diameter of saucer 14.5cm (5¾in), *c.*1815, Godden of Worthing.

Chocolate cups

| *See* picture 41

The same 1783 auction of Chelsea-Derby porcelain also contained chocolate cups as did many other sales: "six chocolate cups and saucers, enamelled with roses, festoons of green husks and purple and gold border". Chocolate cups are usually larger than teacups, often with twice the capacity and with one or two handles. Some originally had covers, as is evidenced by the Chamberlain-Worcester accounts in July 1799, "2 chocolates, two-handled, with covers and saucers. Best Queen's (pattern)", and in May 1803, "6 rich figured chocolates, complete with covers and stands, pattern 305 at £4/4/0d."

Dinner services

| *See* pictures 43, 45, and 182

After teawares it might be easy to assume that the next most important standard ceramic product would be dinner sets or, as they were called, "table services", with

41

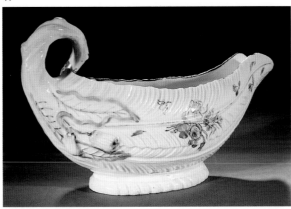

42

43

41 A rare Chelsea-Derby cabinet, chocolate, or caudle cup and saucer decorated in the general Sèvres style. The figure panels were perhaps by Fidelle Duvivier, incised cursive "N" mark on saucer and gold-anchor marks, diameter of saucer 15.75cm (6¼in), c.1775, formerly in the Godden collection.

42 A finely moulded large-size Worcester cos lettuce-form sauceboat of characteristic shape, enamelled with typical floral sprays. This shape was made in different sizes and decorated in various styles, painter's tally mark, 21cm (8¼in) long, c.1755, Godden of Worthing.

43 A colourful Chamberlain-Worcester circular tureen and cover (missing its stand) decorated in the popular "Japan" style. The complete service was originally £63. Printed "Chamberlain-Worcester" mark, pattern number 886, 25cm (10in) high, c.1825, Godden of Worthing.

their long runs of plates and dishes. This was not the case for, with the notable exception of the Bow factory, the English manufacturers before 1765 were largely content to let the imported Chinese porcelains supply the need for inexpensive table services. I say "content", but in fact they had little choice as they could not compete with the imported wares. The Chinese potters could produce thousands of thin hard-paste plates without a trace of warping or other blemish while English manufacturers using a heat-prone artificial porcelain could not approach these standards. The Worcester factories, for example, did produce some magnificent tureens (*see* picture 43) but the surviving pre-1760 plates and dishes can almost be counted on the fingers of one hand! It is simply impossible to find complete 18th-century dinner services, but such items as tureens, large meat or vegetable dishes, and sauceboats (*see* picture 42) originally adorned the dinner table.

So English manufacturers were undercut in price by the Chinese and came a poor second to their potting skill. This is not to say that no English manufacturer produced dinner services. Several did but not on a large scale, apart from some magnificently rich Chelsea porcelain examples.

A May 1782 sale of Chelsea and Derby porcelains sold by Mr Christie included, "a complete set of table-china enamelled with groups of coloured flowers, and richly finished with a fine blue and gold vine border, consisting of 60 table dinner plates, 24 soup plates, 20 oval dishes in sizes, 1 pair tureens and covers, 4 sauce boats and stands and a salad dish" (sold for £44/2/0d). This is a reasonably representative make-up of a dinner service of the 1770–90 period. There are two points to make about them: first, these early sets did not usually include small-size "side plates" and, secondly, the 20 oval dishes that were supplied in graduating sizes were vegetable dishes, which were flat and also uncovered. The salad dishes are normally somewhat shallower than a punch bowl and they usually have a shaped edge.

On a more mundane and less costly level we find listed in a sale of Worcester porcelain by Mr Christie in December 1769, an underglaze blue-printed dinner service of a tureen cover and stand, 16 oblong dishes in five different sizes, two sauceboats, four oval "compoteers" (comports), two round dishes, 48 dinner plates, and 24 soup plates. The complete set was sold for a mere £5/7/6d, which underlines my point concerning the remarkably low price of the blue-printed wares. You may have noted, in both the sets listed, the inclusion of sauceboats, perhaps the most graceful and collectable of all dinner-service components. These are to be found in amazing variety (*see* picture 42), originating from every pre-1780 English porcelain factory and, although some of these noble boats were included with dinner services, a great many others must have been sold separately, in pairs or sets of four – as of course were silver sauceboats.

Fine tureens are known from many factories and can be found in numerous ornate and fanciful forms, such as a boar's head or carp-form tureens with stands, but these were made as special centrepieces, not as part of a standard service. Early English soup plates made prior to 1770 are remarkably scarce.

In the latter part of the 18th century the imported Chinese dinner services were much more complete than English products, comprising large meat platters, covered dishes, salts, and even hot-water plates and dishes (these were double-walled vessels that could be filled with hot water to retain the heat of the food) as well as the normal tureens (of two sizes), dishes, and plates.

By about 1800, however, the English sets were, or could be, superb, especially those from the Worcester factories, where the compact, durable porcelain and good glazing, coupled with neat potting and quality painting, as well as the tasteful gilding, captured the market that the Chinese had held for so long. Try to picture a fine mahogany table dressed with sets such as the "Stowe" (Buckingham residence) combined dinner and dessert service (*see* picture 45). These pretentious services were almost too good to use but equal potting skill also went into the less expensive services, some of

which were decorated in a very restrained style, with little floral sprays or merely with a gold border. Throughout the 19th century most everyday services were of course made in pottery rather than porcelain. The English earthenwares were world renowned and varied, with such 19th-century strong bodies as the "stone-china" and "Masons Patent Ironstone China" wares. The porcelain services from the Minton or Spode factories were far more expensive and met a relatively small but upperclass market.

Dessert services

| *See* pictures 44–5 and 100

After teawares the main standby of the English 18th-century factories was not dinner services but the related dessert services. This was a class of porcelain strangely neglected by the Chinese potters, or rather by the European traders or East India Companies responsible for ordering and importing the Oriental porcelain.

The dessert service market was a very important one in England and many of the single pieces found in collections or museums today were originally part of such services – certainly most of the plates that have a diameter of less than 21.5cm (8½in), the variously shaped side dishes, and many other objects. Our cabinets would look very bare if we were to withdraw the dessert service pieces, for we would lose not only the standard shapes that have been mentioned above but also most

44 A Flight-Worcester royal plate from the Order of the Thistle service made for the Duke of Clarence in 1789. Blue painted mark – "Flight" under a crown over a small crescent, diameter 24cm (9½in), *c.*1789, formerly in the Godden collection.

45 A typically fine-quality Barr, Flight & Barr period Worcester dessert plate bearing the crests and family motto of the Marquess of Buckingham, impressed "BFB" and crown mark, also with large printed mark, diameter 19cm (7½in), *c.*1813, Godden of Worthing.

of the openwork baskets (*see* picture 54), leaf-shaped dishes, a host of tureens, and even some figures. I will quote three lots from contemporary sales to illustrate my point, first, one from the Chelsea sale of February 1770, "A beautiful complete service for a dessert, consisting of two large basket-work dishes, two oval baskets with handles, two large rosette compoteers, four oval green edge ditto, four vine-leaf dishes, four seven-leaf ditto, four strawberry ditto, four shell ditto, and three dozen of plates, finely enamelled in groups of flowers" (sold for £30/9/0d). Note the inclusion in this service of 16 leaf-shaped dishes of four different forms. The Chelsea sale catalogues also include very many similar fancy dessert forms sold separately, lots such as "four small cabbage leaves enamelled in flowers, after nature, for a dessert" (sold for £1/9/0d).

By no means all Chelsea dessert dishes were of leaf shape. For example, another service sold in the same 1770 sale comprised: "...two large oval baskets, two openwork rosette dishes, two close [not openwork?] ditto, four round compoteers, four oval, twelve scollop'd ditto, four silver-shap'd ditto, four leaves, four round baskets and twenty-four plates with the pea-green edge, all finely enamelled with fruit" (sold for £31/10/0d). In this set there are several baskets but others were sold separately as "one large oval two-handled basket for a dessert" (sold for £1/11/6d). The earlier mention of fruit painting on these dessert plates prompts me to introduce a tantalizing quotation, a Chelsea service that was the property of John Follett, "A small dessert service of beautiful Chelsea china, consisting of a sugar bowl cover and stand, 2 lemons and covers, 2 oval baskets, 15 small fruit dishes, 1 extra large plate, and 2 pairs of partridges on their nests to contain sugar, etc." This lot was sold for a mere £4/6/0d! Admittedly this sale was in 1813 and cannot be considered a contemporary reference to the use of the two-piece partridge tureens or covered sugar boxes. However, it is easy to believe that the small lemon and other fruit boxes graced a table at dessert, although the partridges and other bird-boxes might be more suited to sauces than to sugar; at all events, they were most certainly made for use on the table. While mentioning fruit-shaped Chelsea porcelain boxes I should add that one lot that was sold in 1771 included: four pears, three pomegranates, four lemons, six citrons, eight melons, two figs, two artichokes, five lettuces, four sunflowers, and a rose, all sold for a mere £1/5/0d. You are, of course, unlikely to find a complete 18th-century dessert service, only individual pieces – and mainly plates. A superb range of dessert services were produced in the 19th century, *see* page 50 for more details.

Dessert figures and candlesticks

| *See* pictures 9 and 47

Other articles that were made to grace the table during dessert were vases, and in Chelsea sale catalogue lots there were many such listings as "twelve small dessert vases". A 1760 advertisement for another sale of Chelsea porcelain sheds light on the use of at least some of these vases when it reads, "variety of baskets, leaves, compotiers, sweetmeat vases for dessert and some small figures for ditto". Turning to figures we find these again mentioned in a notice relating to the 1763 sale, "...a large variety of handsome candlesticks, large groups of figures and single ditto of all sizes for desserts..." The groups and figures for a dessert would mainly be those

46 A rare Chelsea rococo-form candlestick (one of a pair), well painted with figure subjects. Gold-anchor period but bearing a brownish anchor mark, 26.5cm (10½in) high, *c.*1760, J.A. Davidson collection.

that incorporate baskets or other containers such as shell-shape bowls to hold comfits (breath sweeteners), small fruits, or the like (*see* pictures 9 and 47). However, many figures or groups were used purely for decoration on the table. In the last quotation there was mention of "handsome candlesticks". Remembering that all 18th-century lighting was candlepower, and mostly at table level, it is obvious that the dinner table must have held candlesticks of one material or another. In the homes of the wealthy many of these would have been made out of porcelain, but far from being simple pillar sticks modelled on brass or pewter examples, these porcelain candlesticks were decorative and ornate focal points of the table (*see* picture 46). Here are a few Chelsea candlestick models as listed in the 1770 sale catalogue:

One pair of large table candlesticks, with dog, fox, grapes, &c
A pair of candlesticks with a sportsman and companion
A pair of large ditto, with an ox, ass &c
A pair of table candlesticks, goat in a well
A pair of boar-hunting candlesticks
A pair of Black-a-moor candlesticks
A pair of candlesticks for four lights, with groups of figures, representing the four seasons, curiously decorated with flowers.

This last item in particular serves to remind us that the fashion for these table novelties, the fruit and other fancy-shaped boxes, the table figures and groups, and the ornate table candlesticks, came to England from the Continent and several English models would have been copied from Dresden (Meissen) porcelain originals. Mrs Elizabeth Adams gives a good account of Chelsea dessert wares, figures, and other dessert table dressings in her book *Chelsea Porcelain* (The British Museum Press, 2001).

Ice-pails
| *See* pictures 48, 49, and 68

Our list of dessert wares is by no means exhausted – some of the more expensive dessert services included open ice-pails, normally of jardinière-form but sometimes oval with two separate compartments. These ice-pails, or fruit-coolers, were for cooling the wine bottle in a bed of crushed ice. From about 1780 the three-piece ice-pail

with an inner bowl and handled cover was produced. These were sold in matching pairs, one such pair being included in Christie's 1785 sale of Derby porcelain, "a pair of elegant ice-pails, basons and covers, enamelled with groups of flowers, fine mazarine-blue ground richly gilt". These three-piece pails were probably for chilling fruit of various kinds, although if the liner and cover were removed they would serve to hold a wine bottle. Fruit-coolers remained fashionable until at least the 1820s; they are quite scarce and costly items and rarely found complete and perfect today. When *in situ* they are imposing items of decoration on a sideboard or on a pair of tables.

Shell centrepieces
| *See* picture 50

Another popular and imposing item of dessert dressage was the shell centrepiece. Christie's 1769 Worcester porcelain sale included, for example, "a curious stand for the centre of a dessert decorated with shells, &c". Such shell pieces were made at Bow, Derby, Plymouth, and Worcester. Probably the last examples made in the

47 One of a pair of early Derby seated figures holding baskets for bon-bons, and suchlike. Note the sharp modelling and restraint of decoration; typical pad marks under the base, 18.5cm (7¼in) high, *c.*1760, Godden of Worthing.

48 One of a pair of Derby ice-pails or fruit coolers, with intricately gilt borders. Inscribed on base "near Broseley, Shropshire" with the Derby mark of crown, crossed batons, and "D", in red, 24.75cm (9¾in) high, *c.*1820, Godden of Worthing.

49

50

18th century were the shell-form "pickle-stands" made at the Chamberlain factory in Worcester in the early 1790s, although the Irish Belleek factory made rather similar shell centrepieces in the 1870s and beyond.

Nineteenth-century dessert services

See pictures 52, 51, 69, 100, 127, 154, 168, 175, 182, 183, 211–12, 215, 217, 222, 223–25, 229, 236

By the 1780s, and certainly the 1790s, the dessert table began to simmer down. It lost its old flamboyance as the novelties gave way to much more utilitarian forms. In place of the fruit-shaped covered boxes or tureens and the partridge tureens there was a pair of circular or oval covered tureens and stands enamelled to match the plates and dishes. Contemporary catalogues and factory records show us that these tureens, or rather covered bowls, were for cream and sugar. Some were equipped with matching porcelain spoons. These delicate articles are nearly always lost or broken today.

The centrepiece settled down to become an almost standard dish mounted on a low stand. This item was usually around 7.5–10cm (3–4in) high. The various shaped dishes were still flat rather than raised on a separate base or stem. Many dessert services of the 1790–1820 period were truly magnificent in the painted and gilt decoration they bore. After about 1820 the side dishes tended to be raised by about 5cm (2in) on

49 One of a pair of magnificent Coalport four-piece ice-pails or fruit coolers in hybrid hard-paste porcelain that would have been part of a dessert service. Very richly gilt and painted. 33cm (13in) high, *c.*1810, Godden of Worthing.

50 A Derby shell-form centrepiece pickle stand, painted in underglaze blue. Such elaborate articles normally show some damage or repair. Typical Derby patch marks and rarer number "1" – perhaps to link it to the correct separate base, 15.75cm (6¼in) high, *c.*1760, Phillips, ex Dr Watney collection.

51 Representative pieces from a Minton dessert service of the mid-1840s, when footed comports of various heights had come into favour. Pattern number 5337, tureen (one of a pair) 15.25cm (6in) high, *c.*1845–50, Godden of Worthing.

52 Representative pieces from a Samuel Alcock dessert service, showing typical shapes of the 1840s. Painted with various decorative scenes, pattern number 2/5718, 15.75cm (6¼in) high, *c.*1845, Godden of Worthing.

53 A two-tier centrepiece from a Minton Sèvres-style dessert service of the 1860s. This shows the attractive use of white unglazed parian in contrast with the glazed porcelain. Typically fine quality, a piece still in daily use. Impressed marks "MINTON", "550" (the model number), and the year mark, 38cm (15in) high, 1868, Godden collection.

feet or a shaped foot. The centrepiece, or comport, was now mounted on a central stem that was at least 15.25cm (6in) high.

The post-1840 Victorian porcelain dessert services almost defy description as they were so varied. The standard sets, if any can be so described, comprised one

51

52

53

or two tall comports, about 20cm (8in) high, mounted on a central stem, two similar comports around 15.25cm (6in) high, and four low comports some 5cm (2in) high. The dished top of the comports matched the outline of the plates, and were basically of circular plan. The standard sets would have included 12, 18, or 24 plates, according to the customer's choice and pocket. The more costly services might still have a pair of tureens – for sugar and cream (*see* pictures 52 and 51).

The major factories such as Minton, Copelands, and Royal Worcester also produced really sumptuous services, the centrepieces often supported by parian-figure bases. On such items, the white matt parian (*see* p.204) contrasts delightfully with the richly glazed porcelain (*see* picture 53), and the plates might well also have delicately pierced borders.

Miscellaneous items

| *See* pictures 54–5

I have mentioned the three main types of tableware – the tea, dinner, and dessert services – but there is also a great variety of miscellaneous articles such as jugs of many sizes, tankards or mugs, salad bowls, and various other containers, as well as large bowls that are normally described as punch bowls, although they would have been used in a great many different ways. Baskets of all sizes were a big feature of the early 19th-century English factories; Rockingham porcelain examples may be painted with various named views. The John Ridgway example shown in picture 55 is of superb quality. Some very decorative inkwells or inkstands were also made by the leading manufacturers in the 19th century.

Of a more utilitarian nature there are a relatively large number of surviving 18th-century toilet bowls and guglets (handleless water bottles of vase shape) as well as relatively few egg cups, egg drainers, eye baths, mustard pots, thimbles, buttons, finger bowls, spittoons, decanter stands, and flasks. Each discovered example proves that such items were made.

54 A pair of Worcester openwork dessert baskets decorated with a pale yellow exterior and floral painted interiors, 25cm (10in) long, *c*.1765, P. Homefield collection.

55 A superb-quality John Ridgway basket. Centre painted by a leading ceramic artist and there is rich gilt applied over a turquoise ground. Printed Royal Arms mark, with "By Royal Appointment" wording, 25 x 20cm (10 x 8in), *c*.1845, formerly in the Godden collection.

56 A square, Worcester bulb pot (one of a pair), with Worcester mark, which is typically decorated with scale-blue ground and panels of exotic birds, 14cm (5½in) high, *c*.1765, Godden of Worthing.

Vases and bulb pots

| *See* pictures 56, 57, and 137

Progressing forward to more ornamental pieces, there is also a great assembly of vases, of all sizes and shapes and bearing every type of decoration. Some of these served as pot-pourri vases, as a pleasant odour arose from the pierced cover to scent the room. Most English porcelain vases were, however, simply for ornamental purposes only, to dress a mantelpiece or cabinet. They had covers so could not have been used for cut flowers. From about 1760, however, there was a fine series of bulb or flower pots showing a distinct Continental influence. At first these were rococo in style (*see* picture 56), but became, in general, a half-moon shape (*see* pictures 57 and 137) from about 1800. The flat back was usually left undecorated as it faced the wall. These bulb pots and the related circular jardinières (with their separate bases) were very richly decorated. The early 19th-century mantel would not have been complete without a pair of often cylindrical spill vases (picture 232), or "match pots" as they were called, which in rare instances were made to match the bulb pot. (Spill vases were for holding rolled-up strips of paper or thin sticks of wood used for lighting candles.)

On 18th- and 19th-century mantelpieces there would also have been perhaps a porcelain clock case and almost certainly a pair of decorative porcelain figures and a pair of animals or birds modelled in the round. These figures, groups, and models from nature were produced from the earliest days of the British ceramic industry and are still made today. They will always be in great demand both as cabinet pieces and as dressing for a table, sideboard, or other furnishings in a room.

Several books have been devoted to this aspect of ceramic art and other specialist books give a good pictorial account of the figure models made at individual factories. Some factories produced extremely few figures while others concentrated heavily on their production. For example, 18th-century Worcester figures and bird or animal models are extremely scarce and by no means up to the modelling standard of the factory's other products. The Liverpool, Lowestoft, and Isleworth factories concentrated almost entirely on useful wares while, in contrast, the Bow, Chelsea, and Derby figures and groups are reasonably available (but not cheap) and certainly outnumber the surviving teapots from these factories. Early 19th-century Worcester figure models are also very scarce* and there are hardly any from the important Spode factory, while this factory's main rival, Minton, excelled in Derby and Meissen-style figures of exquisite quality. After about 1850 the relatively inexpensive parian figures (*see* pictures 255 and 257) and the earthenware models dominated the figure market.

* From about the 1880s the Royal Worcester company produced a superb range of decorative figure models.

5
Decoration and marketing

Having discussed the manufacturing processes and the types of object being made, we will now, firstly, consider the decorating processes or styles. Assuming a ceramic object is to be decorated rather than left in the white, there are two basic types of decoration – that applied before glazing and that applied after glazing (*see* picture 57). These are broadly classed as "underglaze" and "overglaze" decoration. Each of these has subdivisions, such as hand-painted or printed designs. Some porcelain was also originally sold in the white to be decorated outside the factory that produced it, by specialist decorators or amateurs.

Underglaze blue painting

Underglaze painting is normally confined to cobalt blue, as this is the pigment best able to withstand the high temperature of the glost kiln in which the glaze is matured. The cobalt oxide is so powerful a colouring agent that it cannot be used alone but is used either as "Zaffre" or "Smalt". Zaffre is prepared by heating the cobalt ore and fritting the ground powder with sand, sometimes with the addition of borax and calcined flint to act as a flux. Smalt is made by adding potassium carbonate to Zaffre; the resulting glass-like mass is then pulverized. An extremely useful chapter on cobalt is included in Dr Bernard Watney's standard work, *English Blue and White Porcelain of the 18th Century*.

The diluted cobalt in a liquid suspension is then painted onto the unglazed porcelain. To get graduations of tint, detail, shading, etc, different strengths of pigment can be used or, more usually, some overpainting is carried out, so that very dark details may have three applications of the blue pigment. I write "blue", but when applied as cobalt oxide it appears nearly black, and becomes a very fine blue only after glazing and firing (*see* picture 58, left). The glaze seems to have an important part to play in maturing the blue for when, as sometimes happens, the glaze does not completely cover an article the blue at the unglazed part will appear dark and even dirty looking. Although the term underglaze blue is commonly used this might not be the most appropriate. While it is indeed applied under the glaze, on firing the blue rises through the glaze so the term "inglaze blue" may be a better description. In fact you can also paint the cobalt blue on top of the glaze and then on firing it will sink right into it to give the appearance of underglaze blue.

Blue-and-white porcelains have always been very popular and fashionable. This fact probably dates back to the earliest importations of Chinese porcelains. Certainly in the first half of the 18th century, when the large-scale trade in such Oriental wares was being developed, the directors of the English East India Company instructed their agents or ship-borne "Supra-cargos" that "the china ware must all be of useful sorts most blue and white" or noted "always preferring good blue and white to any other colour", to quote from directions issued in 1724 and 1731 respectively.

When, some 20 years later, English manufacturers entered the porcelain market they therefore largely knew what the buying public required and the demand for blue-and-white designs suited the novice porcelain producers remarkably well. This was because it was relatively trouble-free and inexpensive to produce – indeed the Lowestoft factory marketed only blue-and-white designs for the first 12 or so years of its existence, *c*.1757–69. Limehouse and Isleworth also seem to have concentrated on blue and white.

Only two main firings were required for such wares: the normal biscuit and the glost (glaze) firings, with none of the subsequent firings that would have been necessary had overglaze enamels or gilding been employed. The manufacturers did not have to bother about preparing enamel colours and were spared the cost of the gold, which made these designs cheaper to produce. Blue-painters could be young or apprentice painters earning a low wage, which also meant that the manufacturers could save even more money. The majority of the blue-and-white porcelains were of a repetitive nature; it is easy to picture youngsters painting the same mock-Chinese designs day after day, week after week. These remarks may appear to be somewhat disparaging, since even the normal run of 18th-century blue-and-white porcelain gives nearly all collectors the greatest visual pleasure. However, although some pieces are indeed ceramic masterpieces in their way, it must be remembered that they were commercial productions.

57

From the serious collector's point of view English blue-and-white wares have several attractions. They are, or were, relatively common, which means that a good representative and instructive collection can be formed at a fraction of the price of enamelled pieces. Obviously this general statement does not apply to rare or very early specimens, which always command a high price. An extremely wide assortment of shapes were enhanced with blue-and-white designs, and indeed many forms are known only in blue and white. A range of inscribed and dated pieces enables us to plot the development of various pastes and factory styles. The value of such documentary pieces cannot be overstressed but to the true collector the importance of blue and white probably lies in the difficulties of attribution that these everyday wares pose. Take, for example, a blue-and-white teabowl and saucer. Is it Bow, or Lowestoft, or perhaps Derby or Isleworth? Was it made at one of the Liverpool factories, at Bristol, or even in hard-paste, bone ash, or soapstone? To find the answer knowledge of the potting techniques used at different factories is needed. These and other facets of ceramic knowledge assist such a diagnosis, for very few examples of blue-and-white porcelain bear a factory mark.

If you have mastered blue and white then your knowledge of all English porcelain has been built on

58

57 One of a pair of Derby bulb pots with a central panel in the manner of George Complin, crowned crossed batons and "D" standard mark, 25cm (10in) long, *c*.1805, formerly in the Vera Browne collection.

58 Left, a biscuit (fired but unglazed) waster from the Worcester site, with sharply painted unglazed blue. Right, a glazed and refired Worcester moulded milk jug with the matured blue decoration. Painter's mark under the handle, 10cm (4in) high, *c*.1760, Godden collection.

very reliable foundations. Or, as W. B. Honey, of the Victoria and Albert Museum, wrote in the year of my birth, 1929, "the classification of blue and white is likely to provide a severe test of its owner's knowledge and judgement". How true but I have enjoyed this test for over 60 years and revelled in the charm and beauty of the pieces. Some of the many changes in our beliefs that have occurred in my lifetime are recorded with a selection of examples that have given me great pleasure in my *Godden's Guide to English Blue and White Porcelain* (Antique Collectors' Club, 2004) published over 70 years after Mr Honey's still valid truism.

Overglaze printing

Overglaze designs are those patterns or motifs added to the glazed and fired blanks. In some ways overglaze pieces present less trouble to the manufacturer than the inexpensive blue-and-white pieces. The reason for this lies in the fact that the enamels (as overglaze pigments are called) do not have to endure the high glazing temperature of the glost kiln. They are matured at the relatively low temperature of 700°C (1,292°F) in a small "muffle kiln". A visit to any factory site provides evidence of the high kiln-loss of blue-and-white wares and of the almost total lack of wasters or failures in lower-fired enamelled designs.

I have not explained how the colours for overglazing are mixed or otherwise prepared from metallic oxides and applied, as the painting process varies little from the normal technique. I must point out, however, that, when applied, the pigments bear little or no visual relation to the colour after firing and, in some cases, the pigments have to be applied in a given order and fired separately, as they mature at different temperatures. The high temperature colours are applied and fired first, working down to those requiring the lowest firing.

Transfer-printing

It would appear that in about 1760 the demand for blue-and-white porcelains, especially the less expensive tablewares, led to the introduction of transfer-printing. This meant that the standard designs could be run off at speed so that, for example, 500 blue-printed saucers could be produced with identical designs. The ceramic printing process was first developed in England and applied in the 1750s (or perhaps even the late 1740s) over the glaze onto various earthenwares, porcelains, or enamel wares. In about 1760, the same process was adapted to the application of cobalt-tinted pigments to the unglazed porcelain, as can be seen in pictures 59

and 60. Further details and numerous illustrations of blue-printed wares are included in my specialist book *Godden's Guide to English Blue and White Porcelain*.

Creating designs

The engraver or the designer (if they are not the same person), has to dream up a pleasing design suitable for placing on a variety of shapes – such as teapots, saucers, teabowls, and narrow coffee cups. The design not only has to fit the various shapes but also to sell – to induce the buyer to choose a Worcester tea set rather than a Bow or Lowestoft set.

The initial design is usually drawn onto paper, with a series of possible designs having been submitted to the factory owner, partner, or manager. Traditionally these drawings were often adapted from paintings or prints of the period or copied from popular designs introduced by a rival firm. (Printed versions of popular hand-painted Chinese, Continental [Meissen or Sèvres], or English porcelains), were produced. Few would have been completely new patterns. Once the design has been approved it can be transferred, probably by "pouncing", to the face of a copper plate. This technique consists of piercing a series of small holes through the paper to mark the main lines or details of the composition. The

59

59 A blue-printed Worcester mask-head jug of characteristic graceful form. The blue-printed design is typical of the 1770s. Blue-printed (filled in) shaded crescent mark, 17cm (6¾in) high, *c*.1775, Godden collection.

60 Right, a Worcester moulded cabbage-leaf jug with mask spout – a popular form at several factories. Printed in underglaze blue with a selection of typical floral groupings, printed (shaded) crescent mark, 20cm (8in) high (sizes vary), *c*.1765–70, Godden of Worthing.

prepared paper is then laid on the sheet of copper and a porous bag of finely powdered material is scattered on or over the surface so that the powder drops through the holes or pin-pricks to mark the copper plate with the outline or main details of the desired design.

Engraving

A temporary outline image can then be lightly engraved into the relatively soft copper with sharp and fine engraving tools and further details added until the required design is fully shown on the copper plate.

This preliminary design must then be worked over. Parts of the design that are to show a bold, dark line must be cut deep so that they can hold more pigment; parts that have to be shaded must be cross-hatched using a series of closely spaced lines, while delicate shading or the merest outline – such as the edge of a rose petal – must be left as the finest and shallowest incised cut into the copper plate. Many of the finest copper plates have delicate details added through the etching process with the help of acids. I have referred to just one copper plate here but to introduce a single new teaware pattern 20 or more different copper plates must be painstakingly prepared to suit the different size of article – the teapot, its cover and stand, the cream or milk jug, the waste bowl, the sugar bowl and cover etc. With small subjects that are used as space fillers – such as butterflies, insects, or flowers – several are engraved on one copper plate. However, for objects made in quantity, such as saucers or teabowls, several copper plates are required. Such items are almost mass produced and can differ slightly in the engraving detail.

From about 1780 specialist engraving firms began to supply sets of engraved copper plates to potters who did not have their own highly paid engraver. Obviously, if a small factory required only four or five new printed designs each year then it was far cheaper to buy the copper plates ready engraved. The majority of 19th-century printed pottery designs therefore originated from a few specialist engraving firms.

The master-engravers were key men who could sell their services and copper plates to the highest bidder. So, even apart from the normal copying of one factory's popular designs by another, precisely the same design could appear on porcelains of a different manufacture when the original engraved copper plates were sold. Several of the 18th-century Worcester copper plates, including at least one signed by Robert Hancock, were found at the 19th-century Coalport factory. When one factory was sold or changed ownership the existing copper plates also passed on, so that former patterns

could still be produced. You may like to consult Colin Wyman's specialist English Ceramic Circle paper "A Review of Early Printing Techniques", published in the *Transactions of the English Ceramic Circle*, Vol. 16, Part 3 of 1998 for further details of this.

Transferring

Once a set of copper plates has been engraved hundreds of articles can be adorned with the same design before the copper plates need touching up or re-engraving. The initial engraving is a time-consuming, skilled job, but after that, low-paid, semi-skilled labour can transfer the design to the waiting porcelain. The procedure involves heating the copper plate and then charging it with a thick, oily, treacle-like mixture containing the cobalt (or other) pigment. Having forced this into the engraved lines the surplus pigment is cleaned from the face of the copper leaving the "ink" just in the recessed lines. A special tough yet thin tissue-like paper is then laid over the charged and reheated copper plate and pressed firmly onto it using a printing press, so that the pigment is transferred from the lines onto the paper.

After peeling off, the charged transfer paper is trimmed, discarding surplus pieces of the paper or dividing the design as required to fit the pot. For underglaze printing, the inked paper can then be carefully positioned onto the unglazed but biscuit-fired article. The paper is then pressed firmly but carefully in order to transfer the pigment onto the ware. The paper is then soaked off, the ware dried, and the pigment lightly fired or hardened on, which burns off the oil and fixes the design. Factory wasters often usefully illustrate the importance of the "hardened-on" process – for when such pieces are washed the unglazed pattern remains, but with pieces that were discarded before the all-important light firing the pattern dissolves almost at the sight of water. Even hand-painted blue designs were hardened on to avoid the design running in the glaze (*see* picture 58).

The next stage is to glaze the object bearing the hardened-on design and then glaze and glost fire it. If on examination the wares are cleanly fired with a well-matured blue and clear covering glaze, the objects can be passed to the warehouse, where they will later to be made up into sets and dispatched to wholesale or retail outlets. Examples that have a slightly "flown" glaze (those which display a blue that has run), would be separated and sold as "seconds", or "thirds" if of much inferior quality, at a reduced price.

Overglaze printing differs only in that it is fixed into the glaze by another firing that is longer than

61

62

63

the underglaze hardening-on process. The bat-printing process was employed to give a more delicate result at lower cost, *see* p.61.

This account of the printing technique may well give the impression that it is extremely complicated but in practice this is not so. During the 18th century it enabled tasteful, well-drawn designs to be applied by cheap labour – a team of one adult and several young (often female) helpers being paid only a few shillings a week. In all probability the following two notices of 1763 and 1772 refer to such blue-printed porcelains, both being Worcester in origin:

The most valuable part of all, and which principally calls for notice, is the extraordinary strength and cheapness of the common sort of blue and white Worcester porcelain...

Complete tea services of blue and white Worcester china from £1 to £1.5s the set, consisting of 43 pieces.

61 A Chinese hard-paste saucer dish, printed over the glaze in England. The Hancock "Tea Party" is neatly coloured over and slightly gilt, perhaps at Giles' London studio. The print is signed "R. Hancock, fecit. 1757", diameter 15.25cm (6in), 1757, Godden collection.

62 A relief-moulded Worcester cream or butter boat, the reserve panels "jet-printed" with figure and landscape designs. The inner border is hand-painted, 10cm (4in) long, *c*.1755–60, Sally & Jonathan Godden collection.

63 The front and reverse of a Worcester King of Prussia mug, which is "jet-printed". The central print is signed with an R.H. monogram for Richard Holdship, and there is also "Worcester" and Josiah Holdship's anchor rebus, 15.25cm (6in) high, but these patriotic mugs were made in various sizes, *c*.1757 onwards, Godden collection.

The blue-printed porcelains are often decried as mass-produced wares. I do not agree with this general dismissal. Originally the process enabled the articles to be produced at a price the customer could afford, and it must be remembered that a factory's success depends not on the quality of the relatively few superb pieces it produces specifically for the rich but on the success of the low-price, "bread-and-butter" goods that are made for the mass market. Chelsea ultimately failed at just this, while the Worcester factory has continued to the present time. I also contend that most blue-printed designs of the 1760–90 period are superior to the run-of-the-mill hand-painted designs. The latter are mainly repetitive and degenerate with endless copying, while the printed designs retain the original quality. If there is a fault in the printed designs it lies in the fact that the engraver had time to rework and perfect the design so that in some cases there is a certain tightness or lack of spontaneity – the pattern can actually be too perfect!

The late W. B. Honey (Keeper of the Department of Ceramics at the Victoria and Albert Museum when I started collecting in the late 1940s), a noted authority and discerning author, observed that overglaze "transfer-printing is one of the few entirely English contributions to the art of porcelain…the earliest work done in the technique has a peculiarly English eighteenth-century charm, which a close acquaintance can only increase…" Quite apart from the need to reduce costs and speed production, try to visualize the amateur appearance that would result from a factory hand having to paint hundreds of copies of the very complicated printed design shown on picture 59. Not only would he have to paint the figures as best he could but in order to make a living he would have to paint rapidly, for the factory hands were employed on a piece-rate basis. As it is, the printed design is by the doyen of ceramic artist-engravers, Robert Hancock (c.1730–1817). His work can be found on enamels, on Bow porcelain, even on Chinese blanks (see picture 61), and notably on Worcester porcelain. This artist engraved a wonderful array of designs, and each one is a charming little masterpiece. The standard work on Hancock and his designs is still Cyril Cook's *The Life and Work of Robert Hancock* (Chapman & Hall, 1948, with a supplement privately published in 1955). In the 18th century, a great many other talented engravers were employed at various different factories or supplied engraved copper plates on a freelance basis.

Robert Hancock's prints are complete in themselves and were not usually further embellished at the factory, except in some cases (such as picture 62) a hand-painted border might have been added. The normal colour of the design is black. At the time of production this was known as "jet" and, somewhat misleadingly, such Worcester porcelains were described as "jet-enamelled" rather than printed. In the Worcester porcelain sale by Mr Christie in December 1769 we find listed, "A compleat tea and coffee equipage, jet enamelled L'amour, 43 pieces." (This was sold for £1.18s.)

The purchaser of this black-printed tea set bearing the L'amour design was James Giles, a talented London decorator of Worcester and other porcelains. The rare and delightful examples of Worcester jet-printing that are tastefully coloured over (see p.93) are now generally attributed to the Giles decorating studio in London, but others could also have been engaged in this trade.

Early Worcester prints are superb. Most are now rare and deservedly costly. The well-known King of Prussia design (see picture 63) occurs in several versions on different shapes and sizes of mugs. In general the Hancock-type overglaze printed designs were made only within the period c.1756–74. (See my *Eighteenth-Century English Porcelain*, section XIV.) There was some overglaze printing after this but by then fashion would seem to have favoured printed designs in underglaze blue.

A good range of blue-printed patterns as well as hand-painted wares are covered in Dr Watney's *English Blue and White Porcelain of the 18th Century*. My personal love of blue and white is explained in my *Eighteenth-century English Porcelain* as well as in the specialist work *Godden's Guide to English Blue and White Porcelain* (Antique Collectors' Club, 2004). Most books on 18th-century Worcester porcelain will include representative examples of overglaze printed designs and some underglaze blue-printed patterns. One superb publication featuring just one personal (husband and wife) collection is *Worcester Porcelain 1751–1790 the Zorensky Collection*, by S. Spero and J. Sandon (Antique Collectors' Club, 1996).

Standard designs

With a few exceptions all designs, blue-and-white or enamelled, are stock patterns linked to a pattern book, list, or to pattern pieces retained within the factory. The exceptions to this general rule mainly comprise the pieces made to the special order of a customer. While some traditional motifs permitted a certain licence, in that flower compositions or scenic designs with standard borders could be changed at the whim of the artist, most patterns remained reasonably constant.

The 18th-century housewife shopping for perhaps a new tea service no doubt had a larger choice than her present-day counterpart, but, whether she shopped in the cities of Bath, Bristol, or Cheltenham she would have seen largely the same selection of patterns. The reason for this is simple: the painting of stock designs enabled the management to employ mainly semi-skilled hands at low rates. It also enabled the retailers to re-order popular designs over and over again, and the customer was able to purchase replacements or enlarge existing services. Obviously new designs were added to a factory's range, slow-selling patterns were discarded, popular ones retained or slightly updated, but it was not until the 1780s or early 1790s that the system of adding pattern numbers to the wares was gradually adopted.

Printed outline designs

Apart from the superb Hancock overglaze prints on Worcester and other porcelains, designs complete in themselves, some simple, printed designs appear on Bow porcelains. These patterns mainly comprise Chinese figures and they would seem to be little more than outlines that a young apprentice would have coloured in. This ceramic technique has continued down to modern times and was much used in the 19th century when very finely engraved floral compositions were coloured in by hand – the purchaser and present-day owner fondly believing they owned, or own, an entirely hand-painted object, not a mass-produced printed design that had been coloured over by a young boy or girl. Remember, the existence of a name or signature does not definitely guarantee that the design was hand-painted! The 18th-century Vauxhall factory in London produced some fine-quality outline prints using different colours (*see* picture 29).

Bat-printing

The engraved designs that I have already written about were in the main made up of lines or cross-hatching, but from about 1800 another style of engraving and/or etching technique of printing was applied overglaze to English ceramics. In this particular technique the engraved pattern was made up of a series of dots rather than lines, the dots being smaller or larger, closer or more widely spaced according to the depth of colour that was required. Instead of using paper, the image was transferred from the copper plate to the glazed article by means of a pliable bat of glue and isinglass, or like substance, hence the term "bat-printing". The copper plates were charged with oil or another similar medium, the glue bat transferred this design to the article, and then powdered colour was dusted over the article, adhering to the oiled parts. This indeed is how the New Hall and Spode firms managed to print in gold (*see* picture 64), and is the method described by William Evans (a knowledgeable contemporary author), in 1846. The engraved or etched copper plate could then be most delicately engraved, as the plate did not have to be charged with the old thick colouring compound and so no heat was needed to soften this

before it would transfer. Certainly bat-printed designs of the period of around 1800–20 can be a real delight and are generally underrated. The bat-printed saucer (*see* picture 65) from a New Hall tea service is a typical example, and each piece in this set bears a related, but different, hand-engraved, tasteful design. The gilt borders were applied by hand.

The bat-printing technique is very well explained and illustrated in David Drakard and Paul Holdway's book *Spode Printed Ware* that was originally published by Longman in 1983. An enlarged and revised edition was published by the Antique Collectors' Club in 2002.

64

65

64 A Spode bone-china ewer shape vase (one of a pair). The blue panels are overprinted in gold under Warburton's patent of 1810, 16.5cm (6½in) high, c.1815, Godden of Worthing.

65 A New Hall hybrid hard-paste porcelain saucer from a tea service of pattern 511. Printed in gold under Warburton's 1810 patent. The major pieces of the service are marked with "Warburton's Patent", which is painted under a crown, diameter 13cm (5¼in), c.1805–10, Godden collection.

Gilding

Apart from printing and painting in enamel colours there is one further class of overglaze decoration – gilding, which is a rather neglected study as gold ornamentation on early porcelain was not as rare as some authorities would have us believe. Much of the imported Chinese and Japanese porcelain was enriched with gilding. For example the instructions given to the Supra-cargos of the East Indiamen Loyal Bliss in 1712 mention gilt wares, "20,000 plates in colours and gold, 10,000 with a border inside and gold edges". When English manufacturers commenced production in the mid-1740s and early 1750s, the gilding process must have caused some concern and added to the cost of the article. This cost was not so much due to the value of the gold, as very little was in fact used, but more to the skill and trouble of applying it, re-firing the object, and then hand-burnishing the gold, which appears brown, dull, and slightly rough until the final polishing process.

We must bear in mind that gold is applied as the last form of embellishment. A Worcester plate, such as that shown in picture 66, may have had its decoration applied in the following way: first an underglaze blue edge (matured at *c*.1,000°C (1,832°F) in the glost kiln), then enamel decoration added after glazing that has been matured in a muffle kiln at approximately 700°C (1,292°F), and finally the intricate gilding added to complete the design. The gilding is fixed at a lower temperature still, in the last firing process, and then it needs hand-burnishing. The gold is obviously the least permanent form of decoration.

The application of gold to ceramics is a separate craft that was traditionally carried out by gilders rather than by painters. In the 18th century, and for at least the first part of the 19th century, almost pure gold was used. It appears that in some early factories the gold was applied in leaf form adhering to the glaze only by the application of size or a like substance. It was not fixed by firing. This is, in fact, a standard technique that is fine for picture frames or for other objects that are not handled or washed, but for porcelains a more permanent method is required. It is still possible to find early white figures or groups that reveal, in protected crevices, traces of the original unfired (or cold) gilding, or unfired colours.

The very earliest fired gilding was called "honey gilding" because the powdered gold or gold leaf was mixed with honey before being painted onto the glazed ware. After firing the gold fluxed slightly with the glaze and became a permanent part of the decoration. The dull fired gold could then be burnished by being rubbed

66

67

66 A fluted-edged Chamberlain-Worcester dessert (or cabinet) plate, with underglaze blue edge. Richly painted and gilt in a highly typical manner. Gilt mark "Chamberlain-Worcester", diameter 22cm (8¾in), *c*.1795, formerly in the Godden collection.

67 A highly decorative Cauldon cabinet or show plate in the Continental manner, inscribed "Unser Liebling". Intricate raised-gold border design. Printed "Cauldon/England" mark, diameter 26cm (10¼in), *c*.1920, private collection.

quickly with a polished and smooth bloodstone or agate mounted on a short handle; such tools were handed down in the family as the more they were used the better they worked. From the 19th century to the present time burnishers have been women.

Honey gilding did have a certain body or thickness that permitted "tooling" or "chasing" of floral or other motifs with a metal point, in the Sèvres style (*see* p.216). The tooled or chased design usually shows bright against the only slightly burnished or "sanded" dullish gold, to provide a pleasing contrast. Some of the Chelsea and Worcester tooled gilding of the 1760–70 period can be extremely fine and was probably more time-consuming to complete than the main painted decoration. Tooled gilding on a dark blue ground has a magnificently rich effect, and perhaps the painters were responsible for the tooled butterflies, insects, and flowers that are drawn or incised into the gold (if not the painters then only the most skilled gilders would have been employed). Most useful wares would have borne only simple burnished gold borders or other enrichments, while the cheaper bread-and-butter lines would not have been gilt at all.

The great difficulty with the necessarily low-fired gilding is to induce the gold to adhere to the glaze, which is a difficulty that has by no means always been overcome. Some factories, notably Bow in about 1750, used a brown-coloured undercoat or fluxing agent, which at one and the same time added depth to the gold and assisted the fixing. Similar but lighter underlays can be seen on some later porcelains, such as Bristol, where the gold has worn or partly flaked away.

In about the 1785–95 period the old honey gilding gave way to mercury gilding. The gold, once it has been mixed with mercury to form a paste-like substance, can then be painted, stippled, or otherwise applied to the porcelain. The mercury is then vaporized in the muffle kiln, leaving the gold to be sanded to a dull polish or burnished to a fine polish as required. Mercury gilding, to a trained eye, is rather harder and more brassy than the soft honey gilding and in some cases (such as in Minton of the 1825–35 period and Rockingham) the colour has acquired a distinct coppery tint.

The Regency period saw some magnificent gilding on English porcelains, although there were instances of copying of the then current Paris porcelains where vase handles etc were gilt to emulate ormolu, and matt or frosted dull gold effects were used to great advantage, contrasting well with the bright, burnished gilding. The leading firms in this field – Spode, Minton, Davenport, Daniel, and the Worcester companies – employed very talented gilders who also made good use of raised gilding or relief designs in gold. The relief design (*see* picture 67) was first worked with a mixture of colour and ground porcelain, the relief work then being gilt, "sanded" to a dull polish, and the perhaps chased or tooled. The technique, the introduction of which has been attributed to Henry Daniel (*see* Chapter 8, p.176), when used with restraint can be superb (*see* picture 68) but often the effect can be spoilt by excess. Magnificent gilding of this type is best seen on the reverse side of

68 A very finely decorated Daniel porcelain fruit cooler or ice-pail from a large Royal service, which included three-tier cake stands. It has the retailers' name mark "Mortlocks" in gold, 25cm (10in) high (taller examples were also made), *c.*1825–30, formerly in the Godden collection.

Alcock, Daniel, Davenport, or Minton vases of the 1820–40 period – the side that is normally turned to the wall.

Obviously time-consuming, quality gilding of the type just described is only found on the most expensive products from the leading firms. There were short cuts, however, for less expensive wares. Peter Warburton (he was one of the partners in the New Hall company at Shelton) patented methods of bat-printing in gold and silver (platinum) in 1810 and a rare and attractive class of gold-printed New Hall (Staffordshire) porcelain is to be found with the mark "Warburton's Patent". The Spode company also printed in gold, normally on a deep-blue ground (*see* picture 64). Minton introduced a patented technique of acid-gilding, a tasteful style that was subsequently taken up by many late Victorian firms (*see* picture 69), and in the 1870–80 period German "liquid" or "bright" gold was used on some wares made by the smaller potters. This "liquid gold" did not need burnishing but the finished effect is unfortunately watery and cheap looking.

Returning to 18th-century gilding, the fact that it needed only a soft firing in a muffle kiln meant that some of the independent decorators could quite easily enhance slightly decorated wares with gilding, or simply gild white porcelains. Several of the London decorators, from about 1780, added gilt borders etc to

69 Representative units from a Cauldon bone-china dessert service. The centres were painted by S. Pope and are signed. The wide borders are ornamented with acid-gilding on two levels. Printed mark "Cauldon/England", pattern number "P/1949", diameter of plate 22cm (8¾in), c.1920, Godden of Worthing.

Chinese blue-and-white porcelains,* and they may also have added gilding to some English blue-and-white wares. The Giles Studio in London during the 1760s and 1770s is also a source of some tasteful gilt designs found on Worcester and perhaps Caughley porcelains. It is also true that the low-fired gilt designs could be erased or fired away, which permitted the addition of more "collectable" enamel decoration at a later period (*see* p.238)

I find some of the simple 18th-century and early 19th-century gilt patterns far more pleasing than the fashionable and very expensive Worcester porcelains with coloured grounds. In a less rich style the gilt patterns of the 1785–1810 period can be extremely pleasing, as can the white-and-gold Caughley or Worcester porcelains (*see* pictures 16, 70, and 92).

Decoration

I do not wish to fill the remaining part of this general book with a class-by-class coverage of the various styles of ceramic painting, as the range can be endless.

There are many well-illustrated reference books on the styles. For example, my own two works *An Illustrated Encyclopaedia of British Pottery and Porcelain* (1966) and *British Porcelain, an Illustrated Guide* (1974) contain well over a thousand illustrations between them. My later books, such as *Staffordshire Porcelain* (1983) and the *Encyclopaedia of British Porcelain Manufacturers* (1988), contain good colour plates that show the skill of the English painters and decorators to advantage.

Some consideration of styles of decoration will be given later, in the coverage of individual factories. In general I would suggest that minimal decoration is the most successful for useful wares and in this regard I, like many present-day collectors, favour the early porcelains of the 1750–75 period to the more flamboyant wares

---

* I have such an English gilt Chinese teapot bearing the mark or name of a leading London dealer – "Hewson, Aldgate", but many others were engaged in this enhancing exercise.

of the next decade. There is, however, a case for richly decorating vases and such ornamental pieces that were specifically made to dress a mantel or cabinet.

Many manufacturers made the error of completely covering the surface of the object with ground colours or other painted decoration – a fault not confined to the Victorian period. In so doing they hid the attribute of porcelain: the wonderful white or near-white body, which is a material with a real beauty all of its own. Decoration should always complement and enhance the porcelain and the white body set off this added decoration. Of all the overglaze enamel decorations I respect most the floral patterns, the scattered sprays (rather than large masses), and the restrained Oriental-style designs. These seem to me well suited to the medium on which they are painted and could hardly offend the eye or appetite of the person eating from them.

70

71

70 One of a pair of Caughley dessert dishes from a set with four shapes of flat dishes, neatly decorated in gold. The glaze is "pegged" away from the foot-ring in the Worcester manner, 26.5 x 20cm (10½ x 8in), *c.*1785, Mrs P.A. Britain collection.

71 A Chamberlain-Worcester dish from a harlequin dessert service, each piece having a different central design (*see* picture 175). Printed "Chamberlain-Worcester" Prince Regent mark, 24 x 19cm (9½ x 7½in), *c.*1815, Godden of Worthing.

Obviously we must all make our own judgements about what we like or wish to collect. However, apart from individual taste there are many good reasons for collecting a particular style of decoration. For example, one collector I know seeks porcelain painted with named views – a reasonably common interest – but has extended this interest to revisiting the location and photographing the scene or building as it appears today, perhaps 200 years after the scene was first painted on his porcelain. A keen gardener might collect wares painted with botanical specimens. Many people collect porcelains painted with a yellow ground or with yellow bands for their decorative merit or because these pieces suit the furnishing of a room so well. (Such people need a healthy bank balance as yellow is the rarest of ceramic colours and therefore the most costly.) If you are indeed wealthy you can also consider the rare porcelains painted with shells or feathers (*see* picture 71), for such pieces are always of the finest quality.

There are endless interesting styles of decoration or types of porcelain to consider, ranging down to the early 20th-century crested Goss china perhaps at a few pounds per piece. There is, however, no need at all to specialize in any one type and most collectors follow the healthy practice of buying simply what appeals to them at the time. The late Bernard Leach (the famous potter from St Ives), had the right idea when he replied to the question, "Why on earth did you buy that?" with, "Because I like it". There is no better answer.

The distribution of finished wares

We have discussed, in general terms, the different types of decoration found on English porcelain so before turning our attention to the major factories we will look at how the finished wares were distributed and reached the customer. We must remember that in the 18th century roads as we know them today were non-existent; they were generally little better than muddy, rutted tracks. This means that the easiest and cheapest mode of transport for goods – if not for people – was by water so the porcelain factories were mainly situated at ports like London, Bristol, Plymouth, and Liverpool, or on important rivers. The river Severn, for example, permitted raw materials to be shipped to Worcester, to Coalport, and the nearby Caughley factory and it also formed the main artery for the dispatch of the finished wares. Derby was likewise well served by river transport as were the Staffordshire Potteries, particularly so after the establishment of the Midland canal system.

Many people have a mind's eye picture of hawkers travelling the country districts and markets with their wares. This system may indeed have been employed for the commoner types of pottery but more sophisticated porcelains were certainly not hawked in this manner. Prospective buyers living, for example, within 32km (20 miles) of a porcelain factory would probably have been inclined to purchase their wares direct from that source, particularly when a special order was being placed. Both the main Worcester factories had separate retail establishments in that city where a full range of wares was on display and where orders could be taken.

Other cities and towns would each have had at least one "chinaman". Contemporary records retained by the present Worcester company are quoted at length in my specialist book *Chamberlain-Worcester Porcelain 1788–1852* (Barrie & Jenkins, 1982). One chinaman (dealer) may have stocked Derby porcelains, another acted as agent for Worcester, Caughley, or Bristol wares so that the buyers, in the main centres of trade, had quite a good choice not only of English porcelains and earthenwares, but also of Chinese blue-and-white porcelains, glass, papier-mâché, and other related goods. Also many 18th-century china dealers stocked teas and coffee. On the evidence of the Chamberlain records it would seem that these retail shops would not only have carried a stock of the more saleable patterns and items but would also have had a good selection of sample pieces to assist the buyer in choosing a tea or dinner service to suit his or her taste. Orders could then be relayed back to the factory. In March 1790 we find, for instance, "Patterns sent to Mr P. Bushly, Yorks". These were pattern cups and saucers but each price quoted is for the full tea set:

1 cup and saucer Prince of Wales' border set at £13-10-0
1 do. [ditto] new Royal Festoon at £8-8-0
1 do. new Royal Star at £7-7-0
1 do. new gold festoon at £6-6-0
1 do. Broseley blue & gold sprigs at £5-5-0
1 do. plain blue & gold sprigs at £3-13-6
1 do. plain gold sprigs at £3-3-0

In some cases the order books also provide details concerning transport: for example when Chamberlain supplied porcelain blanks to William Billingsley's decorating firm at Mansfield they were dispatched from Worcester "per canal to Nottingham", which underlines my point about the advantages of water transport.

Pattern pieces

Apart from sample pieces showing one pattern, some factories also produced pattern plates in which the surface or border was divided into segments and each part bore a different, numbered design. The customer could then visit the local chinaman and order a service to be made with border number 10 or 11, stipulating, for example, a scenic or floral centre, or give orders that his or her armorial bearings or crest be added to the chosen standard pattern.

A few, very rare, single-pattern plates are known inscribed on the front with the pattern number. It is not, however, known if such plates were kept at leading retailers, as with wallpaper patterns, or if they were used inside the factory to guide the decorators when re-orders came to hand.

London showrooms

Several of the major porcelain manufacturers also had London showrooms or wholesale warehouses. Not only did these London establishments serve the nobility but, even in the 18th century, there was quite a thriving export trade and overseas buyers could find the pick of English pottery and porcelain within London. The London factories of Bow and Chelsea had local retail establishments and the Worcester China Warehouse in Aldersgate Street was issuing price lists of available porcelain by about 1760 – such as delightful scallop-shell dishes in blue and white from 4d to 1s each, depending on size, or their charming double-handled sauceboats from 2s to 3s 4d each!

William Duesbury of Derby opened his "large and elegant suit of rooms" (as proudly stated on his trade-card) in Bedford Street, Covent Garden in June 1773. The tradecard (see p.87), a copy of which is in the Victoria and Albert Museum, includes engravings of typical wares for "the nobility Gentry and Public in General". The Caughley or "Salopian China Ware-house" was at 5 Portugal Street, Lincoln's Inn Fields, and was later taken over by Spode. St. Paul's Church Yard was a very fashionable centre for the retailers.

Apart from the London establishments of various manufacturers it would seem to have been fashionable for the chief firms to have offered their products to the public by auction, not only at "Mr Christie's Great Room in Pall Mall" but at several other auction rooms too. Many notices of these London sales are printed in J. Nightingale's fascinating book *Contributions towards the History of Early English Porcelain from Contemporary Sources*, which was privately printed at Salisbury in 1881. This rare book is among the most useful and interesting of our ceramic sourcebooks. It also shows that the study of English ceramics was being taken seriously during the 19th century. One modern study, however, explains very well the difficulties faced by china dealers in London during the latter part of the

72 Three pieces from a Daniel bone-china, miniature tea set (originally on a small tray with shell-shape handles). The shapes and decorations are very much in the Spode-style, teapot 4.5cm (1¾in) high, c.1830, Godden of Worthing.

18th century, and the general shortage of money there was. I refer here to A.P. Ledger's 2002 study *The Bedford Street Warehouse and the London China Trade, 1773–96*, which is Vol. 2 of the *Derby Porcelain Archive Research*, published by the Derby Museum & Art Gallery.

Independent decorators

Another means of supply for the porcelain-buying public in London was the independent decorators, of which James Giles is the best known, but by no means the only, practitioner. Giles advertised in January 1768 that he had Worcester porcelain that was "useful and ornamental, curiously painted in the Dresden, Chelsea and Chinese tastes…as the Proprietor had a great variety of white goods by him, Ladies and Gentlemen may depend upon having their commands executed immediately and painted to any pattern they shall chuse". The sources of supply were many, the choice varied. (*See* p.93 for a fuller coverage of James Giles.)

Toy wares

I have already stated that the finer porcelains were not hawked about the country as the cheaper utilitarian pottery was, and in this regard it is convenient to scotch the idea that charming little miniature pieces were travellers' samples. However, such items were made and sold purely as children's playthings, as contemporary accounts well illustrate. Chamberlain of Worcester, for example, ordered various articles from Thomas Turner of the Caughley factory in 1789, and noted, "The toy china is too small but send a few". Chamberlain ordered such items as "2 Toy teasetts, pleasure boat pattern

4/8d" and "toy" dinner and tea sets were included in the 1799 sale of Caughley porcelains on Thomas Turner's retirement.

In several cases the patterns found on these toy wares, and indeed the shapes themselves, do not occur on full-size wares, so they definitely cannot have been travellers' samples! If travellers did in fact travel the country with porcelains, it was only in order to visit wholesalers and retailers. The housewife, I believe, had an extremely good selection of fashionable porcelain on display in every sizeable town. The country was well supplied with china dealers ranging from the great and influential London dealers to a host of much smaller shops stocking the cheaper types.

The large range of delightful 18th-century English porcelain miniature wares has been witnessed by two recent trade exhibitions of such "toys". The first was a show held by Stockspring Antiques (*see* p.33) and another, specialist blue-and-white exhibition was held in spring 2003 by Simon Spero (Kensington Church Street, London). His catalogue of *The Simpson Collection of 18th Century Blue and White Miniature Porcelain*, gives us a permanent reminder of this fine collection and of the range of such porcelains. Other leading dealers can be expected to have at least some toy items in their stock. The Caughley examples are perhaps the most usual, but at the same time this factory produced the largest range of miniature articles.

6
The major English 18th-century porcelain factories

In the next four chapters we will discuss the various English porcelain manufacturing factories or firms. My coverage in this chapter is somewhat brief for in most cases detailed and reliable modern books, which I list in the bibliography, are readily available to give the complete story of the major 18th-century manufacturers, and these works also provide a very good pictorial coverage of the firms' output and styles. In particular my *Godden's Guide to English Blue and White Porcelain* (Antique Collectors' Club, 2004) gives a good illustrated review of this style of decoration. I do not seek here to compete with these specialist books, yet I do wish to give you an overall picture of what factories were in existence, as well as what they were producing.

The following coverage of soft-paste (*see* p.16) porcelain factories has been arranged in alphabetical order, for the several factories that were established in the 1745–55 period continued for so long that a chronological coverage would present great difficulties and lengthy overlaps. The two factories that produced true, or "hard-paste", porcelains are discussed later in Chapter 7, together with those producing the so-called hybrid hard-paste type of porcelain (*see* p.132).

Below I have arranged the soft-paste porcelain factories into their approximate chronological sequence as a quick reference list so that you can see which one started first etc. Unfortunately I have simply had to give approximate dates in most cases as we have no firm dates of establishment that can be proven by evidence. Also some manufactories produced earthenwares before turning to porcelain, or porcelain was only produced for a limited period within a longer period of a factory's existence. This was, we believe, the case with Isleworth (*see* p.97). My plus signs (+) indicate that the period was extended into the 19th century.

Chelsea	c.1745–69
Limehouse	c.1746–8
Bow	c.1746–76
Bristol (Lund's)	c.1749–52
"Girl in a Swing" (St James's)	c.1749–54
Derby	c.1750–1800+
Longton Hall	c.1750–60

Worcester	c.1751–1800+
Vauxhall	c.1753–64
Liverpool factories	c.1754–1800+
Lowestoft	c.1757–99
Isleworth	c.1760–90s
West Pans	c.1764–77
Plymouth	c.1768–70
Bristol (R. Champion)	c.1770–81
Caughley	c.1775–99
Baddeley-Littler	c.1777–90
Neale	c.1778–92
New Hall	c.1781–1800+
Chamberlain-Worcester	c.1788–1800+
Pinxton	c.1796–1800+

Of these, only Derby and Worcester survived for a lengthy period, although the small East Coast factory at Lowestoft soldiered on for over 40 years, outliving most of its more pretentious competitors.

The factories featured in Chapter 7 that produced the hybrid hard-paste body included as their leader the New Hall partnership. This too was a success, being in production from the early 1780s to the early or mid-1830s (*see* pp.139–145). My discussion of our main, known, 18th-century porcelain manufacturers starts with the little-known Baddeley-Littler porcelains.

Baddeley-Littler, c.1777–90

| *See* pictures 73–76

Baddeley-Littler is a relatively new name in the story of British porcelains as the double name was first suggested by myself in an effort to attribute, or name, a puzzling class of late 18th-century porcelains that had previously been attributed to Thomas Wolfe & Co. of Liverpool. However, many specimens seem to predate this c.1795 Wolfe period by many years.

The reasons behind the new names, which have now been generally accepted, are given at some length

73 A well-painted Baddeley-Littler moulded mask-head jug and a well-potted mug. Both finely painted with the same main group of flowers, which was a favoured design at this manufactory, jug 20cm (8in) high, c.1780, Godden collection.

74

75

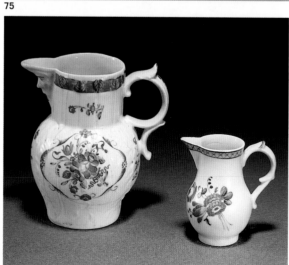

76

in Chapter 3 of my 1983 book *Staffordshire Porcelain*. The various porcelains that are now attributed to Baddeley-Littler are believed to have been made at Ralph Baddeley's factory at Shelton under the management of William Littler. Littler is very well known for his porcelain making at Longton Hall in the 1750–60 period. He subsequently moved to West Pans near Edinburgh but this Scottish venture seems to have failed in about 1777. William Littler is believed to have then returned to Staffordshire and to have been engaged as the manager of Baddeley's pottery, where he introduced (or reintroduced) the manufacture of porcelain.

By chemical analysis the Baddeley-Littler porcelain body is remarkably similar to that previously employed by Littler at Longton Hall and at West Pans. Visually, too, there are distinct similarities: the thick wax-like glaze tended to bubble and discolour in the firing, a scum line often occurs where the glaze ends, open body cracks occur, and in general the potting is heavy. The decoration includes several simple, Worcester-style, overglaze printed designs (*see* picture 74). These prints and border designs are also found on earthenwares, which were Baddeley's main concern. Other enamel designs are in the style of the popular, contemporary, Chinese export-market porcelains (*see* picture 75) but few underglaze blue patterns were produced as the soft glaze did not prove suitable.

The range of shapes and patterns that can now be attributed to this little-known group is continuing to grow. Several basic teapot forms were produced and the little sparrow-beak cream or milk jugs made by Baddley-Littler are particularly charming (*see* picture 76). The popular mask-head jugs were made in various sizes, with differing handle forms. The flower painting on these can be extremely good – *see* picture 73. No factory mark is recorded but a range of typical shapes and added patterns is shown in my book *Staffordshire Porcelain*. Interest in this group is growing, as is my collection. Do remember, though, that my name for this group is only one of convenience.

74 A Baddeley-Littler class small teapot with overglaze-printed designs each side and on the cover within characteristic hand-painted feather-like borders, 14cm (5½in) high, *c*.1780–85, Godden collection.

75 A globular Baddeley-Littler class teapot with typical floral knob. This teapot is hand-painted with a standard mock-Oriental design. Note the bubbled glaze at the foot and on top of the spout. 14cm (5½in) high, *c*.1780–85, Godden collection.

76 A small-size Baddeley-Littler moulded cabbage-leaf jug and a well-potted, neatly painted, sparrow-beak milk jug. The larger jug is 14cm (5½in) and the sparrow-beak jug is 9cm (3½in) high, *c*.1780–85, Godden collection.

Bow, *c.*1746–76

| *See* pictures 77–80

The Bow porcelain factory (which was originally termed "New Canton"), is one of the earliest English porcelain factories. It was situated in what we would now loosely term the East End of London, or more accurately on the north side of Stratford High Street at Stratford Langthorne in the parish of West Ham in Essex*. It was reasonably near the Limehouse factory.

An interesting early reference to this factory appeared in Daniel Defoe's *Tour of Great Britain*, which was published in July 1748, "...the first village we come to is Bow where a large manufactory of porcelaine is lately set up. They have already made large quantities of tea cups, saucers, etc which by some skilful persons are said to be little inferior to those brought from China...". In this account, presumably written in 1747, we have the main facts: the works were on quite a large scale; indeed, it was no back-street pottery employing just six or seven persons. The main products were of a useful nature and could be compared with the fashionable Chinese porcelains; in this factory's blue-and-white wares the Oriental influence is actually quite startling.

The reference to the factory being "lately set up" is of particular interest. Some four years earlier, in December 1744, a patent was taken out by Edward Heylyn and Thomas Frye, persons who at a slightly later date were undoubtedly connected with the Bow factory, although Alderman George Arnold, a very successful London businessman, was probably the main investor, and until 1750 the partnership traded as Arnold & Co. This patent was for:

a new method of manufacturing a certain mineral, whereby a ware might be made of the same nature or kind and equal to, if not exceeding, in goodness and beauty, china or porcelain ware imported from abroad... The material is an earth, the produce of the Cherokee nation in America, called by the natives Unaker... The articles are put into a kiln and burned with wood, called "biscuiting", if they are very white, they are ready to be painted blue...they are then dipt in glaze...

It has been believed that no porcelain was ever made under this first patent** and you will note that

77 A simple Bow "sparrow-beak" milk or cream jug, which is painted in the Chinese Famille Rose manner, 7.5cm (3in) high, *c.*1760, W.A. Bowler collection.

the wording is tentative and reads "whereby a ware might be made". The patent also reveals that the wares were apparently intended to emulate the imported Chinese porcelains and that underglaze blue designs were favoured. As Defoe records, the factory was already producing useful wares such as cups and saucers by 1747, or at least 1748, and in November 1749 Thomas Frye took out a further patent. Bones as such are not mentioned, but then he would not have wanted to give away trade secrets – instead we find the all-embracing grouping "animals, vegetables and fossils by calcining, grinding and washing". Chalk, limestone, sand, and flints are all mentioned too although no new process was publicized, but certainly by the period of this patent, in November 1749, the Bow factory was well established and continued to produce porcelains on conventional lines (*see* pictures 77–81). There is evidence that Bow employed a few Germans in the late 1740s and it can be surmised that they were refugees from Meissen, which was, at that time, being badly affected by the War of Austrian Succession. Saxony

---

* See The Reverend David Thornton's English Ceramic Circle paper "The Bow Factory Site and Environs" (*Transactions of the English Ceramic Circle*, Vol.16, Part 3, 1998).
** Recently (2002) it has been suggested that the "A" marked porcelains (*see* p.73) represent the earliest type of Bow porcelain, of the mid-1740s. The "A" mark could relate to Arnold & Co.

being a Protestant state, it followed that England was their natural refuge.

The Bow porcelain body is of the English artificial type, being soft-paste with a high percentage of bone ash (calcined and ground animal bones) in the mix to increase the workability and the strength. It is what we call a bone-ash body, such as that employed at the Lowestoft factory. Analysis of a typical early example would give a result similar to this table:

Silica	43.58%
Alumina	8.36%
Lime	24.47%
Phosphoric acid	18.95%
Lead oxide	1.75%
Magnesia	0.60%
Potash	0.85%
Soda	1.20%

The bone-ash content is shown by the high percentage of phosphoric acid, which indicates 45 per cent bone ash. Other Bow pieces analysed by the late Herbert Eccles (*see* p.75) contained between 48 and 28 per cent bone ash.

From the late 1740s through the following decade the body tended to be rather creamy in tint (except when overlaid with a slightly blue glaze) and examples have a compact appearance. This body is heavy and on occasions can seem remarkably hard.

From the 1760s the standard body became more open or floury, lighter in weight as well as in colour. The potting is normally rather thick and consequently the pieces will feel heavier than contemporary Chelsea, Derby, or Worcester porcelains. The glaze is rather soft, prone to knife scratches and, in some cases, to staining and glaze-crazing.

The factory made a great feature of blue and white, nearly always comprising tablewares decorated in the popular Oriental style. The pieces with powder-blue ground can be extremely fine. These blue-and-white Bow wares do not bear a true factory mark but normally show the painter's personal tally mark or reference number painted under the base (not on the inside angle of the foot-ring, which is a position favoured by the Lowestoft painters).

Some blue designs bear very ornate Chinese-style character marks, such as those shown at the top of the next column (A). Some printing in underglaze blue was practised from c.1765, but, in the main, the factory produced hand-painted designs in underglaze blue from the late 1740s until its closure in 1776.

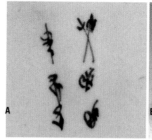

The later wares, decorated in overglaze enamels, often bear an anchor and dagger (B) rather boldly or hastily* painted in red enamel. Pieces made before 1765 do not normally bear such a mark – if marked at all, they would bear various letters or devices such as an arrow-like sign incised into the body. A capital "A" painted in blue can occur on figures. A rare class of early Bow porcelain produced from a compact feeling heavy body can bear an incised capital "R" initial mark. See Anton Gabszewicz's paper "Bow Porcelain: The Incised "R" marked Group and Associated Wares", published in the *Transactions of the English Ceramic Circle*, Vol. 17, Part 2, 2000.

A range of decorative figures and animal models were made, particularly in the 1760s and 1770s. In general these are somewhat heavier in appearance than the finely modelled Chelsea examples and small areas

78 A Bow porcelain dish, probably originally part of a dessert service. Neatly painted in a popular Japanese style – a pattern not confined to the Bow factory, 24.75 x 26cm (9¾ x 10¼in), c.1755–60, Godden of Worthing.

* The rendering of this double mark can vary greatly.

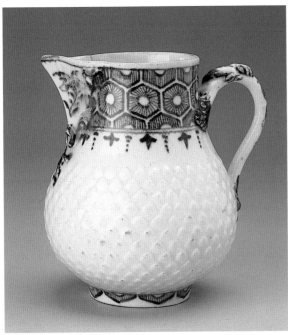

79

80

of underglaze blue can augment the overglaze enamels. Turning a Bow figure you may often find at the back a square hole made to hold a metal candle-holder fitment. The Bow figures were press-moulded (*see* p.21) so they are thickly walled and heavy for their size in comparison with the slip-cast Chelsea or Derby pieces of the same period.

The Bow porcelains seem to have enjoyed a good export market in North America and there is evidence of American clays being initially used at this London factory. It also seems likely that some of the workmen went on to find employment within the Philadelphia porcelain works of Bonnin & Morris.

The Bow factory closed down in 1776. Many books indicate that William Duesbury of the Derby porcelain works purchased the concern, or at least its working materials, but I do not know of any evidence to support this belief. Certainly if such a purchase took place it had no visual influence on the Derby products, and we can say that the history of this London factory closed in 1776, when England was losing the American colonies. In its modest way it was a success, producing for nearly 30 years a pleasing range of seemingly then inexpensive porcelain – mainly for the tables of the middle class – and surviving for a relatively long period the very real competition from the imported Chinese porcelains, the slick Chelsea productions, and the well-potted Worcester porcelains with their superior body.

For further reading you should consult Dr Watney's *English Blue and White Porcelain of the 18th Century* and *British Porcelain 1745–1850*, edited by R.J. Charleston (Benn, 1965) – the chapter on Bow written by Hugh Tait of the British Museum. This authority was also the author of the splendid British Museum catalogue of the 1959 Bow exhibition held at that museum. More recent excellent specialist books include *Bow Porcelain* by Elizabeth Adams and David Redstone (Faber, revised edition 1991), *Bow Porcelain – The Collection Formed by Geoffrey Freeman* by Anton Gabszewicz, as well as Geoffrey Freeman (Lund Humphries, 1982) and Anton Gabszewicz's 2000 catalogue *Bow Made at New Canton*.

There is also the splendidly helpful *A Treasure of Bow* published by the Ceramics and Glass Circle of Australia, under the editorship of Chris Begg, in 2000. I should also direct readers to an interesting joint paper, by W.H.R. Ramsay, A. Gabszewicz, and E.G. Ramsay entitled "Unaker or Cherokee Clay and its relationship to the Bow Porcelain Manufactory", as published in *Transactions of the Englsih Ceramic Circle* Vol.17, Part 3. The suggestion is also made that the mysterious "A" marked porcelains could represent the earliest Bow.

79 A quite large Bow moulded milk jug, with a well-modelled spout and handle. The underglaze blue borders are similar to some Derby designs. This model was issued with a cover, 10cm (4in) high, *c*.1760, Godden collection.

80 A typical, rather late and showy Bow figure, which is one of a pair. The rococo-style base and floral bocage is not restricted to Bow. It has a red-painted anchor and dagger mark, 24cm (9½in) high, *c*.1765–70, Godden of Worthing.

81 A rare, large, rather thickly potted moulded sauceboat, painted in underglaze blue with panels of mock-Oriental landscapes. It has a "Bristol" name mark moulded in relief under the base, 21cm (8¼in) long, c.1749–50.

Bristol, c.1749–52 (Lund's-Bristol)

| *See* picture 81

There are two distinct types of Bristol porcelain. First there are the soft-paste wares of the 1749–52 period, which used to be called "Lowdin's" but which are now more correctly termed "Lund's-Bristol", and secondly there are the hard-paste porcelains of the 1770–81 period, which are covered in more detail in Chapter 7, p.135. Strangely, both were continued at different ceramic centres, respectively at Worcester and at the New Hall works in the Staffordshire Potteries.

The first porcelain made at Bristol (which is a city with several claims to ceramic renown for its excellent tin-glazed delft-type ware and other earthenwares and stonewares) was of the soapstone type. In March 1749 Benjamin Lund and William Miller (a grocer and banker) were granted licences to mine this mineral (steatized granite) in the neighbourhood of the Lizard. Little or nothing is known of how this "soapy-rock"

first came to be used in a ceramic mix, or if any earlier trials had been made (perhaps at Limehouse) before Lund and Miller set up their small works at Redcliff-Backs, Bristol. If they were the first to try soapy-rock they were lucky, for its inclusion in a porcelain mix results in a very workable, compact, and crisp body, and one with a pleasant visual appearance. The Worcester factory was to be founded on this Bristol recipe.

A very interesting contemporary reference to the local material was made in the diary of Dr Richard Pococke when he visited the Lizard on 13 October 1750 "to see the soapy rock...which is mostly valued for making porcelain and they get five pounds a ton for it, for the manufacture of porcelain now carrying on at Bristol". In November 1750 Dr Pococke visited the works at Bristol where he recorded, "I went to see a manufacture lately established here by one of the principal manufacturers at Limehouse which failed". In recent years we have been able to identify porcelains from the London Limehouse works, which were made in the late 1740s (*see* p.100), and interestingly soapstone has been detected in a few wasters from this London site. Unfortunately we do not know if Dr Pococke was referring to either Lund or Miller when writing of a potter from Limehouse being at Bristol. Dr

Pocoke also recorded seeing at Bristol in 1750 "very beautiful white sauceboats adorned with reliefs of festoons which sell for sixteen shillings a pair".

This description has enabled us to identify some of the products of this early West Country factory – the now very rare but delightful festooned sauceboats. Other pieces have been identified by the relief-moulded place name "Bristol" or "Bristoll" that is to be found under the base of some sauceboats, low creamers or butter boats, and rare figures of a standing Chinese sage in the *Blanc de Chine* style – the white Chinese porcelains of the approximate period 1680–1720 so much used for figures of this style. These marked pieces, of which probably under 25 are known today, give us a very good idea of the early Bristol porcelains. Much, perhaps even nine-tenths of the output, was decorated in underglaze blue, normally with Chinese-style water scenes with boats, islands, and the like (*see* picture 81). They are sparsely decorated as if, rightly, to show to the best effect the early porcelain body. Also noteworthy are the relief-moulded panel surrounds on the sauceboats. Such designs were to be used at Worcester, Lowestoft, and other English porcelain factories. This style was earlier employed at Limehouse.

The porcelain body is not all that translucent but, in use, as long as the body is white, unblemished, and stable the translucency of, say, a sauceboat is of little consequence – as it is not generally held to a light source!

The glaze is good, tight, and does not craze, but it is prone to bubble and spot where thickly applied or where it has run in the firing. The cobalt blue is often somewhat lighter than on the later Worcester pieces and there is a tendency for the blue to have run slightly in the firing, giving a somewhat smudged or hazy effect perhaps because it was not submitted to a hardening-on firing. However, for their period (1749–52) the available marked pieces show a good mastery of the art of porcelain manufacture that was then relatively new in England. It is not surprising to find that the partners found themselves being courted for a takeover bid by a consortium of rich merchants and others from Worcester led by Dr John Wall who wished to participate in the porcelain adventure and obviously were in need of technical know-how and a supply of raw materials. This development is further explained in the Worcester section at the end of this chapter (*see* p.121). Here I simply record the fact that in June 1751 the Worcester partners drew up articles of association to purchase the secrets of the Bristol works, the proprietors of which were not to continue to make porcelain or to disclose

the processes to others. The raw materials, moulds, and other working materials, as well as some (or all) of the Bristol workforce, were transferred to Worcester where the transplant prospered. The final moments of the Bristol venture are recorded in the *Bristol Intelligencer* of 24 July 1752, where it states the manufactory was "now united with the Worcester Porcelain Company where for the future the whole business will be carried on".

"United" is definitely the right description – the great difficulty left to us is to differentiate between Bristol and early Worcester porcelain. It is as difficult as differentiating between Worcester or Chelsea or Derby porcelain made in 1755 from that made in 1756, for there is a seemingly uninterrupted continuation. Some collectors will argue the point *ad infinitum* but really it makes very little difference if one of these delightful early pieces was made at Bristol in 1751 or at Worcester in 1753.

The late Herbert Eccles* analysed one of the typical low sauceboats of the type shown in picture 81. The result, published in the Victoria and Albert Museum booklet *Analysed Specimens of English Porcelain* (1922) reads:

Silica	67.62%
Alumina	4.61%
Lime	2.64%
Phosphoric acid	2.00%
Magnesia	13.28%
Soda	1.61%
Potash	1.15%
Lead oxide	8.01%

The magnesia content is the most important one, as it represents approximately 40 per cent of soapstone, although the amount of lead oxide is surprisingly high and unusual. It should be noted that these old analyses seldom, if ever add up to a precise 100 percent. This one totals 100.92, which is pretty good when you consider the small quantity of material available.

There are very few early Bristol pieces outside the larger museums but the following books offer some help: Dr Watney's *English Blue and White Porcelain of the 18th Century*; *The Illustrated Guide to Worcester Porcelain* by Henry Sandon (Barrie & Jenkins, 1969); *Worcester Porcelain and Lund's Bristol* by Franklin A. Barrett (Faber, 1953, revised edition 1966); H. Rissik Marshall's *Coloured Worcester Porcelain of the First Period* (Ceramic Book Co., 1954); and my *Godden's Guide to English Blue and White Porcelain*.

---

* Herbert Eccles FCS was joint author of this V&A booklet with Bernard Rackham. He carried out the various analyses, which are still referred to.

Caughley, c.1775–99

| See pictures 5, 8, 22, 37, 70, and 82–93

The Caughley porcelain works, which was also known as the Royal Salopian Porcelain Manufactory, was situated on high ground in still open countryside to the west of the river Severn, some 3.2km (2 miles) south of Broseley in Shropshire. The place itself is pronounced "calf-ley", and it was to a pottery or earthenware factory already in existence there that Thomas Turner originally went in the early 1770s. Turner had formerly worked at the Worcester porcelain factory. He probably had a good all-round knowledge of porcelain production or was able to take with him key personnel from Worcester. Certainly Robert Hancock, a fellow engraver from that factory (*see* p.58), advertised in July 1775 that, "having disposed of his share in the Worcester work, he is now engaged in the Salopian china manufactory...the sole province of dealing in this manufactory, except in the London trade, being assigned over by Mr. T. Turner & Co."

The "& Co." in the firm's trading style included Ambrose Gallimore, who had been granted a 62-year lease of the original earthenware pottery in 1754. At least two early examples of Caughley porcelain are known to have a circular printed mark that reads "Turner Gallimore Salopian", and one is shown in picture 83. The former pottery was rebuilt in about 1772 and a quite large open-plan porcelain factory was erected on the site. This had three kilns, as is evidenced by old estate maps. The site was conveniently situated as clay for the saggers was readily available locally, as was coal, which was mined in the next field – and the site was reasonably near (but not on) the river Severn, linking to the north with the Midland canal system and to the south with Worcester, Bristol, and the coast shipping. The Caughley factory was also secluded; it still was when my wife Jean and I enjoyed many a pleasant picnic there searching for wasters (*see* pictures 5 and 8). It has since become an open field, but its historical significance is marked by a small inscribed monument that was erected in 2002.

For a long period the Caughley wares were regarded as inferior imitations of Worcester; if an example under discussion was finely made it was classed as Worcester, if poor it was relegated to Caughley. While it must be admitted that many shapes and patterns were made at both factories, their classification is by no means as simple as the old rule would suggest. I submit that much Caughley is superior to Worcester of the same post-1775 period and I think pieces in my collection substantiate my opinion. For example, take a look at picture 83 or the "low Chelsea ewer" shown in picture 84. They are superb, every bit as good as Worcester, and the little

82 Left to right: A superbly potted Caughley French-style dessert tureen; an early Caughley blue-printed jug in the Worcester-style; and a small blue-and-gold "Dresden-flower" pattern teapot. There is a printed "Turner Gallimore" circular mark on the jug, which is 16.5cm (6½in) high, c.1780–90, formerly in the Godden collection.

83

84

85

83 A neatly potted, relief-moulded early Caughley small-size jug.
There are two panels of blue-printed figure subjects and one floral
panel. Unglazed base with printed "Turner Gallimore Salopian"
circular mark, 13cm (5¼in) high, c.1775, Godden collection,
formerly in the Dr Watney collection.

84 A particularly well-moulded Caughley "low Chelsea ewer", a form
made at most factories. Simply painted in underglaze blue, this
is a simple, trim, example. Painted, open "C" mark, 6.25cm (2½in)
high, c.1775–80, Godden collection.

85 A small, trimly potted, Caughley creamer or melted butter boat
that is neatly painted and well modelled. Impressed star device
on the inside edge of the foot, 5.75cm (2¼in) high, c.1780–85,
Godden collection.

The basic Caughley body is of the soapstone type, and
it is very similar in make-up and appearance to Worcester. An analysis of one of my "S"-marked pieces
bearing the standard blue-printed "Fisherman" design
(*see* picture 90) gave the following result:

Silica	75.25%
Magnesia	11.06%
Alumina	5.54%
Potash	2.14%
Phosphate	1.78%
Lime	1.75%
Soda	1.68%
Ferric oxide	0.49%

enamelled creamboat shown in picture 85 is likewise a
delight. Happily, the old view used to enable Caughley
pieces to be purchased for much less than would be
charged for a Worcester example of the same type!
Alas, that situation no longer holds true.

The Caughley factory produced, in some 24 years,
a very wide and interesting range of porcelains – from
studs and buttons through to large dinner services.
Many of the standard patterns are not particularly rare
or unduly costly even today and the Salopian wares can
be considered one of the most collectable and generally
available classes of English porcelain. We now, rightly,
have the Caughley Society, which is devoted to the
study of these interesting Shropshire porcelains.

The Caughley body often shows an orange tint by
transmitted light, although it can also be quite greenish,
like the Worcester porcelains. The Caughley glaze is a
good, close-fitting one – it is colourless when applied at
normal thickness but when gathered in pools it can
have a greeny-blue tint. On many examples it is very
slightly matt, as if the piece has been breathed upon.

The body and glaze was extremely workable, which
is again like Worcester. This stable body, coupled with
the wide application of printed patterns in underglaze
blue (probably three-quarters of the factory's output
comprised blue-printed designs), enabled Turner to

compete not only with the established and renowned Worcester porcelains but also with the fashionable, and by now also inexpensive, Chinese blue-and-white porcelains. (A typical blue-printed Caughley teapot is shown in picture 88.) Speaking in terms of blue and white, Caughley, Worcester, and the imported Chinese wares practically monopolized the market in the 1775–95 period, though from 1785 the Worcester firm had almost ceased to produce these traditional blue-and-white wares, leaving Turner to fill the gap. This he did very successfully (*see* picture 89).

As to enamelled patterns, the Caughley factory produced relatively simple overglaze designs. These can be very attractive, often combining deep underglaze blue with gilding; of course the cost was quite low so that the durable wares must have sold readily in the vast middle-class market that Turner catered for with such success.

I find some of the simple gilt Caughley tewares particularly attractive. This vast class of decoration is very neglected and does not, as yet, find the same favour as even the simplest of the underglaze blue designs. (I illustrate a tastefully gilt presentation jug in picture 92.) It is often thought that Thomas Turner was preoccupied with copying Worcester shapes or designs, and collectors have jumped to the conclusion that it was Caughley that copied Worcester pieces. With the most popular of Caughley printed Oriental-style designs, the "Fisherman" (or "Pleasure Boat" design, to give it the original title), it seems more than likely that Worcester copied Caughley. Other designs found on both types of porcelain may have been introduced by Turner or Hancock himself while engraving for Worcester before they moved north to Caughley so, in a sense, they would have been Turner's or Hancock's own designs. I would also like to make the point that many Caughley patterns do not occur on Worcester or any other porcelains; they are completely unique to the Caughley factory.

There is an interesting class of Caughley porcelain that displays a decided French influence, sometimes in the adaptation of Continental forms but more commonly in the use of simple sprig motifs in the style of French Chantilly and other Continental porcelains that enjoyed an international market (*see* pictures 82, left, and 91). These simple floral motifs* could be in underglaze blue or in overglaze enamels. Once again Thomas Turner successfully copied popular designs that could be produced at little cost, which was an almost certain road to success.

Much Caughley porcelain was shipped down to Chamberlain's Worcester decorating establishment in order to be embellished before being forwarded to Turner's London warehouse or shipped back upriver to Caughley for distribution from there. Many of the popular designs combine underglaze blue with gilding to complete the design (*see* picture 82, right). Much of this additional gilding was added at Chamberlain's decorating studio before about 1795 (*see* p.82)

I cannot in this general book deal with the mass of accounts and other records that we have relating to Caughley porcelain or with the tons of wasters found within recent years at the factory site. I certainly cannot give detailed information on the slight variations between the very similar Caughley and Worcester shapes and patterns; all this is given at length in my specialist book *Caughley and Worcester Porcelain, 1775–1800* (revised edition, Antique Collectors' Club, 1981). I can however, make some basic points as my book is long out of print and a collector's treasure in its own right!

(1) The Caughley glaze was often cut back from the inside of the foot-ring like Worcester. This fact is shown time and again in wasters from the factory site and by clearly marked completed pieces (*see* picture 93). This is not a sure sign of Worcester origin (*see* p.26).
(2) The shaded printed crescent mark was not used at Caughley; it is a Worcester mark.
(3) The "disguised numeral marks" similar to those shown are Worcester marks not Caughley.

(4) You cannot tell Caughley from Worcester by simply judging quality alone.

86 Three early Caughley sparrow-beak milk jugs, painted in underglaze blue. The left example has an unglazed base. Painted "S" marks, 9cm (3½in) high, c.1775–8, Godden collection.

87 A selection of Caughley blue and white, showing the variety of patterns and shapes. The two dessert dishes are hand-painted and the smaller items are transfer-printed. The square dish is impressed-marked with "SALOPIAN", 20cm (8in) square, c.1780–90, Godden of Worthing.

---

* Similar designs were also produced at Isleworth (*see* p.99).

86

87

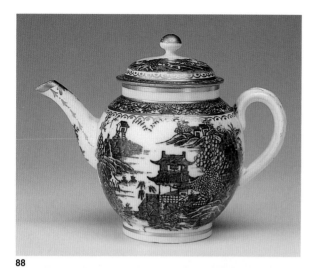

88

90

89

91

88 A typical Caughley mock-Chinese globular teapot and cover, printed in underglaze blue with quite a rare design and some slight gilding. Printed "S" mark, 13cm (5¼in) high (sizes vary), c.1780–85, Godden collection.

89 A Caughley Chinese export-market shape platter from a dinner service. Printed in underglaze blue with the "Full Nankin" pattern, one much favoured for Caughley dinner services, 24 x 17.75cm (9 ½ x 7in) but such dishes were made in various sizes, c.1785–90, Godden of Worthing.

90 A Caughley saucer-shaped plate from a tea service, printed in underglaze blue with the popular "Fisherman" or "Pleasure Boat" pattern. This design is found on a wide range of products. The glaze is "pegged" away from the foot-rim, diameter 21cm (8½in), c.1785, Godden collection.

91 A Caughley handled dish from a dessert service. Neatly painted in a bright underglaze blue with French-style floral sprigs. Impressed-marked "SALOPIAN", in capital letters, 20 x 21cm (8 x 8¼in), c.1790, Godden collection.

Caughley wares were *not* sent to the main Worcester factory to be decorated. All underglaze blue decoration is Caughley factory work although some enamelling and gilding was added at Chamberlain's works at Worcester (*see* pictures 94 and 95). Some other reference books do make exactly opposite suggestions but my points are supported in detail in my specialist work on the Caughley and Worcester porcelains.

The Caughley factory marks comprise the word "Salopian" or "SALOPIAN" impressed, but in practice this mark is found only on dishes, plates, and such flat-based objects. The initial "S", however, occurs printed in underglaze blue on a multitude of objects large and small. On pieces bearing a blue-printed design the "S" will be printed too, but sometimes a small, hand-painted "o" or "x" was added to this, which resulted in "So" or "Sx" markings. On hand-painted blue designs the "S" is also painted on and the extra letters do not occur on the wares at all.

The capital initial "C" from Caughley was also employed both in hand-painted (*see* picture 93) and, more often, printed versions. On the rare powder blue ground pieces (*see* picture 87, top right) mock-Chinese characters (not numerals) occur. With the exception of the very rare and early "Turner Gallimore" mark (*see* p.76) Thomas Turner did not use his own name as an identification, relying on the initial "C" for the little-known place-name Caughley, the county designation "Salopian" (Shropshire), or its initial letter "S". "Turner" marked wares are actually Staffordshire.

It seems likely that in the late 1790s the basic soap-stone-type body was changed to a type of hybrid hard-paste; this development is covered within the next chapter (*see* p.148).

In October 1799 Turner sold the Caughley works as a going concern to the partners working the nearby Coalport factory – John Rose, Edward Blakeway, and Richard Rose. He then sold much of his remaining stock by auction in Shrewsbury but the Caughley factory was continued by John Rose, along with his Coalport factory, for some 15 years and the story of this later period is told in the Coalport section.

Most books published before the late 1960s are rather unreliable concerning the Caughley wares as the authors did not have access to the finds since made on the factory site. This means that pieces we now know to be Worcester are shown as Caughley, and incorrect facts are given on the factory marks as well as on other important matters. Our current knowledge is, I believe, well explained in my own specialist book *Caughley and Worcester Porcelain, 1775–1800*, which features over 300 helpful illustrations. Several magazine articles also shed light on our new knowledge; these include *Collectors Guide* 1967, August 1968, and the same magazine's "World of Antiques" issue of October 1968. *The Connoisseur*, May 1969, and *Burlington Magazine* of January 1969 are also very useful. The catalogue of the 1972 Bicentenary Exhibition held at the Shrewsbury Art Gallery is a most interesting record too. The miniature or "toy" pieces are well covered in Dr C. Holloway and Felicity Marno's well-illustrated exhibition catalogue or monograph *Caughley Toy Wares* (Stockspring Antiques, London, 2001). See also Simon Spero's 2003 exhibition catalogue (*see* p.67). My *Encyclopaedia of British Porcelain Manufacturers* should also be helpful while my *Godden's Guide to English Blue and White Porcelain* (Antique Collectors' Club, 2004) gives an up-to-date résumé of Caughley porcelains in relation to its competitors.

Good collections of Caughley porcelain can be seen at the Victoria and Albert Museum in London, and particularly at the Coalport factory site – the Ironbridge Gorge Museum in Shropshire. The meetings of the Caughley Society are often held in the former Coalport works, now part of the Museum complex.

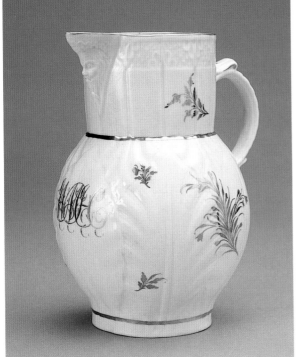

92 A Caughley moulded cabbage-leaf jug, decorated with gilt floral sprays and initial monogram at Chamberlain's decorating studio, Worcester. (Existing documents and accounts relate to this trade.) 19cm (7½in) high, *c*.1790, Godden collection.

93 A superbly potted Caughley teabowl. Painted in underglaze blue with a rare pattern. The rest of this tea service is in the Victoria and Albert Museum. Painted "C" mark, as shown, 8cm (3in) in diameter (at top), *c*.1776–80, Godden collection.

92

93

94

95

94 A Caughley moulded cabbage-leaf, mask-head jug. The decoration, apart from the underglaze blue borders, was added to the jug at Chamberlain's Worcester decorating studio. This is a superb piece – for a one-off order. Blue "S" mark, 22cm (8¾in) high, c.1788–92, formerly in the Godden collection.

95 A superb-quality Caughley mug. The decoration, apart from the underglaze blue borders, was added at Chamberlain's decorating studio at Worcester. The gilding is of very high quality, the gilt initials being typically highlighted or shaded with enamel. Blue "S" mark, 11.5cm (4½in) high, c.1788–92, Godden collection.

Chamberlain, *c.1788–1800+*

See pictures 17, 36, 40, 47, 66, 94, and 95

The place name "Worcester" is normally added to the name Chamberlain, which gives rise to descriptions such as "A fine Chamberlain-Worcester figure-painted vase". We cannot use the place name alone to describe such pieces as, from the 1780s to the present century, there were two and sometimes three different firms producing fine porcelain within the city of Worcester.

Robert Chamberlain, the founder of the firm we are discussing, was apprenticed to the main so-called Dr Wall porcelain company. In fact he is said to have been its first apprentice in the 1750s. Robert specialized in the decorating side of the Dr Wall concern and, in 1770, it would appear that he and his son Humphrey were in charge of this all-important part of the company. However, after Thomas Flight took over the Worcester works in 1783 Robert Chamberlain and his son left, and in about 1786 they established their own decorating establishment. At first, and for a period of about two years, they, with their team of decorators, seem to have been employed in embellishing the Flight porcelains by contract or other arrangement but in 1788 or early in 1789 the Chamberlains broke with the Flight management at the former Dr Wall factory. After this they were supplied with blanks (undecorated porcelain) by their former colleague Thomas Turner of the Caughley porcelain factory. Turner had also loaned Robert Chamberlain a large sum of money and they were in fact at this early period business partners – the Chamberlains were not only decorating for Turner but also affording a valuable retail outlet for Caughley porcelains within Worcester. Some of this Caughley porcelain was enamelled and gilt to Turner's express orders and was returned to him or forwarded to his London warehouse on completion. Other Caughley wares were purchased outright by the Chamberlains and sold by them after being embellished.

In June 1789 the Chamberlains opened their retail shop at 33 High Street, Worcester. These premises were in fact previously used by Flight's, so the Chamberlains must have gained some of Flight's former customers who returned to a shop that had now changed ownership. In reading contemporary documents the impression is gained that Chamberlain and Flight were very keen rivals and that they were hardly on speaking terms, enticing away each other's decorators!

The typical Caughley cabbage-leaf jug shown in picture 94 was probably ordered at the Chamberlain shop and then decorated to a special order. As this was before Chamberlain started to produce his own porcelain, a Caughley blank was used for the piece. This form was extremely popular and examples were made in various sizes.

In approximately 1791 (certainly by 1793), the Chamberlains had decided to branch out and become porcelain manufacturers as well as decorators. They continued to decorate some Caughley porcelains but by 1796 the majority of the porcelains originated in Chamberlain's own manufacture and he was receiving Royal orders and had built up an export trade.

The early Chamberlain porcelains, especially their tea services, were decorated in a very simple manner, with floral sprigs etc or with Chinese-style designs (*see* picture 171), but many vases and other ornamental pieces were decorated in the richest style (*see* picture 173) rivalling contemporary Flight or Derby porcelains. The post-1800 history of the Chamberlain partnership is given in Chapter 7 but I have purposely started the story in this present section to make the point that the Chamberlain manufactory was established in the 18th century and that very fine pieces were being produced. Some have regarded Chamberlain's as being a second-class factory, but this is not so. In workmanship and decoration the Chamberlain wares excel many other types; it is a very underrated factory.

The Chamberlain-decorated Caughley porcelains of the late 1780s and early 1790s do not appear to bear any special mark and so they are normally regarded purely as Caughley pieces – examples with blue borders may well bear the Caughley "S" mark, (*see* picture 95). We could call these pieces "Caughley-Chamberlain".

For further information on Chamberlain wares see my out-of-print specialist book *Chamberlain-Worcester Porcelain 1788–1852* (Barrie & Jenkins, 1982), which illustrates a very good range of standard shapes. For personal details of the Chamberlains see Dr Sonia Parkinson's "Chamberlains of Worcester. The Early Years of a Family Enterprise", *Journal of the Northern Ceramic Society*, Vol. 8 (1991). (See also my coverage of the later wares in Chapter 7, p.145).

Chelsea, *c.*1745–69

| *See* pictures 10, 26, 27, 30, and 96–101

Chelsea is the most famous English porcelain factory and yet we are still not at all sure of its exact location in the Chelsea district of London or of the exact year of its establishment.

What we do know is that it was producing quite sophisticated pieces by 1745, such as the moulded

96 Early Chelsea porcelains. Centre: an incised triangle-marked covered coffee or chocolate pot. Right: a rare child model – a similar example, in the British Museum, is dated 1746, and on the left is a raised-anchor marked copy of a Chinese figure of Kuan Yin. Pot 23cm (9in) high, *c.*1745–50, formerly in the Godden collection.

Goat and Bee fancy small jugs – some of which bear the date 1745 incised under the base. Other objects of the same period owe much in inspiration to contemporary silverware and we should remember that Nicholas Sprimont (1716–71), the manager of the factory for most of its history, was originally a silversmith.

The Chelsea porcelain body varied greatly during the factory's life, but it was always of the soft-paste variety. This and the related glazes have a warm, friendly feel and prior to around 1755 the glaze was slightly whitened by adding a small quantity of tin oxide to its make-up: such pieces have a waxy cream-like appearance.

Apart from the very early examples that were often unadorned with enamels or gilding (see picture 96), the Chelsea porcelains were the most richly decorated of all the English 18th-century ceramics. In general, therefore, it seems that the Chelsea management set its sights on the higher-class market, producing ornate pieces for the rich.

Extremely few examples from the factory seem to have been decorated in underglaze blue. Many of the Chelsea products were sold by public auction, usually in London. These fashionable gatherings today afford us valuable information on the changing styles and models of the company, as some of the original printed catalogues have survived and are quoted in several specialist books on Chelsea wares.

The various periods of Chelsea porcelain have been conveniently classified by reference to the marks then employed, normally the anchor in various forms and colours. Before turning the discussion to these marks, however, I must mention two earlier ones. First, we have the incised triangle mark as found on the Goat and Bee form jugs and other pieces of about 1745 (see picture 96, centre). Do note that I said "incised" not impressed or ground in: in other words the triangle device should have a spontaneous appearance with a slightly ploughed-up look, as if the mark had been drawn with a matchstick in butter or cheese. The other early mark regarded as being of Chelsea origin is painted in underglaze blue (although this colour may not have been used in the decoration) and comprises a small trident-like device piercing a crown.

We can now discuss the various anchor marks used by Chelsea. The first version of the anchor was relief moulded on a small applied oval pad; this is called the "raised anchor" mark and its probable period of employment was but three years, 1749–52 (see pictures 30 and 96, left). (The raised anchor can be picked out in red enamel.) Such examples may represent transitional pieces made in the raised-anchor period but decorated

in the following red-anchor period. The standard body was a glassy frit paste with the waxy cream-like whitened or semi-opaque glaze. This same body and glaze was carried over to the early years of the next period, c.1752–6, known as the "red anchor" period because a small anchor was neatly painted in a red enamel. Note how in the bowl shown in picture 97 the anchor mark is quite small. Large, blatantly positioned marks should be treated with great caution, see p.237. Do note that relatively few examples bear any of these so-called standard marks. Most pieces are unmarked.

If an early Chelsea saucer dish or plate is held up to a light, small light-coloured "moons" or "stars" can be seen, which were caused by small air pockets within the piece. Although some of the Longton Hall and Derby porcelains can display the same faults, these "moons" are a good guide to pre-1760 Chelsea porcelains. When defects appear on the surface of the ware, such as exploding "stars" or spots in the glaze, the painters very often camouflaged these by overpainting them with insects or floral sprays, for manufacturing processes had by no means been perfected and slight faults were accepted. Also foot-rings would normally need to be ground flat before the plate, dish, or bowl would "sit" on a table. The three little pimple-like marks under the Chelsea bowl shown in picture 97 are not defects but rather the marks left by the "stilts" or "spurs" on which the piece rested in the glost kiln, so raising the glazed article from the kiln shelf or from another piece in the sagger, to prevent the glaze gluing the pieces together (see picture 10). Notable, pleasing, and characteristic enamelled designs included animal fable subjects attributed to the hand of the ceramic

97 An attractive and typical red-anchor period Chelsea fluted bowl, with the scenes painted in monochrome. Red-anchor mark and stilt marks, diameter 17.75cm (7in), c.1755, Godden of Worthing.

artist J.H. O'Neale as well as various botanical studies, although flower sprays remained the standard mode of decoration, supported by the simple old Japanese-style patterns that had perhaps been copied second-hand from Continental copies of the Oriental originals (*see* picture 98).

The next main period of Chelsea porcelain is the "gold anchor" period, *c.*1756–69. Here the mark is in gold providing the pieces bear some gilding. This is by far the longest period, and in fact continued into the so-called Chelsea-Derby period, but I must point out that some late red-anchor and early gold-anchor wares of a more ordinary nature (such as picture 100) bore anchors of other colours. An anchor painted in brown enamel tends to be of a rather larger size than the red anchor, and some of the very rare blue-and-white pieces bore a blue anchor. In general the gold-anchor marked porcelains are very richly decorated (often with ground colours) and ornately gilt, as pictures 26 and 101 show. In my early days of collecting it was popularly thought that the colour of the anchor was related to the quality of the piece, not to its period of manufacture, but this is not the case. Indeed modern taste prefers the earlier, rather sparsely decorated, wares to the more richly decorated and once extremely popular and expensive later gold-anchor examples.

In this gold-anchor period, or late in the red-anchor period, the porcelain body was of the bone-ash type containing about 40 per cent bone ash. A gold-anchor plate that was analysed by the late Herbert Eccles gave the following result:

Silica	45.52%
Alumina	12.06%
Lime	26.00%
Phosphoric acid	14.27%
Soda	0.73%
Potash	0.93%

The change in make-up is most apparent in the lead glaze that, being thickly applied, tends to break up into that network of fine lines we call crazing. It is also clear or only slightly coloured rather than being whitened by the addition of tin oxide, as were the early pieces. These different glazes can readily be contrasted by examining pieces in available collections.

While Chelsea porcelain has always enjoyed a very high reputation, at least in England, it must be stated that the potting is often thick, the pieces are on the heavy side, and the glaze is far from being perfect (if we accept that such a covering should be translucent, well-fitting, and free of crazing).

98

99

98 Two early Chelsea creamers copying Japanese forms and patterns. Note the ground foot on the left-hand example and lack of factory marks, 6.25cm (2½in) and 4.5cm (1¾in) high, *c.*1750–55, Godden collection.

99 A standard red-anchor period Chelsea plate from a dinner service, painted with scattered flowers – some covering defects in the body or glaze. The reverse side is shown in picture 10. Small red-anchor mark, diameter 23.5cm (9¼in), *c.*1755, Godden collection.

I have pointed out that the various periods into which we divide up the Chelsea porcelains are related to the different types or colour of the anchor marks: the raised anchor, the red anchor, and the gold anchor. We must remember, however, that the dates given are dates of convenience for us today. They are approximate only and there was probably some overlap during which time two different marks were used. It must also be remembered that by no means all Chelsea porcelain is marked; probably less than half is and that is why a study of the body, the glaze, and the potting features is

100 A boldly painted oval dish from a Chelsea dessert service. The exotic birds in landscape designs were popular at most English factories. Small brown-anchor mark, 25 x 18.5cm (10 x 7¼in), c.1758, Godden of Worthing.

so important and why collectors should familiarize themselves with the key marked and authentic pieces.

There are many fakes and reproductions on the market to be careful of. These pieces normally boast a prominent anchor (usually in gold) about twice the size of the real Chelsea anchor. Always question any anchor mark that measures over 0.5cm (¼in) in height. The fakes are nearly always in a glittery Continental hard-paste porcelain but some were made well over 100 years ago so they are "antiques" in their own right and have acquired a pedigree. Remember, a mark is easy to fake and several factories other than Chelsea used this anchor device. Until you are quite sure of your subject you are well advised to only buy your Chelsea from a reputable source. You should bear in mind that wares bearing a painted or printed designation "Chelsea" are *not* from there. Such markings usually related to the style of decoration applied to some 20th-century porcelains or even earthenwares (*see* also p.238).

There is simply not room here to discuss the many fine figures and groups produced at Chelsea or the charming little "toys", the seals, and the scent bottles, but these aspects of the factory's production are well covered in specialist books, such as *English Porcelain Figures of the Eighteenth Century* by A. Lane (Faber, 1961) and G.E. Bryant's *Chelsea Porcelain Toys* (Medici Society, 1925). See also Kate Foster's E.C.C. paper "Chelsea Scent Bottles – Girl in a Swing and another group", *Transactions of the English Ceramic Circle*, Vol.6, Part 3, 1967.

In August 1769 the Chelsea premises, plus all the working materials, were put up for sale. The factory continued for a further period until 1784, as it was continued by William Duesbury of the Derby factory. These later wares, of the 1770–84 period, are termed (I think incorrectly) "Chelsea-Derby", *see* right.

The modern standard book on Chelsea porcelain is Elizabeth Adam's *Chelsea Porcelain* (Barrie & Jenkins, 1987, and The British Museum Press, 2001). Another very well-illustrated work is *Chelsea Porcelain at Williamsburg* by John C. Austin (Colonial Williamsburg Foundation, 1977). Other older books on Chelsea porcelain in general include *Chelsea Porcelain, The Triangle and Raised Anchor Wares*; *Chelsea Porcelain, The Red Anchor Wares*; and *Chelsea Porcelain, The Gold Anchor Period*, all three by F.S. Mackenna (F. Lewis, 1948, 1951, and 1952 respectively). The Chelsea section by J.V.G. Mallet in *English Porcelain 1745–1850*, edited by R.J. Charleston (Benn, 1965), is also instructive. Various papers also provide specialist information on various aspects of Chelsea porcelain. There is, for example, John Mallet's "Chelsea Gold Anchor Vases (I). The Forms", *Transactions of the English Ceramic Circle*, Vol.17, Part I, 1999.

101 A richly decorated gold-anchor period Chelsea handleless cup. The gilt border helped to tidy up the run blue ground. Rare but typical figure subjects, anchor mark in gold, 9.5cm (3¾in) high, c.1765, private collection.

Chelsea-Derby, *c.*1770–84

The Chelsea premises and working materials were put up for sale in August 1769 and were sold to James Cox but were quickly resold to the well-known, established Derby porcelain manufacturer William Duesbury in February 1770. He must have been well pleased with the prestige that this new acquisition gave him.

William Duesbury continued production at Chelsea and employed several of the former hands, which is evidenced by the wage records and other documents quoted by Llewellynn Jewitt in his book *The Ceramic Art of Great Britain* (Virtue & Co., 1878). The wares made at Chelsea within the Duesbury period, 1770–84, are usually referred to as "Chelsea-Derby". However, the Derby influence is hardly marked and Duesbury himself in his advertisements and sale notices rightly and understandably referred to the goods being offered as Chelsea Porcelain. His post-1773 tradecard (*see* below) in the Victoria and Albert Museum (other examples can be found in the British Museum) reads, "Duesbury & Co., Manufacturers of Derby & Chelsea Porcelain". The engraved articles shown in this card illustrate the trim, classical nature of Derby porcelains of the 1770s, "Biscuit Groups and Single Figures" are mentioned, as are some non-ceramic types of room decoration. These showrooms opened in June 1773.

The term used for porcelain of this period is today complicated by the fact that a large class of figures and groups that seem to have no links at all with the Chelsea factory are often referred to as "Chelsea-Derby". Indeed, they appear to be purely of Derby manufacture and of a period before Duesbury took over the Chelsea factory!

It would be very convenient if we could designate all porcelain made at Chelsea before the buildings were demolished in 1784 as "Chelsea", regardless of the ownership of the works. This would mean all porcelain made at Derby could be known as "Derby", but at the moment the terms seem muddled. The situation was, and is, admittedly complicated for there was some interchange of moulds, clay, and workmen between the two factories, and the very real difficulty distinguishing between the Chelsea and the Derby porcelains of the 1770s probably gave rise to the joint term Chelsea-Derby as an easy way out of the problem at the time.

The tableware designs that we normally attribute to the Chelsea-Derby period are often decorated in a restrained classical manner with swags and festoons of flowers etc and seem much more associated with the Derby factory than with Chelsea. The wares are thinner in the potting than the earlier gold-anchor period Chelsea wares and the gilding has a tendency to peel from the body, which is a fault found with Derby wares of about this period. The foot-rings are often not ground flat, as Chelsea feet were. The accounts relating to the early period of Duesbury's ownership of the Chelsea factory were available in the 19th century and some of these are quoted in Llewellynn Jewitt's *The Ceramic Art of Great Britain*. These show that small "toys" such as seals, thimbles, and scent bottles were being made in large quantities, as well as many vases and busts on pedestals. We also find entries such as "48 compotiers [dishes] all made with the Darby clay, 24 ornamental plates, made with ditto". Such Chelsea-made objects of "Darby clay" puzzle us today but I believe they should be regarded as true Chelsea and certainly they were decorated at this famous London factory.

The Chelsea works under Duesbury appear to have been gradually run down as workmen were transferred to Derby or were otherwise lost to the London factory. The main value of the purchase was probably prestige and the right to use the Chelsea gold-anchor mark. As time wore on Duesbury no doubt found that he could not efficiently manage both factories, so in 1784 the last of the Chelsea buildings was demolished and the remaining useful materials transferred to Derby.

Apart from the so-called "Chelsea-Derby" figures – which I regard as purely Derby – the "Chelsea-Derby" wares are often marked. These marks are normally in gold and comprise the following basic devices.

The crowned-anchor mark (A) is quite rare and should probably be regarded as a post-1775 Derby mark, while in general the gold anchor occurs on pieces that I regard as being of Chelsea manufacture.

The conjoined "D" and anchor mark (B) is found largely on porcelains that I believe to be of Derby manufacture; the mark perhaps signifying the joint management controlling both the Chelsea and Derby factories. This broad and general classification by marks may well be questioned by many and we will probably be debating the true origin of the porcelains classed as Chelsea-Derby for years. These porcelains of the 1770–84 period do not bear a pattern number and it should be noted that the "D" and anchor mark can also occur on 19th-century Continental hard-paste porcelain fakes.

Typical Chelsea-Derby porcelains are featured in several different books on Derby porcelain, such as F. B. Gilhespy's *Crown Derby Porcelain* (F. Lewis, 1951) or his *Derby Porcelain* (Spring Books, 1965). These wares are also featured in Elizabeth Adam's book *Chelsea Porcelain* (Barrie & Jenkins, 1987) and the revised 2001 edition.

Coalport, *c.*1796 to the present day

The Coalport porcelain works were established and in production at least by June 1796 but the discussion of these little-known early wares is found in Chapter 7 as the body was of the hybrid hard-paste variety. The post-1820 examples are featured in Chapter 9.

Derby, *c.*1750–1800

| *See* pictures 9, 38, 41, 47, 48, 57, and 102–108

Although I have already indicated that the production of porcelain in the city of Derby has been spread over at least 200 years or more, it has not been a continuous progression on just one factory site. There are several periods and types of Derby porcelain and we are only concerned here with the 18th-century pieces, as later developments are revealed in Chapters 9 and 10.

The early history of the Derby works is not at all clear but on the evidence of some white jugs with the incised initial "D", and in one case also the date 1750, the factory was in production at this period. I must point out in passing that these jugs now seem similar to some early Chelsea and "Girl in the Swing" porcelains of the same period. Andrew Planche, chinamaker, had a largely unknown but probably important part to play in the establishment of the porcelain industry in Derby, with John Heath. However, the prime mover from the mid-1750s was William Duesbury, who had started his ceramic career as a ceramic decorator and, after

building up the reputation of the Derby factory as the "Second-Dresden" (to use his description!), he was able to purchase the Chelsea works in 1770 (*see* pp.86–7).

The Derby porcelains were made from about 1750 by Heath & Co, that is by John Heath and Andrew Planche. There is an unsigned agreement dating from 1 January 1756 that shows that William Duesbury "Enammelor" then agreed to join Heath and Andrew Planche as co-partners to produce "English China". Duesbury continued until his death in 1786, when he was succeeded by his son of the same name.

The early Derby porcelains are soft-paste porcelain, which is somewhat open in texture and lighter in weight than contemporary Bow or Chelsea. The figures and other moulded wares are slip-cast (*see* p.22), which accentuates the light feeling of the wares. The colours on the early examples of the 1750s tend to be very pale and the decoration is restrained, (*see* pictures 47 and 102). The glaze is normally free of crazing and is tight-fitting and thinner than the Chelsea glazes, and has less of a tendency to pool or run. Great care was taken to keep the bases of figures clear of glaze so that they would not stick to the kiln furniture and would need little or no grinding after the pieces came from the kiln. To accomplish this, the glaze was stopped short of the bottom edge or the edge was chamfered or trimmed at an angle, which gave rise to the description "dry-edge". Later, from about 1755, the Derby wares were generally kept clear of the sagger or other kiln furniture by being placed on three or more clay blobs or "pads" These separators left slightly darker "pad-marks" or "patch marks", which are a good guide to a Derby origin (*see* picture 9 and the base detail shown below.)

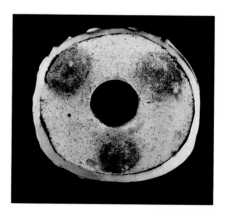

Duesbury's pre-1770 porcelains are rarely gilt; they are not as pretentious as the Meissen and Chelsea pieces that had inspired so many of his productions (especially the figures and groups, and it is his figure models that built Duesbury's reputation). His early

102 Two rare and early Derby figures from a set of four, which represent the elements – Fire, Air, Earth, and Water. These are shown in a damaged, unrepaired state, and one is turned to show its base. Note the early, pale colouring and simple bases; the crude inscription on the base reads "Water" in reference to its subject, 10cm (4in) high, *c.*1750–52, formerly in the Godden collection.

useful wares of the 1750s and even of the 1760s are now quite scarce and not really startling, and while some blue-and-white porcelains were produced they do not have the charm and "life" of some other makes, nor do they show the crisp workmanship of the Worcester examples. The enamelled tablewares are normally painted with flowers in rather dry-looking colours (*see* picture 104); the flowers typically grown on very thin cotton-like stems! Other pieces are painted with simple Chinese-figure designs.

The figures and groups of the general type often classed as Chelsea-Derby are, as I have noted, almost certainly purely of Derby manufacture. In the 1770s the beautiful white biscuit (unglazed) Derby figures and groups were introduced. These were produced into the early 1800s but most are 18th century. These are of superb workmanship, as only the finest unblemished examples were sold in this white state (*see* picture 106). The slightly faulty models were glazed and coloured to mask the defects, which means that, originally, the unblemished, undecorated examples cost more than the coloured pieces. In general these white models, with

their wonderfully sharp modelling, are not appreciated as they should be. You should bear in mind that by no means all unglazed white figures are of Derby origin, for the idea came from the French Sèvres factory and many other Continental manufactories made such wares, but these to British eyes are too white and cold-looking and, in many cases, the hard-paste porcelain has an unpleasant feel (I am not speaking here of the early Sèvres examples, which are delightful but simpler than the Derby pieces.) A good account of the Derby biscuit wares is given by Timothy Clifford in *Transactions of the English Ceramic Circle*, Vol. 7, Part 2, 1969.

By the 1780s the Derby body had become very smooth and almost waxy to the touch. It was coated with a soft, warm, and pleasant-feeling glaze (slightly whitened rather than clear), which tended to form a scum line at the edges near the foot. Useful tablewares became a much more important feature of the factory's production at this time. Very tasteful simple forms were embellished with fine-quality painting, notably landscape subjects and floral designs, and one painter,

103

104

103 A Derby jug with typical large spout and small handle. Decorated with a rare pale yellow ground and flower-painted panels, 17cm (6¾in) high, c.1760, Godden of Worthing.

104 A Derby rib-moulded globular teapot and cover, attractively painted with floral sprays. Ground foot-rim, 15.25cm (6in) high, c.1765, Miss A. Blist collection.

105 Right, a typical, well-modelled, large Derby figure on simple base, with slight gilt embellishments. Three pad-marks on base, 34.25cm (13½in) high, c.1770, Godden of Worthing.

William Billingsley, is perhaps better known than Duesbury himself. Unusual seascapes, battle scenes, classical figure subjects (*see* picture 108) and the like can also be found if you are lucky (or very rich)! The superb-quality coffee cans, such as is shown on picture 108, were individual items with plainer "stands". They were not usually part of a matching service. These expensive Derby porcelains of 1780–1800 may be regarded as the finest of the period, as they surpass, in delicacy and charm, the Worcester porcelains and totally outclass the Caughley, Isleworth, Liverpool, and Lowestoft wares. Derby's nearest rival in the late 1790s was the almost related small works at Pinxton, which was nearest in geographical terms as well as in quality (*see* p.115).

Before about 1774, the Derby porcelains were very seldom or never marked, but then various marks became more usual and by 1800 it is almost possible to say that if a piece is not marked then it is not Derby in origin. The first real standard Derby porcelain mark comprised the cursive capital letter "D" under a crown (*see* below). This normally occurs painted in blue enamel but it can also occur in other tints. Being hand-painted, many slight variations in drawing may be expected (all within the period *c.*1775–82). This mark is by no means common.

The Derby porcelains made before May 1775 should not be called "Crown Derby". This term, if it is used at all, relates to the post-May 1775 Royal Appointment period and therefore "Duesbury Derby" is preferable for 18th-century wares. Many Derby porcelain useful wares made before, say, 1790 bear an incised cursive "N". This is under the glaze and would have been added during manufacture. Although its significance is now uncertain it serves us today as a useful guide to a Derby origin. By this period the Derby body contained some 40 per cent of bone ash.

A very rare mark comprises the words "Duesbury London" painted in a neat manner, one word above the other (see p.92). This mark no doubt relates to the London showrooms, but its rarity means that not all pieces sold there could have been so marked.

The next standard painted mark (found also incised on figures) is the first of a series of so-called "crossed baton" marks. Here, placed between the crown and the initial "D", are two crossed sticks or batons with three dots added at each end. This mark would seem to have been introduced in about 1782. At first it was very neatly painted, often in a puce-coloured enamel (but occasionally in blue, black, or gold), and, for the first time, with this mark was a pattern or other number added below. This application of pattern numbers to Derby porcelains of the 1780s could mark the first use of such numbers on any English ceramics (*see* p.234)

The red-painted version of this mark is post-1800 and, as time progressed, the mark was sometimes very hastily painted, as you can observe by comparing a neat puce-colour mark of the 1790–1800 period with a typical specimen of the red mark of the 1820s. Derby figures and groups produced from about 1790 can have the model number incised into the porcelain base.

106

107

106 A superbly modelled and produced Derby biscuit porcelain figure, which is part of a set of four French seasons. These were made in three sizes (priced at £2-2-0 to £4-4-0). They were also issued in a glazed and coloured version at a cheaper price. Incised crown, crossed batons, and "D" mark and "no 123", 17cm (6¾in) high (smallest size), *c.*1800, Godden collection.

107 A graceful Derby dancing group, model number 16. Typical rococo base and pale colouring. Incised number "16", three pad-marks, 19cm (7½in) high, *c.*1790, Godden of Worthing.

108 A Derby coffee can that is attractively decorated in the style of the 1790s but which nevertheless bears a later mark. Red-transferred circular "Bloor Derby" mark with crown, 6.25cm (2½in) high, c.1815–20, Godden of Worthing.

Bradley (Thomas Heneage & Co., 1990), *Derby Porcelain 1748–1848 An Illustrated Guide* by John Twitchett (Antique Collectors' Club, 2002). There are also several advanced or specialist publications, such as Volume I of Derby Porcelain Archive Research study entitled "European Competition, Trade and Influence 1786–1796", compiled by A. P. Ledger and published by the Derby Museum and Art Gallery, in 1998. Vol. II of 2002 deals with the London trade. Later volumes will, I'm sure, continue the vital research, using original letters and documents.

Serious collectors or students of Derby porcelain should definitely consider joining the Derby Porcelain International Society (*see* p.264). Not only does this Society publish a regular newsletter containing new research and information but it also sponsors or publishes well-illustrated journals, under such titles as *Recent Research on Ceramics of Derbyshire*.

Most ceramic museums will feature some examples of Derby porcelains. Apart from the Victoria and Albert Museum and The British Museum, in London, the local City Museum (The Strand, Derby) and the Museum at the Royal Crown Derby works have good specialist collections covering all periods of porcelain production in Derby. The later aspects of the story are continued on pp.191 and 218.

Continental copies of Derby porcelain occur with standard Derby or with the Chelsea gold-anchor mark, but the porcelain is hard and the gilding flat. The later so-called Stevenson & Hancock porcelains made at the separate King Street works in Derby can mislead some people, as at first the old Derby mark was employed and even when the additional initials "SH" appear some new collectors do not realize their significance (*see* p.193).

The second William Duesbury succeeded his father in 1786, but he in turn died in 1797, having from Christmas 1795 formed a partnership with Michael Kean. I will leave the discussion of Derby porcelains at this point and to take it up afresh in Chapter 9.

Useful specialist books on the Derby wares are: *Crown Derby Porcelain* by F.B. Gilhespy (F. Lewis, 1951); his *Derby Porcelain* (MacGibbon & Kee, 1961); *Derby Porcelain* by F.A. Barrett and A.L. Thorpe (Faber, 1971); *Derby Porcelain* by J. Twitchett (Barrie & Jenkins, 1980); *Derby Porcelain, The Golden Years 1750–1770* by D.G. Rice (David & Charles, 1983); *Derby Porcelain Figures 1750–1848* by P. Bradshaw (Faber, 1990); *Derby Porcelain 1750–1798* by Gilbert

James Giles, *c.*1760–80

| *See* picture 109

I am not really dealing with a make of porcelain in this short section but rather with an independent decorator – independent in that he was not employed by a factory but decorated on his own account white blanks that he had purchased from various sources.

There were many such independent decorators in the 18th century but James Giles is probably the best known of these. However, few books give any clear account of his work and the available information is rather scattered. I must exempt from this statement the excellent account of Giles's work given by H. Rissik Marshall in his book *Coloured Worcester Porcelain of the First Period* (Ceramic Book Co., 1954) and G. Coke's very well-illustrated book *In Search of James Giles* (Micawber Publishing, Wingham, 1983).

James Giles was born in 1718, the son of James Giles. An apprentice record of June 1729 describes James Giles senior or his son Abraham (the record is not clear which is meant) as a "china painter" bound to Philip Margas, the London china dealer. Two points are interesting here – first that there was a trade of china painting at this early date, which was long before the English had learned to make porcelain – but this is perhaps explained by my second point, that Margas was a leading "chinaman" or dealer of the period and was a very large purchaser of Oriental porcelains imported by the English East India Company.

James Giles (junior) was apprenticed to John Arthur, jeweller, of St Martin- in-the-Fields, London, in 1733 and by November 1747 he was described in a Poll list as a chinaman at Berwick Street. At this period the porcelains he dealt with would most probably have been Chinese but he could also have stocked some early Bow, Chelsea, or even early examples of Limehouse porcelain.

If we are to believe the history accompanying the "Craft" bowl of Bow, now in the British Museum, Giles (or Gyles as his name was sometimes written), had a kiln for firing enamelled porcelains at Kentish Town in about the year 1760 and he may have been practising as an independent china painter a few years prior to this. Mortimer's Directory of 1763 lists James Giles "China and Enamel Painter" at 82 Berwick Street, Soho. The entry continues, "This ingenious artist copies patterns of any china with the utmost exactness…either in the European or Chinese taste…". By 1767 Giles also had a warehouse in Cockspur Street, which he called the "Worcester Porcelain Warehouse", and in a 1767 advertisement he claims to have available "a great variety of articles of the said manufactory, useful and ornamental…"

A sale notice relating to Giles's decorated porcelain held in May 1770 gives us a good idea of the range of his decorating achievements on Worcester blanks:

the whole consisting of elegant dessert services, fine tea sets, Caudles etc, curiously enamelled in with Figures, Birds, Flowers, etc, and ornamented with mazarine and sky blue and gold. Every article in this sale is the sole property and has been enamelled in London by and under the Direction of the Proprietor of the said warehouse, who having at present a large quantity of white china, continues to execute all orders to any pattern, at the shortest notice…

This decorator obviously had a thriving business and was apparently capable of embellishing Worcester (and other porcelains) in the most elaborate manner. The jug and plate shown in picture 109 are Worcester porcelain, while the teabowl is Chinese porcelain.

In broad terms we can divide the work that is today attributed to the Giles Studio into the following classes: dishevelled birds in the landscapes (*see* picture 109); Teniers-type figure subjects; fruit painting, which usually includes some sliced fruit; landscape and figure designs, often in monochrome – although such designs can of course occur on factory-decorated wares or on pieces painted by other decorators depending on their skill and markets. Giles, or his painters, also enamelled other orthodox styles, such as boldly painted floral compositions often featuring a large full-blown tulip and, as he advertised to "execute all orders to any pattern…", armorial and other devices and perhaps also "matchings" to services made by other firms.

No signed specimens of Giles's painting are known to me and the identification of his work has been largely built up by the study of four plates that were given to the Victoria and Albert Museum by Mrs Dora Edgell Grubbe. These specimens have been referred to in several books as the "Grubbe" plates. They are of Worcester manufacture of the 1765–70 period and it has been well documented that Giles purchased Worcester blanks to decorate. There seems little or no doubt, therefore, that these Grubbe plates were at least decorated in Giles's workshop or studio. It is often forgotten that he must have employed several painters and gilders and we do not have firm evidence that he himself painted the objects so readily accredited to him! So, was he merely the leader of a talented team? Probably not, as it is possible to see the master's hand on so many pieces.

Once he had given up the shop or warehouse in Cockspur Street, Giles retained the Berwick Street premises, "where he continues to paint and enamel all sorts of china" (as stated by one of his several adverts in newspapers). As well as decorating Giles also acted as a normal chinaman, selling the wares of various manufacturers – at this period mainly Derby porcelain but also glassware and even Chinese lacquer ware. His surviving account books of the 1770s show he dealt with the Bow, Caughley, Derby, Liverpool (Philip Christian), and Worcester concerns. The sale catalogue of his stock also suggests that he decorated, or at least dealt in, some Continental porcelains – including Frankenthal and Nymphenburg wares. He sold to Thomas Pitt a pair of plain white biscuit groups that would not have borne any added Giles decoration.

Giles also purchased from the Worcester factory much blue-and-white porcelain. It has been suggested that he embellished this with slight gilding but at this period very little blue-and-white bears gilding and such additions were mainly fashionable after Giles's death in 1780. It does seem, however, that his studio was responsible for some simple and attractive gold designs on Worcester blanks. These are quite different from the sumptuous pieces that we traditionally associate with Giles's decoration. Perhaps too much attention is paid

109 Porcelains decorated in James Giles's London studio, in typical styles. Left to right: Worcester milk jug, Worcester plate with rare special-order armorial bearings, and a Chinese porcelain teabowl. Diameter of plate 23cm (9in) c.1765–70, Godden of Worthing.

to the more pretentious Giles decoration and his more ordinary decoration is neglected as a result.

Much research still remains to be carried out on the Giles Studio. The known facts are to be found in the following publications, which will give you a very good groundwork to build upon: a paper by Aubrey J. Toppin in *Transactions of the English Ceramic Circle*, Vol.1, No.5, 1937 (he illustrates as Plate II the four "Grubbe" plates now in the Victoria and Albert Museum); *Coloured Worcester Porcelain of the First Period* by H. Rissik Marshall (Ceramic Book Co., 1954); *Worcester Porcelain and Lund's Bristol* by F.A. Barrett (Faber, revised edition, 1966); and *The Illustrated Guide to Worcester Porcelain* by Henry Sandon (Barrie & Jenkins, 1969).

An important document is Mr Christie's catalogue of the sale of "Elegant Porcelaine of English and Foreign manufacture, part of the Stock in Trade of Mr James Giles, Chinaman and Enameller, quitting that business, brought from his shop in Cockspur Street…" The sale was held on 21–25 March 1774. Details of

this sale catalogue are given by R.J. Charleston in *Transactions of the English Ceramic Circle*, Vol.6, Part 3, 1967. A well-illustrated article by Mrs A. George, "James Giles's London Atelier", is contained within the *Collectors Guide* of June 1974. In March 1977 Mrs George, who was then of Albert Amor Ltd, the well-known London dealers in antique porcelains, held an important loan exhibition of various porcelain and glass that had been decorated at the Giles workshop. This magnificent array was featured in the excellent exhibition catalogue, entitled *James Giles China Painter 1718–1780*. This is definitely a most useful source of information on this branch of ceramic decoration, but the most important single work on the Giles decorated porcelains remains G. Coke's *In Search of*

110

111

110 A very rare "Girl in a Swing" porcelain bird model. Note the characteristic shaped base, typical flower painting, modelled flowers, and leaves, 13cm (5¼in) high, c.1750–55, Godden of Worthing.

111 A very rare "Girl in a Swing" small covered porcelain pot. This is very thinly and delicately potted and the leaf and flower knob matches those elements found on the figure models. Flat unglazed base, 7.5cm (3in) high, c.1750–55, Godden collection.

James Giles, as mentioned at the beginning of this section. A good selection of Mr. Coke's collection can be seen at the Worcester Works Museum.

"Girl in a Swing" Factory (St James's, London) c.1749–59

| *See* pictures 110 and 111

This interesting and early class of English porcelain is named after the well-known white porcelain model of a girl in a swing, an example of which can be seen in the Victoria and Albert Museum today. That model is a typical example of this very rare class of design that has rather wooden modelling and overgrown leaves – many of which are larger than the girl's head! These porcelains, which show on analysis an unusually high lead content (about 16 per cent), were sold through the Chelsea China Warehouse in St James's, the manager of which reported in January 1751 that, "My China Warehouse is not supply'd by any other person than Mr Charles Gouyn late Proprietor and Chief Manager of the Chelsea-House, who continues to supply me with the most curious of goods of that manufacture, as well useful as ornamental". Confirmation of Charles Gouyn's involvement in this small and short-lived enterprise came about in the early 1990s as a result of the researches of a Paris dealer, Bernard Dragesco, and the 1759 account of a French traveller, Jacques Louis Brolliet. Dragesco's discovery was first revealed at a lecture given at the annual 1993 London International Ceramics Fair & Seminar, and was later published and distributed personally.

These St James's or "Girl in a Swing" porcelains are extremely rare and costly, and so much interest is raised whenever a specimen comes onto the market. Some of the "toys" by the same factory, such as its fancy scent bottles and seals, are attractive and relatively common while the tea-wares and figures are very rare but have little technical excellence. However, if you see any little figures or birds standing on a base like that shown in picture 110, then you are almost certainly looking at one of the rarest class of English porcelain, which may have continued up to 1759.

Strangely the figures and bird models outnumber the tablewares but this is probably only because we as yet know so little about these London porcelains. The Girl in a Swing useful wares do still largely await identification, for as yet only one type of enamelled decoration – floral sprays (*see* picture 111) seems to have been recognized.

For further information on these rare porcelains refer to R.J. Charleston and Arthur Lane's paper in

Transactions of the English Ceramic Circle, Vol.5, Part 3, 1962. Interesting views on these porcelains are also put forward in Elizabeth Adam's *Chelsea Porcelain* (Revised edition, The British Museum Press, 2001), which is a work that includes helpful illustrations too. Bernard Dragesco's finds are outlined in the *Transactions of the English Ceramic Circle*, Vol.15, Part 2 (1994), in an important paper by the late Mrs N. Valpy entitled "Charles Gouyn and the Girl in a Swing Factory".

Isleworth, *c.1757–90s*

| *See pictures 112–17*

Although very good accounts of this small London-district pottery and porcelain manufactory existed as long ago as 1866, over the years this history has been discounted! Yet there were even simple, seemly contemporary notices such as that given by the Revd Daniel Lyson in his *Environs of London* (Vol.III, 1795), which stated, "There is a china manufactory at Isleworth belonging to Messrs. Shore & Co."

It has been learned from William Chaffers (the well-known author of *Marks and Monograms*, which was written in the 1860s) and from insurance records that the Isleworth works was situated on the east side of the rail head near to the ferry across the river Thames at Isleworth, by the River Crane and Kew in Middlesex. The founding owner was Joseph Shore, the chief painter was Richard Goulding, and the manager or "superintendent" was Benjamin Quarman, who was also a partner in the business. The Shores, Gouldings, and the Quarmans were all related by marriage. Joseph Shore possibly received his ceramic training at the Worcester factory. Joseph Shore's son William joined the partnership in 1769. The firm variously traded as "Joseph Shore" and then "William Shore & Co.", but no true factory name mark was employed.

Seemingly under 20 persons were employed; there was one kiln for the biscuit firing and one for the glazed wares. Both earthenwares and porcelains were produced, but we are not sure over what period the porcelains were manufactured. One unglazed factory waster, a base, was found with the clearly incised date "November ye 22nd, 1754". Yet no completed examples that can reasonably be dated to the 1750s are known to me. On analysis this early specimen contains gypsum, lead, and potash and is not a phosphate – that means that it does not contain calcined bone – and rates were paid from October 1757. My dates under the section heading may not therefore be exact. We have dated blue-and-white examples for 1770, 1779, and 1782, and so on style and form we can

112

113

112 A superbly painted Isleworth mug with simple and characteristic ribbed handle. Wide, unglazed, foot-rim. This piece was formerly attributed to Derby, 14cm (5½in) high, *c.*1775–80, Godden collection.

113 A relief-moulded Isleworth sauceboat of a type made by several English factories. It is unusual as it is painted with flowers, rather than with a mock-Chinese landscape. It has a deep foot, 15.75cm (6¼in) long, *c.*1770–75, Godden collection.

judge that porcelains were produced at the small Isleworth factory within the period 1765–95. Judging from an insurance policy the manufactory was then enlarged in 1786. It seems to have concentrated on the production of blue-and-white useful wares and by at least the mid-1790s the production seems to have been restricted simply to press-moulded, slip-trailed pottery dishes.

The standard post-1770 porcelain mix from this factory is of the phosphatic-type, containing bone ash. It is consequently like that produced at Bow, Derby and Lowestoft, and so can be mistaken for these porcelains. Indeed, most of the porcelains that have now been attributed to Isleworth have come from other cabinets!

This reattribution has come about mainly through wasters initially found by Ray Howard and Norman Bayliss in the Thames mud near the site of this 18th-century pottery, and later finds further extended our knowledge. Other indications took the form of a small cache of Isleworth blue-decorated porcelains that were still preserved by a descendant of Richard Goulding. These family pieces, along with the wasters, show a selection of patterns that were used, as well as some of the characteristic shapes of the factory's wares. They also point to a generally poor translucency and a rather blued glaze that has a tendency to craze (often in a large-size network of glaze cracks). The glaze can pool and also creep away from the cobalt blue. These faults do not, however, occur on all pieces and some Isleworth porcelain is of a very high standard (see, for example, the splendid mug that is illustrated in picture 112. This example has hitherto been attributed to Derby).

Joseph Shore, much like the Bow and Lowestoft managements, favoured relief-moulded wares, with reserved panels for underglaze blue designs of floral or Oriental-style landscapes. The rather small sauceboat shown in picture 113 is of this type. In general such relief-moulded wares are usually from the 1760s or the early 1770s so they represent a relatively early period of Isleworth porcelain. Most of these examples are hand-painted in underglaze blue.

However, a good range of underglaze blue-printed designs were also employed. Several of these are in the style of contemporary Worcester or Caughley. One Oriental-style design in particular is helpful, Shore's copy of the "Fisherman" or "Pleasure Boat" pattern. The Isleworth versions have an extra seated figure (*see* picture 114), a fisherman holding out a fish. I had two teabowls and saucers of this design, both inscribed and dated "1782". This extra, third, figure does not appear on other classes of this pattern. It should be noted that these Isleworth versions are, as yet, rarely found and at this time very few examples of Isleworth porcelain have been identified.

A favourite floral blue-printed design comprises a carnation with supplementary small sprays and insects. This subject is found on a surprisingly large range of shapes (*see* pictures 115, left and 116, right) but again this motif is by no means confined to the Isleworth factory alone. Several other Caughley or Worcester-style blue-printed designs also occur and lend weight to the idea that Shore was competing for the same market that those factories were catering for. I show typical examples of this blue-printed design in picture

114 The reverse side of an Isleworth waste bowl, which is printed with a version of the Fisherman pattern. Note the characteristic extra, seated fisherman in underglaze blue, which does not occur on other makes of this pattern, diameter 12.75cm (5in), *c.*1775–80, Godden collection.

115 A group of Isleworth blue-printed porcelains. Left to right: a rare ink pot with typical prints, a fluted plate (originally from a tea service) printed with floral sprays, and a waste bowl from a tea service. Note the extra, seated fisherman (see picture 117). Diameter of plate 19cm (7½in), *c.*1775–80, Godden collection.

116

117

116 A rather deep Isleworth fluted plate (originally from a tea service). This plate is printed with typical floral prints, diameter 15.75cm (6¼in) and depth 3.25cm (1¼in), c.1775–80, Godden collection.

117 A French-style Isleworth tumbler cup and its deep "trembleuse"-type stand. These were made in at least two sizes. Typical French-style floral sprigs, diameter of stand 14cm (5½in) and depth 4.5cm (1¾in), c.1785, Mr and Mrs Roger Edmundson collection.

115. Standard Isleworth tewares were made in simple turned shapes, or fluted or ribbed forms.

A range of Continental-style, simple, hand-painted floral patterns were also being produced in the 18th century. On the Continent these designs are known as "La Brindille" and they are found on various French and Luxembourg wares. In England the Caughley factory was the main factory that was producing such French-style patterns and forms. However the Worcester factory also produced similar patterns for a time (during the 1770s or 1780s), and so did the Isleworth factory.

The Middlesex versions in this style were in the softer bone-ash body, not the rather more compact Caughley and Worcester soapstone body. A very rare Isleworth beaker with a deeply recessed Continental-style "trembleuse" saucer or stand is shown in picture 117. This recess keeps the cup in place.

At present our study or knowledge of the Isleworth porcelains is still very much in its infancy. I cannot, for example, illustrate here a single example decorated in overglaze enamel colours as all my specimens are painted or printed in underglaze blue. No pieces bear a true factory name or initial mark either, although a rather curly version of the Worcester crescent mark has been recorded. A Bow-like arrow mark painted in blue occurs on some wasters. It is also possible that a more normal version of the Worcester crescent mark was sometimes employed. Some unglazed wasters bear incised initials or numbers, as these were workmens' tally marks.

Our present knowledge about this factory can be found within: "Isleworth Pottery, Recognition at Last" by Ray Howard (*English Ceramic Circle Transactions*, Vol.16, Part 3 [1998]), "Isleworth Porcelain" by Anton Gabszewicz and Roderick Jellicoe (this is an exhibition catalogue published by R. Jellicoe, London, 1999), three short papers on Isleworth site finds published in the *E.C.C. Transactions*, Vol.17, Part 3 (2001), and *Godden's Guide to English Blue and White Porcelain* by G.A. Godden (Antique Collectors' Club, 2004).

At an English Ceramic Circle meeting held on 19 January 2002, two important papers were delivered. One was given by Professor Ian Freestone of the British Museum and it dealt with the composition of the factory's porcelain. The second, by Roger Massey, was concerned with the factory's accounts (of a late period) and with some insurance policies (see *Transactions of the English Ceramic Circle*, Vol 18, part 2, 2003). A mass of helpful wasters are retained at the Museum of London, or in its stores. Many of these are featured, with complete examples, in *Isleworth Pottery and Porcelain, Recent Discoveries*, an exhibition catalogue by R. Massey, J. Pearce, and R. Howard (Museum of London and English Ceramic Circle, 2003).

It should be noted that earthenwares that bear impressed initials such as "S & G", "S & Co.", "F.G." or "G" are likely to be 19th-century German products, often in an earlier and English style. The impressed mark "SHORE & CO.", while being English, is not necessarily to be associated with the Isleworth works.

Limehouse (London), c.1746–8

| See pictures 118–20

Excavations that were undertaken by specialists from the Museum of London in 1990 unearthed a number of factory wasters that had suffered from various manufacturing faults. These wasters seem to link to at least some underglaze blue-painted wares that have in the past been attributed to William Reid of Liverpool or to the Pomona Pottery at Newcastle-under-Lyme in Staffordshire, see p.113. The very short period of this factory's existence, and the many fire-damaged wasters found on the site, might suggest that the factory was a failure. We should, however, bear in mind the very early period, as Bow and Chelsea were perhaps the only other porcelain factories in the British Isles. The quality of the potting of the finished pieces can be superb, the shapes are mainly unique to Limehouse – as are the added underglaze blue designs. The body, while not showing much translucency, does not discolour or craze like the later Isleworth mix. This was probably the earliest English porcelain factory ever to include European figure and landscape underglaze blue designs in its repertoire. The decoration is predominantly in underglaze blue and is variable in tone, but usually a little dull, due to the slightly whitened glaze. Yet the pieces were fit for their purpose and can be charming (see pictures 118–20, for example). The moulded forms are noteworthy, these include some recessed, rather than raised, patterns. These seem unique to Limehouse.

Evidence that there was a porcelain manufactory near Dick (or Duke) Shore on the Thames at Limehouse in London has been known for many years and some contemporary notices even mention the types of wares made at this pottery. A notice published in September 1746 sought "pot-painters that are good hands...for the Pot Works at Limehouse". Various advertisements dating back to at least 1 January 1747 refer to "a large assortment" of the "new invented blue and white Limehouse Ware". Another advertisement in the *Daily Advertiser* of 4 April 1747 is more detailed, drawing to the public's attention that, "The new-invented blue-and-white Limehouse ware, which as to duration etc is no ways inferior to China, consisting of great variety of Sauce Boats, Tea Pots and other useful and ornamental vessels, is to be had at most of the Dealers...in Town...at the Factory near Duke Shore, at Limehouse". However, the same London newspaper of 3 June 1748 carried a note calling on the creditors of the manufactory to meet "upon affairs of importance". Such a notice normally only had one meaning – financial difficulties.

Contemporary references mention two names in connection with the Limehouse Works – William Tams, and Joseph Wilson. Records relate to the firm of Wilson & Co. occupying the Limehouse premises. Seemingly Joseph Wilson soon moved to Staffordshire, to the pottery we now term the Pomona Works at Newcastle-under-Lyme. Dr Richard Pococke, writing on 14 July 1750, noted when visiting this "market town and Capital of the Pottery villages" that "Newcastle-under-Lyme is a small well built town...they have a handsome church and a market house...: there are some few Potters here, and one I visited whom I saw at Limehouse who

118 Two rare Limehouse specimens, painted in underglaze blue with European figures in landscapes. These are perhaps the earliest essays in non-Oriental designs on English blue and white. Vase or tea canister 10.75cm (4¼in) high, c.1745–8, Godden collection.

119

seemed to promise to make the best China ware but disagreed with his employers". This could refer to William Tams rather than Joseph Wilson, but "Joseph, son of Mr Wilson, Potter" was baptised at St. Giles Church, Newcastle, in November 1751, which shows that the Wilson family had moved to Staffordshire. The factory wasters found some years ago on the Pomona site in Newcastle-under-Lyme, Staffordshire, bear a certain likeness to the Limehouse wasters, but the Newcastle venture seems to have been more short-lived than that at Limehouse, as far as the production of porcelain is concerned.

Useful reading on this factory includes Dr B. Watney's "Limehouse in the Limelight", *Antique Collecting*, September 1983; Simon Spero, "Pomona Related Ware", *Collectors Guide*, May 1989; and Dr Watney's interim report, "Recent Excavations on London Porcelain Sites: Vauxhall and Limehouse", *Transactions of the English Ceramic Circle*, Vol.14, Part 1, 1990.

The well-illustrated standard on the excavations at Limehouse and the related wares is *Limehouse Ware Revealed*, a multi-author work that was published by the English Ceramic Circle in 1993. This is important because the possible connection between Limehouse and the Pomona wasters are discussed, by Dr Bernard Watney, in Chapter 6. The 2000 Museum of London publication *The Limehouse Porcelain Manufactory* is another multi-author report on the site excavations. Wasters that have been found on the factory site are kept

120

119 Three rare Limehouse specimens. The cream or butter boat is recess (not relief) moulded – a technique that was possibly unique to this early factory. Small teapot 12cm (4¾in) high, *c.*1745–8, Godden collection.

120 The exterior and interior of a Limehouse sauceboat, which is sat on typically large-sized lion's head, paws, and feet, 19cm (7½in) long, *c.*1745–8, Godden collection, previously in Dr B. Watney's collection.

at the Museum of London. The reader is also referred to my own 2004 specialist book on English blue-and-white porcelain.

As the small factory had such a short duration the surviving products are rare and highly desirable so are likely to be very costly (*see* p.247).

Liverpool *c.*1754–1800+

| *See* pictures 121–6

Our knowledge of the Liverpool porcelains has both increased and decreased over the years as various authorities have researched these interesting and yet puzzling different makes of porcelain. Our knowledge can be said to have decreased because in the 1988–90 period finds on two sites in London, at Limehouse and Vauxhall, have necessitated the reattribution of two classes of "Liverpool" porcelain to London. Briefly, the delightful wares formerly attributed to William Ball of Liverpool are now believed to have been produced at Vauxhall in London and the wares formerly attributed to William Reid of Liverpool or to the Pomona Works at Newcastle-under-Lyme have now been re-attributed to the Limehouse factory. It is possible that in future years other amendments may have to be made to our traditional understanding of Liverpool porcelains, for the situation is complicated in the extreme. There were, in the important city and port of Liverpool, many potters producing a variety of earthenwares* and stonewares for the home trade as well as for export to North America and other markets. Several of these, at one time or another, turned their attention to the manufacture of porcelains.

The Liverpool porcelains are of variable quality. Some fully equal Worcester and specimens may well be misplaced in Worcester collections, but other examples are very inferior copies of contemporary Worcester, Caughley, or Chinese wares. It is perhaps too easy to group together all Liverpool porcelains – Bow and Chelsea are not, for example, grouped under a London heading, and there is the danger of placing any problem example under the simple designation "Liverpool".

The fact that few authorities readily understand the different types of Liverpool porcelain, coupled with the low regard given to the later pieces by many collectors, means that interesting examples can still be found at reasonable cost. Be warned, however, the study is not easy; no name marks occur. So-called key pieces are not

as certain as we would wish, although our knowledge has greatly increased in recent years with the discovery of factory wasters. Still our knowledge of Liverpool porcelains is far from complete. Take, for example, the really charming small teapot shown in picture 121. Dr Bernard Watney in his last book *Liverpool Porcelain of the Eighteenth-Century* (Richard Dennis, 1997) illustrated this or a similar pot. After a lifetime's study he could only state that these rare hexagonal steatitic (soapstone bodied) teapots were "perhaps made for Chaffers by Podmore as they have close links with Lund's Bristol and early Worcester". They also are very similar to some Limehouse examples. Current thought is that this example is Lund's-Bristol. What a mixture, but what a delightful result!**

My following brief notes on the main Liverpool makes of porcelain are arranged in chronological order of their establishment.

Richard Chaffers & Co., *c.*1754–65

This pottery was established on Shaw's Brow, and a soapstone-type soft-paste porcelain was being made by about 1756. In general, these Chaffer's porcelains are, along with William Reid's, the most accomplished of all the Liverpool makes, closely rivalling Worcester. Much blue and white was made for the middle-class markets and, with the related enamelled designs, they display the popular Oriental influence.

Richard Chaffers died in 1765 and his pottery was continued by Philip Christian & Co.

William Reid & Co., *c.*1755–61

The porcelains formerly attributed to William Reid of Liverpool were in recent years tentatively reattributed to the Pomona Works at Newcastle-under-Lyme in Staffordshire. However, finds of factory wasters on the site of the Limehouse factory in London match at least some of the wares formerly thought to have been made by William Reid while he was at Liverpool. Now, with the publications of two specialist books on the

121 An interesting and attractive, perhaps early, Liverpool small teapot that has visual links with Limehouse or Lund's-Bristol. This is a treasure wherever it was made. 9.5cm (3¾in) high, *c.*1755–60, private collection.

122 A well-potted, relief-moulded William Reid of Liverpool sauceboat, with underglaze blue panels. Painter's mark 7 (or 4) in blue, 20cm (8in) long, *c.*1755–60, Godden collection, ex Dr B. Watney.

---

* Gore's Liverpool Directory of 1766 lists only two "china makers" – William Ball and Richard Chaffers & Co., but twelve "Potters", one mug maker plus Sadler & Green's "Printed ware manufactory".
** This piece was sold by Bonhams for over £20,000 ($30,000), in November 2003. I originally purchased it as a Liverpool piece, and paid approximately a tenth of that sum.

121

122

excavations at Limehouse, we are reasonably certain that the porcelains formerly attributed to William Reid at Liverpool were made in the late 1740s at Limehouse in London. Details of this factory and the works of reference are given on page 264.

In my previous (1992) edition I wrote: "One should remember that if William Reid did make porcelain at Liverpool, major rethinking will be required to fill the vacuum left after his believed wares have been reattributed to Limehouse."

We now (from c.2000) have a rich accumulation of shards or factory wasters that are believed to relate to William Reid. These have indeed resulted in a re-think, indeed a breathtaking reshuffle among the porcelains attributed to several Liverpool manufacturers. It is almost as if all the best Liverpool pieces have been allocated to William Reid as a result. Research is still in its early stages and we seek to find finished examples to match the newly discovered broken fragments and fire-damaged wasters.

Much still remains to be done – perhaps further excavations will be possible but the site is in the middle of a busy city. At present, the best guide to the history of the factory and the wasters is Maurice Hillis and Roderick Jellicoe's joint well-illustrated exhibition catalogue *The Liverpool Porcelain of William Reid*. Roderick, the London dealer, held an exhibition of the excavated material and matching porcelains at his London premises (3a Campden Street, off Kensington Church Street, London W8 7EP) in the spring of 2000. It was a real eye-opener and revealed superb shapes and potting, quality enamelling and interesting blue and white – all hand-painted. Dr Maurice Hillis's excellent E.C.C. paper "The Liverpool China Manufactory of Wm. Reid & Co. A Survey of the Wares", is also worth referring to – it was published in the *Transactions of the English Ceramic Circle*, Vol.18, Part 1, 2002.

Samuel Gilbody, c.1758–61

By 1758 this Liverpool potter was advertising "China Ware of all sorts, equal for service and beauty to any made in England". He was perhaps the first manufacturer from England to claim his products were beautiful as well as serviceable and certainly they have charm and quality of workmanship and painting. Gilbody is one of the few Liverpool makers to have produced figures, but these are now extremely rare – or perhaps mainly unrecognized.

The identification of Samuel Gilbody's productions owes much to the first site finds of Alan Smith published in the *Transactions of the English Ceramic Circle*, Vol.7, Part 2, (1969). Also full of useful information is M. Hillis's excellent survey *The Liverpool Porcelains*

123

124

123 An amusingly painted Samuel Gilbody, Liverpool porcelain bowl, diameter 15.75cm (6¼in), *c.*1760, which was formerly in the Godden collection.

124 A Pennington-Liverpool high "Chelsea ewer". This piece is painted in underglaze blue and incorporates a standard Oriental-island pattern. It is overpainted in red and gold and has a glazed-over, rather speckled base, 9cm (3½in) high, *c.*1780–85, Godden collection.

(Northern Ceramic Society, 1985) and M. Hillis's and R. Jellicoe's, "Further Finds of Gilbody Porcelain", *Journal of the Northern Ceramic Society*, Vol.8, 1991, featured other wasters. However, some doubt has now been placed on the source of these wasters and on their attribution to Gilbody. Certainly since the spring of 2000 some, but not all, porcelains formerly classed as Gilbody have been reclassified as William Reid. A little time may elapse before the picture becomes clear. At the moment some former Gilbody specimens are illustrated in Roderick Jellicoe's exhibition catalogue, cited above.

I trust the attractive ex-Godden waste bowl shown in picture 123 is still Gilbody, but much fine Gilbody has recently been transferred to the William Reid shelves!

William Ball, c.1761–3

The attractive porcelains formerly attributed to William Ball have, since 1988, been reattributed to the Vauxhall factory in London. It is now believed that William Ball did not own a factory and that he was not a porcelain manufacturer in his own right, only a manager.

The Penningtons, c.1763–1805

Various Penningtons played an extremely large part in the history of porcelain manufacture in Liverpool over some 40 years and much research will be required to differentiate between the different types. The list given below provides the basic details.

James Pennington & Co., Brownlow Hill – c.1763–8
James Pennington & Co., Park Lane – c.1768–73
John Pennington, Copperas Hill – c.1769–79
John Pennington, Folly Lane – c.1779–86
Jane Pennington, Folly Lane – c.1786–94
Seth Pennington & John Part, Shaw's Brow – c.1778–99
Pennington & Edmundson, Shaw's Brow – c.1799–1803
Pennington & Edwards, Shaw's Brow – c.1803–5

Further information is given within Dr Bernard Watney's standard work *English Blue and White Porcelain of the 18th Century* (Faber, revised edition, 1973). The reader is also referred to John J. Murray's "The Potting Penningtons of Liverpool", *Journal of the Northern Ceramic Society*, Vol.4, 1980–81, and to Maurice Hillis's paper, *Journal of the Northern Ceramic Society*, Vol.6, 1987 and his *The Liverpool Porcelains* (1985). Dr Bernard Watney made a last, noble, effort to sort these later Liverpool porcelains in his generously illustrated 1997 book *Liverpool Porcelain of the Eighteenth-Century* (Richard Dennis, 1997). Alas, the task will still occupy future generations of collectors.

In general the Pennington porcelains, especially the pieces made after about 1785, tend to be of average or poor quality. The forms relate mainly to tablewares, usually parts of tea services. The cobalt blue tends to be dark and unattractive, and the glaze can speckle quite badly. Nevertheless they interest many researchers, and now and again there is a jewel among the dross. Picture 124 represents an average Pennington example. Further examples are featured in my *Godden's Guide to English Blue and White Porcelain*.

125

126

125 One of a pair of relief-moulded small-size Liverpool mugs, painted in underglaze blue. Such mugs were made in various sizes, as were similar jugs. Probably Philip Christian, 9.5cm (3¾in) high, c.1770, Godden collection.

126 A large Liverpool coffee pot and cover – note the typically elaborately moulded spout and the intricate handle. The floral spray, palette, and border are typical of Philip Christian, 25cm (10in) high, c.1770–75, Godden of Worthing.

Philip Christian & Co., c.1765–78

Christian took over Chaffer's factory on the latter's death in 1765 and the production of a soapstone-type body continued. The underglaze blue of this body tends to be slightly grey and rather pale, but is finely painted. The overglaze colours are often rather dull in tone but good flower painting occurs. Pictures 125–6 show typical good-quality Christian examples and a fair quantity of Christian pieces should still be available. Helpful information and illustrations are given in Dr Watney's *English Blue and White Porcelain of the 18th Century* and Maurice Hillis's, "Late Christian and Early Pennington", *Journal of the Northern Ceramic Society*, Vol.5, 1984. Dr Watney's well-illustrated 1997 book *Liverpool Porcelain of the Eighteenth-Century* (Richard Dennis) should also be helpful, but do bear in mind that the history of Liverpool porcelains is in a state of flux!

Other Liverpool porcelains

I will discuss the Liverpool porcelains made by Thomas Wolfe, John Lucock, and Miles Mason at the Islington Pottery in Chapter 7, as they are of the hybrid hard-paste type. The Liverpool porcelains that were made at the Herculaneum Pottery 1796–1840 are discussed in Chapter 9.

Our understanding of Liverpool porcelains is based on very slender clues and subsequent research may well result in the further reclassification of some classes. The discovery of dated or otherwise documentary specimens is awaited with interest. Our confusion is confounded by the fact that the types of body appear to have changed at the various factories from time to time – indeed the Liverpool potteries produced every known type of English ceramics. None of the 18th-century examples have helpful marks, although some painters' numbers or other tally type devices can occur on the blue-painted pieces. Some porcelains bearing signed "Liverpool" printed designs were not necessarily made in that city, although the printed decoration may have been added there – probably by the specialist printers Sadler & Green.

Longton Hall, c.1750–60

| *See* pictures 28 and 127

For very many years we have believed that the first porcelains produced within the Staffordshire Potteries area were those produced at the Longton Hall factory, which was established in 1750 or perhaps in 1749. However it seems now that this honour might be presented to the Newcastle-under-Lyme works of the approximate period 1745–55 (*see* p.113). Even if this is the case, the Longton Hall porcelains are still of great interest to collectors and well worth study. Once again we owe much of our present-day appreciation of the history of the Longton Hall factory to the researches of the late Dr Bernard Watney as published in the books listed at the end of this section.

The name Longton Hall stems from the situation of the pottery at the building known as Longton Hall, east of the road between Stone and Newcastle-under-Lyme. We used to associate only one man with this factory – William Littler – but the works now seem to have been established in 1749 or in 1750 by William Jenkinson, who claimed to have obtained, (unfortunately we know not where from), "the art, secret and mystery of making a certain porcelain ware in imitation of china". In October 1751 William Nicklin and William Littler were taken into partnership. Nicklin, a lawyer by profession, may have supplied the very necessary funds, for the trading style Nicklin & Co. was apparently employed in 1751. William Littler almost certainly supplied the expertise, being an experienced "earth potter" making saltglazed wares. The early Longton wares would have included the white figures and animal models that we now term the "snowman"-class on account of the smothering mass of white glaze that clogs the modelling.

In 1753 Jenkinson retired and Nathaniel Firmin and his son Samuel joined the partnership. They, with Robert Charlesworth, were a source of new working capital in 1755 but this came to an end in 1760. In July 1760 the stock of the London warehouse in St Paul's Church Yard was sold and in September 1760 a great sale of Longton Hall porcelain was held in Salisbury. This was surprisingly advertised as including "upwards of ninety thousand pieces". These sales mark the end of the Longton adventure but Littler later went to West Pans (*see* p.119) before returning to Staffordshire.

The Longton Hall porcelain is of the glassy soft-paste type, showing on analysis a high percentage of lead. The glaze on occasions seems to have been clouded with tin oxide or a similar whitening agent and a scum line can often be seen at the glaze edge. In general the pieces are thickly potted and often rather crudely finished, especially the insides. Chelsea-type "moons" can also appear in Longton porcelains. Separators in a similar form to matchsticks were used and their shadow can often be seen on the foot. Natural forms were popular: leaf-shaped sauceboats, fruit-shaped boxes, leaf-dishes, etc. Most pieces were enamelled over the glaze (*see* picture 127) but blue-and-white useful wares (*see* picture 28) were also made and some specimens bore a rich blue ground – one that was very prone to

127 A rare Longton Hall oval dish. The leaf-moulded edge is characteristic but matching plates are more common. The centres are usually painted with floral sprays, 33cm (13in) long, *c.*1755, Godden of Worthing.

run in the glaze. Some Littler porcelains, mainly mugs, were embellished with the overglaze-printed designs added at Liverpool.

Longton Hall porcelain is unmarked. Workman's marks such as crosses, letters, or chemical signs do occur but similar marks are found on many types of porcelain. It should be noted that the two crossed "L's" with dots below – a device in the past cited as a Longton Hall mark – was not found on any Staffordshire-site wasters. This mark was probably used by Littler at West Pans in Scotland at a later period, *see* p.120.

Within approximately a ten-year period, in the 1750s, the Longton Hall works managed to produce a relatively large range of wares. A very good selection is shown in Dr Watney's standard work *Longton Hall Porcelain* (Faber, 1957); his contribution on Longton Hall to *English Porcelain 1745–1850*, edited by R. J. Charleston (Benn, London, 1965) is also important, as is his *English Blue and White Porcelain of the 18th Century*. Some typical pieces are shown in my *An Illustrated Encyclopaedia of British Pottery and Porcelain and*

British Porcelain, an Illustrated Guide. A paper on William Littler's early career, by Miranda F. Goodby, is contained in *E.C.C. Transactions*, Vol.17, Part 3 (2001).

Lowestoft, *c.*1757–99[*]

| *See* pictures 6, 11, 21, and 128–34

The charming and unpretentious Lowestoft porcelains were my first love. I still remember the thrill of buying a complete tea service from a leading West End dealer, for what I thought at the time was a king's ransom price of £25! That was in the mid-1940s when I was 14 or 15 and only later did I realize how generous that dealer – the late David Manheim – had been to the young upstart of a collector that I was then. The Lowestoft porcelains have always given me the greatest pleasure

128

129

128 A pair of relief-moulded Lowestoft large-size tea canisters
(covers missing). Painted in underglaze blue and inscribed at
the ends "H/Tea" and "G/Tea" and "Hyson Tea" and "Green Tea".
Flat glazed bases with painter's number "5", 12cm (4¾in) high,
c.1765, Godden collection.

129 A typical Lowestoft mug, painted in underglaze blue in a
characteristic naïve style. Note the handle form. Painter's number
"5" in blue on the inside edge of the foot, 14.5cm (5¾in) high
(other sizes were made), c.1770, Godden collection.

and even excitement, especially when I managed to find
a rare specimen lurking in some unexpected place.

I should explain that many people still refer to a
class of hard-paste Chinese export porcelain as being
"Lowestoft". Most of us now know better but you may
find this term sometimes used to describe 18th-century
Chinese wares, made for the European market. The
contradictory term "Chinese-Lowestoft" may also be
employed. Remember the real Lowestoft porcelain is
soft-paste. Like Bow or Isleworth bodies it contains a
relatively high percentage of bone ash, 40–45 per cent.

The modest factory was situated in Bell Lane at the
resort and fishing town of Lowestoft, the most easterly
part of the British coastline. Lowestoft and its nearby
rival Yarmouth were very important places for coastal
shipping and also for trade to Holland. However, the
ambitions of the proprietors of this porcelain factory
seem to have been very simple and limited to producing
a range of useful wares for the locality rather than to try
to compete with the leading manufacturers of the day.
This policy gave rise to the production of a number of
special pieces inscribed with names, places, and dates,
which were made to commemorate family occasions.
This side of the production is exemplified in the unique
little circular "birth tablets" made to mark the birth of
local children. These modest aims paid dividends, for the
factory existed for over 40 years, outliving Chelsea and
other great names in the history of British ceramics.

There are many rather unlikely stories surrounding the establishment of the Lowestoft factory. It is said that an unsuccessful attempt to make porcelain from local clay was made in 1756. A successful attempt seems to have been made in 1757 under the partnership of Philip Walker (a local potter) and Robert Browne (factory manager). Browne was succeeded by his son of the same name, Obed Aldred, and John Richman in 1771. Walker and Robert Browne were the key figures in the concern. They were curiously described within a Directory of 1795 as "China manufacturers and Herring curers" and in many ways their porcelains have an attractive, almost amateur appearance.

The Lowestoft factory was unusual in that for some years from 1757 only blue-and-white designs were issued, no dated overglaze coloured pieces being known before 1774, and this fact underlines the modest aims of the proprietors: to produce useful tablewares for the local middle-class market. An advertisement in the Norwich Mercury of 2 February 1760 gives notice that Walker & Co. (the factory's trading style at that time):

Will be offering for a sale a great variety of neat blue and white china or porcelain at the manufactory in town.

'Tis humbly hoped that most of the shopkeepers in the County [Suffolk] and the County of Norfolk, will give encouragement to this laudable undertaking by reserving their spring orders for their humble servants.

We can see here that the blue-and-white wares were sold direct from the factory. The strange aspect of this advertisement is that it would appear to herald the first endeavour of the management to market their wares.

These blue-and-white patterns (*see* pictures 128–30) remained the staple of the factory until its closure, and we have contemporary reports that women were employed in this branch of the trade. The standard blue-and-white designs in the main comprise attractive, almost child-like Chinese-style landscape designs often reserved in panels amid relief-moulded borders and floral motifs. Some of these moulded designs incorporate the initials "IH" of Hughes (the modeller) with a date 1761 or 1764. A fine and rare pair of Hughes-type moulded tea canisters is shown in picture 128.

Apart from the Oriental-type designs many formal floral patterns are to be found and, very rarely, pieces painted with local views. Turning from the unique pieces with their hand-painted design, there is also a repetitive class of ware bearing blue-printed designs. Such pieces date mainly from the 1770s and, with a few notable exceptions, these printed designs are copies of popular Worcester or Caughley prints. The engraver had a strange hesitant touch and often the shaded or darker areas are painted in by hand. The Worcester crescent mark was often copied on such printed pieces.

Midway between blue and white and the enamelled pieces there is a class of Oriental-inspired patterns incorporating both modes of decoration. These are referred to as the Redgrave patterns as this family, or rather several families of this name, are believed to have been responsible for these simple but attractive designs in underglaze blue with overglaze red, green, and thin gilding (*see* picture 131).

Studying a list of dated examples* – which provides a yearly sequence of nearly 200 pieces from 1761 to 1799 excepting only 1785 – the first dated *enamelled* example is as late as 1774. From this date onwards we have a good selection of enamelled wares. Especially notable are some pieces boldly painted with tulips, but many figure subjects occur in both European and Oriental-style (*see* picture 132) patterns, and of course a wide range of simple floral designs. In the 1790s a now scarce class of mugs, inkwells, and the like were produced and inscribed with "A trifle from Lowestoft" (*see* picture 133) or with the names of nearby villages Bungay, Holt, Wangford, etc, which is where they'd have been sold.

130 A Lowestoft jug, of a very typical shape but painted in a perhaps unique style, with three marine subject panels, approx. 23cm (9in) high, *c*.1775–80, stolen from the Godden collection.

---

* Such as "Inscribed and Dated Lowestoft Porcelain" by A.J.B. Kiddell, in the *Transactions of the English Porcelain Circle*, No.3, 1931.

131

132

131 A very rare shape of Lowestoft cylindrical teapot. The cover of this teapot has Continental-style locking lugs. It is painted in underglaze blue and overglaze enamel colours in the Regrave style. This pattern seems to have been confined to Chinese and Lowestoft examples, 12.75cm (5in) high, c.1785–90, Godden collection.

132 A rare large-size Lowestoft tea- (or punch) pot. This is painted very much in the style of the popular Chinese export-market porcelains of the second half of the 18th century. There is also gilding to the spout and handle, 22cm (8¾in) high and 29.75cm (11¾in) long, c.1780, formerly in the Godden collection.

Also of great rarity are the Lowestoft figure models: a pair of *putti* and a pair of standing musicians (*see* picture 135), small cats, a swan, a sheep, a ram, and perhaps one or more dog models. Rare and desirable as these models are, I prefer the simple pieces made to use on the table. Although small, the Lowestoft factory produced a surprisingly assorted selection of articles, the many sauceboat and smaller creamboat forms being particularly noteworthy.

The date of closure is open to some doubt. Most books give this as 1802 or 1803 but I believe that it closed down in 1799, making it a purely 18th-century concern. I return to this point on page 111.

No true Lowestoft factory mark exists. The early blue-and-white porcelains, which were made before about 1774, often bear a painter's number: this in itself is not helpful as several factories used such painter's identification numbers, but at Lowestoft they were usually placed on the *inside* of the foot-ring.

The later blue-and-white pieces do not bear a painter's number, nor do the enamelled pieces (although one solitary example is known to me). Some copies of Worcester blue and white bear a crescent mark and some Continental-inspired designs bear a copy of the Meissen crossed-swords mark. Some Continental hard-paste copies or fakes of inscribed Lowestoft porcelain occur but most of these are unlikely to deceive you once you are familiar with the true Lowestoft soft-paste and the rather naïve style of painting found on the originals. Fortunately the more ordinary Lowestoft wares – their most charming and typical products – have not been copied, although recent high prices may change this!

Good collections of Lowestoft porcelains can be seen at: the Castle Museum, Norwich; at Christchurch Mansion, Ipswich; at the new Lowestoft Museum at Nicholas Everitt Park, Lowestoft; the Fitzwilliam Museum, Cambridge; and at the Victoria and Albert Museum in London.

If you are unable to see these porcelains in the flesh, several well-illustrated reference books should prove helpful. The earliest of these, W. Spelman's *Lowestoft China* (Jarrold & Sons, London, 1905) includes illustrations of several moulds and factory wasters but the other illustrations serve mainly to show how our knowledge of true Lowestoft porcelains has changed over the years. More up-to-date works include: *English Blue and White Porcelain of the 18th Century* by Dr B. Watney (Faber, revised edition 1973); *Lowestoft Porcelain in Norwich Castle Museum, Vol.1: Blue & White* by S. Smith (Norfolk Museum Service, 1975); *Early Lowestoft* by C. Spencer (Ainsworth & Nelson, 1981); *Lowestoft Porcelains* by G. Godden (Antique Collectors' Club, 1985); *Lowestoft Porcelain in Norwich Castle Museum, Vol.2: Polychrome* by S. Smith (Norwich Museum Service, 1985), *Variety in Lowestoft Porcelain*, by Margaret Corson (Lilac Publishers, Cambridge, 1992) and *Lowestoft Porcelain Illustrated* by R. Oddy (Thrift Cottage Antiques, 2003). My own book *Godden's Guide to English Blue and White Porcelain* reflects my love of these porcelains.

In addition various *Transactions of the English Ceramic Circle* contain learned papers on various aspects of Lowestoft porcelains. The latest contains an interesting paper by John Howell on the quite rare later Lowestoft porcelains of the 1790s. This is entitled "Lowestoft Porcelain: The Final Decade", *E.C.C. Transactions*, Vol.17, Part 3, 2001. This noted authority

133

134

on and collector of Lowestoft porcelains questioned my belief that the factory closed in 1799, suggesting 1801 was more likely. In the absence of a sale or closing-down notice, it is perhaps a matter of opinion. Yet while we have an almost unbroken array of dated examples from 1761 to 1799* (except for 1785) none are known for 1800 or 1801. Neither have late shapes such as oval teapots been noted.

In my book *Lowestoft Porcelain* (published by the Antique Collectors' Club in 1985) I made the point that some known Lowestoft work people were taken on by the Chamberlains factory in September 1799. Mr Howell states that these were few and may not indicate the closure of the factory at that period. But we only

133 Two rare Lowestoft "Trifle" mugs. Enamelled in typical 1790s style and palette. One mug "A Trifle from Bungay" has been turned to show the characteristic late Lowestoft handle shape, 12cm (4¾in) high, *c*.1790–95, formerly in the Godden collection.

134 Two late Lowestoft coffee cups shown with a small "A Trifle from Lowestoft" mug. All with characteristic late ear-like handle, 6.25cm (2½in) high, *c*.1790s, Godden collection.

know a few names and I have only been able to check the wage records of one factory. Other Lowestoft work people may well have sought employment at the main Worcester factory or in Staffordshire. Therefore I feel that there are more pointers for a closure in 1799, than for any other later date.

* A birth tablet, inscribed "John Ward. Born Febry 15th 1799" and probably post-dating that event.

In 2000 a local potter commenced work emulating old shapes and patterns. Such modern essays are clearly marked "Lowestoft Porcelain". However, 19th-century hard-paste fakes also occur.

Neale, *c*.1778–92

| *See pictures 25, 35, and 136*

James Neale, a leading London pottery and porcelain dealer, in effect took over Humphrey Palmer's Church Works at Hanley, in 1778. Superb Wedgwood-type ceramics were made under the Neale name, but Robert Wilson was the manager (and partner from *c*.1783) while James Neale was concerned with the London retail premises. At an unknown date in the mid- or late 1780s Neale and Wilson seem to have added porcelain to their output. This is usually extremely finely potted and neatly decorated (*see* pictures 25, 35, and 136). It often displays a Derby-like charm and some shapes seem to follow closely forms of the 1785–95 Derby period.

All Neale porcelain is rare. Impressed marks "Neale & Co." and "Neale & Wilson" are recorded – this double-name mark should indicate a period prior to the dissolution of their partnership in April 1792. Typical but rare specimens are featured in Chapter 4 of my book *Staffordshire Porcelain* (Granada, 1983). The standard book on all Neale products is Diana Edwards's *Neale Pottery and Porcelain, Its Predecessors and Successors 1763–1820* (Barrie & Jenkins, 1987).

New Hall, *c*.1781–1835

The New Hall works in the Staffordshire Potteries must certainly rank as a leading 18th-century concern, although it seemingly produced only useful wares. As the body before about 1815 is of the hybrid hard-paste type the New Hall wares are discussed in the next chapter.

Newcastle-under-Lyme, *c*.1746–54

There is not a single finished piece that was definitely made at this early Staffordshire factory – only one or two pieces that may have been made there. Research is still in its infancy. In fact before 1973 there were no published references to this manufactory, or rather to its porcelain products, at all. In 1969 Paul Bemrose, the then Curator of the Newcastle-under-Lyme Museum,

136 A neatly potted Neale porcelain coffee cup, with simple loop handle – from a tea service painted with similar views in monochrome by, or in the style of, Fidelle Duvivier, 6.25cm (2½in) high, *c*.1785, formerly in the Godden collection.

with a team of helpers, started excavations on the site of The Pomona Inn. The inn is on the site of an early pottery, one in which we believe a type of porcelain was made – the first ever produced in Staffordshire. The excavations were difficult and very limited but a mass of these wasters were painted in underglaze blue. The wasters appeared to have been overfired and the kiln opened too quickly before the contents had cooled as the body fractured. All were perhaps the result of just one faulty firing. As yet we are unable to tell if so high a proportion of wares were so spoilt that the production of porcelain ceased after a short period or indeed if it ever reached a marketable quality.

The pottery, which we can conveniently now call the "Pomona Pottery", was established by Samuel Bell Jr. He is believed to have produced only earthenwares (see A.T. Morley Hewitt, "Bell's Pottery, Newcastle under Lyme", *Transactions of the English Ceramic Circle*, Vol.4, Part 1, 1957) . Bell died in 1744 and the property was placed on the market. Luckily a 1746 London newspaper advertisement is preserved in the Staffordshire Record Office and this includes some interesting points:

To be Lett at Lady Day next at Newcastle-under-Lyme Staffordshire:

A very commodious house (late in the occupation of Mr Bell, and now in the possession of Mr Steers) with three parlours, a hall, and two kitchens, on the ground floor, chambers and garrets answerable, lately built and fash'd, a large garden, well planted with all

135 A pair of very rare Lowestoft figures of musicians, missing the instruments. Note the typical bases, floral bocages, and decoration at the rear, 17cm (6¾in) and 17.75cm (7in) high, *c*.1780–90, stolen from the Godden collection.

sorts of useful fruits, sundry warehouses, workshops, laths, throwing wheels and other utensils useful in making fine earthenware or china; three pot-ovens, one lately built on purpose to burn china; good stabling and yards; all entire in itself.

For further particulars enquire of Mr Crowther at St Katherine's near the Tower; to Mr Bell, in Aldermary Church-Yard, Bow-Lane, London, or of Mr Brittain*, at Newcastle aforesaid, where the premises may be seen.

N.B. It's cheap country for coals and provisions.

We can here see that during 1746 Mr Steers was in the occupation of Samuel Bell's pottery, which boasted three ovens or kilns, one of which had been "lately built on purpose to burn china". We might also observe the mention of Mr Crowther and Mr Bell in London who were possessed of "further particulars" and both may well have had an interest in the property, the "Mr Bell" being perhaps related to the late proprietor.

Among the spoilt factory wasters there was the base of a small bowl, much bubbled and fire-damaged but with an indistinct date, which has been read (perhaps incorrectly) as 25 July 1746. If this reading is indeed correct, it represents the earliest-known dated example of English underglaze blue-decorated porcelain. The maker was possibly William Steers, a merchant from Hoxton in Middlesex who had, some four years earlier, filed a petition for a patent claiming the invention of a new method of making a transparent body in imitation of porcelain. Steers seems to have left Hoxton by March 1745, and by early 1746 he was more than likely working Bell's former potworks on the Pomona site. He had, however, left there by June 1748, which is when he recommenced paying rates at Hoxton.

The Newcastle Pomona Pottery would seem to have been purchased in about 1747 by Joseph Wilson. As we already know, Wilson's name is also associated with the Limehouse factory in London (*see* p.100), the important link being shown in the letter that was written by Dr Richard Pococke on 14 July 1750, after his visit to Newcastle-under-Lyme (and which is also quoted on p.100).

Dr Pococke does not seem to be saying that the ex-Limehouse potter was making chinaware at Newcastle, rather that while at Limehouse he seemed destined to make the best chinaware the Doctor had ever seen. This link between the two potteries is of great interest to us. The potter concerned would appear to be Joseph Wilson and both he and Joseph Wilson & Company

paid taxes at Limehouse in 1748. Apart from Dr Pococke's unnamed mention we of course know that a Joseph Wilson was at Newcastle-under-Lyme in November 1751 due to the baptism entry occurring in the church register (*see* p.101). Joseph Wilson is also mentioned in an abstract of a property agreement that relates to the sale of the pottery in 1754.

Dr Pococke, in his letter, continued to describe the types of wares made at that time at Newcastle. In it he does not mention porcelain or china, although he does mention some "which when they are quite plain and well done look like china teapots". The site wasters in many cases were of earthenware bodies and I should point out that even the porcelain pieces were not readily identifiable as of this body, showing little translucency and with a rather creamy tint, but then they were spoilt, overfired fragments not necessarily representative of any correctly fired articles offered for sale. Here lies the trouble; we have still to find some finished examples from this particular manufactory. Some earthenware pieces seem to closely match shapes in the porcelains that we have formerly attributed to William Reid of Liverpool and which are now being attributed to Limehouse. These include a moulded cup that has prunus decoration on it, as well as some leaf-shaped dishes.

These notes have been based on a paper read to the English Ceramic Circle by Paul Bemrose in November 1971 and published in the Circle's *Transactions*, Vol.9, Part 1, 1973. This paper should be read by all keen collectors and ceramic students. They should carefully study the illustration of the wasters and keep a good look-out for pieces that match these fragments.

An account of this factory and the site wasters is contained in the 1973 edition of Dr Watney's *English Blue and White Porcelain of the 18th Century*. In a rather controversial manner I illustrated as Newcastle a series of porcelains that were formerly thought to be of Reid's Liverpool make, in my *Encyclopaedia of British Porcelain Manufacturers* (Barrie & Jenkins, 1988), p.601–4. However, finds made on the Limehouse site in 1990 suggest strongly that some of these Pomona-type wares were in fact made by Wilson & Co. at Limehouse. Wilson seemingly moved from London to Staffordshire where he continued to make (or tried to make) similar wares. This aspect of study was discussed by the late Dr Watney in Chapter 6 of the multi-author book *Limehouse Ware Revealed* (English Ceramic Circle, 1993). This was considered to be the definitive work

---

* This is unlikely to have been the much travelled John Brittain (various spellings occur), an experienced hand connected with several factories as he was born in 1735, far too late to have been involved in the trade in the mid-1740s.

on Limehouse ceramics. It has been, however, more recently succeeded by *The Limehouse Porcelain Manufactory, Excavations at 108–116 Narrow Street, London 1990*, by K. Tyler and R. Stephenson (with others). This Museum of London Archaeology Service monograph number 6 was published in 2000.

Pinxton, *c.*1796–1813

| *See* pictures 137–8

This Derbyshire factory can hardly be considered one of the major 18th-century English porcelain factories but it is convenient to include it in this chapter. It was quite a modest concern, perhaps best thought of as an offshoot of the Derby factory, which was some 24km (15 miles) away. John Coke, of a well-known local family, would seem to have acquired an interest in porcelain making in the mid-1790s. It is believed that William Duesbury of the Derby factory tested some local clays for John Coke and that William Billingsley, the talented Derby porcelain painter, followed up the enquiry in July 1795 by discussing the possibilities of establishing a porcelain manufactory at Pinxton with Coke, mainly, it would appear, to produce teawares. Various very interesting letters from Billingsley to John Coke, together with factory accounts, are published in C.L. Exley's excellent little book *The Pinxton China Factory* (Mr and Mrs R. Coke-Steel, 1963).

Work was started on the new factory in October 1795, with a trial firing in April 1796, and Billingsley settled at Pinxton in October 1796. The Billingsley-Coke partnership was dissolved in April 1799, after which time Billingsley established his own decorating establishment at Mansfield and later moved on to Brampton, near Torksey, then to a succession of other now famous ceramic centres. Coke continued alone at Pinxton until September 1801, when he took Henry Bankes into partnership, but this arrangement was terminated in January 1803. Later, from 1806, John Cutts, a Derby-trained landscape painter, leased the factory from John Coke. Some available accounts are inscribed "Brought of John Cutts, Pinxton Works, Derbyshire", but in March 1813 Cutts wrote to Josiah Wedgwood in Staffordshire regarding his forthcoming employment there, stating "…I am under the necessity of removing from this place this Lady Day, or otherwise engaging the premises for another year", and after Cutts joined Wedgwood as a porcelain painter the Pinxton factory was closed.

We therefore have a possible duration of 17 years for the Pinxton works, but it is by no means certain that porcelain was *produced* during the whole of this period.

I believe during the Cutts period, at least, the pottery works were used merely for decorating blanks that had been made in earlier years or white porcelains that had been purchased from other sources.

Pinxton porcelain and glaze from the Billingsley period (1796–9) is very similar to that made at the Derby factory. The body is a glassy one containing calcined bone. It has good translucency and the covering lead glaze is warm and pleasing to the touch. It can almost be said that unmarked Derby-type porcelain is of Pinxton make, so similar are they in appearance. The later wares are not so trim or of such a good body and, as I have stated, it is possible that no porcelain was made at Pinxton in the Cutts period between 1806 and 1813.

137

138

137 A Pinxton "D"-shape bulb pot – this shape is unique to this Derbyshire factory. The flower painting was almost certainly by William Billingsley, 12.75cm (5in) high, *c.*1796–9, Godden collection.

138 A rare Pinxton coffee can and saucer with a rare but typical pale yellow ground. The scenic panels are painted in monochrome and were probably done by William Billingsley. Note the handle form. The can has an impressed letter "N" (or "Z") and is 6.25cm (2½in) high, *c.*1796–9, formerly in the Godden collection.

139 An oval Pinxton porcelain teapot, with a typical, rather Continental-inspired, handle form. The scenic panels were almost certainly by William Billingsley. Impressed "Y" letter in printer's type, 25cm (10in) long, *c.*1796–9, Godden collection.

The often characteristic Pinxton shapes, such as that shown in picture 139, are shown in the books listed at the end of this section. The decoration often comprises small-scale landscapes – sometimes named local views – and some good flower painting, the best of which may have been by William Billingsley (*see* picture 137), although most standard patterns were of a very sparse nature with simple sprig motifs or elegant gilt designs. Ground colours were sometimes applied and these are rather pale and can be uneven (*see* pictures 137 and 138), but the quite rare Pinxton porcelains have great charm and are among the most pleasing productions of the period.

Very few pieces have written marks "Pinxton"; other pieces have a script capital "P", which may be followed by a pattern number, but most examples are unmarked or bear only the relevant pattern number. Some Pinxton wares bear small impressed letters, and a notation in the factory account book of 25 February 1797 seems to refer to the purchase of these typeface letters, "By 20 letters to mark ware at 1½d, 2/6d". Similar impressed letter markings were employed at the Derby factory.

What may be called the Pinxton sourcebook is C.L. Exley's *The Pinxton China Factory*. The late Mr Exley's researches and manuscript were edited by F.A. Barrett and A.L. Thorpe. The book is well illustrated, and the Exley collection has been on display in the Usher Gallery Museum, Lincoln. Other Pinxton pieces are in the Derby

Museum and the Victoria and Albert Museum. You should also refer to the Pinxton chapter by A.L. Thorpe in *English Porcelain 1745–1850*, edited by R.J. Charleston. (E. Benn, London, 1965).

Two recent, very well-illustrated books are evidence of the growth of knowledge and interest in Pinxton porcelain. These are Nicholas D. Gent's *The Patterns and Shapes of the Pinxton China Factory* (Privately published, 1996) and C. Barry Sheppard's *Pinxton Porcelain 1795–1813* (Privately published, 1996). There has been some excellent and surprisingly large exhibitions of Pinxton porcelain, and there is also a thriving Pinxton Porcelain Society, which publishes an illustrated newsletter.

Vauxhall (London), *c.*1753–64

| *See* pictures 29 and 140–42

The identification of these mid-18th-century London porcelains arose from the discovery of a relatively few porcelain wasters on or near the site of John Sanders & Co.'s pottery at Vauxhall (near Lambeth) on the south side of the river Thames in the late 1980s.

This class of porcelain has been known and collected for many years but before the London finds had been

140 A Vauxhall porcelain small-size sauceboat that is painted in a typically bright underglaze blue, 16.5cm (6½in) long, *c.*1760, Godden collection.

141 A Vauxhall teabowl and saucer that has been painted in underglaze blue, and finished with enamels and gilding. This man on a bridge pattern was popular at Vauxhall and can be found on several shapes, such as the cream or butter boat that is shown here. Diameter of saucer 12cm (4¾ in), *c.*1760–64, Godden collection.

140

141

142 A rare Vauxhall globular teapot that is decorated with multi-colour printed outline designs and coloured over by hand, 12.75cm (5in) high, *c.*1760–64, formerly in Mrs Margaret Cadman's collection.

classified as William Ball's Liverpool porcelain. Typical but rare examples are shown in pictures 29 and 140–42. The few books that do refer to Vauxhall porcelains tend to associate them with Nicholas Crisp but John Sanders (a practical potter) was the mind behind the enterprise. Crisp, in my opinion, supplied the funds and ran the retail sales shop under his name in Bow Churchyard, in Cheapside.

The existence of the Vauxhall pottery, and also its diversification into porcelain, has been known for some considerable time but the late Mrs Nancy Valpy's discovery of an advertisement in the Public Advertiser of 21 May 1753 has enabled us to pinpoint a date of commencement: such information is extremely rare! The opening paragraph reads: "At Mr Sanders' near the Plate Glass house, Vauxhall is now to be sold, a strong and useful manufacture of PORCELAINE WARE made of English materials…"

Note that at this time, in May 1753, only John Sanders' name was mentioned and seemingly the new wares were available direct from the pottery. However, Nicholas Crisp had been commercially associated with Sanders since at least June 1751 when they jointly took out a licence to mine soaprock in Cornwall. The soaprock was an ingredient of the porcelain mix, as it was with Worcester and some other porcelains (*see* Chapter 2). The Sanders & Crisp partnership had paid

for soaprock by November 1752, and experiments in porcelain-making probably date from around mid-1752 up to May 1753, which is when finished wares were first advertised.

The firm was variously mentioned as "John Sanders & Co.", "Sanders & Co.", "Crispe & Sanders", "Sanders & Crisp", or "Crispe & Co." in contemporary accounts, the surname Crisp being spelt with or without an "e". John Sanders died in 1758, leaving the pottery to his son William and his son-in-law Henry Richards but Nicholas Crisp retained an interest. Crisp (*c.*1704–74) was a jeweller with many other interests and was a leading member of the Haberdashers' Company and a founder member of the Society of Arts. Nevertheless Crisp, along with his brother and nephew, was declared bankrupt in November 1763, and this seems to have brought the Sanders' porcelain-making venture to an end. A closing-down auction sale of "all the entire stock of their Messrs Crisp's valuable Porcelain Manufactory at Lambeth…consisting of curious Figures, all sorts of the ornamental Toys, knife-handles and Variety of all Kinds of Useful sorts" was advertised in May and June 1764. Nicholas Crisp later reappeared at Bovey Tracey in Devon.

The Vauxhall porcelains made within the 1753–64 period (and previously attributed to William Ball's factory at Liverpool) can be most attractive. Although figures and other fancy articles were the main output, or at least the pieces known to us today, the company also made useful tablewares, mainly tea services or parts thereof. In accordance with the fashion of the period the added patterns mainly comprised mock-Oriental landscapes and other motifs that are painted in underglaze blue. This blue is usually bright (*see* picture 140) and the glaze is very glossy. The pieces have a rather oily appearance. A typical cream boat (or butter boat) and teabowl and saucer combining overglaze enamels with underglaze blue are shown together in picture 141 – this pattern was popular in the early 1760s.

A rare class of Vauxhall porcelain is decorated with printed outline designs, and coloured in by hand. The prints, however, are unusual if not unique in that the outlines appear in different colours relating to the floral or other subject – as if the engraved copper plate was charged with different colours at various points. Picture 142 illustrates a very rare teapot embellished in this manner, the spoon tray shown in picture 29 is also decorated in this unique printed outline* manner.

Most earlier books will not mention Vauxhall as a porcelain centre but further information is given in my

143 A group of porcelains that were either produced or simply decorated at William Littler's West Pans pottery. Note the handle form on both the mug and coffee pot. Crossed "L"s mark in blue on large dish, coffee pot 24.75cm (9¾in) high, c.1770, Godden of Worthing.

Encyclopaedia of British Porcelain Manufacturers (Barrie & Jenkins, 1988) under Nicholas Crisp and John Sanders (& Co.), where further specialist papers are mentioned. A selection of the wasters that led to the 1988 reappraisal of these porcelains is illustrated in Dr. Bernard Watney's important paper "The Vauxhall China Works 1751–1764", *Transactions of the English Ceramic Circle*, Vol.13, Part 3, 1989. The reader is also referred to *Godden's Guide to English Blue and White Porcelain* (Antique Collectors' Club, 2004).

West Pans (Scotland), c.1764–77

| See picture 143

This section, like that on the Newcastle-under-Lyme manufactory, owes its origin to comparatively recent research and again you will not find mention of it in books published before the mid-1960s, nor in some books that were published at later dates!

West Pans is near Musselburgh in Scotland and the proprietor was none other than William Littler, better known for his connection with the Longton Hall factory (1750–60) in Staffordshire. A West Pans bill-head for 1766 reads:

BOUGHT OF WILLm. LITTLER
China maker at West Pans near Musselburgh in Scotland
Where is made all kinds of usefull and ornamental china. Particularly mazareen and gold enameld china, also all kinds of stone ware, such as fine gilded and Japan'd Black and Tortoise shell ware &c

The items listed below the quoted October 1766 bill-head were supplied to the Duke of Atholl and the account was preserved, fortunately, within the Blair Castle papers.

The West Pans goods comprised:

Two large cabbage leaves fine mazareen & gold china	£2/ 0/0
Six pansey leaves do.	£2/14/0
A butter tub and stand	£1/ 0/0
Two dozen dessart (sic) plates	£5/10/0

For the additional work and expense
   of ye crest on each piece of ware   £0/18/0

These leaf-shaped dishes, the matching plates, and the butter dish of "fine mazareen and gold china" would seem to be very similar to the pieces shown in Plates 357 and 359 of my *Illustrated Encyclopaedia of British Pottery and Porcelain*, with their rich streaky blue borders. We cannot, however, be quite certain that these listed pieces were of porcelain although they probably were. The question of body arises from the discovery of earthenware copies of Longton-type leaf dishes, plates, etc. These relief-moulded earthenwares were embellished with a blue glaze giving an overall blue appearance. On this blue glaze gilt floral sprays were added on at least some pieces of this class.

While speaking of earthenwares we could recall that Littler's bill-head read: "also all kinds of stone ware, such as fine gilded and Japan'd Black and Tortoise shell ware". The stoneware could well have included white saltglazed wares. The description "fine gilded and Japan'd Black" may relate to the glossy black wares we so readily refer to as "Jackfield", although they seem to have been made at many pottery centres. Many of these black pieces bear impermanent enamelled and gilt decoration of the type Littler may have applied. We may assume that Littler, while at West Pans, made, decorated, or at least sold, porcelains, stonewares, Jackfield-type black glazed wares, and creamwares.

As to the establishment of the Littler enterprise, we read of one such venture in the *London Chronicle* of 25–27 December 1764, "We hear from Edinburgh that some gentlemen are about to establish a porcelain manufacture in Scotland, and have already wrote up to London to engage proper persons to carry it on." Some six weeks later the *Daily Advertiser* reported, "Four persons, well skilled in the making of British china, were engaged for Scotland, where a new Porcelain manufacture is going to be established in the manner of that now carried on at Chelsea, Stratford, and Bow." These newspaper accounts may relate to what was to become the West Pans pottery but it would seem that Littler was settled in nearby Musselburgh slightly before these reports, for the list of Honorary Burgesses gives under 30 October 1764: "Mr Wm Littler, china manufacturer at West Pans".

In February 1766 Littler applied to the Musselburgh Town Council for permission to build houses for his workpeople, to erect a windmill to grind flint and other materials, and also for liberty to take "as much clay as his manufactory required". The last request was apparently not granted but he may have had some clay available on his own original site; in fact in a council minute of December 1765 it refers to clay let to William Littler, china manufacturer. This local clay would hardly have been suitable for the making of porcelain but pottery of various types could have been made from it.

An advertisement in the Caledonian Mercury of 4 February 1765 lists at this early date a remarkable selection of wares to be sold by auction at the Palace of Holyrood. The advertisement reads in part:

...a neat collection of the productions of the Scotland manufactory china ware, it being made at the West Pans, near Musselburgh, and a good part of the china is not inferior to the foreign china both in transparency, beautiful colours and uses; consisting of fine mazareen blue jars and beakers, neatly enamelled and gilded; great variety of figures, chandeliers, candlesticks, flowers mounted in flower pots representing natural flowers; various sorts of beautiful leaves richly enamelled being calculated for the use of desart services. Also tea pots, cups and saucers, milk jugs, sugar cups and coffee cans, quart jugs and mugs, potting pots and sundry sorts of sauce boats. All these articles both in blue, white and enamel, with many other sorts, too tedious to mention. This being the first offered to public sale and for the sale of ready money, will be sold reasonable...

N.B. A good assortment of enameled cream coloured ware, which will be sold very cheap.

Other slightly later advertisements of wares offered as of West Pans manufacture are quoted by Dr Watney in a paper listed below. Dr Watney (and others) have carried out limited excavations on the site and have found evidence that porcelain was made at West Pans. He had also shown that Littler was seeking a partner to put new funds into the apparently failing works in June 1777. He seems to have failed in this endeavour and it is believed that he then returned to the Staffordshire Potteries and acted as manager at Ralph Baddeley's Shelton pottery, where he produced Longton and West Pans-type porcelain in the approximate period 1777–90 (*see* Baddeley-Littler entry on p.68).

The underglaze blue devices that are shown on p.121 have previously been attributed to William Littler's Longton Hall venture, *c.*1749–60, but no pieces with this device were found on the Staffordshire site and it could well be that this rather puzzling mark was used by him at West Pans. The unfinished or worn blue-edged dish shown in the centre of picture 143 bears a version of this double "L" mark. The other enamelled pieces are typical of this type.

Many people have added to our knowledge of the West Pans venture and the available facts have been ably summarized in the following illustrated papers: Arthur Lane (with appendix by Dr Bernard Watney) "William Littler of Longton Hall and West Pans, Scotland", *Transactions of the English Ceramic Circle*, Vol.5, Part 2, 1961; Mavis Bimson, John Ainslie, and Bernard Watney, "West Pans Story – The Scotland Manufactory", *Transactions of the English Ceramic Circle*, Vol.6, Part 2, 1966. For those who do not have access to these, there is a brief account in Chapter 4 of Dr Watney's *English Blue and White Porcelain of the 18th Century* (Faber, 1973 edition) and see also my *Encyclopaedia of British Porcelain Manufacturers* (Barrie & Jenkins, 1988).

Worcester, 1751–93

| *See pictures 4, 7, 13, 16, 23, 31, 32, 34, 42, 44, 45, 54, 56, 58, 59, 62, 63, 144–55, and 278

As I mentioned when discussing early Bristol porcelains in this chapter, a body of men from Worcester under Dr John Wall made a successful takeover bid for the Bristol enterprise in June 1751. A list of the Worcester partners and the full agreement for the carrying on of the "Worcester Tonquin Manufacture" is given in Henry Sandon's excellent and early book *The Illustrated Guide to Worcester Porcelain* (Barrie & Jenkins), first published in 1969.

As this takeover included working materials, moulds, and some of the former Bristol workpeople (even Benjamin Lund went up to Worcester), the new

144 The reverse side of a rare relief-moulded Worcester "Wigornia"-type cream or butter boat. This example, picked out in underglaze blue, is particularly rare. Oriental-style workman's mark in blue, 6.25cm (2½in) high, c.1755, Godden collection.

145

146

enterprise, which is now centred at Warmstry House in Worcester, was able to make a flying start, obviating the teething troubles often experienced by other new porcelain manufacturers*. Right from the start the Worcester wares display remarkable quality in body, glaze, workmanship, and decoration. The porcelain, which on analysis shows some 30 per cent soapstone, proved to be extremely workable and to behave very well in the kiln during the firing processes. To the touch it is compact but does not feel over heavy; it is smooth and pleasant. Pieces are rarely warped and foot-rims are normally true (they did not need grinding flat). Almost from the start attractive relief-moulded designs were produced. Superb sauceboats and cream ewers were made in a profusion of different moulds. I show such little pieces in this book (see pictures 62, 84, and 144–5**).

I have to mention a sweet creamboat that was illustrated in black and white in earlier editions as Plate 52. This piece set a very temporary world record price for English porcelain when it was sold in 1973 for £20,000 – and it stands no more than 6.25cm (2½in) high. Happily, it can be seen at the former Dyson Perrins Museum at the Worcester works, having come "home" after spending many years on the other side of the Atlantic. You may ask why such a sum was given for this little ewer. Apart from its obvious charm it boasted one special feature – the word "Wigornia" (the latinized name of Worcester) was relief-moulded under the base and, as far as is known at present, this is the only piece to have survived with such a mark. I would not be surprised if other specimens turn up because the name would have been part of the mould and moulds were usually reused for a run of similar pieces. However, when bought, this piece was believed to be unique, a fact that accounts for the price, as two or more wealthy collectors or museums were competing for it.

Postcards that illustrate this piece state "cream boat 1751 reported to be the earliest piece of Worcester porcelain in existence" – a bold claim that would surely have been difficult to substantiate. The creamer's fame rests on the mark, not on the possible date. To celebrate the factory's 250th anniversary this little creamer was reproduced in 2001.

Other smaller creamers of this general type, but without the mark, may be purchased for a fraction of the cost of the "Wigornia" example, especially those that are decorated in underglaze blue, and for the average collector these more ordinary examples will give just as much visual pleasure as the marked creamer. As a general rule, however, 18th-century Worcester porcelain does tend to be costly. It rightly attracts discriminating collectors from all over the world. Examples decorated with an apple-green ground or with very rare yellow ground are always expensive but the range of the factory's products is so large that (to me) equally attractive pieces can still be found at modest prices.

Much delightful Worcester, painted or printed in underglaze blue, is, I believe, still undervalued, although prices have rocketed in recent years. The overglaze printed pieces (see pictures 62, 63, and 150) are likewise often reasonable as are the white-and-gold designs. These simple gold designs show off to good effect the graceful shapes and the workman-like finish, and in general they are typical of the Worcester taste and potting skill.

I am deliberately avoiding retelling the history of this factory as this is well set out in so many books that you can readily consult (see the Bibliography on p.266). Instead I shall make some general points that are not made in most conventional books.

You may be told by some authors that a sure sign of a Worcester origin is glaze shrinkage inside the foot-ring. Yet, as I have already noted, glaze does not shrink, it spreads during the firing process. This fact gives rise to the practice after about 1760 of wiping the glaze away from the inside of the foot-ring so that the molten glaze would not run down the foot and glue the piece to the kiln-furniture. However, you should note that other porcelain factories employed the same method of wiping or "pegging" glaze away from the inside of the foot: most Caughley displays this feature as do some Liverpool porcelains and many 19th-century factories followed the practice too. You must also observe that the pre-1760 Worcester porcelains do not normally show this feature. So, to sum up, a glaze-free line inside the foot-ring is not an infallible guide to a Worcester origin.

145 A selection of early Worcester porcelains. Left to right: a rare early dinner plate with mock-Oriental markings on the reverse; a relief-moulded plate from a tea service; and a "Wigornia"-type moulded cream or butter boat (see also picture 144). Diameter of large plate 23.5cm (9¼in), c.1752–6, Godden collection.

146 A group of early Worcester blue-and-white wares, which are highly collectable. The leaf-moulded dish is particularly rare, but the creamers and the leaf dish would delight most collectors. Various painter's tally marks – note the rather later crescent marks, diameter of dish 21cm (8¼in), c.1755–65, Godden of Worthing.

---

* It is, however, believed that some early experiments in porcelain manufacture were made before the Bristol factory and "know-how" was purchased.
** See also pictures 4, 7, 14, and 145–8 for other early Worcester relief-moulded delights.

147 A rare relief-moulded oval dish, which was possibly used for holding butter, enamelled with charming Oriental-style scenes (on the front and back). 18.5 x 14.5cm (7¼ x 5¼in), c.1755, Godden of Worthing.

It is often stated that the Worcester paste is green by transmitted light. This is generally true but it can vary to a considerable degree and some Caughley porcelains also display a very similar greenish tone as both of these factories seem to have drawn their raw materials from the same source.

While some Worcester porcelains are really superb (*see* picture 153*) and neat in all respects, it must be acknowledged that *some* pieces – especially those made in the 1770–80 period – are of rather ordinary quality, made to cater for the vast market for low-priced useful wares. The Worcester management, like others, sold off slightly faulty pieces, "seconds" and even "thirds", at reduced prices. Make no mistake, Worcester porcelain is *nearly* always faultless, but not always.

Some 18th-century Worcester is of extreme rarity, and not only figures. Strangely the manufacturers seem to have experienced great difficulty in firing large

plates and dishes before the mid-1760s or even the early 1770s. The tea sets had two saucer-shaped plates (or stands) but the number of known flanged meat or soup plates can almost be counted on the fingers of one hand. The management seem not to have competed with the imports of Chinese dinner services, which were a staple item of the Chinese export porcelains. Instead, the Worcester management concentrated happily on the production of a host of table accessories, sauceboats, creamboats, leaf-shaped dishes, shell-shaped dishes, pickle-dishes, and, of course, relief-moulded teawares. These pieces, so English in their way, were decorated with Oriental-inspired figure or landscape patterns painted with such charm that, to British eyes at least, they have far more appeal than the wares that inspired them (*see* pictures 4, 7, 14, 145, and 146).

I have already written of the overglaze printed designs. Worcester was probably the very first factory to have employed this technique of mass production, and certainly it was used to the greatest advantage and has probably never been bettered. Printing in underglaze blue seems to have been introduced in a somewhat hesitant manner in about 1760. Some of these designs are of great rarity but many of the more common ones are very successful. There is a tendency to decry printed pieces but, as I explained earlier, the original copper plates were engraved by talented artist-designers and such patterns are far superior to a stock design painted by a young apprentice hour after hour, day after day. We should remember that the majority of hand-painted designs were themselves mass produced or were stock designs that were produced by the hundred if not by the thousand.

The famous Dr Wall retired in 1774 and he died two years later. However, most authorities continue the first, or Dr Wall, period up to 1783, which is when Thomas Flight purchased the works as a going concern, to be joined in 1793 by Martin Barr, thus giving rise to the Flight & Barr period. Henry Sandon, the former Curator of the Dyson Perrins Museum, has suggested

in his *The Illustrated Guide to Worcester Porcelain* that we should designate the 1776–93 period the Davis/Flight or middle period. William Davis had been one of the original partners or "inventors", his name being linked with Dr John Wall's in the 1751 agreement. Davis was to continue after 1774 and take the firm into the Flight period.

Within this middle, Davis/Flight period we can fit a selection of Worcester porcelain that is of rather mediocre or commercial quality. We can perhaps excuse this slight lowering of standards when we remember the position that the management would have been facing at this troublesome time in Britain's history, with the loss of the American colonies. Apart from the loss of markets and hard times at home, Thomas Turner had left to establish the Caughley factory, which started production in about 1775 and made mainly good but inexpensive blue-and-white useful wares that very often copied Worcester shapes and designs. The Derby factory was producing some extremely fine decorative porcelains and the Staffordshire potters were also producing not only New Hall porcelains but a huge

148 A group of three early Worcester useful tablewares, each enamelled in a typical delicate and charming manner and showing characteristic shapes and styles. Jug 17cm (6¾) high (sizes do vary), c.1753–8, Godden of Worthing.

149 A typically well-potted, neatly enamelled Worcester teapot and cover, of a graceful form. Like most Worcester of this type and period it is unmarked, 14.5cm (5¾in) high, c.1755–60, Godden of Worthing.

range of good-quality earthenware that must have cut into the Worcester porcelain trade significantly.

The Worcester factory surmounted the difficulties by concentrating to a large degree on the production of blue-printed useful wares – the staple of the industry. In many cases the patterns were traditional ones that were kept in production year after year. It is difficult to date such pieces, for the use of the standard crescent mark was continued well into the Flight period. The typical "Dr Wall" tankard shown in picture 152, for example, is in fact dated "1784", which was eight years after the Doctor's death, and some pieces bearing well-known first-period blue-printed designs bear also the post-1783 impressed mark "FLIGHTS".

There is, however, one very interesting new class of Worcester blue-printed porcelain that is seemingly confined to this Davis/Flight period. Very many pieces of this type bear a fresh series of related marks, the so-called disguise numeral marks. We have the numbers "1" to "9" each used separately and disguised with Oriental-looking curves or other embellishments. Three typical examples are reproduced on page 128. Up to the time of my researches that were published in 1969 (*Caughley and Worcester Porcelain, 1775–1800*, Barrie & Jenkins, revised edition Antique Collectors' Club 1981), these marks and the whole class of the porcelains on which they occur were incorrectly classed as Caughley. These devices are found associated with a charming range of well-engraved underglaze blue landscape and figure patterns often featuring prominent classical ruins. Sometimes these landscapes are set in a small panel; at other times the design fills all but the edge of the piece. These European subjects are quite rare, some excessively so, and the same disguised numerical marks (as well as the crescent mark) also occur on some of the later standard prints – the floral designs and the Oriental-inspired patterns including the Worcester version of the ever popular "Fisherman" or "Pleasure Boat" print.

It would appear that the Worcester enamelled porcelains of the post-1774 Davis/Flight period were usually unmarked and in general the overglaze design became very restrained. By the 1780s the former richly coloured Worcester style had given way to simple patterns combining underglaze blue with overglaze gilding. The teapots and sugar basins tended to be oval rather than circular, which perhaps followed the Chamberlain examples. The "cabinet pieces" can, in contrast, be extremely finely decorated and such pieces often bear clear name marks of the period.

With the exception of the one known "Wigornia" creamboat the early Worcester porcelains do not bear a factory mark. If marks occur before about 1755 they are painters' marks, which are small signs that take various individual forms. These normally occur on blue-and-white wares only, and usually only on the pre-1755 examples. The devices were often painted under the handle of a creamer or other article. The early enamelled pieces are usually unmarked.

After about 1755 or later the well-known factory marks were used (these are shown on the next page). The crescent is painted unshaded (A) on hand-painted objects, and with shades with lines on printed designs (B). We also have the initial "W" (C) in various forms painted in underglaze blue, and versions of the Meissen crossed-swords mark (D). This device sometimes has the unexplained numerals "9" or "91" placed between the blades.

You will also find many slightly different versions of the "square" or "seal mark" (E), which is a device found on many of the scale-blue ground (blue ground with scales) wares. Some Oriental-type designs bear fanciful Chinese-looking character marks (F). Marks C to F will appear on Worcester porcelains made in around 1760–75. The crescent mark was continued into the Flight period – that is into the 1790s.

150 A small Worcester milk jug "Jet"–printed in black over the glaze. Each item in the complete tea service would have been embellished with a different printed view engraved by Robert Hancock, 8.25cm (3¼in) high, *c*.1760, Godden collection.

151 A fine, large-size, Worcester moulded cabbage-leaf jug. It has a rare pale yellow ground and minutely painted panels of Chinese-style figures in landscapes. This is a grand piece but perhaps a little fussy, 26cm (10¼in) high (sizes vary), *c*.1760–65, Godden of Worthing.

150

151

Do note that the square mark (E), in particular, can occur on hard-paste and other reproductions of Dr Wall porcelain. However many of the original Dr Wall porcelains are completely unmarked.

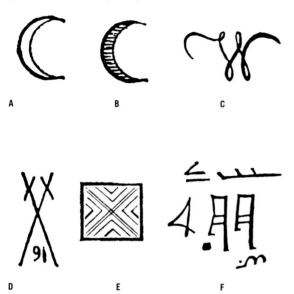

A   B   C

D   E   F

Below are three of the nine "disguised numerical" marks found on some good-quality blue-printed Worcester porcelains of the approximate period 1775–85. These comprise the numbers one to nine disguised or adorned with Oriental-style flourishes, although the subjects are usually European rather than Chinese. The standard shaded or filled-in Worcester crescent device was also used up to this period and into the early Flight period.

For the novice, as yet unfamiliar with the Worcester body or glaze, the best guide to identification is the shape of the object. Close comparison should be made with actual specimens or, where this is not possible, with pieces illustrated in standard reference books. Apart from the forms some, but by no means all, patterns are unique to the Worcester factory. It should be noted that fakes occur (see picture 277) and that some sparsely decorated pieces were repainted in an expensive style, see picture 278. You should find the following specialist books most helpful, but most works on English ceramics also give a fair coverage of this

important factory: *Coloured Worcester Porcelain of the First Period* by H. Rissik Marshall (Ceramic Book Co., 1954); *Worcester Porcelain and Lund's Bristol* by F.A. Barrett (Faber, revised edition 1966); *Caughley and Worcester Porcelain, 1775–1800* by G. Godden (revised 1981 edition, Antique Collectors' Club); *The Illustrated Guide to Worcester Porcelain* by H. Sandon (Barrie & Jenkins, 1969, third edition 1980); *Worcester Blue & White Porcelain 1751–1790* by L. Branyan, N. French, and J. Sandon (Barrie & Jenkins, revised edition 1989); *Worcester Porcelain – The Klepser Collection* by S. Spero (Lund Humphries, 1984); or my *Godden's Guide to English Blue and White Porcelain* (Antique Collector's Club, 2004).

Apart from these titles, there is also a mini library on various types of Worcester porcelain. *John Sandon's The Dictionary of Worcester Porcelains Vol.1, 1751–1851* (Antique Collectors' Club, 1993) is a most convenient sourcebook. You must also – and I do mean must – visit the splendid collection at the Museum

152

152 A well-potted Worcester mug, with underglaze blue border that is neatly painted with floral swags and trim gilding. Such a piece might be attributed to the mid-1770s, but it is dated, in blue under the base, "1784", 9cm (3½in) high, 1784, Godden of Worthing.

153 Right: a large-size Worcester moulded cabbage-leaf jug with underglaze blue ground. The reserved panels are finely painted with colourful, exotic birds in landscapes and finely detailed butterflies. Square mark in blue, 29.75cm (11¾in) high (sizes vary), c.1765–70, Godden of Worthing.

154

155

adjoining the Royal Worcester works in that city, and the Worcester pieces found at the Victoria and Albert Museum in London are well worth many visits.

I shall return to the subject of the 19th-century Worcester porcelain products in Chapter 9.

Other 18th-century British porcelain manufactories

I have given details of the main British manufactories in this chapter, though some are listed in the following chapter as they made a different type of porcelain. Other manufactories were very small and are mainly known to us from a few contemporary records: no porcelains have as yet been attributed to these particular makers. Known makers are listed in my standard book, *Encyclopaedia of British Porcelain Manufacturers* (Barrie & Jenkins, 1988).

William Billingsley

Some well-known names do not fit conveniently into the general arrangement of this book. For example, William Billingsley (1758–1828) is a case in point. His fame as a flower painter has spread far and wide – indeed some people seem to have the impression that any rose painted on porcelains must be by Billingsley! In fact, the reality is that every major factory employed several competent flower painters.

William Billingsley was born at Derby in 1758, and his father was also a flower painter. Young Billingsley was apprenticed to William Duesbury at the Derby factory in September 1774. He acquired a technique of wiping out the highlights to expose the underlying white porcelain body, which gave a novel, delicate naturalistic effect. It must not be thought that this technique remained unique to Billingsley, however, although he was probably the first to use it.

In 1795 Billingsley was approached by John Coke of Pinxton, who wished to open his own porcelain works with Billingsley as manager (*see* Pinxton entry, p.115). Billingsley also decorated Pinxton porcelain during his short stay there (*see* picture 137). However, Billingsley left Pinxton in April 1799 and moved to

Mansfield where he established a decorating workshop painting bought-in white blank. By 1802 he had moved on to Brampton (Torksey) in Lincolnshire. It would seem that Billingsley made porcelains at Brampton in the 1802–7 period. During 1808–13 Billingsley was in Worcester painting for Barr, Flight & Barr but in 1813 he moved on into Wales where he endeavoured to produce fine porcelains at Nantgarw (*see* Chapter 9, p.200). Billingsley and his partner Samuel Walker soon moved to Swansea but then returned to Nantgarw (*c.*1817–20). He reputedly moved on to Coalport but it is not clear if he was employed by John Rose. Billingsley died in January 1828, aged 70. Possibly no other English ceramic painter established such a long-lasting reputation or created so many porcelain works.

Most books on Welsh, Derby, or Pinxton porcelain will give a good account of Billingsley's life and work. There is also the scarce and costly specialist book *William Billingsley* by W.D. John (Ceramic Book Co., 1968) and the later multi-author book *Not just a Bed of Roses. The Life and Work of the Artist, Ceramic and Manufacturer William Billingsley 1758–1828*, which is published by the Usher Gallery, Lincoln, 1996.

154 A colourful, if rather late, Worcester dish from a dessert service. The animal subject is unusual but the groups of fruit are typical of the late 1770s or early 1780s. Crescent mark in underglaze blue, 26.5 x 24cm (10½ x 9½in), *c.*1775–85, Godden of Worthing.

155 A Worcester globular teapot with hand-modelled floral knob. Decorated, in underglaze blue, enamels, and gold with an old Japanese design. Matching plates and saucers are also finished on the underside in Oriental-style with mock marks. Teapot 15.25cm (6in) high, *c.*1770, Godden of Worthing.

7
The hard-paste and hybrid hard-paste porcelains

We have, in the previous chapter, learned something about the major 18th-century English porcelain factories that produced artificial or soft-paste porcelains. There is, however, a further type of English porcelain, a sort of hybrid hard-paste, which is midway between hard-paste and soft-paste. Many English factories in the approximate 1790–1810 period made such porcelains and they have been little researched. Indeed many standard reference books will not mention this quite large group of porcelain at all! This is hardly surprising for so little is known about the different makers, or even about the type of body employed. Shapes and patterns of one firm were closely followed by others and very few marked pieces exist to help study today.

I first began to be interested in these porcelains some years ago when working on my book on Coalport and after excavations on the Caughley factory site. My research widened when I was asked in 1973 to read a paper at the Morley College "Hard-Paste" Seminar. This paper was to follow David Holgate's, which was on New Hall porcelain, and he in turn followed learned authorities speaking on Bristol and Plymouth hard-paste porcelains. I was to tidy up the loose ends and discuss the other hard-paste wares. Tidy up? Indeed I posed more questions than I answered and certainly set myself rethinking the whole puzzling question of this class of English porcelain.

It is strange but true that we know today far more about early British porcelains made in 1750–70 than we do about many of the wares made at the beginning of the 19th century. There are two main reasons for this. First, ceramic students have concentrated on the earlier period and second, the later wares were routine useful objects, mainly teawares, which in their period excited little or no contemporary comment.

156 A Chinese porcelain teapot and coffee cup from a tea service, which is attractively painted with English figures in landscapes. The overglaze decoration was added in England by a leading but as yet unknown ceramic painter. There is slight gilding on the pieces too, teapot 13cm (5¼in) high, *c.*1750–55, Godden collection.

157 A large, deep Chinese porcelain dish from a dinner service. The floral painting and crest were added in England by a specialist ceramic painter. This example is a happy marriage of Eastern potting skills and European painters' art, diameter 38cm (15in), *c.*1750–55, Godden of Worthing.

But before proceeding to discuss the hybrid hard-paste porcelains we must consider the true, high-fired, hard-paste porcelains and firstly those made in the East, which were then imported to Great Britain. There is no generally accepted or acceptable definition of hard-paste porcelain. We have several often-repeated tests but on re-examination I find that they are in fact unreliable. I have already mentioned that a good file will cut into most hard-pastes, certainly into New Hall. So throw away that file! Secondly, some accepted hard-pastes show a granular, rather than conchoidal, fracture, a feature that is regarded as a characteristic of soft-paste porcelains. Also, the degree to which the enamels stand up on top of the glaze is an unreliable guide as this depends not so much on the underlying porcelain as it does on the make-up of the glaze and the enamels, the amount of flux used, and also on the firing temperature. Therefore, all the traditional tests used for detecting hard-paste porcelain are negated, so we are left simply with the feel and individual experience of each collector.

Chinese

| *See* pictures 156–7

The majority of porcelains in use in the British Isles during the 18th century, particularly teawares, were made in China. Most were decorated in that country, especially those made for the European market, and were sometimes special orders on which the owner's armorial bearings, crest, or initials was enamelled.

Apart from these decorated importations some other Chinese porcelain was imported in a white, undecorated state. Such Oriental blanks were often enamelled in England by specialist decorators such as James Giles (*see* p.93). This class of English-decorated Chinese hard-paste porcelain is interesting, decorative, but scarce. The basic types of decoration enhance floral groups or sprays (with insects as in picture 157), exotic birds in landscapes, or, more rarely, landscapes and figure compositions (*see* picture 156). In pictures 156 and 157 I show three good examples of the probable period *c.*1750–55. Some Chinese porcelain was even printed in England (*see* picture 61). I have written on this class of Anglo-Chinese ceramics within *Eighteenth Century English Porcelain. A Selection from the Godden Reference Collection* (Granada, 1985). See also my *Oriental Export Market Porcelain*, (Granada, 1979).

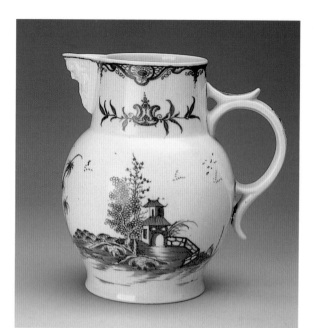

158

159

Plymouth, c.1768–70

| *See* pictures 158–9

The rare West Country Plymouth porcelains are of the true or hard-paste type and this was the invention of the local Quaker chemist William Cookworthy. As early as 1745 Cookworthy had been interested in manufacturing porcelain, possibly using clay from North America. We do not have any knowledge about whether his early experiments met with any commercial success, but partial success was to crown his endeavours when later he came to use raw materials found nearly on his own doorstep. These were the vital petuntse and kaolin as used by the Chinese (*see* Chapter 2).

William Cookworthy took out a patent for making porcelain using these materials in March 1768. The patent was no idle boast for one finished piece predates the patent by three days, showing that he was indeed possessed of the knowledge of how to produce hard-paste porcelain and to fire it successfully at the very high temperature required, which was *c.*1,400°C (2,552°F). However, the Plymouth works were closed in 1770, after which Cookworthy continued to work his patent at Bristol. Indeed it seems probable that some experiments were carried out by Cookworthy at Bristol before his own works were successfully established at Plymouth. Apparently the early porcelains would discolour in the kiln, which is a not uncommon fault that is found even on the so-called successful Plymouth porcelains. Quite wide cracks might also occur, as well as distortion of the shape. The handle to the jug that is

158 A rare Plymouth hard-paste porcelain jug with mask spout. The dull underglaze blue is typical of Plymouth. Stresses in the firing have separated the bottom of the handle away from the body – yet the decoration was completed with overglaze enamel, unmarked, 17cm (6¾in) high, *c.*1770, Godden collection.

159 A rare Plymouth hard-paste porcelain candlestick group (the candle holder is missing). There are firing cracks at the back and under the base, 18.5cm (7¼in) high, *c.*1770, Godden collection.

shown in picture 158 has come away from the body at the lower joint, although it was completed and sold!

Cookworthy was ambitious; he was not content to make only useful wares and blue-and-white porcelains emulating the Chinese imports. He also produced figure models and groups (*see* picture 159), shell-shaped centrepieces, and similar designs. His downfall may have been the difficulty he experienced in firing flat wares. The cobalt employed on the blue-and-white wares were fired to a rather unattractive inky-black (*see* picture 158) and the overglaze enamels tended to remain on the very surface of the hard glaze. Although these Plymouth porcelains are important, being the first successful essays in English hard-paste porcelain, I much prefer the technically poor relations – the soft-paste wares.

The Plymouth porcelains are often unmarked but the sign for tin – the numbers "2" and "4" conjoined – was often employed. I have added a drawing of such a mark on the next page. However, as with other hand-painted marks, many variations occur as the devices were hastily rendered. Many later copies of Plymouth porcelain may also be seen – often bell-shaped mugs painted with exotic birds in landscapes. Such later fakes bear copies of the Plymouth tin mark while other Continental fakes can have full, misleading inscriptions such as "Plymouth Manufactory".

4

For further information you can consult F. Severne Mackenna's *Cookworthy's Plymouth and Bristol Porcelain* (F. Lewis, 1947), Dr B. Watney's *English Blue and White Porcelain of the 18th Century*, and the well-illustrated general books such as *English Porcelain 1745–1850*, edited by R.J. Charleston. See also Dr F. Severne Mackenna's paper "William Cookworthy and the Plymouth Factory, an Updating", *Transactions of the English Ceramic Circle*, Vol.2, Part 2, 1982.

160 A simply decorated Bristol hard-paste waste bowl from a tea service. There are various firing cracks and tears in the body. Painted Bristol cross mark with painter's number – "18", diameter 14.5cm (5¾in), *c.*1775, Godden collection.

Bristol hard-paste porcelain, *c.*1770–81

| *See* pictures 23, left, and 160–63

The name of William Cookworthy is a very important one in English ceramics. As I have stated he found in Cornwall the vital raw materials and had the necessary knowledge to make use of his discoveries, although it is doubtful if he profited greatly from the venture.

William Cookworthy seems to have carried out early, probably unsuccessful, experiments in hard-paste porcelain in the mid-1760s at Bristol before establishing his famous Plymouth works in 1768. However, he soon returned to Bristol, in 1770, to establish a factory that continued production for just eight years. Richard Champion succeeded Cookworthy late in 1773 and it was Champion who later resold the patent rights to produce translucent bodies containing Cornish kaolin and petuntse – the true or hard-paste type of porcelain. It is really Richard Champion's name that we associate with the Bristol porcelains of the 1770s.

The Bristol true porcelains are neater and cleaner than the related earlier Plymouth porcelains. The glaze is noticeably better but the body did tend to tear slightly in turning, causing faults. The modest waste bowl shown

in picture 160 illustrates some of these characteristic defects. First, the body shows "wreathing", a series of little ridges running like a spring or the thread of a screw around the piece. These marks are formed by the pull of the fingers or turning tool as the piece is thrown or trimmed. Secondly, we can see the small tears where the body was dug into during the turning or trimming process, and finally there is a "firing crack" or opening of the body. Such firing cracks can occur in almost all porcelains but they are quite usual on these early hard-paste wares. A firing crack differs from a later impact crack in that it is slightly open and glaze has flowed into the opening. Such cracks are caused by the body contracting unevenly during the firing process. Unless very disfiguring or serious, these manufacturing faults are normally overlooked by collectors or rightly regarded as a helpful indication of origin or age.

The Bristol factory seems to have concentrated on producing tasteful enamelled designs, often with a decided Continental air. To me the most attractive of its enamelled designs are the well-painted simple floral patterns or festoons of flowers (see pictures 161 and 163) painted with wet-looking overglaze colours. The gilding on these is restrained and elegant. Less successful are the rather poorly painted copies or adaptations of Chinese figure designs. These are normally painted on simpler teaware shapes and this general class gave rise to the old term "cottage-Bristol".

Apart from its tablewares, mainly tea and dessert services, the Bristol factory made some very attractive figures (see picture 162), some of which bear the impressed mark "T" or "To" of the "repairer" John Toulouse, but the factory is perhaps best known for the very rare, small, oval biscuit floral encrusted plaques, some of which bear personal initials or even armorial bearings in the centre.

The Bristol enamelled wares often have a copy of the Meissen crossed-swords mark painted in a rather dull underglaze blue. By the side of this the painter or gilder added his personal tally number in overglaze enamel or gold. Such a mark is shown but very many examples of Bristol hard-paste porcelain are unmarked.

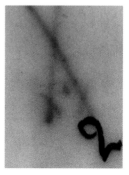

The blue-and-white Bristol porcelains are decidedly scarce. In comparison with Worcester pieces (and such wares were regularly copied at Bristol) they are rather unsatisfactory. If they were not the product of a short-lived and collectable factory they would cause little or no excitement, although an advertisement in Aris's *Birmingham Gazette* of 1 February 1779 made the following claim: "The blue and white is now brought to the greatest perfection equal to Nankeen, which with the very great strength and fine polish [glaze] renders it the best for use of any china now in the world". Alas, this is an unwarranted claim but it does show us today that these underglaze blue designs were made up to the final period of the factory's existence. We are in fact not very sure of the date of closure: the works were seemingly being run down as early as 1778 and Champion was in Staffordshire trying to sell his rights in November 1780. The Bristol factory closed in 1781 but probably production had ceased some time before this.

The blue designs were, in the main, Chinese-style landscapes, and some not very successful printing was practised. When Bristol blue and white is marked the simple cross would be expected rather than the crossed-swords mark, but remember that this simple cross device can occur on non-Bristol wares, especially as a painter's tally mark.

161 A pleasing selection of Bristol tearwares, showing a characteristic shaped teapot and typical enamelled festoons of flowers. The initialled plate and teabowl and saucer were painted by William Stephens. Blue cross marks, diameter of plate 20cm (8in), *c.*1775, Phillips.

162 Right, a Bristol hard-paste porcelain figure depicting Water, which would have been part of a set of the four Elements. The piece has numerous firing cracks, 26cm (10¼in) high, *c.*1775, Godden of Worthing.

Herbert Eccles analysed a Bristol enamelled saucer and published the following result:

Silica	69.96%
Alumina	24.43%
Lime	1.50%
Phosphoric Acid	0.17%
Magnesia	trace
Potash	1.36%
Soda	1.92%
Lead oxide	1.50%

This is remarkably close to his analysis of a fragment of 18th-century Chinese hard-paste porcelain.

The literature on Bristol is sparse, but there are two classics from the 1940s: F. Severne Mackenna's *Cookworthy's Plymouth and Bristol Porcelain* (F. Lewis, 1946) and the same authority's *Champion's Bristol Porcelain* (F. Lewis, 1947). Of more recent vintage we have Dr Watney's *English Blue and White Porcelain of the 18th Century* (Faber, 1963, revised edition 1973). Some typical Bristol forms and styles of decoration are featured in my *British Porcelain, an Illustrated Guide* (Barrie & Jenkins, 1974).

163 A good grouping of Bristol hard-paste dessert wares, painted in a classic Bristol style and of the finest quality. Blue cross marks with painters' numbers – in one case the gilder's initial "C", oval dish 25cm (10in) long. *c.*1775, Phillips.

In September 2001 Phillips, the London-based auctioneers, sold Peter Stephens' collection of Bristol (and Plymouth) porcelains. The illustrated catalogue shows a very good and varied selection of English hard-paste porcelain. It also shows the value of modern sale catalogues as mini works of reference. Pictures 161 and 163 are from his collection.

Firing processes

One characteristic of hard-paste lies within the firing procedure. The Chinese potters used a single firing or perhaps hardened off the biscuit porcelain at a very low heat, after which it was glazed and then subjected to the high temperature of 1,400°C (2,552°F) – at which the body vitrified, the glaze matured, and the two fused together as a whole. Most Continental manufacturers of hard-paste porcelain continued following this traditional method of a low initial firing, followed by a higher firing after glazing.

The English soft-paste porcelain manufacturers reversed the firing sequence so that the first (biscuit) firing was the highest and vitrified the porcelain. This was then glazed and refired at a lower temperature to mature and fix the covering skin of glaze.

The hybrid hard-paste porcelains appear to have been fired in the English soft-paste manner; they are therefore of a type of hard-paste porcelain fired in the soft-paste manner. There is a great advantage to the potter employing this method for, once a piece has been fired and vitrified, its body is strong and will withstand much rougher handling than unvitrified wares. Printed designs can, for example, be applied, the transfer paper pressed on in a positive manner and then soaked off again. It is difficult to carry out such processes on a lightly fired blank.

The firing temperatures to which the different mixes matured also have a bearing on the type of porcelain produced. Hard-pastes mature or vitrify at about 1,400°C (2,552°F), some 200 or so degrees higher than soft-paste or artificial porcelains.

With the help of Henry Sandon and Paul Rado, then of the Worcester Royal Porcelain Company, I submitted various types of porcelain to different firing temperatures, first in their standard hard-paste kiln, which reaches 1,435–1,450°C (2,615–2,642°F) in the normal course of firing the Worcester special high-temperature porcelains. As you may have expected, the 18th-century Chinese hard-paste porcelains came through this temperature with flying colours. I was, however, surprised to find the glaze had just started to melt and flow from the porcelain in this range of temperatures. Obviously the Chinese porcelains (at least the seemingly typical pieces that were tested) would have failed if fired at over 1,450°C (2,642°F). The Meissen fragments also survived the 1,435–1,450°C (2615–2642°F) firing, as did Bristol porcelains. So we have shown that the hard-paste Chinese, Meissen, and Bristol porcelains matured in approximately the same high-temperature fire. Of course, as you may have expected, the overglaze enamel decoration fired away at this high temperature.

These firing experiments led to tests on New Hall porcelain. The first piece submitted to the hard-paste kiln came out a shapeless blob whereas a Chamberlain-Worcester fragment kept its shape perfectly at this temperature. A further New Hall piece from the same specimen lost its shape and the glaze bubbled into a "moonscape" at 1,250°C (2,282°F) and a further fragment remained perfect at 1,100°C (2,012°F). The firing temperature of the New Hall paste was probably within the 1,150–1,200°C (2,102–2,192°F)

range, hardly consistent with the temperature that is needed to mature a true hard-paste porcelain. In fact a Coalport/Caughley site waster of the 1800–10 period of the type I call "hybrid hard-paste" stood up better to the fire at 1,350°C (2,462°F) than the New Hall example did at 1,250°C (2,282°F). I must, however, point out that the New Hall partners themselves claimed to be "Manufacturers of Real China"; but they did not claim to produce a porcelain body under Cookworthy's, or any other, patent. I make these points as old books state that Plymouth, Bristol, and New Hall are all true hard-paste porcelains. The analysis of the body as carried out by Herbert Eccles on a New Hall bowl of the 1795–1800 period is very similar to that of standard and accepted hard-paste porcelains. It is the firing sequence that differs. His analysis showed:

Silica	73.56%
Alumina	19.30%
Phosphoric Acid	0.24%
Lime	4.02%
Soda	2.10%
Potash	0.92%
Lead oxide	0.67%
Magnesia	Trace

It should be noted that on the Continent the term "hybrid porcelain" is used in a different context, as it relates to some porcelain mixes containing magnesite, as was used, for example, at Venice.

The study of these hybrid hard-paste porcelains is very closely related to the New Hall porcelains and I propose to start our discussion with these wares. You will find the standard books on New Hall porcelains at the end of the following section on New Hall.

New Hall (Staffordshire), 1781–1835

| *See* pictures 18, 24, 33, 64, and 164–69

The New Hall porcelains are linked historically with the two hard-paste factories of Plymouth and Bristol, which worked William Cookworthy's original patent of 1768 (this was extended in 1775 to take its coverage up to 1796). When the Bristol hard-paste factory failed, Champion sought to cash in on his most valuable asset, the patent, which permitted the holder to make translucent porcelains using the vital raw materials – china-clay and china-stone. With this in mind, Champion visited the Staffordshire Potteries and sought the help of his old adversary, Josiah Wedgwood. On 12 November 1780 Wedgwood reported to his partner Bentley:

164

165

164 A rare moulded early (pre-New Hall) Tunstall porcelain mug, with typical handle form. Simple early decoration in a typical palette, 9cm (3½in) high, c.1781, Godden collection.

165 A very rare form of early New Hall milk jug, with a bridge across the spout. The handle form is very similar to that of a Bristol piece. The early pattern is a version of the popular pattern 3, 15.75cm (4¼in) high, c.1785, Godden collection.

...Mr Champion of Bristol has taken me up near two days. He is come amongst us to dispose of his secret – his patent etc... He tells me he has sunk fifteen thousand pounds in this gulf, and his idea is now to sell the whole art, mystery and patent for six and he is now trying a list of names I have given him of the most substancial and enterprising potters amongst us...

One may wonder why the leading Staffordshire pottery manufacturers should have been interested in laying out the then considerable sum of six thousand pounds to purchase Champion's patent when his own efforts to work it had been rather unsuccessful, but the manufacture of porcelain was a compelling goal. At that time Caughley, Derby, and the Worcester factories were obviously prospering and practically had the market to themselves while not one potter in Staffordshire was then making porcelain (except perhaps James Neale and Baddeley, *see* pp.113 and 68).

In his letter to Bentley, Wedgwood stated that Champion was selling the "whole art, mystery and patent". There would seem to have been a further saleable commodity: Champion's licences to mine and take the all-important Cornish clays, and if Champion retained the licences he certainly hoped to sell the raw material to make a profit.

It occurs to me that while Champion was producing his own hard-paste porcelain he would obviously seek to protect his patent right to be the sole producer, but once he had ceased to make porcelain himself, and provided he had access to a supply of the raw materials, it would be in his interests to permit, by licence or otherwise, as many potters as possible to use and buy from him the materials he no longer required. This reasoning is supported by two letters that were written by Champion when reporting on his progress in Staffordshire. The first, dated 6 August 1781, merely touches on this aspect of extending the trade, "The present plan has a clause in it giving liberty to every potter to make the porcelain in his own works, on payment of a certain fine to the company". A letter written on 3 September 1781 is rather more detailed and I have quoted the more interesting passages:

...I have now entered into an agreement with ten Potters only, who if they like the Manufactory on its Establishment in the County are to give me a certain sum for liberty to use in their own works, but I have also liberty to sell to any other I please. In this situation I naturally look to some Advantages from the sale of Materials but the high price of them compared with these of Trethewys (12 guineas a year) and Carthews

166 **Three small "Robin creamers"** (partly so-called due to their chirpy robin-like nature), displaying typical early New Hall enamelled patterns – the right-hand example being number 22, 6.25cm (2½in) and 7cm (2¾in) high, c.1785, Godden collection.

equally cheap, make me have very little hopes of advantage...You will please always to carry this in your view, that the Potters will buy where they please, and that there is no way of engaging them than by selling cheap.

It can be deduced from this letter that Champion would have been only too glad to grant a licence to any potter that approached him and was willing to pay the price of the china-clay and china-stone. We may also guess that Champion knew his patent rights were not all that watertight, for if they were the question of price would not have arisen: the potters would simply have had to pay his price or licence fee or not make porcelain with these ingredients.

The earliest printed account of Champion's efforts to sell his art and patent in Staffordshire is given by Simeon Shaw in his book *History of the Staffordshire Potteries* (privately published, Hanley, 1829). After giving a brief account of Cookworthy's discovery and of Champion's purchase of the patent, Shaw explained that Champion:

...sold the patent to a company in Staffordshire: Mr Samuel Hollins, red-china potter of Shelton; Anthony Keeling, Potter of Tunstall; John Turner, Lane End; Jacob Warburton of Hot Lane; William Clowes and Charles Bagnall, Potter, Shelton.

After this agreement Mr Champion directed the processes of the manufacture for the company from

November 1781 at the manufactory of Mr Anthony Keeling at Tunstall but when that gentleman [Champion] removed to London in April 1782, a disagreement ensued among the partners; Mr Keeling and John Turner withdrew and they who continued together engaged as managing partner Mr John Daniel...and settled the manufactory at the New Hall, Shelton only a short time previously erected by Mr Whitehead, of the Old Hall, Hanley; on which account the Porcelain had the appellation of New Hall china and during the lifetime of the several partners, the concern has been carried forward to their great profit...

If we can believe Shaw's account, and after all he was writing at a time when the factory was still in being, we can deduce that these leading Staffordshire potters, whom are spoken of as partners in the New Hall concern, did little more than put up money for the new adventure started by Champion and continued by their manager, John Daniel, while the practising partners continued to run their own potteries where they made various types of high-grade earthenware. It should be noted that the partnership rarely traded under the name "New Hall" in the 18th century, but rather traded under the names of the main partners, generally as "Hollins, Warburton & Co.". However, the partners, and therefore the trade name, changed from time to time.

The initial porcelains of the 1782–3 period can often go unacknowledged because, in form and style of decoration, they are very different from the later pieces – the silver-shape teapots and simple cottagey floral designs that are to so many people typically "New Hall". The pieces that we now regard as the earliest are usually moulded with corrugated surface (perhaps to give added strength). A typical small mug of this rare early type is shown in picture 164. However, not all pre-1784 pieces were corrugated; many were of simple hand-thrown form. The early teapots were often globular in form. Many of the early designs comprised only elegant gilt borders or bands. The early pieces produced before about 1790 are devoid of a pattern number or other mark.

We have a few original accounts relating to New Hall wares, but one for goods purchased by Josiah Wedgwood is of considerable interest. It is dated 7 September 1789 and reads:

Bt. of Hollins Warburton & Co.
Manufacturers of Real China, Shelton, Staffordshire

1 sett cups and saucers enameld
    of 6 diff'rt [patterned] cups and 6 saucers 6/-
4 cups and 4 saucers blue & white
    of 4 diff'rt patterns 3/6d
1 cup and saucer white & gold 2/5d

These cups and saucers, of 11 different patterns for under 12 shillings, were probably samples. This brief account shows that in 1789 at least four blue-and-white patterns were in production, but more remarkably we can see that a single gilt cup and saucer cost nearly two and a half times the price of enamelled coloured examples. We can also see that the blue-and-white cups and saucers (the designs were almost certainly printed) were only marginally cheaper than the hand-painted coloured designs. (These quoted prices were probably the retail ones for, from the total of 11s 11d, Wedgwood was allowed 25 per cent discount.) The tasteful gilt pieces are far superior to the simple, very repetitive enamelled designs, most of which have the appearance of having been painted by inexperienced boys rather than by trained ceramic artists.

Fidelle Duvivier

In contrast, some rarely found New Hall porcelains were painted by talented artists, the most famous of

167 A New Hall milk jug, with a typical "clip-handle". The monochrome painting is by Fidelle Duvivier – the front of the jug shows a girl in a swing, 13cm (5¼in) high, c.1785–90, Godden collection.

which was Fidelle Duvivier – indeed I think he is the only proven New Hall painter known to us by name. Duvivier was born on the Continent in August 1740. He was painting for Duesbury of Derby in the 1769–73 period; he also worked at Worcester, or at least his work is known on a single signed teapot dated 1772 (but this may have been an example of Duvivier's independent ceramic painting, rather than a work carried out for the Worcester management).

In the 1781–90 period Duvivier was at New Hall, where he painted in a characteristic, pleasing style mainly figure and landscape compositions. These very often include smoking kilns in the background and the distant views are wonderfully shaded off into the haze. A rare milk jug in Duvivier's typical style is shown in picture 167 and picture 168 is a tureen stand from a magnificent scenic-painted dessert service painted by Duvivier for John Daniel, the factory manager. Other superbly painted pieces from this unique service are illustrated in my specialist book on New Hall, where the work of Duvivier is discussed at length. Duvivier may also have been employed at Chamberlain's factory at Worcester for a short period, and his painting also occurs on a rare class of well-potted Neale porcelain (*see* pictures 25 and 136). This work may be the nature of part-time independent decoration.

On 1 November 1790 Fidelle Duvivier wrote to William Duesbury in Derby. I have quoted this letter in part below:

...[I] take the liberty of addressing you with a few lines as mine engagement in the new Hal Porcelaine manufactory is expierd, and the propriotors do not intent to do much more in the fine line of painting, therefor [I] think of settling in New-Castle under-lime being engag'd to teach drawing in the boarding school at that place, one school I have at Stone, so as to have only three days to spare in the week for painting which time could wish to be employ'd by you preferable to eany other fabricque, because you like and understand good work ...

Duvivier then goes on to ask Duesbury to send him porcelain each week by wagon from Derby. Duesbury is hardly likely to have agreed to this troublesome process when he had such good ceramic artists working under his own roof and under his own watchful eye. However, we can see from this letter that Duvivier was seeking part-time work and he may well have continued to paint special pieces for the New Hall management (or other local firms such as Neale) for several years after 1790.

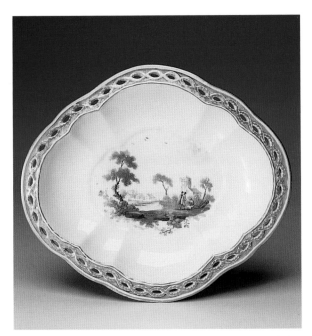

168 A rare openwork-edged New Hall sugar tureen stand, attractively painted by Fidelle Duvivier. Part of a superb dessert service painted for John Daniel, the factory manager, 23.5 x 19.75cm (9¼ x 7¾in), c.1785–90, Godden collection.

Other wares and marks

Do not think for one moment that the so-called silver-shape or turreted teapot (as shown in picture 18) is typical of New Hall. It (and there are very many variations of the basic form) was only employed for a limited period, probably c.1790–1805, and many other teapot shapes were made before and after this. Certainly over 12 totally different New Hall teapot shapes were made. Remember also that several firms other than New Hall made this basic shape of teapot (*see*, for example, pictures 170 and 198).

Apart from the gilt patterns and the enamelled designs the New Hall firm also produced a range of blue-and-white porcelains, normally printed designs having distinct Chinese influence (*see* picture 169); one pattern at least occurs on hand-painted Chinese porcelains of the period. Apart from these blue-printed pieces some fine overglaze prints are to be found on New Hall porcelains. These are normally of the "bat" type (*see* Chapter 5, p.61) with a delicate stippled effect. Some of these prints were dusted with gold rather than with black or other pigment. Such rare specimens are normally marked "Warburton's Patent" in large writing letters and this mark relates to Peter Warburton's 1810 patent for printing in metallic colours.

These often charming stipple-engraved bat-prints provide a convenient link between the early hybrid hard-paste and the later New Hall bone china, for a completely new body was introduced in the 1813–15 period. The new body (*see* picture 220) was lighter and whiter and on some of these later bone chinas there appears for the first time the name mark "New Hall", printed within a double lined circle (*see* page 144). This name (but not the mark) was certainly in use at an earlier period – it occurs in catalogue descriptions as early as 1802 and Duvivier used the term "the new Hal porcelaine manufactory" in his 1790 letter to Duesbury.

It would seem that most writers have confused the issue of marks by illustrating written pattern numbers

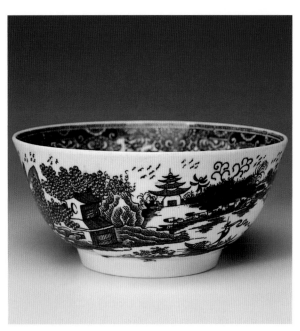

169 A large New Hall bowl, transfer-printed in underglaze blue, with typical mock-Chinese landscape and intricate inner border design. This and similar prints occur on a large range of New Hall porcelains but mainly teawares. Diameter 22cm (8¾in), c.1785–90, Godden collection.

or describing these in words, stating that the New Hall pattern numbers were prefixed with "No" or "N". It is often so written but by no means invariably, and I could quote ten or more firms of the same period that also used such common abbreviations for the word "number" when marking their standard designs with the relevant pattern number. Do remember that the pre-1790 New Hall porcelains seldom bore a pattern number at all. The (ungilt) blue-and-white pieces were not marked and, in the case of the standard tea sets, it was only the main pieces that bore a pattern number. Saucers, teabowls, and coffee cups were to all intents and purposes never marked with a number, although New Hall-type pieces from other factories often bear pattern numbers.

No standard factory mark appears on the early hybrid hard-paste New Hall porcelains. A blue-printed crowned lion rampant mark does very rarely occur on some blue-printed porcelains, which may or may not be of New Hall origin, c.1785. This device has been referred to as a copy of the earlier Frankenthal factory mark but the crest bears little resemblance to the German mark. I have mentioned previously the hand-written "Warburton's Patent" mark (with crown above) that occurs on gold-printed wares of the 1810–14 period. Some painted workmen's or painters' personal tally marks also occur in the 1800–20 period,

of which the most frequent and characteristic is the "F"-like device shown. The retailer's name mark "E. Cotton" of Edinburgh also occurs on some teawares of the same period. The bone-china wares made in the approximate period 1815–20 can, but do not always, bear a printed name mark (*see* pictures 221 and 222 and Chapter 8, p.178).

The later New Hall bone china, produced after about 1825, had little character, or rather individuality, and the factory was ill-equipped to compete with the very many large and small firms producing the same basic body. The main partners had died; there was no drive and the works seem to have gradually declined until, in March 1831, the factory, flint mill, and land were offered for sale by auction. They were not then sold but were advertised to be let in August and September 1832. In October 1835 the stock of the "Valuable & Extensive stock of burnished gold china" was offered for sale, the auction notice then stating, "The New Hall Company are declining business and have let the premises, which they now occupy, with immediate possession".

Nevertheless the name "New Hall" was continued up to 1956 by various firms situated on the original site, the last being the New Hall Pottery Co. Ltd, in the 1899–1956 period, and some of these later firms legitimately used the description "New Hall" on their usually earthenware products. Strangely these 20th-century New Hall earthenwares are rarely come across.

The standard books on New Hall porcelains are G.E. Stringer's *New Hall Porcelain* (Art Trade Press, 1949); David Holgate's *New Hall and Its Imitators* (Faber, 1971) and his updated *New Hall* (Faber, 1987); Anthony de Saye Hutton's *A Guide to New Hall Porcelain Patterns* (Barrie & Jenkins, 1990), which lists or illustrates many of the New Hall patterns; and my more recent contribution, the large *New Hall Porcelains* (Antique Collectors' Club, 2004). G. Grey's New Hall chapter in *English Porcelain 1745–1850*, edited by R.J. Charleston, is a most useful contribution as is the same authority's paper in *Transactions of the English Ceramic Circle*, Vol.8, Part 1, 1971. The *Collectors' Guide* of April 1971 contains articles by Mrs Holgate and myself under the general heading

170 A neat "Factory Z" silver-shape teapot and matching milk jug, from a grouping having possible links both with Liverpool and with Staffordshire. The factory or factories produced attractive New Hall-styled tewares. Pattern number "114" on both pieces, creamer 10.75cm (4¼in) high, c.1790–1800, Godden Reference collection.

"The Total Look of New Hall". The reader is also referred to Pat Preller's *A Partial Reconstruction of the New Hall Pattern Book* (privately published, 2003).

Note that not all simple floral sprig designs are of New Hall origin. The so-called New Hall patterns were popular, inexpensive period designs and, as such, featured in the pattern book of nearly every factory. In particular the products of the then unidentified factories that Mr Holgate originally termed "Factory X", "Factory Y", and "Factory Z" can be very close in style to the New Hall productions (*see* pictures 170, 196–201, and 205).

All these New Hall simple floral designs have a timeless charm and even now such teabowls and saucers are very reasonably priced, although this is obviously not the case with the rare patterns or the scarce shapes.

Chamberlain, *c.1788–1852*

| *See* pictures 17 and 171–6

The trail of hybrid hard-paste porcelains takes us to the city of Worcester next, to the works of Robert Chamberlain. I have explained in the preceding chapter

how, in 1788, Chamberlain left the main Worcester factory to set himself up as a decorator and retailer and how at first he was content to decorate blanks made at the Caughley factory in Shropshire (*see* pictures 94–5 and p.76). But at an unknown date sometime between 1789 and December 1793 Chamberlain commenced the manufacture of his own porcelains at Worcester.

A sample of this Chamberlain porcelain (a cup of pattern 55) was analysed at the North Staffordshire College of Technology with the following result:

Silica	68.61%
Alumina	23.52%
Potash	3.61%
Soda	1.27%
Lime	1.14%
Ferric Oxide	0.34%
Magnesia	0.16%
Loss (calcined at 950°C/1742°F)	0.34%

This is remarkably similar, in its main constituents, to a Bristol analysis and to a New Hall one published by G.E. Stringer. A piece was also tested at the British Museum Research Laboratory by x-ray diffraction analysis and reported as being a hard-paste porcelain.

Henry Sandon, Paul Rado, and I also submitted a fragment of a hunting pattern tea set of about 1795 to the Worcester hard-paste kiln, which reaches 1,435°C (2,615°F), at which temperature a New Hall fragment had melted into a shapeless mass. Of the Chamberlain

171

172

pieces, Henry Sandon commented: "The Chamberlain piece was a great surprise – it certainly looks to be a hard or near hard-paste body but which was never fired up as high as its potential. At our 1,435°C temperature the body held well and even became more translucent."

Although the thin fragment retained its shape in the hard-paste kiln, it was probably originally fired at about 1,300°C (2,372°F), still quite a high temperature. The glost firing was, as might be expected, lower and in this case the glaze bubbled and blistered in a kiln reaching 1,220°C (2,228°F).

On all counts the early Chamberlain body can be regarded as a hybrid hard-paste and it was certainly able to stand a hard firing very much better than the New Hall body.

As to the introduction of Chamberlain porcelain, entries in the Chamberlain account books suggest that he was making, or about to make, his own wares in 1791, and monies paid to modellers and throwers in the latter part of this year confirm this impression. The production of Chamberlain's earliest porcelain was probably rather limited and he certainly continued to decorate some Caughley blanks for several years after he was making his own porcelains. By January 1796, when the following letter was sent from the factory, the output would seem to have increased:

Sir,

By a later material improvement of our kilns we have been enabled to make much larger quantity of china, in consequence of which Messrs Chamberlain will be now happy in the favour of your orders… On every painted teapot we write 'warranted' which never having in one instance failed…

In other words the teapots did not crack when filled with near-boiling water.

The early Chamberlain porcelains that were made between 1791 and 1796 were seldom marked and even pattern numbers were not used before about 1794, although there were at least 32 numbered designs in production by February 1794. The early unmarked examples (such as picture 171) are rare and little known.

171 Three early Chamberlain-Worcester milk or cream jugs, which are decorated with simple, early, Oriental-looking designs. Right example 11.5cm (4½in) high, c.1791–5, Godden Reference collection.

172 A collection of Chamberlain hybrid hard-paste porcelain: a rare pickle stand, a cabbage-leaf jug that was decorated to a special order, and a moulded tumbler – all in the style of the modeller John Toulouse. Pickle stand 23cm (9in) high, c.1795–8, Godden collection.

173 A Chamberlain-Worcester spiral-fluted teabowl and saucer, finely decorated in typical Worcester style. Dated "1794" under saucer. Diameter of saucer 14cm (5½in), 1794, Worcester Works Museum collection.

The later oval standard shapes (*see* picture 17) are described in the January 1796 inventory as "Bell fluted" or as "shanked" and "new fluted". In fact, shanked and fluted teapots, creamers (*see* picture 171), and other teawares were included in a stock-taking list of December 1793 in the biscuit, or unglazed, state, so they were of Chamberlain's own make, not Caughley blanks. This December 1793 list includes:

40 teapots, sorted in biscuit	valued at	6/8d
50 teapot stands and spoon trays in biscuit	" "	8/4d
70 dozen (840) ewers, sorted	" "	£7/0/0d
160 sugar boxes	" "	£1/6/8d
230 dozen pressed and plain coffee cups	" "	£23/0/0d

The low value that was put on the undecorated stock is quite remarkable. Teapots at 2d each, 120 cream ewers to the pound, etc show, if the figures were truly realistic, the basic low cost of the initial manufacturing process.

Let us look in more detail at the first entry "40 teapots, sorted". I think "sorted" must mean that more than one shape was included in the accounts. It could also refer to the different sizes. It can hardly refer to the pattern because the pots were not yet glazed. I feel sure that one of these Chamberlain teapot shapes was very similar to the contemporary New Hall turreted teapot of the "silver-shape". Tea sets of the same early period included spoon trays – a component soon discontinued – and sometimes low Chelsea-ewers (*see* picture 171, centre) of the type made at Caughley, Derby, Lowestoft, and at the New Hall works.

Many of the early patterns were simple Chinese-figure designs often rather naively painted (*see* picture 171). The shape is very much in the New Hall style, but then several manufacturers made rather similar shapes. This painted pattern also occurs on Dr Wall Worcester wares and it occurs again in the Chamberlain list as number 9 "Hunting pattern in compartments" (at £2-12-6 for a complete tea service). Here we have a little-known early Chamberlain pattern on a rare jug form of about 1795.

I will not dwell too long on the Chamberlain useful wares for the subject and the range of patterns is vast. But it is important to point out that at an early date Chamberlain was making ornamental wares (*see* picture 174) and quite complicated and imposing centrepieces for the table. The January 1796 inventory lists (in the biscuit room) a figure of Apollo and in the Christmas 1795 stock-taking list we find listed "1 pickle-stand, Apollo, glazed 10/6d" (*see* picture 172, centre). Such a completed piece was sold to Michael Loveley of Honiton in November 1798; the sales entry then read "1 rich 4-shell pickle-stand with figure of Apollo, £3/3/0d".

In the late 1790s Chamberlain's produced a huge array of finely and often richly decorated porcelains ranging from magnificent dinner and dessert services (*see* picture 175) to thimbles. It would seem, however, that Chamberlain's did not really seek to compete with Thomas Turner of Caughley in the production of blue-and-white wares, except in their traditional "Royal Lily" or "Queen Charlotte" pattern (a very formal compartmented floral design) and in a single mock Oriental landscape design. The story of this factory is completed in Chapter 9, which is where I relate how the present Royal Worcester company came to be formed and how it related to the Chamberlain firm. You would be well advised to keep a good look out for examples of this early Chamberlain-Worcester porcelain.

For a full account of the history of Chamberlain's as porcelain manufacturers and for a good selection of illustrations I refer the reader to my earlier book *Chamberlain-Worcester Porcelain 1788–1852* (Barrie & Jenkins, 1982).

Grainger, *c.*1805–87

Just as in 1788 Chamberlain left the main Worcester company and set up on his own account, so in turn did Thomas Grainger leave Chamberlain. The early Grainger-Worcester porcelains are seldom marked, and in shape and in the added patterns they are very similar to the Chamberlain pieces of the same period. I give more details of this factory in Chapter 9, but I should mention here that his early porcelains are of the class of hybrid hard-paste. Some of the teawares are featured in my *British Porcelain, an Illustrated Guide* but the standard specialist book is *Grainger's Worcester Porcelain* by Henry and John Sandon (Barrie & Jenkins, 1989). These researchers have questioned the accepted date of establishment of the Grainger Works (which is claimed in later printed marks to be 1801), showing that it must have been between the date Grainger became a Freeman of Worcester (September 1805) and the earliest dated Grainger porcelain of 26 September 1807.

Late Caughley, *c.*1795–9

| *See* picture 177

I have already given a general account of the standard Salopian or Caughley porcelains in Chapter 6, where I explained that the body was a soapstone one similar to that employed at the Dr Wall factory at Worcester. This was the case for the major part of the factory's existence under Thomas Turner, *c.*1775–99.

174 A superb but typical Chamberlain-Worcester vase, decorated with a titled (inscribed under the picture) classical figure-subject panel in the style of John Wood. The gilding is typical of this factory. Painted "Chamberlains Worcester" mark, 31cm (12¼in) high, *c.*1795, Godden of Worthing.

175

176

177

175 Representative parts of a Chamberlain-Worcester dessert service.
The different centres make a popular harlequin service – the
dolphin-supported centrepiece has a view of Worcester and the
factory. Printed (Prince Regent) marks, tureen 23.5cm (9¼in)
high, c.1815, Godden of Worthing.

176 A Chamberlain-Worcester teapot and stand, richly and finely
decorated. This is basically the popular Oriental-inspired
pattern 75, but it was adapted to take the Arms of Sir Charles
Malet. Painted mark "Chamberlains Worcester, Warranted.
No 75" inside the cover, 25cm (10in) long, c.1802–5,
Sothebys (this piece was formerly within the Nelson A.
Rockefeller collection).

177 A rare, late Caughley oval hybrid hard-paste sugar basin. It is
rather thickly potted and has body tears. Impressed oval Royal
Arms mark, 14.5cm (5¾in) high, c.1798–99, Mr and Mrs Roger
Edmundson collection.

There are, however, some pieces which appear to
be of Turner's period that are of a totally different
body, having only a trace of magnesia and therefore
soapstone and having a cold, hard appearance. This
is in fact a type of hard-paste porcelain. The difficulty
is to determine if these pieces are pre-1799, true
Caughley porcelains that were made under Turner's

management, or if they were made after the Coalport
partners had acquired the works. The trouble is that
the new owners worked the same site and used the old
moulds and the Turner copper plates.

To ascertain this information we need an impressed
"Salopian" example of this hard-paste type, or a piece
bearing a date prior to October 1799. There are some
pieces of this Shropshire hard-paste bearing an
impressed Royal Arms device, a mark that is found
on several wasters at the Caughley factory site. The
significance of this mark is unknown but it may be
relevant that in the closing-down sale of Turner's stock
he advertised it as the stock "of the Royal Salopian
porcelain manufactory". The Coalport partners did
not, as far as I am aware, claim any royal association
and this Royal Arms mark was probably used by
Turner before his retirement.

Picture 177 shows an oval covered sugar basin
bearing this mark. In general style it is very different
from our picture of the normal Caughley porcelains but
it does have near parallels in Chamberlain-Worcester,
New Hall, Coalport, and other porcelains. The body

itself is well worth study. It is very cold and hard-looking, but is also very poorly potted with prominent firing cracks and other faults. This is in sharp contrast to the standard Caughley soapstone body, which, like that used at Worcester, seems to have given few manufacturing problems. On the evidence of this one piece the introduction of the new harder body was not a success. The reason for its introduction is not absolutely certain – perhaps Turner was trying to emulate the Chamberlain body or the one employed by his competitors just up river at Coalport.

When a factory such as Caughley suddenly changes from its proven and highly successful soapstone body to a completely different hybrid hard-paste porcelain, we can judge there was some good reason – even if it was a case of following the fashion. Usually it happens as a cost-cutting device. A good account of the putative Caughley hybrid hard-paste wares is given by R.S. Edmundson, "Separating Caughley from Coalport", *Journal of the Northern Ceramic Society*, Vol.7, 1989.

Coalport (Rose & Co.), *c.*1791–1815

| *See* pictures 178–81

We cannot at present be sure when the main Coalport porcelain factory commenced production. The early writers had access to some documents that maintained that the first works were at Calcut on the Jackfield side of the river Severn, opposite Coalport. These works, carried on by "Mr Rose, in conjunction with a Mr Blakeway", were soon transferred across to Coalport. The Chamberlain factory records contain a reference to a letter sent on 13 June 1791 to "Mr Rose, manufactory, Salop" but this could have been intended for Rose while first employed at the Caughley factory, not at Coalport. However, early in 1793 there were seemingly two separate factories in the locality, Turner's (at Caughley) and Blakeway's (presumably at Coalport), for there is a letter dated 16 February 1793 that states: "...I could not get any oval trifle dishes at the price you mention, nor any round ones from Blakeways...the cream ewers I had off Turner are cheaper than Blakeways".

Unfortunately we do not know if the Blakeway (and Rose) factory was then situated at Jackfield or if it was then at Coalport. We do, however, have a diary entry made on 1 June 1796 that clearly states that it was then at Coalport near the famous tar springs: "about 100 yards from this...a porcelain manufactory lately established".

The *Shropshire Journal* of 24 August 1796 reported that the Prince and Princess of Orange visited the Coalbrookdale ironworks, the cannon foundry, and the tar springs and then proceeded to the Coalport china factory "where His Highness bought some pieces of Mr Rose". This report serves to remind us that the factory was in the heart of the Industrial Revolution country, a district steeped in history and with many popular sights for the traveller. The locality is now an interesting and thriving open-air museum. This 1796 report also tells us that Mr Rose was probably the dominant partner, having superseded Edward Blakeway. The Coalport firm now traded as Rose & Co. or, rarely, as Rose, Blakeway & Co. There were in fact three partners in the 18th century – John Rose, Richard Rose, and Edward Blakeway.

Joseph Plymley's *General View of the Agriculture of Shropshire* of 1803 tells us, "At Coalport coloured china of all sorts and of exquisite taste and beauty is made...and in which...including its dependencies, the most china is manufactured of any works of that sort in Great Britain, there are employed about 250 persons." The "dependencies" no doubt included the Caughley factory, which had been purchased by the Coalport partners in October 1799 and which was continued by them until about 1814. The claim that Rose & Co. produced at Caughley and Coalport more porcelain than any other manufacturer was probably true.

Our present-day knowledge of the early wares is somewhat restricted. We do not know about the very

178

178 Three early John Rose, Calcut, or Coalport hybrid hard-paste examples. Printed in underglaze blue incorporating typical mock-Oriental landscape designs. The mug has some gilding, including initials and the date "1795". Centre jug (dated "1798") 20.5cm (8½in) high, *c.*1795–1800, jugs: Godden collection, mug: Revd Maurice Wright.

179 Right, a rare, spiral-fluted, Coalport moulded jug, in hybrid hard-paste, with elaborate handle. Printed in underglaze blue with a mock-Oriental landscape, engraved in a typical basic style, 20.5cm (8¼in) high, *c.*1798–1800, Godden collection.

earliest pieces that were made on the Jackfield side of the river and we have little knowledge of the earliest true Coalport pieces too. In contrast, however, we do have a very good idea of the post-1799 porcelains made by the Coalport partners at their newly acquired Caughley factory, for the site has yielded thousands of interesting wasters. These Caughley wasters were of a very hard type that, when submitted to the Worcester kilns, stood up to a temperature of 1,350°C (2,462°F), far better than a piece of New Hall of the hybrid hard-paste period.

I had a John Rose & Co. example analysed and this gave the following result:

Silica	75.94%
Alumina	18.95%
Potash	2.12%
Soda	1.21%
Lime	0.78%
Ferric oxide	0.34%
Magnesia	0.17%
Titanic oxide	0.02%
Loss (calcined at 950°C/1742°F)	0.33%

I think most authorities will acknowledge that such a body is of the hybrid hard-paste type. Certainly it looks it. It would be difficult to find a more compact and heavy body, and a fracture appears conchoidal.

Now the hybrid hard-paste Rose & Co. porcelains of the type found on the Caughley site would post-date October 1799 and so the problem remains: what

180 Fragments of hybrid hard-paste porcelain tewares from the Caughley site but dating from the period when the site was run by John Rose, of Coalport. They reveal simple Chinese Export Market- or New Hall-style enamel designs and are shown here with a similarly styled Caughley-Coalport coffee cup. The cup is 6.25cm (2½in) high, *c*.1800–1805, in the Godden Reference collection.

porcelain did the Coalport partners produce before this? There is some reason for accepting that in the mid-1790s this body was of the soapstone-type similar to that made at Worcester and at Caughley. This is the most likely theory and is one supported by Charles Hatchett's diary. On Saturday 28 May 1796 this very knowledgeable and enquiring traveller and diarist visited Worcester where he "went to see the porcelain manufactory belonging to Messrs Flight and Barr. I have observed [he noted] that the Steatites of Cornwall is used as an ingredient…" This would be the Cornish soapstone which, as we already know, formed a vital part of the Worcester mix. When Hatchett visited the Coalport factory four days later he observed: "The ware is like that of Worcester and the materials are the same" (*The Hatchett Diary*, edited by Arthur Raistrick, D. Bradford Barton Ltd, Truro, 1967.) If we can believe this account, the Coalport porcelain of the 1796 period was of the soapstone type – and yet the post-1799 Rose & Co. Caughley fragments are of a completely different body with only a trace (0.17 per cent) of magnesia.

As the New Hall hard-paste patent ran out in 1796 other manufacturers would then have been free to experiment with and use (if they so wished) the china-clay and china-stone to make a translucent hybrid hard-paste porcelain. At some time between June 1796 and 1800, the Coalport partners switched to a harder body. We can narrow the period to the two years 1796–8, when we consider the blue-printed jug shown in picture 178. The jug in the centre is of the hybrid hard-paste porcelain and is dated 1798. The mug on the left is dated 1795, and therefore is of the pre-Coalport, Calcut period. The jug on the right relates to a class of post-1796 John Rose Coalport porcelains.

While most blue-printed Coalports are tewares, some imposing moulding jug forms were produced (*see* picture 179). In general the Rose & Co. pieces are thicker in the potting and heavier in weight than the earlier Caughley examples and of course the body itself, or rather the thickly applied glaze, looks and feels harder. The blue is a lighter and brighter tone too.

Moving away from the blue-and-white porcelains, which in general terms emulate the Caughley styles, mention must be made of the overglaze simple floral designs in the New Hall manner. Much teaware was decorated in this popular style and (helpfully to us now) the shapes were quite different from those employed by the Staffordshire New Hall company. I show a few sample fragments from the Shropshire site in picture 180. The basic and characteristic Rose & Co. shapes are featured in my book *Coalport and Coalbrookdale Porcelains* (revised edition, Antique Collector's Club, 1981). Please also refer to R.S. Edmundson, "Separating Caughley from Coalport", *Journal of the Northern Ceramic Society*, Vol.7, 1989.

Surveying Coalport porcelains of the 1800–15 period, the richness of decoration is impressive. Of course many pieces are modestly decorated and some have only a slight pattern in gold, but the so-called "Japan" patterns (*see* picture 181) really stand out, with their areas of a deep underglaze blue with overglaze red, green, and gilt embellishments. Such Japan patterns are normally associated with the Derby factory but they were common to most ceramic manufacturers. They were relatively cheap to produce, being repetitive broad designs that could be painted by apprentices*, and yet to the buying public they looked rich and a "good buy". The John Rose company produced a great many such patterns and probably made more of this class than the Derby factory at that period. These Japan patterns were extremely popular in the 18th and 19th centuries. In general they emulate the earlier Japanese Imari styles**.

181

182

181 An "old oval" John Rose Coalport teapot and cover decorated with a very popular colourful "Japan" pattern. Several other factories produced rather similar shapes and patterns, teapot 14.5cm (5¾in) high, *c*.1805, Godden of Worthing.

182 A selection of John Rose Coalport lobed-edged plates, decorated in a variety of styles but all of good quality. Unmarked, except for the top centre plate, which bears the rare name mark "Coalbrookdale". Average diameter 23.5cm (9¼in), *c*.1805–10, Godden of Worthing.

---

* Some versions, particularly the Worcester Japan patterns, are of a superb quality and would have been costly.
** See my *Oriental Export Market Porcelain* (Granada, London, 1979).

The hybrid hard-paste Coalport examples occur on teawares and dinner services – as well as on mugs, jugs, and ornamental objects. Remember, however, that these colourful, popular designs were by no means confined to Coalport.

The Coalport factory, being a market leader in the early 1800s, produced a bewildering range of shapes and patterns (*see* picture 182 for some examples). The picturesque location of the works in the valley of the river Severn, just downstream from Ironbridge, is shown on the front of the large Coalport vase that is illustrated in picture 186. This piece was like many other Coalport vases decorated at Thomas Baxter's London decorating studio (*see* p.156 and pictures 187–8).

I can mention here only the blue-and-white pieces, New Hall-type designs, and the Japan patterns, which represent the main types of Rose's early Coalport hard-paste porcelains. Very many other designs and shapes

are featured in my Coalport book and further New Hall-type designs and characteristic John Rose Coalport shapes are illustrated within David Holgate's paper "Polychrome and Hard-Paste Caughley Porcelain", *Transactions of the English Ceramic Circle*, Vol.7, Part 1, 1968. The later post-1815 John Rose porcelains will be discussed in Chapter 9.

Reynolds, Horton & Rose; Anstice, Horton & Rose, 1800–1814

| *See* pictures 183–5

I have in the previous section deliberately mentioned "Rose & Co." on many occasions rather than refer in a general way to Coalport as one factory. The reason is simply that there were at Coalport, in this period, two separate thriving factories, a mere stone's throw apart.

The rival factory was established in June 1800, with the first partners being William Reynolds, William Horton, and Thomas Rose, but three years later, after Reynolds's death, Robert Anstice joined the two remaining partners and they traded as Anstice, Horton & Rose, or as Anstice, Horton & Co. The factory was sold on to the John Rose company in 1814, after the partnership had been dissolved, on 7 February of that year. For seemingly the whole life of the factory, 1800–14, it was only hybrid hard-paste porcelain that

183 Representative pieces of a Thomas Rose Coalport dessert service. These pieces have been painted with a colourful, but broadly painted, "Japan" pattern. The tureen (which is one of a pair) is 13cm (5¼in) high, *c*.1805–10, all pieces Godden of Worthing.

184 A colourful Thomas Rose (Anstice, Horton & Rose) hybrid hard-paste Coalport part tea service, showing typical shapes. Pattern number "1339", teapot 26cm (10¼in) long, *c*.1812–14, Godden of Worthing.

183

184

185 An Anstice, Horton & Rose Coalport punch bowl painted with a popular pattern. Pattern number "696", diameter 20cm (11in), c.1805–10, Godden of Worthing.

was produced. In the main, useful tablewares were made decorated with at least 1,419 different patterns plus the unnumbered blue-and-white designs. A sale advertisement published in *The Times* in January 1814 most probably relates to the auctioning off of the stock that belonged to the Anstice partnership. The advertisement, quoted below in part, suggests a large and varied output including very colourful patterns:

...on account of the manufacturers and in consequence of a dissolution of partnership.

The genuine and extensive stock, consisting of several superb and costly dinner and dessert services, in imitation of fine old Dresden and rich Japan pattern déjeuné services and supper sets, cabinet and ornamental vases, cups and cans, tea and coffee equipages and bowls, pencilled [a contemporary name for painted] in landscape, birds, fruit and flowers, figures and various designs and painted in rich colours, and superbly gilt; an assortment of blue and white of every description and a profusion of white china ...

The Anstice, Horton & Rose shapes are very close copies of the standard John Rose forms, although there are slight differences when the two versions are placed side by side. (Such comparisons are featured in my *Coalport and Coalbrookdale Porcelains*). Apart from the key shapes shown there, and in specimens included

in my reference collection, we have a further source of information on these little-known wares. Strangely, this source is the pattern book of the rival John Rose company, where there are various references to the Anstice, Horton & Rose numbers – for some designs were made by both firms. For example, in the John Rose pattern book is the design on the punch bowl that is shown in picture 185. The John Rose number for this pattern is 319 but there also appears the notation that it was the rival partnership's design number 696. The higher number appears on this bowl. This particular design was popular, colourful, and occurs on several Anstice shapes – however, note that the pattern number must read "696".

An array of these unmarked Anstice porcelains will startle most collectors for the diversity and decorative merits of the wares. This was a short-lived factory that is almost unknown to many ceramic students, and yet the porcelains must surely repay any close study and attention. There is a display of such porcelains at the Ironbridge Gorge Museum on the original factory site – this, and the research on these Coalport porcelains, is due to the works of the Shropshire historians Mr and Mrs Roger Edmundson.

186

187

Thomas Baxter decorated porcelains

| See pictures 186–9

Thomas Baxter senior (*b*.1760), assisted by his son of the same name and a few other painters and gilders, established their decorating studio at Goldsmith Street, Clerkenwell, by May 1797 – having moved to London from Worcester. At the Baxter studio a wonderful array of porcelain was embellished. The white blanks came from the Coalport factory in the main but some Chinese and French hard-paste porcelain was also used. The Coalport porcelains at this pre-1815 period were of the hybrid hard-paste type.

The finest compositions are usually signed with "T. Baxter", and with the year added. It is assumed that such signed work is that of Thomas Baxter Jr (1782–1821), owing to the fact that his work can postdate the likely date of death of his father. Much of the studio decorated porcelain bears groups of closely arranged flowers (*see* pictures 187 and 189), unsigned but with its origin usually indicated by the additional use of one or more of the characteristic gilt borders (*see* pictures 187–9). In addition to this some Coalport porcelains, mainly teawares, were embellished with simple designs and gilding was also applied to otherwise inexpensive blue-printed wares.

The Baxter studio was but one of several such establishments that flourished in the approximate period 1790–1820 but it is the best known, as the important examples are signed or initialled. A detailed watercolour drawing of the studio by Thomas Baxter Jr was exhibited at the Royal Academy and is now in the Victoria and Albert Museum. It is reproduced in my *Coalport and Coalbrookdale Porcelains* (Antique Collectors' Club, 1981), Plate 42. That work and the more recent *Encyclopaedia of British Porcelain Manufacturers* (Barrie & Jenkins, 1988) illustrate typical Baxter decorated porcelains.

The London studio seemingly closed in about 1814 if not before (I do not know of any signed and dated pieces after 1809). Thomas Baxter Jr then returned to

186 A magnificent Coalport covered vase. The front panel has been painted with a titled view of the "Coalbrookdale China Manufactory" and the river Severn. The panel of fruit on the reverse side was painted by Thomas Baxter, 54.5cm (21½in) high, *c*.1805, Wells Collection, Los Angeles County Museum of Art.

187 A John Rose Coalport squat vase, in hybrid hard-paste porcelain. The flower painting and gilt borders are typical of Baxter's London decorating studio, 19cm (7½in) high, *c*.1805, Godden of Worthing.

188 A superb set of John Rose Coalport vases in the hybrid hard-paste body. The panels were painted by Thomas Baxter. The figures reputedly depicting Lady Hamilton. The floral painting and gilding is typical of Baxter's London studio work. Signed "T. Baxter" and dated "1801", centre vase *c*.25cm (10in) high, 1801, unfortunately stolen from Godden of Worthing.

189 A large John Rose Coalport moulded bulb pot of a characteristic shape (pieced cover missing). The flower painting and gilding is typical of Baxter's London decorating studio. 28.5cm (11¼in) long, *c*.1805, Godden of Worthing.

188

189

his birthplace, Worcester, where he was employed by the Flight, Barr & Barr management. He then moved to Swansea where he remained during the 1816–18 period. In 1818 he returned to Flight at Worcester but by July 1819 he had moved to the Chamberlain factory. He died on 18 April 1821. Signed examples of Thomas Baxter's work are rare and rightly costly.

Davenport, 1794–1887

Davenport is actually a family, not a place, name. The Davenport factories (there were four of them) were situated at Longport in the Staffordshire Potteries. At first only earthenwares were made but, from an unknown period (about 1800), good-quality porcelains were also produced. The early pieces made before around 1810 were of the compact hybrid hard-paste type but later bone china was adopted.

The earliest Davenport teawares have not yet been identified, but they were probably rather similar to the New Hall porcelains. There are some attractive and well-potted dessert wares, some of which bear the standard impressed Davenport name mark along with the anchor device. Typical forms are shown in *Davenport China, Earthenware & Glass 1794–1887* by T.A. Lockett and G.A. Godden (Barrie & Jenkins, 1989). The later Davenport bone china is discussed in Chapter 9.

Miles Mason, *c.*1804–13

| *See* pictures 190–91

Miles Mason (1752–1822), the London china dealer, had, in the late 1790s, been engaged in two different manufacturing partnerships, one at Liverpool for the production of porcelain and the other at Lane Delph in Staffordshire Potteries for the making of earthenwares. These two partnerships were dissolved in June 1800.

The Lane Delph pottery was subsequently worked by Miles Mason as a "china manufactory" and had been so occupied "for some years past", to quote from a November 1805 sale advertisement. We cannot, however, be sure when this was opened as a porcelain works, for Miles Mason's famous and oft-quoted advertisement of October 1804 gives the impression that the Mason porcelains were a recent innovation and Mason appears to have been directly engaged with his London business until 1802: "...Miles Mason, late of Fenchurch Street, London...has established a manufactory at Lane Delph...upon the principle of the Indian [meaning Chinese] and Seve [Sèvres] china..." The advertisement from the *Morning Herald* is quoted in full in my *Godden's Guide to Mason's China and the*

190 A Miles Mason Staffordshire hybrid hard-paste porcelain jug, of a characteristic shape. Painted with a widely popular simple design (often termed the "knitting-wool" pattern due to the tangled wool-like motif at the top), 15.25cm (6in) high, *c.*1805, Godden collection.

Ironstone Wares (Antique Collectors' Club, 1980) and in my more recent *Godden's Guide to Ironstone, Stone & Granite Wares* (Antique Collectors' Club, 1999).

Miles Mason moved from Lane Delph to Fenton in 1807 and a second factory was opened there in 1811. By this period he had built up a good reputation, as is shown by the following report written by the manager of Wedgwood's London retail showroom, "Mr Mason of Lane Delft is in town and he called upon me and in the course of conversation said that we should sell immense quantities of china here, if we had it and that he should be very happy to make it for you. His china is I believe very good and he has great orders for it..."

In general the early Miles Mason porcelains are, in decoration, very similar to those that were made earlier at Liverpool. Many simple floral designs in the New Hall tradition occur, but on Mason shapes (*see* picture 190). Other teawares bear coloured-over prints of Chinese figures (*see* picture 191) and a large selection of the early wares bear blue-printed Chinese-style landscape designs – the Pagoda or Broseley pattern – rather similar to the later willow pattern. These underglaze blue prints link with the earlier Liverpool porcelains and it is often impossible to tell in which site the unmarked Mason porcelains were made, though the shapes can be a good guide.

The later, post-1807 porcelains became much more decorative. Finely painted vases were made, as were dessert services, but the teawares predominate and are often just as fine as the Spode or Flight, Barr & Barr porcelains. Some of the Mason stipple-engraved or etched bat-printed designs are of the highest order and quite individual. The Mason porcelains are of the hybrid hard-paste type, at least the examples made before 1810 are, after which the paste appears to have been changed to the bone-china body.

A fragment of a mandarine pattern oval teapot stand of the 1805–10 period was analysed:

Silica	63.46%
Alumina	26.46%
Potash	3.25%
Soda	1.79%
Magnesia	1.76%
Lime	1.28%
Ferric oxide	0.04%
Not determined	1.64%

This result is very near the hybrid hard-paste Chamberlain body, although this Mason analysis may have been affected slightly by glaze on the sample submitted. In firing tests the Mason fragments stood up well to high temperatures nearing 1,400°C (2,552°F) and, using this method, the body seems very much harder than New Hall. The translucency of some Mason pieces can, however, be rather poor and in general the pieces are thickly potted.

In 1813 the famous Mason's Patent Ironstone China, a hard, durable earthenware, was introduced. The patent had been taken out in the name of Charles James Mason, who was Miles Mason's third son. I believe that by this period Miles had all but retired. Certainly the new ironstone body proved extremely popular and I think his sons would have been more interested in developing and producing their new body than in producing porcelains in keen competition with many other manufacturers. For all practical purposes I think that the manufacture of Miles Mason's porcelain practically ceased in 1813 after being in production for about ten years only. Miles Mason died in April 1822. Subsequent Mason firms produced bone china after 1813. It should be noted that some early ironstone examples can show a degree of translucency, as the mix is vitrified in the high firing temperature.

The early Mason porcelains sometimes bear the impressed mark "M. MASON" but this normally occurs only on the more important pieces, such as teapots and by no means on all such pieces. A small impressed circle can occur on the foot-rims of some specimens.

Some blue-printed designs have a mock Chinese seal mark with "MILES" above and "MASON" below. It should be noted that many other manufacturers used the basic Oriental seal device in various forms (without the name) so you should not assume that all such seal marks indicate a Mason origin.

191 A selection of Miles Mason hybrid hard-paste porcelain teawares showing characteristic forms. Printed outline pattern (termed "The Boy at the Door"), coloured in and finished by hand. The pattern occurs on other makes but these shapes are Mason, teapot 14.5cm (51/2in) high, c.1805, Godden of Worthing.

Much research remains to be carried out on these porcelains. Reginald Haggar gave us a good foundation to build upon – see *The Masons of Lane Delph* (Lund Humphries, 1952), his excellent paper "Miles Mason", *Transactions of the English Ceramic Circle*, Vol.8, Part 2, 1972, and, importantly, his joint work with Elizabeth Adams, *Mason Porcelain and Ironstone 1796–1853* (Faber, 1977). Mason patterns and the characteristic forms are also featured in my specialist book *Godden's Guide to Mason's China and the Ironstone Wares* (Antique Collectors' Club, 1980 revised edition 1991) and in Deborah Skinner and Velma Young's book *Miles Mason Porcelain. A Guide to Patterns and Shapes* (City Museum & Art Gallery, Stoke, 1992). Also see Gaye Blake Roberts' book *Masons. The First Two Hundred Years* (Merrell Holberton Publishers Ltd, 1996).

Good selections of Mason Porcelain can be seen at The Potteries Museum at Hanley and, by appointment, at The University of Keele. For the latter see *The Raven Mason Collection* by Gaye Blake Roberts and John Twitchett (Keele University Press, 1997).

192 A selection of rare Turner hybrid hard-paste porcelain teawares. The teapot shown here bears the "Traveller" blue-printed design, which occurs on marked "Turner" earthenwares. The covered sugar bowls have characteristic moulded knobs and are hand-painted, teapot 14cm (5½in) high, *c*.1795–1805, Godden Reference collection.

Turner, *c*.1759–1806

We are concerned here with a famous Staffordshire earthenware potter, or rather a family of potters, who on occasions turned their attention to the manufacture of porcelain. The standard mark on their varied but always fine quality wares is the impressed name mark "TURNER". The founder of the firm was John Turner, 1738–87. His pottery was continued by his sons William (1762–1835) and John (1766–1824). John Turner was apprenticed in 1753 to Daniel Bird, a famous potter, and he seems to have been established on his own account at Lane End in 1759. I do not propose to discuss the various Turner earthenwares for you can readily turn to the standard book *The Turners of Lane End* by Bevis Hillier (Cory, Adams & Mackay, 1965) or see typical pieces featured in my *British Pottery, an Illustrated Guide*.

Turning to the very rare Turner porcelains, it seems likely that John Turner made some experiments in this field in the 1780s, just before his death in 1787. There is an impressed-marked "TURNER" small mug or tankard in The Potteries Museum at Hanley that relates to this period. Also there exists somewhere a documentary beaker that is inscribed "Lane End, July 1787", showing the interior of a pottery. This piece is linked with the much travelled Louis-Victor Gerverot, who reputedly agreed to teach Turner the secrets of

porcelain manufacture and to build his kilns in the 1786–7 period. This beaker is signed by the former New Hall artist Fidelle Duvivier and you may recall that Turner had been one of the original partners in the New Hall concern, c.1781–3.

It would appear that the young Turners, when they succeeded their father in 1787, ceased to manufacture porcelain for a period of years, but it seems on the evidence of some rare marked examples that they returned to this branch of the trade in about 1800. Some simple oval teapots and covered sugar bowls exist with the very rare impressed name mark "TURNER" (see picture 192). These were made in the hybrid hard-paste body. Other pieces were produced in a softer-looking body, the blue-and-white patterns included in picture 192 are typical Turner designs. The Turner porcelains can be extremely fine – perhaps too good and costly for the market. They are also very difficult to find today. As with other classes of English porcelain, the Turner wares offer very good scope for the keen collector, student, or researcher and no doubt in time we will be able to attribute with more certainty more porcelains to this famous family.

193 A selection of biscuit wasters from the Wolfe-Mason Islington site at Liverpool. The hardened-on but unglazed Oriental-style printed landscape patterns are typical and match finished examples. Left: waster fragment 10cm (4in) long, c.1797–9, Liverpool City Museum.

In 1803 the two Turners took John Glover and Charles Simpson as partners but in November John Turner retired from the partnership to join Minton, and on 27 March 1806 the last partnership was dissolved. The works were advertised and the wording is of some importance in our consideration of the porcelains: "An old established…manufactory, lately occupied by Messrs Turner & Co. at Lane End, in the Staffordshire Potteries; where the making of porcelain and earthenware, in all its branches, has been carried on to a great extent, for a great number of years…"

Any Turner porcelain must pre-date 1806 and in July of that year the two brothers were declared bankrupt. For further illustrations and information see Chapter 6 of my *Staffordshire Porcelain* (Granada, London, 1983).

Islington China Manufactory, Liverpool (Thomas Wolfe & Co.), c.1796–1800 +

| *See* pictures 193–95

In 1796 Thomas Wolfe, who had occupied and worked the Islington China Manufactory in Folly Lane, Liverpool, from February 1790, took two partners. These were John Lucock (or Luckcock) and Miles Mason, (see p.158) and the three traded at the factory as Thomas Wolfe & Co. Miles Mason was a leading

194

195

194 Two Wolfe-Mason milk jugs and a small (sugar) bowl. These are decorated in typical styles emulating the much favoured imported Chinese porcelain teawares. Jugs 11.5cm (4½in) high, c.1797–9, Godden Reference collection.

195 Two rare Wolfe-Mason hybrid hard-paste porcelain teapots, of characteristic shapes, and a hand-painted Chinese-shape plate with tinted foot-ring. Diameter of plate 19.75cm (7¾in), c.1797–9, Godden Reference collection.

chinaman in London and had been a great purchaser of the imported Chinese porcelains. When the East India Company decided to cease large-scale importations of this commodity in the early 1790s Mason must have looked round for an alternative source of supply and then to the partnership with Thomas Wolfe. Porcelain of the hybrid hard-paste type was made by this partnership working Pennington's old works. At the same time Mason was in partnership with George Wolfe at Lane Delph in the Staffordshire Potteries but this partnership was seemingly for making earthenwares, not porcelains.

Miles Mason had "married money" so he may well have provided the financial backing for both of these enterprises. He would also have provided a valuable retail outlet for their products in London for he was firmly established there as one of the leading dealers of the period.

We owe our initial knowledge of the porcelains produced by Wolfe & Co. at Liverpool in the late 18th century to the excavations of Professor Alan Smith. His finds, in the form of site wasters (*see* picture 193), are featured in the *Transactions of the English Ceramic Circle*, Vol.8, Part 2, 1972. These factory wasters include simple New Hall-type floral patterns and, as you might expect from a factory partly owned by a London chinaman, much blue-printed teawares with Chinese-style designs (*see* pictures 194 and 195).

I have located some of the Wolfe-Mason enamelled simple patterns in the style of New Hall and Chinese export teawares (*see* pictures 194 and 195) and one day the other articles that were made at the Islington China Manufactory will no doubt be identified and show the range of these Liverpool hybrid hard-paste porcelains of the 1796–1800 period.

The *London Gazette* of 5 July 1800 records the dissolution of this Liverpool partnership as from 7 June. The Staffordshire partnership had been dissolved two days earlier and we next hear of Miles Mason setting up on his own account in the Staffordshire Potteries. The Liverpool-made Wolfe & Co. porcelains do not bear a factory mark or a pattern number, and much further research needs to be carried out on this interesting class.

For further information refer to Chapter 2 of my *Godden's Guide to Mason's China and the Ironstone*

Wares (Antique Collectors' Club, 1980), *Godden's Guide to English Blue and White Porcelains*, and Trevor Markin's paper "Thomas Wolfe: Teawares at Liverpool and Stoke", *Journal of the Northern Ceramic Society*, Vol.7, 1989 is also helpful.

Other, unidentified manufacturers

I have already set out basic details about some of the known manufacturers of this class of hard-looking porcelains, those makers who sometimes at least marked their products. We are, however, left with a large number of pieces, very often of New Hall type, which do not seem to link with the known makers. The trouble is that we have more types of porcelain than known manufacturers! If we accept that the majority of these porcelains – of which the attractive teawares shown in picture 196 are a sample – were made in the 1785–1810 period, and if we then search the pottery directories and other contemporary records, we still don't get much closer to solving the problem.

Taking first William Tunnicliff's *Directory of Staffordshire* of *c*.1786, the only potters that were listed as making porcelain were (a) Heath, Warburton & Co., the New Hall partners and (b) Hugh Booth of Cliff Bank, Stoke.

Hugh Booth's working period at Cliff Bank would appear to be *c*.1781-9; he died in 1789. However that is not the end of the story, for the works were then continued by his brother Ephraim and, in the 1791–1802 period, the trading style was Ephraim Booth & Sons, and from 1802 to 1808 these sons, Hugh and Joseph, continued the pottery, which was later taken over by William Adams. The various Booths working at Stoke therefore cover the years 1781–1808, a period vital to our present researches. They were evidently of some standing as they are mentioned in contemporary Derby, Minton, and Wedgwood accounts, and yet I do not know of any marked examples of their products – but then the New Hall porcelains of the same period are unmarked, except for one special teapot now in the Victoria and Albert Museum.

I think we should seriously consider the Booths as probable manufacturers of very, very close copies of New Hall teawares. We must remember, however, that I have assumed that all the Booths working at the Cliff

196 Representative parts of a tea service, which is superbly potted and neatly decorated. The pattern was produced at several factories but this set is as yet not positively identified. It is a charmer nonetheless. Painted pattern numbers "11", ".11.", or "(11)", teapot 16.5cm (6½in) high, *c*.1790–1800, Godden Reference collection.

197 Two rare "Factory X" Oriental-shape sugar bowls, with their covers. They are neatly potted and decorated. The "X" class is now attributed to the Staffordshire partnership of A & E Keeling. The right example is marked with pattern number "94." in underglaze blue, 11.5cm (4½in) high, *c.*1800–1805, Godden collection.

Bank Pottery produced china or porcelain based purely on the evidence of one entry in Tunnicliff's *Directory* published in 1787. Hugh Booth's entry reads: "Booth Hugh, manufacturer of china, china glaze and Queens ware in all its various branches". The majority of the potters had the simplest of descriptions against their name – even Josiah Spode and John Turner had the one word "Potter". Here lies one of the problems: the brevity of the contemporary directory entries.

In the early 1800s there were several new firms listed in one or more directories as making porcelain, but of course not all these would have made the hybrid hard-paste wares we are now discussing. There was William Adams of Cobridge and Stoke, but one would have expected some at least of his porcelains to have been marked. I know nothing of potter John Blackwell of Cobridge, except that his working period was *c.*1784–1814. John Davenport of Longport worked from 1794 onwards. As previously stated, the marked Davenport dessert wares seem to post-date 1800 and we do not know if slightly earlier unmarked porcelain teawares were made. John and George Rogers of Longport (1784–1814) are also recorded as making porcelain, and John Yates of Shelton (1784–1835).

My researches on the various different Dissolution of Partnership notices of porcelain manufacturers has

also brought back to our attention several forgotten firms, such as Anthony & Enoch Keeling (*c.*1795–1815). In the Victoria and Albert Museum there is also an interesting pattern book as well as hybrid hard-paste teawares, but we still cannot link the book or the wares to a potter's name – the linking porcelains (*see* picture 205) being at present known as the "Pattern Book" class.

The late David Holgate (a friend of a great many collectors) introduced the classifications "X", "Y", and "Z" classes*, to distinguish the main types of New Hall-type problem pieces. The identifications of these mainly hybrid hard-paste porcelains has occupied many of us for over 20 years now and we have formed a "X Y Z Study Group" in order to research this area further and discuss any findings. I am now able to report that we have, collectively, made some headway.

Factory X

See pictures 197–8 and 200

The largest of the group, in terms of the number of examples known to us, is undoubtedly the "X" class. The probable span of the factory's existence is *c.*1790 (or earlier) through to *c.*1815. Like New Hall, the earliest specimens seldom bear a pattern number, but within the range 80 to 400 we have a fair number of reported patterns bearing their numbers – written without the prefix "N" or "No". In the main the over-glaze enamel designs are simple border designs and floral sprays, of the type that can be painted by semi-skilled or young workers on low wage rates. Most of

---

* As mentioned on p.145. See also David Holgate's *New Hall & Its Imitators* (Faber & Faber, London, 1971).

these, often attractive, original low-price designs are devoid of gilding. Others are rather upmarket and rival most New Hall (I show some of the typical specimens in pictures 197–8). The majority of the known pieces are teawares, and of these a pleasing selection of milk or cream jugs have survived.

Both Michael Berthoud and I have been fortunate enough to locate specimens (a very, very few) that bear the name "A.E. Keeling" or the initials "AEK". As a result of these finds, the former "X" class is now becoming attributed to this potter or to the various linked Keeling partnerships with factories at Tunstall and Hanley in the Staffordshire Potteries.

Anthony Keeling was one of the original partners in the New Hall adventure, but left (with John Turner) in the early 1780s. It was Keeling's pottery at Tunstall that the so-called New Hall partners first adapted to produce their porcelains. Keeling seemingly continued the production of his own porcelains after the main partners moved to the "New Hall" at Shelton. For a fuller discussion of the Keelings see my *Encyclopaedia of British Porcelain Manufacturers* (Barrie & Jenkins, London, 1988). A range of illustrations of "Factory X" teawares is given in *Staffordshire Porcelain* (Plates

119–30). The teapot shown here in picture 200 is from a part tea service, some pieces of which are marked. This teapot is of a characteristic, if late, shape.

Factory Y

In terms of the number of pieces known this is the smallest of the "X Y Z" grouping. The pieces that are attributed to it are usually rather heavily potted, and a little clumsy looking. Pattern numbers can occur but most are completely unmarked. The probable period is *c.*1795–1810, but as yet we have not been able to suggest a possible maker. With all these problem classes the likelihood is that they have a Staffordshire origin, but other possibilities do exist. I show a rare coffee pot and a creamer in picture 199, but both the pattern (number 141) and near versions of the shapes were also made at other factories.

198 A selection of "Factory X" or Keeling Staffordshire porcelain showing distinctive forms. They have simple, neat patterns in gold. Gilt pattern number "152", coffee pot 28cm (11in) high, *c.*1800–1805, Godden collection.

199 A coffee pot and silver-shape milk jug of "Factory Y" class (pattern number 141) – a little clumsy in comparison with the contemporary and larger classes "X" and "Z". Coffee pot 24cm (9½in) high, *c.*1805, Godden collection.

200 An oval teapot from a part service, some pieces of which bore the rare painted mark "A & E Keeling". This shape helps to identify other teaware forms and patterns to this Staffordshire manufacturer, 25cm (10in) long, *c.*1805–10, private collection.

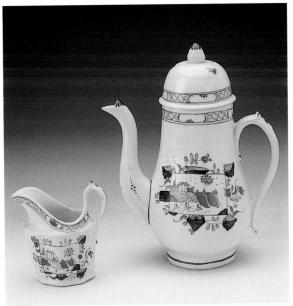

199

198

200

201

202

201 A grouping of "Factory Z" tewares, all painted with pattern 25. This pattern seems unique to this factory. As with other factories, various shapes were in production – for example there are three different coffee cup handles here. Teapot 18.5cm (7¼in) high, *c.*1800–1805, Godden collection.

202 Three charming moulded small milk or cream jugs, decorated in simple Chinese or New Hall-style inexpensive patterns. Possibly early "Factory Z", associated with Thomas Wolfe of Liverpool and Staffordshire. Centre jug 10.75cm (4¼in) high, *c.*1795–1805, Godden Reference collection.

203 Right, a rare "W(***)" class hybrid hard-paste porcelain vase with intricately gilt but rather clumsily painted figure subject panels. Impressed mark "W(***)" (as yet unidentified), 25cm (10in) high, *c.*1800, unfortunately stolen from Godden of Worthing.

Factory Z

| *See* pictures 170 and 201–2

The third of David Holgate's three mystery factories produced some really delightful porcelains during the approximate period 1780–1815. The earlier essays appear to be in the hybrid hard-paste body but the later examples (such as that shown in picture 201) are in a softer bone china, with a pleasing glossy glaze.

While the Chinese export market-type simple floral patterns predominate (*see* pictures 170 and 202), this manufactory also produced some chaste, restrained patterns and some high-quality bat-printed designs. Of our three "X Y Z" factories the products of the last are superior to the others. The porcelains are unmarked, except in some cases where the pattern numbers are shown. These are usually neatly painted and may be prefixed with an "N" or "No". Such markings are often in gold and may be enhanced with one or two dots. These "Z" pattern numbers are much neater than the usual large, hastily painted New Hall numbers but obviously not all neatly rendered numbers can be attributed to this factory.

I show some "Factory Z" porcelains in pictures 201–2 but also in *Staffordshire Porcelain* (Plates 131–2, 650–55, and Colour Plate XXIV). The current feeling is that these porcelains were produced by Thomas Wolfe or one of his Liverpool or Staffordshire partnerships, within the period of *c.*1796–1818. See my *Encyclopaedia of British Porcelain Manufacturers* (Barrie & Jenkins, 1988).

The "W(***)" Porcelains

| *See* pictures 203–4

Few classes of late 18th-century and early 19th-century English ceramics have aroused so much discussion as the ceramics which sometimes bear the unhelpful impressed mark "W(***)" .

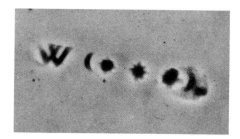

These wares of the 1790s, 1800s, and possibly also the 1810s include creamwares, basalt wares, and some other earthenwares as well as the hybrid hard-paste porcelains that we are concentrating on here.

The porcelains that do not seem to bear a pattern number include ornamental pieces such as vases, bulb-pots, and even small figures as well as tablewares. Some pieces bear early lustres of a steel-like tone.

I set out the basic facts on these varied wares in *Staffordshire Porcelain*, Appendix VI, in which I illustrate a good range of examples (Plates 713–35). Other examples are featured in my *Encyclopaedia of British Porcelain Manufacturers* (Plates 397–9). The problems of attribution are great but there is a link with William Billingsley's decorating establishment at Mansfield in the 1799–1802 period. This is not to suggest that all examples were decorated at Mansfield. I have suggested that the Whitehead's at Shelton produced these wares. In particular the creamware shapes seem to link with James and Charles Whitehead's 1798 printed catalogue. (See Robin Garrett's private 1996 publication *Chatterley & Whitehead, Potters of Hanley & Shelton*). It has, however, been suggested by Michael Bailey that the pieces bearing the impressed mark "W(***)" were made by different firms for a single merchant or wholesaler. Nevertheless, the porcelains all seem to have a family likeness, one that is not associated with other known classes of English porcelain. For example, the glaze often has a strangely dull appearance – almost verging on opaqueness – where it has pooled.

These mystery porcelains can be well decorated and attractive. Résumés of Michael Bailey's two lectures given to the Northern Ceramic Society are contained in NCS newsletters No.123 of September 2001 and in No.125 of March 2002. This last issue helpfully

contained a report by Noel Boothroyd (assistant archaeologist at the Potteries Museum) of an unglazed creamware waster found at Hanley (quite near the Whitehead factory site) bearing the impressed "W" mark. We still have yet to find wasters of porcelain so the problem remains.

The "Pattern-Book" Class

See picture 205

This class of early 19th-century English hybrid hard-paste porcelain is named after an unnamed pattern book now in the Victoria and Albert Museum. (Print Room – ref. 8822, press marks 93.C.21). This book is inscribed "No.4. Painters Pattern Book, begins N.323. Ends June 7th 1809". (Presumably the previous three books containing patterns 1 to 322 originally existed.) The examples shown in picture 205 are of this rare and interesting class.

The pattern book contains in the main sections of teaware, patterns of at least six basic shapes: "Worcs", "French", "Pear", "Bute", "Hamilton flute", and "Shankered". Named painters (or gilders) for patterns between 323 and 457 include: Arrowsmith, Brewer (landscape subjects), Meigh, Sherwin, and Spratt. I discuss these hybrid hard-paste porcelains at length in *Encyclopaedia of British Porcelain Manufacturers* (Barrie & Jenkins, 1988), pages 579–85. In 2002 Michael Berthoud of Bridgnorth published as *Ceramic Bulletin No.10* (Micawber Publications) reproductions of the V&A pattern book, with a helpful résumé of the current position and some porcelains that link with the pattern book.

Other types

This chapter does not by any means cover the whole range of English hybrid hard-paste porcelains that were produced in the approximate period 1790–1810, but it does list the main known types. These usually comprise middle-class market tablewares made to sell for perhaps under £2 per complete service. It follows that the designs will therefore be reasonably simple, in the style associated with the Chinese imports of that period or with the less-expensive New Hall patterns. Such wares were popular and catered for a large market. Today they are decorative, typical of their period, and are of interest to those of us who like to trace the maker of our porcelains.

Before we leave the subject of hard-paste porcelains and the hybrid types, let us briefly review the supply of porcelains available to the housewife seeking a tea or dessert service in the 1780s or 1790s.

204 A "W(***)" class bulb pot and cover and a figure of Winter from a set of the four seasons. The pot has a distinctive shape while the figure is very rare. Impressed "W(***)" marks, figure 19cm (7½in) high, c.1800–1810, Godden of Worthing.

205 An oval spiral-fluted teapot and two milk jugs, in hybrid hard-paste porcelain. These pieces link with an unnamed pattern book in the Victoria and Albert Museum. Pattern number "405" on left-hand jug, teapot 15.25cm (6in) high, c.1800–1810, Godden collection.

In a lecture I startled many of the audience by stating, "I contend that by the 1790s hard-paste tea services probably outnumbered all other types in use in the British Isles…" This statement resulted from taking a look at the wares available at the time, balancing the few British makers of soft-paste porcelains, Caughley, Derby, Lowestoft, etc, against New Hall, Coalport, Chamberlain, and the other makers of our hybrid hard-paste porcelains. I had to take into account the porcelains imported into England; imports that were on a very large scale.

First there were the mass imports of the forerunner of all hard-paste porcelains, the Chinese wares. These had been flooding into the country for well over a century. They were reasonably inexpensive and, until rising import duties more than doubled the cost, they undersold British products. Every 18th-century British dealer, or chinaman, stocked such standard wares, which in the main comprised underglaze blue willow-type Oriental landscape patterns and simple overglaze enamelled designs rather similar to many of the standard New Hall patterns. Some of these blue-and-white Chinese porcelains were further embellished in England with gilt borders, etc, giving rise to some novel but saleable Anglo-Chinese productions.

Apart from the Chinese hard-paste porcelains there was a minor but fashionable flood of French porcelains too. Under the January 1787 Treaty of Commerce and Navigation these porcelains were imported at the reduced rate of 12 per cent as opposed to the old 80 per cent tax. Flight, of the main Worcester porcelain factory, for example stocked his London showroom with French porcelains that he had journeyed across the Channel to purchase. Thomas Turner of Caughley also visited France and, on the evidence of some of his own products, he found the French wares well worth emulating. English china painters also found the French hard-paste blanks a good "canvas" for their craft. The French porcelains were often of new shapes that found favour with the public and, more importantly, the china itself was of a refreshingly white colour contrasting with some of the English soft-paste and with the greyish tones New Hall-type hybrid hard-paste porcelains. I discuss the French porcelains in my *Godden's Guide to European Porcelain* (Barrie & Jenkins, 1993).

Of course the importation of French porcelains was often interrupted by the wars of the period, but the French and the German products had a great influence on English porcelains and on English ceramic forms and patterns generally.

The various makers of English hybrid hard-paste porcelains changed to the rather whiter, lighter, bone-china type body at various periods early in the 19th century. The New Hall partnership was possibly the last to change, which it did in about 1813. Bone chinas are the subject of the following chapter.

8
Early bone china and felspar porcelain

The exact date of the commercial introduction of that wonderful, translucent, ceramic body that is now internationally renowned as "English Bone China" is not known. Various dates are offered around 1800 but it is generally accepted that bone china was perfected and successfully marketed by Josiah Spode, the second, at his Stoke pottery. The Spode firm began by using the description "Stoke China", and it wasn't until later periods that the term "Bone China" was used. The calcined and finely ground bone ash gives the china strength, translucency, and whiteness.

The late and very respected Staffordshire ceramic historian Reginald Haggar defined bone china as, "The standard English porcelain since 1800. It is basically hard-paste, modified by the addition of bone-ash which may be as much as 40 per cent of the ingredients of the bone-china body".

The introduction of bone ash into a ceramic mix, in the form of calcined (burned) animal bones, was by 1800 no new invention. More than 40 per cent bone ash has been detected in Bow porcelains of the 1750s and an equally large percentage was included in the Lowestoft mix. Bone ash was also present in gold-anchor Chelsea porcelains, Derby, Isleworth, and other makes of British porcelain.

Reginald Haggar contributed the chapter "Bone China – a general survey" to the multi-author work *Staffordshire Porcelain* (Granada, 1983). Below I provide the basic details of the main early 19th-century (mainly Staffordshire) manufacturers of English bone china, a now standard ceramic body accepted as nearing ceramic perfection. Further details on the staffordshire manufacturers can be found in specialist chapters in the reference book just mentioned.

I have selected for discussion in this chapter a few manufacturers: two large concerns, Spode and Minton; three relatively small manufacturers, Ridgway, Bourne, and Daniel; plus the Herculaneum-Liverpool and the Wedgwood porcelains. I have also returned to mention the second or bone-china period of the New Hall wares. To cover fully the producers of bone china would mean that this section would extend too far, for almost all of the 19th-century English porcelain manufacturers concentrated on this now standard ceramic body.

I have said "almost all" for there were exceptions – but these were quite short-lived. For example, the New Hall partners in Staffordshire continued to produce their hard-paste-type porcelain until the 1812–15 period, after which they gave way to the whiter bone-china body. The Coalport company likewise changed from a hybrid hard-paste to a bone-china body at about the same time. At least one of the Swansea porcelain bodies of the 1814–17 period is a soapstone rather than a bone porcelain. Perhaps not surprisingly the Worcester firm kept to their well-tried and very successful soapstone-type porcelains at least into the 1820s or 1830s, but, except in that city, bone china was accepted as standard in all English ceramic centres. I state "standard", but of course the various firms favoured slightly different mixes and for the less costly lines the body would be accordingly amended, to give less costly production.

Spode (porcelain), *c*.1800–1833

| *See* pictures 64 and 206

We have very few, if any, firm facts relating to the introduction of bone china, the standard 19th-century and present-day English porcelain body. The very sound ceramic chemist and practical potter William Burton in his excellent book *A History and Description of English Porcelain* (Cassell & Co., 1902) states:

The idea that Spode first introduced bone-ash into the body of English china about the year 1800 is absolutely untenable; but it is extremely probable that the tradition arose because he first abandoned the practice of calcining or fritting the bone-ash with some of the other ingredients and used the simple mixture of bone-ash, petuntse, and china clay, which, since his day, has formed the typical body of English porcelain...

Be this as it may, the Spode factory in Stoke-on-Trent must be regarded as the birthplace of bone china (first marketed as and marked "STOKE CHINA") as we understand the term today. For the commercial production and for the purity of body and trimness of manufacture and excellence of decoration, Josiah

Spode (the second, 1755–1827) led the way. He had come fresh from the London retail shop to manage the earthenware factory at Stoke and so must have been in a position to know just what the public wanted in the way of rich-looking useful porcelains. He set about meeting this demand.

The resulting bone china was a happy marriage of the basic hard-paste materials, china-stone and china-clay, with ground animal bones that had been used previously by several of the soft-paste manufacturers. The result was a fine white body, very workable and capable of being formed and turned to a thin gauge and yet retain its shape in the kiln. As well as being pleasing to the eye, it is strong and compact and reasonably light in weight, and not as cold to the touch or as brittle as the Continental hard-paste porcelains. It is as near perfection as a ceramic body can be – in fact to some eyes that are attuned to the beauties of early soft-paste porcelain it is too perfect and regular!

Leonard Whiter, the former historian of the Spode firm and its products and also the author of that magnificent book *Spode* (Barrie & Jenkins, 1970 and later editions), makes the valid point that there is no one bone-china recipe and, further, that the larger firms would have employed differing formulae at any one time for different types of ware or for different qualities of objects. The expensive "best-body" would not have been used for chamber pots, for example Mr Whiter gave three Spode recipes, the first of which reads:

Bone	35.5%
China-clay	23.5%
China-stone	17.6%
Blue clay	11.7%
Flint	11.7%

He also mentions that all such bodies would have contained a very minute quantity of blue stain to improve the visual whiteness of the body.

I must not dwell on the superb Spode porcelains: you can do no better than consult Leonard Whiter's very detailed and well-illustrated book, which covers the whole field of the factory's wide range of wares. You will find that some 95 per cent of these post-1800 Spode porcelains bear one of several helpful impressed, painted or printed name marks. These marks (ranging from the early "Spode" impressed mark) were used up to 1833 when the new Copeland & Garrett partnership came into being (*see* Chapter 10, p.204). The Spode pattern numbers had climbed to approximately 5,350 by the end of the period, evidencing the large range of fine-quality designs found on these bone chinas. Apart

206 A Spode bone-china jug that is of a typical simple but functional form. It has high-quality figure subject panels on each side, with trim gilding, 14.5cm (5¾in) high, *c.*1810, Godden of Worthing.

from the superb tea, dessert, and dinner services, many ornate decorative objects were produced (*see* picture 206). The Spode firm was the market leader in the 1800–30 period. The story is, however, complicated by the fact that prior to 1823 the decoration was carried out by the Daniels working within the large Spode compound, *see* p.176. The various Spode markings are well covered in Robert Copeland's *Spode and Copeland Marks* (Studio Vista, 1993 and later editions). Vega Wilkinson's *Spode – Copeland – Spode. The Works and its People* (Antique Collectors' Club, 2002) offers a good modern review. There is a Spode factory museum and collection within the works at Stoke, and a "Spode Society".

Minton, 1798–1816 (First period)

| *See* pictures 27, 39, and 207–10

Josiah Spode's greatest commercial rival was Thomas Minton (1756–1836), a one-time apprentice engraver to Thomas Turner at Caughley who later engraved some of Spode's own blue-printed patterns while practising his craft as an independent designer and engraver of copper plates.

I have stated in a previous book, *Minton Pottery and Porcelain of the First Period 1793–1850* (Barrie & Jenkins, 1968), that it was probably Spode's demand for more and more engraved copper plates that first suggested to Minton that if he was to make his mark in the world he must establish his own manufactory and

207

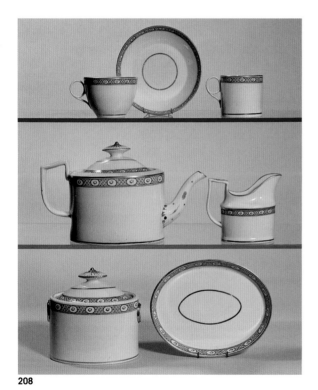

208

207 An oval Minton bone-china sugar box and cover, and a matching milk jug painted with a widely popular enamelled pattern (*see* picture 190) that is number 7 at Mintons and number 195 at the New Hall factory. Painted pattern numbers "N 7." and "N° 7.", sugar box 13.25cm (5¼in) high, c.1800–1805, Godden Reference collection.

208 Representative pieces from an early Minton bone-china tea service showing "Old Oval" forms (original potter's term to describe the straight-sided oval shape) with Bute shape teacup and coffee can. Painted simple border design no. 25, painted pattern number "25", teapot 14.5cm (5¾in) high, c.1800–1805, Godden of Worthing.

not be content to engrave for others. And make his mark he most certainly did. Thomas Minton purchased land at Stoke for his factory in 1793, but it was not until May 1796 that it was in production. The first modest receipts cover the period 23 May to 3 June – the magnificent sum of £33.10.10½ was received for goods sold during this ten-day period. His first productions were purely earthenwares and it was not until December 1797 that we find in the factory records a mention of china or porcelain; the year 1798 would therefore be a reasonable one to mark the tentative entry of Minton into the field of porcelain. Full commercial production probably commenced in about 1800. The body was apparently bone china, closely following Spode's development around the same date*.

Minton's early porcelains mainly comprise tea services, the delicate bone-china body being eminently suited to this staple article of trade. The teaware designs were at first very simple (*see* pictures 207–8) – it appears that Minton may have been endeavouring to capture the market with inexpensive sets. Their border patterns are certainly charming and have a fresh clean appearance. Several of the early designs in the Minton pattern book link with popular New Hall designs – for example Minton pattern 7 (*see* picture 207) is New Hall design 195, one of the most common New Hall floral-spray designs. Other Minton patterns are very similar to Pinxton patterns and several Minton designs are paralleled in the Spode pattern books.

I have yet to find a Minton teapot bearing one of the really early designs below, say, number 20. Such pots of

---

* There is a slight chance that Minton initially produced hybrid hard-paste porcelain. If not, he was a very early manufacturer of bone china.

209

210

the 1798–1800 period may well be similar to the New Hall-type turret teapots, and even of a hybrid hard-paste body. The Minton teapots and sugar boxes bearing patterns from about number 50 are very similar to the Spode forms of the same period (about 1800). From this period onwards we find a close similarity between the teaware forms of the two great rival factories.

Quite apart from the shapes, the post-1800 bone-china body is also similar to Spode's, although the Minton version is somewhat more open and the glaze does tend to craze slightly. Nevertheless we must regard Minton as one of the great early bone-china potters. The Minton patterns became more pretentious and expensive once the Minton porcelains had become firmly established (*see* picture 27). The firm also extended its range of products, and begun making dessert services in porcelain as well as ornamental pieces such as vases – the latter pieces were often very ornately embellished.

However, in or around 1816, Minton discontinued the manufacture of porcelains, although the factory continued to produce various earthenwares on a large scale. After a lapse of eight years Minton returned to the porcelain market. These new Minton porcelains (*see* picture 210) are quite different from those made in the 1798–1816 period and I will discuss these later wares when we examine the major later 19th-century factories in Chapter 10.

The early Minton pieces did not bear a factory mark before about 1805. They did, however, often bear a neatly written pattern number, sometimes prefixed "N" or "No". The occurrence of such pattern numbers is of little help for such markings will be found on most English porcelains of the period, but we can check the Minton numbers against the factory pattern book and from this build up a record of the basic Minton forms.

209 A rare early Minton fluted oval sugar box from a bone-china tea service. It is painted and gilt with a simple and attractive French-style sprig design. Painted pattern number "24", 12.75cm (5in) high, *c.*1805, Mrs M. Browne's collection.

210 A rare early second-period Minton bone-china teapot, cover, and stand. These show that within 20 years the basic forms and styles had vastly changed. Painted (second series) pattern number "127", teapot 15.25cm (6in) high, *c.*1825–8, Godden of Worthing.

This information permits us to identify at least some of the unmarked specimens. These basic shapes are featured in my book on Minton or in other specialist books, listed below.

After about 1805 the Minton porcelain often, but not invariably, bore a hand-painted device that was rather similar to the Sèvres crossed L's mark. This Minton mark was normally painted in blue enamel and, in most cases, the relevant pattern number was added below the device. This mark was used from *c.*1805 to the end of the first porcelain period in 1816. It was not used in the next period and a pattern number above 500 would post-date 1810.

Apart from my pioneer book on early Minton, and the all-embracing books that are mentioned on p.262, see also the following useful titles: *Minton Patterns of the First Period*, by R. Cumming and M. Berthoud (Micawber Publications, 1997) and *Regency Minton Porcelain 1800–1815*, by D. Langford (Langford & Clark, 1997).

J. & W. Ridgway, *c.*1808–30

| *See* pictures 55 and 211–13

I have included this section in my coverage of early bone-china manufacturers to show that some quite large and important firms are not now at all well known, yet their productions closely rival the popular Spode and Minton wares. The brothers John and William Ridgway joined their father Job in 1808. In the same year the production of bone china was added to that of earthenwares at the firm's Cauldon Place Works at Shelton (now Hanley) in the Staffordshire Potteries.

In general terms these new Ridgway porcelains were in the Spode style, with quality scenic bat-prints embellishing some teawares. Other colourful designs were added to the popular "London"-shape teawares (the trade name for the fashionable shapes of the 1810–15 period, *see* pictures 221, 230, and 253) and some superb dessert-services were made. As it happens my present three illustrations – pictures 211–13 – are all from dessert services.

Unfortunately very, very few pieces bore a factory mark and our present knowledge of the wares is based on the existence of all too few name-marked pieces and the discovery of some of the original pattern books. The standard reference book is my specialist work *Ridgway Porcelains* (revised edition, Antique Collectors' Club, 1985) but much research still remains to be carried out on these little-understood Ridgway wares – both pottery and porcelain.

In 1830 the two brothers separated. John continued the Cauldon Place Works and was later appointed Potter to Queen Victoria, making, especially in the 1840s and early 1850s, some magnificently decorated porcelains. William Ridgway concentrated on the production of earthenwares rather than porcelains. The name Ridgway, after changes of trading style, has continued down to recent times, as I relate in my specialist book or in my *Encyclopaedia of British Porcelain Manufacturers*.

Charles Bourne, *c.*1815–30

| *See* picture 214

I have included Charles Bourne in this section on bone china to give a contrast between the big manufacturers and the host of smaller firms who were also producing good-quality porcelains in the same period. In the main these smaller firms did not use a mark. Their products also tend to be attributed to one of the commercially desirable factories!

Charles Bourne (*d.*1836), however, was definitely an exception to this general rule. We can correctly designate some of his pieces as he employed a simple method of identification. The pattern number was often, but not always, placed below his initials "CB" in fractional form, such as "$\frac{CB}{123}$".

Charles Bourne was potting at the Foley Potteries, Lane End, in the Staffordshire Potteries from at least 1802, but his porcelain would seem to date from about 1815. His bone-china porcelain was compact and of a good white tone; the covering glaze was thin, clear, and usually craze-free. In quality and often in form the Charles Bourne porcelains are similar to Spode wares.

Bourne retired "on account of ill health", to quote from the sale announcement, towards the close of 1830. His manufactory then contained three biscuit kilns and three glost kilns, with hardening and enamelling kilns too, and it stood in two hectares (five acres) of land.

The now-rare Bourne porcelains are often very colourful and the gilding is of a high order (*see* picture 214). The standard products comprise teawares, dessert wares, small vases, and some very rare animal models. A selection are illustrated in *Staffordshire Porcelain* and The Potteries Museum at Hanley has a good range of

211

211 A well-decorated moulded dish from a John Ridgway dessert service. Each piece was hand-painted with a different decorative view. Painted pattern number "1895", 29.5 x 22cm (11½ x 8¾in), *c.*1835–40, Godden of Worthing Ltd.

212 A moulded-edged dish from a splendid John Ridgway porcelain dessert service. The panels are painted with different floral compositions. Pattern number "882", 29.75 x 21cm (11¾ x 8¼in), *c.*1825–30, Godden of Worthing.

213 A handled plate from a John Ridgway scenic-painted dessert service. The plate shape is characteristic but not unique to Ridgway. For related pieces see *Godden's Ridgway Porcelain* (Antique Collectors' Club, 1985), Colour Plate I. Pattern number "1078", 23.5 x 21cm (9¼ x 8in), *c.*1825–30, Godden of Worthing.

212

213

214

215

these interesting and well-potted decorative bone-china pieces. Some private collectors are building up interesting collections, and in so doing were expanding our knowledge. I look forward to the publication of a book on these Charles Bourne wares – earthenwares and stonewares as well as porcelains.

Daniel, c.1823–45

| *See* pictures 68, 72, and 215–17

I have just likened Charles Bourne's products to the Spode porcelains. We now consider a class of porcelain that is directly related to the Spode wares, for Henry Daniel, with a talented team of enamellers and gilders, was responsible for decorating all the Spode porcelains. He in effect had a separate decorating studio within the Spode factory. This novel, perhaps unique, arrangement was terminated by mutual consent in August 1822.

By the following July, Henry Daniel had taken over Joseph Poulson's former factory at Stoke and in March 1827 additional premises were acquired at Shelton. Henry had been joined by his elder son Richard and until 1826 they traded as "Daniel & Son", subsequently as "Henry & Richard Daniel" using marks such as "H & R. Daniel., Stoke-upon-Trent, Staffordshire" (hand-painted marks often included full stops as here, though this varied). In 1827 the Daniels produced some truly magnificent dessert and dinner services for the Earl of Shrewsbury. As Simeon Shaw noted in 1829, these

214 A selection of Charles Bourne bone china, of uniformly good quality and very much in the Spode manner. Painted pattern numbers in fractional form under the initials "CB". Diameter of lower plate 22cm (8¾in), c.1820–30, Godden of Worthing Ltd.

215 A selection of Daniel porcelains drawn from the dinner and dessert services made for the Earl of Shrewsbury. These show the typical shapes, uniform ground colour, raised gilding, and panel decoration. Elaborate printed marks "H & R. Daniel., Stoke-upon-Trent, Staffordshire", diameter of marked dinner plate 25cm (10in), c.1827, Godden of Worthing.

sets were "of the most brilliant and costly kind ever manufactured in the district". You will see from picture 215 that this contemporary ceramic historian was right. The two-tier dessert stand (bottom right) illustrates a typical Daniel edge shape. The edging on the dinner wares, however, can be regarded as standard to several high-class factories – and to the silversmiths.

The Daniel decoration, especially the ground colours and the gilding (*see* pictures 215–17), cannot be faulted for quality, although they may be rather too rich for some tastes. The Daniels were, it must be admitted, decorators rather than potters and, although the shapes are novel and characteristic, the porcelain and the glaze can, on many pieces, be below standard. The body is somewhat open and tends to contract, causing open cracks, and the glaze crazes easily. Not all Daniel pieces can be so faulted but the body is by no means as stable as it should have been. (Davenport porcelains that were made during the 1830–50 period also have a tendency to crack). Yet on seeing a selection of these scarce wares, you will surely be astounded by their magnificent decoration.

Some pieces bear written or printed name marks but the majority of specimens are unmarked, except for neatly written pattern numbers. These numbers are normally of four figures and range up to about 9,000.

Henry Daniel died in April 1841 and his son Richard continued the factory at Stoke to at least 1845. These Staffordshire porcelains should not be confused with the later wares sold by the London retailers Daniell (with a double "l") and which often bear this retailer's name mark.

Some of the admittedly rare Daniel porcelain marks are featured in my *Encyclopaedia of British Porcelain Manufacturers* (Barrie & Jenkins, 1988). The reader is also referred to *Staffordshire Porcelain*, Chapter 19; but the specialist book is Michael Berthoud's *H & R Daniel, 1822–1846* (Micawber, 1980). In addition there is *Daniel Patterns on Porcelain*, by M. Berthoud and L. Price (Micawber Publications, Bridgnorth, 1997). These works are updated by the privately circulated newsletters or publications by the Daniel Collectors Circle or by Michael Berthoud in his own bulletins, such as *Daniel Ornamental Wares* (Micawber Publications, 2002).

216

216 **A bone-china jug** of a form made at several factories and in different bodies. This unmarked example is almost certainly Daniel and it has figure subject panels each side. Cursive gilt initial monogram and date 1824, at the front, 23cm (9in) high, 1824, formerly in the Godden collection.

217 **Representative parts of a Daniel porcelain dessert service**, showing typical shapes. The shell-subject centres are unusual and desirable. Painted pattern number "4012", footed comport 34.25cm (13½in) long, c.1835–45, Godden of Worthing.

Herculaneum-Liverpool, c.1796–1840

| *See* pictures 218–19

It was Samuel Worthington & Co. that established the "Herculaneum" factory at Liverpool in 1796. This firm had a large trade in various styles of pottery and for a period from about 1800 some now-rare bone-china wares were made. These pieces were very seldom marked and their identification is in its infancy.

The few pieces known to us, which are impressed-marked with "HERCULANEUM", show the body to be white and pure, and covered with a good glaze that is somewhat prone to very fine crazing. The glaze has a strange soft, warm, almost oily feeling. Some fine bat-printing occurs, also some superb landscape-painting and floral designs as well as a range of Spode-type patterns, although the early designs mainly comprised simple (New Hall-type) border or floral sprig designs of an inexpensive nature. A large impressed capital "L" mark can occur on some Herculaneum-Liverpool porcelains and the pattern number can also be added in gold. A good range of 19th-century Liverpool ceramics is discussed and illustrated in Alan Smith's *Illustrated Guide to Liverpool Herculaneum Pottery* (Barrie & Jenkins, 1970). My *Encyclopaedia of British Porcelain Manufacturers* (Barrie & Jenkins, 1988). There is also a helpful publication *Herculaneum Echo*, which is currently published by Peter Hyland, 26 Plas Newton Lane, Chester CH2 1PJ. Michael Berthoud has also published *Patterns on Herculaneum Porcelain*, which is a checklist of recorded patterns (and is published by Micawber Publications, 2002).

Wedgwood, c.1812–29

| *See* picture 220

The famous firm, founded by Josiah Wedgwood, is of course extremely well-known for its various excellent earthenwares, and one might think that a company with such a high reputation for pottery would not need to enter the porcelain market. Wedgwood did, however, also produce excellent bone-china tea services (*see* picture 220) and other items for a mere 17-year period from about 1812.

The porcelain is of a good white body and it is covered with a clear, close-fitting craze-free glaze. The teawares are trimly potted and are normally decorated with restraint. Other Wedgwood porcelain objects are very rarely found today. Examples usually, but not always, bear the simple red-printed name-mark "WEDGWOOD". Various typical specimens are shown

in the book *Staffordshire Porcelain*, in Chapter 14 – which was contributed by John des Fontaines.

In 1878 the Wedgwood firm returned once again to the porcelain market and from then onwards this body has formed a larger and larger percentage of the company's total production. These later Wedgwood bone-china wares are of course quite different from the earlier designs and shapes. The later examples bear clear, printed "Wedgwood" trademarks.

New Hall, c.1813–35

| *See* pictures 221–2

The various factories that produced hybrid hard-paste porcelains in the closing years of the 18th century and in the early 1800s, as detailed in Chapter 7, turned to the whiter, more workable and pleasing bone-china body by 1810 or before.

Of all the Staffordshire porcelain manufacturers, probably the last to change to the lower-fired bone china body was the New Hall partnership at Shelton (now Hanley). I have already, in pictures 33 and 164–9, shown the earlier types of New Hall wares. Between 1813 and 1815 the management, or rather the factory manager, John Daniel, changed to the softer bone china. This was about the time that ceramic fashion had introduced the so-called London-shape teawares (as shown in pictures 221, 230, and 253). I illustrate in picture 221 three New Hall milk jugs from London-shape tea services. These all bear bat-printed subjects – one of the New Hall company's strong points. They are, however, treated in various ways with coloured borders or gilding. Such delicately printed patterns can be plain or coloured over in a realistic way. The printed "New Hall" circular name mark can occur at about this period. But these three creamers are unmarked – as is the norm. Well, unmarked except for the pattern number, which on New Hall bone china will be in excess of 1000.

218 An unmarked Herculaneum-Liverpool porcelain trio, from a combined tea and dessert service. The moulded handle shapes are characteristic, but the pattern is not (*see* picture 185). Diameter of saucer 13cm (5¼in), c.1805–10, Godden of Worthing.

219 A rare Herculaneum-Liverpool bone-china Empire-type vase that is one of a pair. Various other Continental and English manufacturers made pairs of simple decorative vases, 24.5cm (9⅝in) high, c.1810–20, Godden of Worthing.

220 Representative pieces from a Wedgwood bone-china tea service. The Oriental-styled figure panels are transfer-printed and coloured over by hand. The colour of the groundwork varies but these examples reflect the typical trim potting and graceful shapes. Printed "WEDGWOOD" mark, painted pattern number "565" – for this colour ground, teapot 15.25cm (6in) high, c.1815–20, Godden of Worthing.

218

219

220

221

222

221 Three New Hall bone-china "London"-shape milk jugs from complete tea services. Decorated with different types of bat-printed patterns – scenic, fruit-subjects, and figure designs and coloured over or with different borders. Painted pattern numbers, left to right: "1140", "984", and "1357", all 10cm (4in) high, c.1815–20, Godden collection.

222 A New Hall bone-china handled, dessert dish from a large service. The centre is painted with different Dr Syntax subjects (amusing scenes of a doctor getting up to various antics, which were based on drawings by Thomas Rowlandson from 1809–11) and there are relief-moulded flowers in the border. Painted pattern "N.2679", 21.5 x 19cm (8½ x 7½in), c.1825, Godden of Worthing.

The partnership produced a good range of often very colourful dessert services (but seemingly no dinner services). These services usually bear only a four-figure pattern number. Both hand-painted or coloured-over printed centres occur on a variety of shapes and within moulded borders.

The New Hall partnership (the names of those involved changed from time to time) continued from the early 1780s into the 1830s but then it slowly ran down until the closure in 1835. The last 20 years made up the bone-china period. Much research has been carried out regarding this interesting factory and its mainly unmarked porcelains. For further information and illustrations of the varied shapes and patterns, see

David Holgate's *New Hall* (Faber & Faber, London. 1987), A. (Tony) de Saye Hutton's *A Guide to New Hall Porcelain Patterns* (Barrie & Jenkins, London. 1990), *A Partial Reconstruction of the New Hall Pattern Book* by Mrs Pat Preller (P. Preller, 2003), or my own later book *New Hall Porcelains* (Antique Collectors' Club, 2004).

Felspar porcelain, c.1820–50

One of the major subdivisions of bone china was termed by Josiah Spode II "Felspar Porcelain". A British source of felspar was discovered by Thomas Ryan on the Wales/Shropshire border in February 1819. Leonard Whiter, in his book *Spode*, gave a most interesting account of the introduction of felspar into ceramic bodies and glazes. This authority made the point that felspar porcelain *is* bone china, the felspar merely replaces the Cornish stone, which itself contains some felspar. Felspar is the petuntse of the Chinese true porcelains. Mr Whiter related how the newly discovered British felspar was submitted to John Rose of the Coalport works and how it was at first rejected by him. But, after much prompting, Rose introduced his famous lead-free felspar glaze, a material that won him the Isis gold medal of the Society of Arts. This award, although only for the glaze, was used to great advantage by the Coalport company when a series of prominent printed marks were placed on their porcelains from June 1820. One of these marks is reproduced below, and you will see that Rose favoured the spelling "Felt Spar".

Typical printed Coalport "Felt-Spar" mark. Several variations occur.

Having found a customer in John Rose, Thomas Ryan turned his attention to selling his felspar to the Staffordshire manufacturers, a task no doubt helped by the special Coalport mark and the Society of Arts medal. Other manufacturers would obviously want to produce the well-publicized new felspar porcelain. The Wedgwood archives contain a written account by Ryan of his endeavours to sell this raw material. Here we learn that "Mr Spode gave an order for fifty tons at £15 per ton; the quantity on the wharfs was instantly removed to Stoke and the order was completed in a short time. The cheaper sort of felspar was purchased in large quantity by E. Mayer & Son, T. Minton, Messrs Ridgway and others."

Spode lost little time in placing their new felspar porcelain on the market and they also emulated the large Coalport printed marks with their own – two rare versions of which incorporated the date 1821. One such Spode mark is shown here; such special marks normally occur only on the finest pieces.

Spode "Felspar" printed mark. This is a rare version, incorporating the year "1821".

The Spode felspar body, being regarded as superior to the standard bone china, contained some 15 per cent felspar and about 45 per cent bone. It must also be remembered that a felspar body would have a felspar-containing glaze. This covering and ground for the enamelled and gilt decoration was (to quote again from Mr Whiter's book) "of a quality never bettered...the word 'luscious' has been aptly used to describe it".

Minton also produced a felspar body and had engraved special elaborate marks (such as those below) to be placed on such wares. The term "Felspar Porcelain" was all the rage and I would make the point again that our 20th-century description "bone china" was very rarely used in the 19th century.

John and William Ridgway also produced a fine, compact, white felspar porcelain from the early 1820s but their examples were not specially marked before the 1840s. Ryan mentioned E. Mayer & Son as being purchasers of his felspar. If this was used in a porcelain body, as it probably was, then this was another firm that produced unmarked bone-china and felspar porcelain. Elijah Mayer had potted at the Cobden Works, High Street, Hanley, from the 1780s to c.1804. From c.1805 to 1834 the works were continued by Elijah Mayer & Son, and directory entries list this firm as china and earthenware manufacturers. Simeon Shaw

223 A selection of typical Coalport bone-china dessert service plates. The originally French-style relief-moulded edge was copied at several English factories. For example, the Coalport factory excelled in floral, painted designs such as those shown here. Impressed number mark "2", one with "John Rose 1820 Society of Arts", printed mark, diameters 21–21.5cm (8–8½in), c.1820, Godden of Worthing.

within his *History of the Staffordshire Potteries*, after mentioning Mayer's earthenwares, noted that the works were "now notable for a species of porcelain manufactured only here". Research may in time show that the Mayer firm made a good range of porcelains in addition to the quality earthenwares that are sometimes marked.

There is also scant information on yet another manufacturer of felspar porcelain, James and William Handley, who principally potted at the Kilncroft Works, Chapel Street, Burslem, in the 1822–30 period, but were formerly of High Street, Shelton (1822–3). Simeon Shaw noted, "Messrs James & W. Handley, then of Shelton...introduced a porcelain from feldspar chiefly, of very excellent quality; and of this they made several vases, much larger in size and truly elegant and original in design than any before produced". Very little else is known about this manufacturer, although a very rare marked cup and saucer is featured in my *Encyclopaedia of British Porcelain Manufacturers*.

The following two chapters will concentrate on the important post-1810 porcelain manufacturers, most of whom produced the standard British bone-china body.

9

The major 19th-century factories up to 1850

My coverage of all the major 19th-century British porcelain factories is divided into two sections. In this chapter we mainly look at the factories best known for their products made before 1850, although in some cases the firms continued long after this period. In the next chapter we will consider the firms that came to prominence in the second half of the century.

Samuel Alcock & Co., c.1828–59

| See pictures 52 and 224–9

If instead of "major" I had substituted "well-known" in this chapter's title, I would not have been able to include this very important firm, for Alcock was a major producer but by no means a well-known one to later collectors. Samuel Alcock owned the famous Hill Pottery at Burslem as well as a separate (and earlier) factory at Cobridge. In 1833, some five years after Alcock set up as a potter, a Government Inspector reported that Samuel Alcock's "Porcelain and China Works" employed 400 people. He also noted that 42 painters were employed (one-third of them adult males), "a greater number than I had before observed in one apartment". About five years later John Ward, in his *The Borough of Stoke-upon-Trent* (W. Lewis & Son, 1843), wrote in high praise of the contemporary Alcock porcelains:

The productions of Messrs Alcock & Co., in ornamental china, are of a first rate description, consisting of table and tea services, enriched with exquisite landscape paintings and other devices; of vases, fancy bouquettes, articles of toilette and elaborately modelled subjects from history and romance in biscuit china…

Apart from some portrait busts and other models made in unglazed white biscuit china, most of Alcock's useful porcelains of the 1830s and 1840s appear to be unmarked. That is why the firm is so little known and why many of its productions have been classified as Rockingham (see p.195), Coalport, or other fashionable makes. The quality is there – but not the maker's name.

The Alcock bone-china body is of good quality; it is well potted and often very richly decorated, even with encrusted flowers in the Coalbrookdale (Coalport) manner (*see* picture 228). Rococo Rockingham-style shapes were favoured, especially for the teawares – these include wide teacups in which the tea cools quickly (*see* picture 1). A very good range of animal models were produced, which have impressed model numbers under the base. The one shown in picture 226 (model number 124) is from my grandfather's collection. He, like others of his generation, would have called it "Rockingham" (Rockingham was a much more well-known factory than Alcock and many pieces have been mis-attributed to it).

Samuel Alcock & Co.'s display at the Exhibition of 1851 included porcelain dessert services, tea sets, dinner services (also "white granite" ironstone-type services), centrepieces, individual plates, ornamental pen holders, spill vases, elaborate vases, and relief-moulded jugs as well as single figures and groups. At this period the Burslem works gave employment to no less than 687 people and was run by Samuel's widow with Samuel Alcock Jr, then aged 25, acting as manager assisted by his younger brother Thomas. The founder of the firm, Samuel Alcock, had died in 1849.

Apart from the glazed porcelain pieces the Alcock firm also produced a great quantity of relief-moulded parian jugs from the 1840s and into the 1850s. Many of these are of excellent quality. Other jugs, vases, and other pieces were printed with Classical figure subjects, and a good selection of useful earthenware was also made. Some characteristic pieces are featured in *Staffordshire Porcelain* and a very good account of the early wares is given by S. Bressey and M. Pollinger in *The Northern Ceramic Society Journal*,

224 Two early Samuel Alcock bone-china dessert service plates. The so-called "melted-snow" edge seems restricted to Alcock, as are the raised coloured wheel-like devices. Painted pattern number "843" on left example, diameter 23cm (9in), *c*.1825–30, formerly in the Godden collection.

225 A Samuel Alcock bone-china dessert dish, with moulded "melted-snow" edging. The shape seems unique to Alcock and the rose grouping is also typical. Painted pattern number "956", 24.75 x 21.5cm (9¾ x 8½in), *c*.1830, Godden of Worthing.

224

225

226

227

228

Vol. 20 (2003–4). These Alcock wares should certainly command the collector's respect and attention.

The identification of these porcelains mainly depends on a study of certain key shapes, and these were, in several cases, registered at the Design Registry in Samuel Alcock's name. Few pieces bear a factory mark, except the parian and other jugs. When marks do occur they incorporate the firm's name or the initials "S.A." or "S.A. & Co.", sometimes with the Royal

Arms device. The Burslem pattern number sequence is very high, normally well above 5000, or the number may be given in a "fractional" form such as, for example, 2/5777. The Cobridge numbers are very much lower.

In 1860 Sir James Duke & Nephews succeeded Samuel Alcock & Co. at the Hill Pottery, Burslem, which had failed due to bad management after the founder's death. This new firm also produced good-quality porcelains that were nearly always unmarked, although an impressed hand device was sometimes used, but can be difficult to see.

Chamberlain, c.1788–1852

| *See* pictures 17, 36, 40, 43, 66, 94–5, 171–6, and 230–33

I have already covered the early history of Robert Chamberlain's Worcester porcelain company within Chapters 6 and 7. I now proceed to outline the post-1800 developments at this very important Worcester porcelain factory.

In August 1802, Lord Nelson visited Worcester and he inspected the Chamberlain factory and retail shop but apparently disregarded the rival Flight & Barr establishment. Lord Nelson also ordered several superb Chamberlain services. Then in September 1807 the Prince of Wales visited the Chamberlain works and granted Chamberlain's the honour and style of "Porcelain manufacturers to His Royal Highness the Prince of Wales", a fact recorded in several post-1807 marks, and later amended to read the "Prince Regent". The Prince's patronage was also reflected in the name of a superior and costly new hard-looking body termed "Regent China", which was introduced in 1811.

Apart from Royal orders, the Chamberlain company produced some truly magnificent porcelains (*see* pictures 230–33) and so, not surprisingly, in 1813 a retail establishment was opened within London. This was situated at 63 Piccadilly, and in July 1816 new premises at 155 New Bond Street were taken; in 1840 further premises at 1 Coventry Street were acquired. The addresses of these retail shops are often incorporated in the relevant Chamberlain marks and are helpful in dating an example (*see* p.187). The range and general style of the Chamberlain wares of the 1813 period can be gauged by reading some of the contemporary descriptions of pieces sent to stock the Piccadilly shop. In 1813, 39 cases of porcelain that were valued at £3,279 2s 3d were forwarded from the Worcester factory. Apart from tea, dessert, and dinner services we can also find listed in the contemporary records items such as:

226 One of a pair of Alcock bone-china ornaments. This is typically well modelled and well decorated. Impressed model-number "121" with year or workman's circular mark, 14cm (5½in) high, c.1830–40, Mrs S. Halls.

227 One of a set of Samuel Alcock bone-china jugs. One side of each is painted with landscapes, the other with flowers, and they have typical Alcock gilding, 25cm (10in) high (sizes vary), c.1830–40, formerly in the Godden collection.

228 A very elaborate Alcock flower vase (one of a pair). The hand-made applied porcelain flowers are not confined to the Coalport factory – most porcelain manufacturers of the period made similar Dresden-styled porcelains. Painted fractional pattern number "4/263", 27.25cm (10¾in) high, c.1845–55, private collection.

229 A richly decorated Samuel Alcock dessert plate, showing a characteristic moulded border design. Rich raised and tooled gilding on a coloured ground and is hand-painted with Sèvres-style decoration. Printed "S Alcock & Co" angel mark, diameter 23cm (9in), c.1850–55, Godden of Worthing.

A rich full size Regent vase, painted by Humphrey
  Chamberlain with the Triumph of Mercy,
  £31-10-0d
Two Regent vases painted by Walter Chamberlain
  with King John and the Taming of the Shrew,
  £ 8-8-0d each
Three large mugs pattern "403" painted with dead
  game, £5-5-0d each
Bowls in various rich patterns
Various types of candlesticks
Very many ornamental inkpots, inkstands and
  pentrays
Jugs such as "Quart jug painted with dogs, £4-4-0d"
Baskets, spill-vases
Costly specimen plates such as "1 plate Coriolanus
  at £31-10-0d"
Richly decorated cups and saucers such as "2 cabinet
  cups and stands, figures and gold at £5-5-0d"

There were also house-shaped pastille burners,
figures, and small animals such as cats, greyhounds,
pug dogs, spaniels, and griffins. Among the smallest
articles on offer were porcelain thimbles, which were
valued at 1/6d each.

Some of the sumptuous ornaments or specimen plates
were painted by Humphrey Chamberlain Jr, an artist
and miniature painter who died in 1824 at the early age
of 33. His brother, Walter, also painted on Chamberlain porcelains; they both excelled in figure subjects.
Other fine-quality figure designs were painted by the
justly celebrated and much-travelled Thomas Baxter.
Baxter had been born in Worcester, and after working
in his father's London porcelain-decorating studio
(*see* p.156), Thomas Baxter painted for Flight, Barr
& Barr of Worcester (*c*.1814–16), then at Swansea
(*c*.1816–18), but his last years were spent at Chamberlain's in whose employment he died in April 1821.
Apart from the figure subject artists, there were
talented flower painters such as Samuel Astles, James
Taylor, John Webster, and George Davis the celebrated
bird painter, who was also a fine flower-painter. There
were also talented landscape painters such as Doe,
Muchall, and John Wood.

230 A London-shape Chamberlain-Worcester teapot, cover and stand,
from a colourful Japan-pattern tea service. Painted "Chamberlains
Worcester" mark, with number "623", teapot 24.75cm (9¾in)
long, *c*.1815–20, Godden of Worthing.

The Chamberlain porcelains of the 1810–30 period are really superb, rivalling any manufacturer of the period. In quantity the output seemingly exceeded that of the Flight, Barr & Barr partnership at the old Dr Wall Worcester factory, and in body and decoration the Chamberlain wares were superior to the contemporary Derby productions. However, in the 1830s there seemed to be something of a decline, with the major Staffordshire factories such as Minton and Spode (the Copeland & Garrett partnership after 1833) taking much of the trade. Chamberlain's followed the fashion in changing to a standard bone-china paste. In 1840, no doubt in an effort to pool resources and strengthen the trading position, the two hitherto rival firms of Flight, Barr & Barr and Chamberlain were combined. In effect, the firm established by a mere apprentice had taken over and absorbed the former great Worcester porcelain factory, which had been founded 90 years earlier. The takeover, or "marriage", of the two firms cannot now be counted as a great success. Perhaps the loss of the old rivalry was to blame? Various new lines were tried, such as the mass-production of porcelain buttons and the manufacture of door furniture, but these endeavours could not stem the general decline. Perhaps the times were against them, for in 1848 the famous Derby factory had been forced to close after a lingering death. Chamberlain's remained to display their wares at the 1851 Exhibition but its pieces must have shown up badly against other ceramic pieces.

In 1851 the last of the Chamberlains, Walter, left the partnership, leaving W.H. Kerr in sole command. He turned to R.W. Binns to join him in an effort "to exalt the name and to enhance the reputation of Worcester porcelain". This they succeeded in doing under the trade name of "W.H. Kerr & Co." or, alternatively, "Kerr & Binns", a happy partnership of the 1852–62 period that led to the foundation of the now internationally renowned "Royal Worcester" company (*see* pp.220). We must not, however, consider the Chamberlain period as a mere bridge between the great Dr Wall factory and the present Royal Worcester. Chamberlain's has a long and noble history of its own and within the 64-year life of this factory some of England's most magnificent porcelains were produced, pieces that graced palaces and brightened many a more humble home.

Post-1810 Chamberlain marks normally comprise or include this name, with various addresses or trade styles. A crown may occur from 1811 onwards, and the London shop addresses put on the marks were 63 Piccadilly from *c.*1813–16, and, from July 1816, the New Bond Street address. From 1840 "Coventry Street" may occur but there were many marks; basic types are shown overleaf.

231

232

231 A typically fine-quality Chamberlain-Worcester vase – one of a pair or set of three. The continuous panel scene is taken from *A Midsummer Night's Dream*, 19cm (7½in) high, *c.*1813–18, Godden of Worthing.

232 A superbly decorated Chamberlain-Worcester spill vase or "match pot", originally one of a pair. The subject, "The Mother's Hope", is inscribed on the base along with a neatly written Chamberlain-Worcester mark, including the New Bond Street, London retail address, 9cm (3½in) high, *c.*1818, formerly in the Godden collection.

*Chamberlain's
Regent China,
Worcester,
& 155,
New Bond Street,
London.*

A

CHAMBERLAIN & CO.
WORCESTER
155 NEW BOND ST.
& No. 1
COVENTRY ST.
LONDON.

B

A Printed mark used on the "Regent" body, *c.*1811–20. This mark is mainly found on services that were made from this expensive and special body.
B Printed mark, *c.*1840–5. Note the addition of "& Co." (and the Coventry St address). The first three lines of this mark were also used at this period mainly on small examples.

The standard book on these varied and usually fine-quality porcelains is my own *Chamberlain-Worcester Porcelain 1788–1852* (Barrie & Jenkins, 1982), a work that not only illustrates a large range of products but also quotes many of the original prices and reconstructs the factory list of patterns, which extended to over 4,000.

233 A typical well-modelled and colourful Chamberlain-Worcester
poodle model – one of a pair. This and other factories produced similar animal models. Printed Royal Arms and name and address mark, 10cm (4in) long, *c.*1820–30, Godden of Worthing.

Coalport, *c.*1791–1850

| *See* pictures 49, 178–82,186, 223, and 234–6

I have already given, in Chapter 7, an account of the early John Rose porcelains, as well as details of the other porcelain manufacturers at Coalport and Anstice, Horton & Rose. The porcelains made by these two firms were the first of the hybrid hard-paste variety. The Anstice works were taken over by the John Rose company in 1814 and the two factories, separated only by a narrow canal, were amalgamated. The body too, at about this period, was changed to a bone china, rather softer than most of that period and the wares were in general rather thickly potted. As mentioned in Chapter 8, John Rose had been awarded a Society of Arts gold medal in 1820 for his lead-free felspar glaze (*see* picture 223).

Magnificent dessert services (also tea sets and dinner services) were made with relief-moulded borders (*see* picture 223) in the style so often associated with the Welsh factories (*see* p.200), and the flower painting can equal some of the Swansea porcelains; indeed the talented china painters in London used Coalport as well as Swansea and Nantgarw blanks to enhance, in fashionable styles of the period.

234

235

236

Other very decorative Coalport porcelains were embellished with relief-moulded and coloured flowers (*see* picture 234). Pieces of this class are often termed "Coalbrookdale" and some pieces bear abbreviated marks such as "CDale" or "CD", although other examples bear the standard name "Coalport". You must remember that most factories of the 1820–40 period made some floral-encrusted wares but Coalport (and Minton) led the field in this class of Dresden (Meissen)-inspired porcelain.

Of the more useful wares the Coalport company, which traded as John Rose & Co., produced a fine selection of teawares, often very richly decorated and often mistaken for Rockingham as the shapes tend to be rather rococo (*see* picture 235). Dessert services were another great stand-by of the factory. Most were finely painted with flowers, but other examples can be found in the Sèvres style with coloured borders, as well as some with birds in a landscape depicted in the centre of the plates and dishes.

Apart from the Society of Arts mark (*see* p.180), very little Coalport porcelain of the 1815–50 period is marked. However, the tablewares at least normally bear a (usually fractional) pattern number and, as some of the original pattern books have been preserved, we can build up a series of standard forms to gain a good idea of the Coalport productions. Many of these key shapes are featured in my *Coalport and Coalbrookdale Porcelains* (Antique Collectors' Club, 1981), together with details of the standard styles of decoration and of the artists and gilders who embellished the wares.

The Coalport factory continued into the second half of the 19th century: indeed it still prospers (in Staffordshire) today, having lived through several takeovers. (The later history is given in Chapter 10.)

234 A floral-encrusted Coalport porcelain covered bowl. The general type is often termed "Coalbrookdale" but most English porcelain manufacturers produced similar examples, emulating Dresden floral-encrusted porcelain, 10.75cm (4¼in) high, *c*.1825–35, Godden of Worthing.

235 A superb Coalport early Victoria teapot and cover. Fanciful perhaps, but very well decorated and part of a complete service. Other English factories produced rather similar rococo forms at this period, 21.5cm (8½in) high, *c*.1840, Godden of Worthing.

236 Representative pieces from a Coalport dessert service of the 1830s. The central comport is raised on a stem but the variously shaped side dishes are still only 5 or 7.5cm (2 or 3in) high. Painted pattern number "3/993", comport 21cm (8¼in) high, *c*.1835–40, Godden of Worthing.

Davenport, c.1794–1887

| *See pictures 237–8*

Davenport, like the Coalport firms, initially produced a type of hybrid hard-paste porcelain (*see* p.158), probably during the 1805–10 period, although it is not certain when the production of porcelain was first added to that of earthenware at this Staffordshire factory. However, in general terms, we can consider that from about 1810 the Davenport factory made a range of bone-china porcelains.

It is strange that this important firm, which made glass as well as pottery and porcelain, should have marked so few of its early productions. I do not know of any marked bone-china tewares that can be dated before 1810, although such wares must surely have been made. Some rare dessert-service components are known and these pieces enable us to identify unmarked pieces of the same form. Some few examples bear the painted town mark "Longport", while other examples bear the impressed name mark "DAVENPORT" in curved form over an anchor device. The anchor occurs incorporated in several Davenport marks but do not consider the anchor alone a sign of Davenport origin as it was occasionally used at Coalport and other factories, English as well as Continental. Some of the Davenport porcelain marks are shown here.

237 A fine-quality (almost Welsh-looking) Davenport trio, of the "Etruscan" shape (a name give by the contemporary potter). They are well painted and tastefully gilt. Pattern number "689" and printed "Davenport" and anchor ribbon mark, diameter of large saucer 15.25cm (6in), c.1820–25, Godden of Worthing.

A Impressed mark, c.1805.
B Printed mark, c.1810.
C Printed mark, c.1815, in blue after about 1850.

The printed mark shown at (C) was used from about 1815. Pieces bearing this mark can be of superb quality, rivalling Spode, Swansea, or any other English manufacturer of the period, but alas these marked pieces are all too rare. Some especially graceful Empire-style tewares were made in forms that seem unique to the factory: look out for these rare pieces (the cups shown in picture 238 are good examples).

From around 1825 the Davenport teware and dessert service forms tended to be influenced by the rococo revival and many of the factory's basic shapes are very close to the Coalport forms of this period. I am also sure that much unmarked Davenport porcelain is to be found incorrectly labelled "Rockingham". Attractive as the Davenport body is, it did present difficulties at times and examples of dinnerwares especially are found to have failed to stand up to regular use – as the body developed wide cracks. This fault was soon overcome and the Davenport porcelains continued on a very high level. In the 1870s and 1880s some very colourful Japan patterns were produced in the Derby manner. The firm was turned into a limited liability company in 1881 but failed in 1887. The standard porcelain mark of the 1870–87 period is shown here. Pattern numbers were in simple progressive form without a prefix.

DAVENPORT
LONGPORT
STAFFORDSHRE

The standard book on all aspects of Davenport's many types of pottery and the porcelains is *Davenport China, Earthenware and Glass 1794–1887*.

The Davenport products offer great scope to the collector who wishes to search out unmarked examples and is not content to follow the mass in a search for marked pieces from the more fashionable factories.

238 An elegant Davenport trio, which have been painted with an extremely rare yellow ground. The Paris-style (so-called simply due to their similarity to Parisian porcelain) cups, with moulded face terminals to the cup handles, seems to have been unique to the Davenport factory. Printed "Davenport" and anchor ribbon mark, diameter of saucer 14cm (5½in), c.1825–30, Godden of Worthing.

Derby, c.1750–1848

See pictures 9, 38, 47, 48, 57, 102–8, and 239–42

In Chapter 6 we left our consideration of the Derby porcelain at the point when William Duesbury II had died, in 1797. The works were continued by Michael Kean, seemingly with little or no change in the styles of decoration or in the general high quality production. The body is compact with an almost waxy feel and the slightly whitened glaze has a warm, mellow appearance. The porcelains are trimly potted and tastefully and well decorated. In short Derby at this period set a very high standard and, apart from the useful wares, the factory had practically monopolized the English trade in decorative figures and groups.

Before about 1805 the now standard factory mark (*see* p.92) was neatly painted in a puce or blue enamel.

After about 1805 this same basic mark was painted in a red enamel and the quality of the painting of this mark became worse, haphazard or hasty in the painting (*see* p.92). In the 1811–15 period the management of the factory passed to Robert Bloor. Initially Bloor continued to respect the old high standards and he also continued to employ the old Crown Derby mark.

It is fashionable for people to decry the "Bloor-Derby" porcelains and certainly he took the easy way by producing and selling, often by auction, a mass of gaily-painted Japan pattern wares, some of which we must consider as seconds or slightly faulty pieces. I prefer the earlier, simpler designs, but these Japan patterns were inexpensive and rich looking and so met a vast middle-class market. These colourful Japan patterns are still in great demand today, although they command much higher prices of course!

This decrying of Bloor-period Derby porcelain is somewhat overdone. Of course some pieces were made to a price or rather to a market, but I can show you Bloor examples that any manufacturer of the period would have been happy to have made (*see* pictures 239–40). At the same time Bloor did certainly take measures to cut his considerable overheads. He reduced

The King Street Works, Derby, 1849–1935

| *See pictures 241–2*

The present Royal Crown Derby company is not directly related to the old works that we have been discussing. The new company was established in 1876. There was, however, a continuation, or offshoot, of the old factory, for on its closure a group of the former workmen set up a small works in King Street, Derby. At first they were probably content simply to continue old, established, and popular lines and to match earlier pieces, but they also produced glazed or biscuit figures in the style of earlier Derby models as well as many novelties (*see* picture 241). In later years the great stand-by lay in the production of typical Derby Japan patterns, pieces similar to those that are depicted in picture 242, a page from one of the firm's illustrated catalogues. In 1935 the King Street works were taken over by the Royal Crown Derby Porcelain company.

The King Street company traded under various names: "Locker & Co. late Bloor" in the 1849–59 period, then as "Stevenson, Sharp & Co." in 1859–61, but the next partnership of Stevenson & Hancock is that normally associated with this small firm, and in 1862 the initials "S" and "H" were added – one each

241 A rare King Street, Derby figure of "Dr Syntax on Horseback". This is one of a series of related models that were reissues of 19th-century Derby models. This was the most costly at £3-7s-6d in the 1920s. Painted "S.H." mark, 12.75cm (5in) high, *c*.1920s, E.H. Parker.

239 A superb-quality Bloor-Derby dessert plate. This is a very good example of the wares of this period, and the plate has raised, tooled gilding. Transferred "Bloor Derby" mark, diameter 23cm (9in), *c*.1830–35, Godden of Worthing.

240 Left, a shell-shaped Derby dish, from a scenic painted dessert service – each piece has a different scene on it. (The European views are named on the reverse of each one.) This is a typical, rather heavy looking, Bloor-period design. Transferred "Bloor Derby" mark, in red, 24.75 x 23.5cm (9¾ x 9¼in), *c*.1825–30, Godden of Worthing.

the painting staff, losing flower painters such as Thomas Steel to the Rockingham works. Other talented Derby ceramic artists went on to the Coalport factory, or to Mintons. While in the 1780s and 1790s the Derby factory had the high-class market almost entirely to itself, the position was quite different in the 1830s and 1840s with the competition from the great Staffordshire firms. In 1848, after various changes in management, the original Derby factory in Nottingham Road closed. A selection of Bloor-Derby printed or transferred* marks are shown here, they were usually rendered in red.

Many helpful and well-illustrated books have been published on the subject of Derby porcelains. You should try to locate a copy of John Haslem's classic *The Old Derby China Factory, the Workmen and their Productions* (George Bell & Sons, 1876). More recent works are listed in the bibliography on p.263.

---

* These Bloor-period Derby marks were usually transferred from the engraved copper plate to the porcelain on the thumb. Consequently they can show the lines of a finger or thumb print.

242 A page from the King Street, Derby factory's sales catalogue, which shows reissues of the old Derby patterns described as "Old Crown Derby Rose" etc, c.1920, within the Godden Reference collection.

side of a new version of the old crowned mark, only now the batons became (or looked like) crossed swords. This standard mark of the 1862–1935 period is shown below. Earlier the (rare) name marks used by the previous partnerships were employed or the old, red, crowned, crossed baton mark was copied up to 1862, when Llewellynn Jewitt suggested and sketched the new version. It has been observed that on a very few post-1862 pieces the initials are missing.

A well-illustrated account of the King Street Derby wares is given by John Twitchett and Betty Bailey in *Royal Crown Derby* (Antique Collectors' Club, 1988), see also *In account with Sampson Hancock, 1860s–1880s*, by J. Twitchett (D.J.C. Books, Burford, 1996), and *Old Crown Derby China Works. The King Street Factory, 1849–1935* by R. Blackwood & C. Head (Landmark Publishing Ltd, 2003).

Grainger-Worcester, *c.*1805–1902

| *See pictures 243–4*

This firm's marks after 1890 claimed the firm's date of establishment to be 1801 but, as explained in Chapter 7, Henry and John Sandon, the joint authors of the 1989 standard book *Grainger's Worcester Porcelain*, pointed out that Thomas Grainger could not have made his own porcelain before becoming a Freeman of Worcester, which he did in September 1805, aged 22. Thomas Grainger (1783–1840) was a grandson of Robert Chamberlain (1736–98) and was apprenticed at the Chamberlain factory. The early products were confined to useful wares, closely following in form and pattern the proven Chamberlain porcelains. The early Grainger porcelains are seldom marked. Sometimes one finds painted name marks such as "Grainger Wood & Co." or "Grainger & Co.", but these marks are rare and on teawares would only occur on the teapot and covered sugar bowl, placed inside the covers following the Chamberlain habit.

Between the years of 1812 and 1839 the so-called "New China Works" were under the control of Grainger, Lee & Co. In this period the wares became more richly decorated (*see* pictures 243–4) and the range of objects was greatly extended into the decorative field with large ornate vases and such like pieces, as well as small animal models, rich baskets etc.

Thomas Grainger died in 1839, and was succeeded by his son George, who amended the trading style to George Grainger (& Co.), employing a variety of marks that incorporate the name in full, or, more usually, related initials such as "G.W.", "G.G.W", "G.G. & Co" or "G & Co". Some of these Grainger marks have been reproduced here.

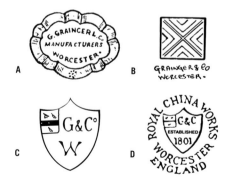

A 1850–75 **B** 1860–80 **C** 1870–89 **D** 1889–1902

Apart from finely painted and gilt porcelains George Grainger also produced a durable (ironstone-type) body, which he termed "Semi-Porcelain", and this description or the initials "S.P." may be found

243

244

incorporated in various Grainger marks during the 1848–60 period. He also produced some very good parian wares (*see* Chapter 10), some of which were glazed and therefore look to the novice very like the standard bone-china body. Some of this glazed parian was reticulated to form an all-over openwork design and other later pieces, made from about 1880, are very similar in general design and tone to the contemporary Royal Worcester pieces. In fact in 1889 this main company took over the Grainger firm, although it continued under Royal Worcester management until 1902 when the Grainger works were finally closed. The Grainger marks were employed up to this closing date, which means that the Grainger porcelains were in production for a little under a century. Thomas Grainger therefore established a factory that added considerable lustre to the history of Worcester ceramic art, a factory that produced a selection of porcelains that must have given the original buyer years of use and pleasure and today's collector considerable interest and delight.

Typical examples of Grainger porcelain are shown in the specialist book previously mentioned.

Rockingham, c.1826–42

| See pictures 12 and 245–6

The porcelain that we know as "Rockingham" was made by the firm of Brameld & Co., which worked quite a small pottery on the estate of Earl Fitzwilliam near Swinton in Yorkshire. The works had for a long period produced various types of earthenware, the translucent porcelains being produced only in the last 16 years of the factory's existence (1826–42). Having made this point and having already stated that the

243 A fine Grainger-Worcester presentation jug, with gilt initials to the front. Quality flower painting and typical Grainger gilding, 16cm (6¼in) high, c.1825–30, Mrs D. Williams.

244 A rare marked Grainger, Lee & Co. (Worcester) letter or note rack showing typical fine flower painting. Painted mark – "Grainger, Lee & Co., Worcester", in red, 19.75cm (7¾in) high, c.1812–22, formerly in the Godden collection.

pottery establishment was quite small, you can deduce that much of the unmarked porcelain attributed to this famous factory could not have been made there. Indeed if all the ceramics attributed to the Rockingham factory had been made there, the factory would have overflowed the not inconsiderable county of Yorkshire!

How do we then know what was, or what was not, made at this Yorkshire factory, (which was managed in this period by Thomas George Frederick Brameld and John Wager Brameld, trading as Brameld & Co.)? Firstly, there are an assortment of pieces bearing one of several different marks that are aptly described as "griffin marks" – this device being taken from the crest of the Fitzwilliam family. Two of these marks are shown here; the pre-1831 versions were printed in red, while the 1831–42 marks appeared in a puce colour. Variations do occur – "Manufacturers to the Queen" can occur on post-1837 examples. Fake Rockingham marks do also occur.

245 A superb Rockingham porcelain mug, finely painted with local (Wath) racing subject. Inscribed and dated "1831", printed griffin mark, in puce, 13cm (5¼in) high, 1831, Christies.

In addition to these marks we have a painted or gilt device comprising the letters "cl" followed by a number. These initials are the abbreviation of "class", as contemporary records include such entries as "Rockingham teapots, class 3" suggest. These initials can, however, also be regarded as a helpful indication of Rockingham origin. They relate to the class of the object, for costing and invoicing.

A picture of the sequence of true Rockingham pattern numbers has been built up, so we can safely regard any piece bearing a number outside these limits as not being of Brameld's manufacture. Rockingham porcelain dessert sets should bear numbers between about 409 and 836; teawares (*see* picture 246) will have numbers within the brackets 400 and 1,600, with some rather late (1840–42) "fractional" numbers 2/1 to about 2/150. Certainly, pieces bearing pattern numbers greater than 2500 or above 2/500 are not true Rockingham.

The Rockingham porcelain is of the bone-china type, a little open or floury in texture, with a glaze somewhat prone to fine crazing – an unhelpful statement as the same description covers so many English porcelains. A general description of the Rockingham shapes and styles of decoration is also rather misleading. There is a long-standing idea of Rockingham porcelains being rococo in form, painted with green or other coloured grounds bearing charming little landscapes, but I can show you far more specimens of Alcock, Coalport, Minton, or Ridgway porcelains that answer this description than I can find Rockingham wares of this type. The Bramelds at the Rockingham works naturally followed the current ceramic fashion; they did not necessarily introduce the style themselves. Many of the specimens are quite modestly decorated with simple sprig designs or only with gold-line borders. Some of the most successful products were the undecorated and unglazed biscuit porcelain figures.

Given the fact that porcelain was produced at this factory for a mere 16 years, it is noteworthy that so many fine ornamental pieces were made and *relatively* few useful wares. This may account for the bankruptcy in 1842, the fault probably lying in the neglect of the bread-and-butter pieces while aiming too high on the production of decorative items, or over-costly wares. These ornamental porcelains, which delight collectors today, include ornate vases and superb baskets – these are often enhanced with raised flowers in the Coalbrookdale style and are painted with scenes or flowers. Inkstands, spill vases, letter or note racks, and a host of other articles were also made. Apart from the figures there are animal models, but the charming house or cottage pastille burners that are so often attributed to this factory do not seem to have been made there – in fact most are of Staffordshire origin.

Apart from the many unmarked pieces incorrectly ascribed to this factory by family tradition (or by a dealer's enthusiasm!) I have to warn you that some reproductions or outright fakes do occur that have a representation of the printed griffin marks. These pieces, although well covered with decoration, lack the spontaneous touch of the originals in the painting, and

246 A Rockingham teapot, which has been produced in one of several unique Yorkshire shapes. The decoration is not typical. The matching saucers bear a printed griffin mark, in puce. 17.75cm (7in) high, c.1834–7, private collection.

the porcelain is lifeless and all too perfect. Some fakes are of Continental hard-paste porcelain.

Try to see a collection of true Rockingham porcelain to familiarize yourself with how examples should look, such as that housed in the Rotherham museum. Several good historical accounts of the factory and the talented artists have been published in recent years: these are *The Rockingham Pottery* by A.A. Eaglestone and T.A. Lockett (revised edition, David & Charles, Newton Abbot, 1973); *Rockingham Ornamental Porcelain* by D.G. Rice (Adam Publishing Co., 1965); and the same author's *The Illustrated Guide to Rockingham Pottery and Porcelain* (Barrie & Jenkins, 1971). The Sheffield City museum published in 1974 a most interesting little book by Alwyn and Angela Cox under the title of *The Rockingham Works*. This includes a lot of new information gleaned from original accounts and letters, indeed our new information on the "cl" marks came from this slim, soft-cover book. A later, very complete, work by the same authors is entitled *Rockingham 1745–1842* (Antique Collectors' Club, 2001).

Worcester, 1793–1862

See pictures 32, 45, 59, and 247–50

In Chapter 6 the early history of the first Worcester porcelain company, which was formed by Dr Wall and his colleagues in 1751, was discussed and the story has been taken up to the Davis/Flight period – 1793.

We will consider here the later partnerships that existed up to the foundation of the Worcester Royal Porcelain company in 1862 (the latter company is

discussed in Chapter 10). Each of these partnerships and their dates have been listed below:

Flight & Barr	1793–1807
Barr, Flight & Barr	1807–13
Flight, Barr & Barr	1813–40
Chamberlain & Co.	1840–52
Kerr & Binns (W.H. Kerr & Co.)	1852–62
Royal Worcester Porcelain Co.	1862–present day
(known as The Worcester Royal Porcelain Company)	

Obviously, between 1793 and the present time the styles have changed greatly, as they had also done in the comparatively short period between 1751 and 1793. In the 1790s the production of the once standard blue-and-white wares had almost entirely ceased, except for the traditional Royal or Queen Charlotte pattern.

The old reliance on Chinese-style designs had been largely left behind, and in the 1790s there was a simplicity in the designs. Teawares tended to have spiral fluting (a fashion not confined to Worcester porcelains) and be decorated with attractively simple sprig designs (*see* picture 32). Dessert services were often rather richer but still had mainly elegant floral or leaf borders rather than overpowering heavy designs.

Dinner services were also decorated with restraint; some admittedly bore rich Japan patterns but most had only a wide, coloured border, often of a pleasing pale colour, remarkable for its evenness of application and tone (*see* pictures 45 and 248). While the useful wares were tastefully restrained, the ornamental pieces – the vases, cachepots (containers for plant pots, *see* picture 247), spill vases, cabinet cups and saucers, ink stands and such objects – were richly decorated. Scenic panels, historical figure subjects, shell and feather studies, and the floral compositions, were painted by a team of ceramic painters who worked in a painstaking and meticulous style, akin to miniature painting. In fact much of the work seems almost too good to enhance a vase because of its jewel-like quality. The main painted subject is often set off against the finest quality gilding and superbly laid ground colours.

I have spoken of ornamental wares, but, strangely, the main Worcester factory in the 1800–40 period did not produce figure or animal models on any scale. Some rare examples are recorded but in the main these decorative articles were left to the two other Worcester factories, Chamberlain's and Grainger's, although from the 1850s to the present day the succeeding Royal Worcester company has specialized in fine figure models.

The Worcester porcelain body has, even at this 1810–20 period, a soapstone base. It is compact or dense

247 A pair of marked Barr, Flight & Barr (Worcester) cachepots. The front panels are finely painted with shells – a favourite high-class form of decoration. Written mark as illustrated, 19cm (7½in) high, c.1810, Godden of Worthing.

and so feels rather heavy, but it is durable and strong in use and has a pleasing, almost waxy, feel. As a base for the decoration it can hardly be bettered. The body was, however, changed to bone china probably in the mid- or late 1830s.

After the Chamberlain & Co. period (1840–52), there was a short-lived but important partnership between R.W. Binns and W.H. Kerr (within the 1852–62 period). Under their directorship the style completely changed and the good name and fortunes of Worcester porcelain were once more set fair. On the success of the Kerr and Binns venture the post-1862 Worcester Royal Porcelain Company and the "Royal Worcester" porcelains were well founded.

Once, when I was really into Victorian ceramics, I decided to form a collection of the rare and always high-quality Kerr & Binns period Worcester porcelain. Examples are rare because the period was short, a mere ten years – 1852–62. Yet I could not shake myself away from my earlier love of 18th-century porcelains and, in particular, from the blue-and-white joys. Now I have but few Kerr & Binns pieces left – one is shown in

picture 249. There is a particular reason for retaining this piece and for explaining its history. In general, the antique trade enjoys a rather bad press! But they are not all "Lovejoys"*, most are highly respectable hard-working traders earning money from their knowledge and love of the articles in which they deal, rather than from questionable practises. When Jean and I became engaged and married in 1964, we were pleased to receive the usual traditional wedding presents to help us set up our home. Those presents had generally been chosen with care and discrimination from shops and stores. But Frank Wilson, a local dealer whom my father had employed in the 1930s and later set up his own business, went a step further. He and his wife invited me into their home. The drawing room (an old term now), was adorned with 100 or so porcelain pieces – plates all around the room, ornamental pieces about on tables or in cabinets. "Geoffrey," said Frank, "I want you to choose any two pieces as wedding presents." He can not have known how embarrassed and overjoyed I was. I obviously could not choose the costly 18th-century pieces, but the two Kerr & Binns Worcester plates sit in our breakfast room, reminding me of the generosity and friendship of fellow dealers.

Back to my résumé, the basic marks used during the "Kerr & Binns" period (during which the alternative title "W.H. Kerr & Co." was also employed) were in circular form, the first with the inclusion of four cursive "W"s, a crescent device and the number "51" (which signified 1751) – this made a connection between the new, Victorian, company and the original Dr Wall one.

A special mark was also employed, mainly on high-quality pieces. This shield-shaped device was novel in that it included the space (middle-right) for the last

248 A fine-quality Flight, Barr & Barr period Worcester centre-dish to a dessert service. The central panels are painted with named birds. Circular printed name and address mark, also "F.B.B." impressed, 35.5cm (14in) long, *c.*1825–35, Godden of Worthing.

two numericals of the year, i.e. "57" for 1857. Also the initials of the artist could be added, by hand, into the bottom left segment. (In the example below the monogram relates to Thomas Bott.) Here we have, I believe, the first British factory mark that records both the year of production and the initials of the decorator.

Apart from the marks, the Kerr & Binns porcelains themselves stand apart from the other British products of the 1852–62 period. The shapes were normally classically pure and simple (*see* picture 250), which was quite a change from the rather fussy Chamberlain & Co. productions. The decoration was again elegant and fine, especially the tooled and chased gilding. Obviously very many styles of decoration were employed in this ten-year period but I will single one out for special mention. I refer to the superb porcelains made in imitation of the celebrated Limoges enamels, although many of the subjects are not antique. It was the style that was emulated, rather than the shape or subject, so they are not mere copies of enamelled metal

249

250

in a ceramic medium. The body continued to be bone china of the standard 19th-century type.

The style of such wares comprised the painting in a slightly tinted and translucent white enamel of subjects laid over a rich deep-blue ground. The covered chalice shown in picture 250, and once in my own collection, perfectly illustrates the style and technique. "Quality" seems to have been the watchword and when, in 1862, W.H. Kerr wished to retire, R.W. Binns was sufficiently encouraged by his shared previous success to form a new firm to continue the production of fine porcelains in Worcester. This was the Worcester Royal Porcelain Company, commonly known throughout the world as "Royal Worcester", the story of which is continued in the next chapter. See also Henry Sandon's *Dictionary of Worcester Porcelain, 1852 to the Present Day* (Antique Collectors' Club, 2001) for the later wares.

The Welsh factories

Nantgarw, *c.*1813 and *c.*1817–20; Swansea, *c.*1814–early 1820s

We can consider the two Welsh porcelain factories together under one general heading as they were so closely connected.

In 1813 the Derby-trained ceramic artist William Billingsley joined with Samuel Walker in establishing a new porcelain factory at Nantgarw on the Glamorgan Canal which linked Cardiff to the Bristol Channel. These first experiments were unsuccessful or at least

249 A very decorative Kerr & Binns dessert plate, which has a characteristic moulded, openwork, border. Each plate in the service is painted with a different fruit composition. Impressed circular (uncrowned) Worcester mark, diameter 23.5cm (9¼in), *c.*1855–62, Godden collection.

250 A superb-quality Kerr & Binns (Worcester) covered chalice. Decorated by Thomas Bott, in the Limoges enamel style. Printed shield mark, incorporating the year numbers "55" and the initials "TB", 26.5cm (10½in) high, 1855, formerly in the Godden collection.

the high percentage of failures in the firing made the production so expensive that the available funds were soon used. The government was appealed to for funds to enable this new Welsh industry to be established and the management of the Swansea Pottery was asked to report on the prospects.

Government funds were not forthcoming – an unsurprising state of affairs – but happily Lewis Weston Dillwyn of the Swansea Pottery had the foresight to realize that if only production difficulties inherent in the very glassy paste could be overcome, the project had great possibilities. Dillwyn therefore invited Billingsley and Walker to join him at Swansea in order to produce a commercially viable porcelain.

At Swansea the venture was a success; some superb porcelains were produced in the 1814–17 period. The great attributes are the very translucent bodies (*see* picture 251), the good glazes, and the fine-quality floral painting. I have written "bodies" for there was no one Swansea body. Several very different mixes were employed and verified specimens must be handled in order to learn the characteristics of each. Some pieces have the appearance and feel of a true hard-paste, very similar to the Paris porcelains of the same period. Many, but by no means all, of the Swansea shapes offer a good guide to their origin and for guidance on these forms you should consult the specialist books listed at the end of this section.

You must not place too much reliance on the "Swansea" name mark, especially the written version, for many fakes have been made. Sometimes the name occurs impressed into the porcelain – occasionally with crossed tridents below. These impressed marks are more reliable than the overglaze mark but until you have a good acquaintance with the Swansea (and Nantgarw) bodies and shapes, and with the hand of the main painters, you would be well advised to buy only from reputable sources and to arm yourself with a fully detailed receipt.

In December 1816 William Billingsley (and later Samuel Walker and William Weston Young) returned to Nantgarw to try again to produce fine porcelains on their own account. At Swansea Dillwyn's successors Bevington & Co. continued to decorate available blanks and they may also have made their own porcelains, which means that the period of Swansea porcelain can be said to have continued into the early 1820s.

At Nantgarw between 1817 and 1820 Billingsley produced fine, delicate porcelains, some very richly decorated. Other useful wares were somewhat sparsely painted with floral sprays or similar simple motifs for sale at competitive prices. It is believed that in or about 1820 William Billingsley and Walker left Nantgarw and were employed by John Rose of Coalport. This seems to be unproven, or at least I do not know of any evidence to substantiate this belief, yet Billingsley, under his assumed name of "Beely", was buried at Kemberton near Coalport on 19 January 1828.

After Billingsley had left Nantgarw, William Weston Young and the artist Thomas Pardoe remained for two years or so decorating the remaining stock of white porcelain and a final stock sale of the porcelain moulds, etc was advertised on 28 October 1822. John Rose of Coalport was reputedly the purchaser of much material from the Nantgarw and Swansea factories, and this is reflected in some later Coalport marks.

The Welsh porcelains had built up a high reputation with the many fine porcelain painters who were practising their craft in London early in the 19th century. The Welsh porcelains had captured a market previously enjoyed by John Rose of Coalport and a market also supplied by the importers of white French porcelains of fashionable new shapes. Many of the Welsh, empire-

251

252

251 A Swansea porcelain plate, with a Sèvres-style relief-moulded edge. Fine flower painting, but the most remarkable aspect of this piece is the high translucency of the porcelain body. "Swansea" name mark faintly impressed, diameter 23.5cm (9¼in), c.1815, Godden of Worthing.

252 A well-decorated Nantgarw porcelain plate, of similar moulding to the Swansea example shown in picture 251. The moulded border is, in this case, very finely accentuated with enamel, and gold. Diameter 23.5cm (9¼in), c.1817–20, Godden of Worthing.

style forms no doubt owe their origin to the London decorators who, I assume, sent novel or saleable French porcelains to Swansea or Nantgarw to be copied in the softer, more pleasing Welsh porcelains. Much of the more ornately decorated specimens you will find referred to as "London decorated". This means precisely that: Swansea or Nantgarw blanks painted in London.

Some of the Welsh blanks were actually decorated at the Chamberlain factory at Worcester (*see* the *Antique Collector*, April 1974, "A Ceramics Enigma").

The Nantgarw porcelains sometimes bear the impressed mark "NANTGARW"* with "CW" below (the initials standing for "China Works") but, like Swansea, a large proportion of the pieces were left completely unmarked. Reproductions occur of both the standard impressed marks and the rare painted name mark, or painted marks have been added to porcelains made elsewhere.

The standard reference books are somewhat costly and difficult to locate, but any serious collector of Welsh porcelain should consult the following: *The Pottery and Porcelain of Swansea and Nantgarw* by E. Morton Nance (Batsford, 1942); *Nantgarw Porcelain* by W.D. John (Ceramic Book Co., 1948, supplement 1956); and *Swansea Porcelain* by W.D. John (Ceramic Book Co., 1958). You could also consult W.D. John's work *William Billingsley 1758–1828* (Ceramic Book Co., 1968), while the most recent work is *Swansea Porcelain, Shapes and Decoration* by A.E. Jones and Sir L. Joseph (D. Brown & Sons, 1988).

The major Museums at Cardiff and at Swansea contain breathtaking collections of Welsh ceramics. The small works at Nantgarw have now been turned into an interesting museum.

Scottish porcelain manufacturers

Very little has been written about Scottish porcelains but undoubtedly some firms mainly known for their earthenwares also produced some porcelain, if only for a brief period. (*See also* West Pans in Chapter 6, p.119).

Apart from the very good-quality examples made by the large firm of J. & M.P. Bell & Co. of Glasgow the Scottish porcelains seem to have been unmarked. There is some evidence to suggest that the following firms, most of which were situated in Glasgow, produced some porcelain. For further details of these firms the reader is referred to the *Encyclopaedia of British Porcelain Manufacturers*.

J. Aitchieson & Co., Glasgow	1807–11
J. & M.P. Bell & Co., Glasgow	1842–20th century
Caledonian Pottery, Glasgow	c.1807+
R. Cochran & Co., Verreville, "	c.1846–56
Delftfield Pottery, Glasgow	c.1748–1823
Glasgow Pottery, Glasgow	c.1800–1807
R.A. Kidston & Co., Glasgow	c.1826–46
Kidston, Cochran & Co., Glasgow	c.1846–7
Lancefield Pottery, Glasgow	c.1824–38
Nautilus Porcelain Co., Glasgow	c.1896–1913
William Reid (& Son[s]), Musselburgh	c.1820s–30s
Reid, Patterson & Co., Glasgow	c.1800–1801
Verreville Pottery, Glasgow	c.1820s–56
West Pans, Musselburgh	c.1764–77

However, most Scottish potteries produced various types of stonewares and earthenwares. The reader is referred to Henry E. Kelly's book *Scottish Ceramics* (Schiffer Publishing, USA, 1999).

Lustre decoration

| *See* pictures 20 and 253–4

I have added here a short section on lustre decoration because up to recently so little has been written on this type of embellishment, and that which has been written seems to give incorrect impressions.

Lustre decoration, emulating silver, copper, or gold effects was much used, especially in Great Britain in the 19th century. Contrary to general opinion silver lustre, derived from platinum (rather than silver, which tarnishes) was first used on porcelains not on pottery**. It was also introduced on the Continent, not in England.

The famous 18th-century German chemist Martin Heinrich Klaproth, consultant to the Berlin porcelain concern, carried out experiments using platinum (then called platina) to emulate silver or polished steel. Some limited use of platinum had been undertaken at Berlin, Sèvres, and probably at the Vienna factory before translations of Kaproth's original 1788 paper were published in two learned English magazines in 1803 and 1804. The first recorded British use of platina or platinum occurs in Henry Daniel's notebook under the date 11 November 1805.

At this period Daniel & Brown and their workforce were decorating, under contract, the Spode porcelains at a workshop within the Spode works. In later years John Hancock (who was employed by Daniel from at least July 1805) claimed in the *Staffordshire Mercury* that he was "the original inventor of lustre…and I first put it in practise at Mr Spode's manufactory, for Messrs Daniel & Brown…" Full details of the events leading up to this claim are given in the specialist book *Collecting Lustreware* by Geoffrey Godden and Michael Gibson (Barrie & Jenkins, 1991).

---

* This word can occur as one word, as two – "NANT GARW", or hyphenated.
** Lustre or metallic effects can, of course, occur on earlier near-Eastern earthenwares, but that is different from the 19th-century English lustred wares.

253

The technique of lustring with both platinum and with gold quickly became widely known and practised. On earthenwares the Wedgwood firm was an early user of lustre but in this book we are mainly concerned with the use of lustre on porcelain. As porcelain is white bodied and as the colour of the lustre effect is, to a large extent, governed by the colour of the underlying body, on porcelains the lustre will in most cases be silver (using platinum) or where gold is used the lustre will be a pleasing pink tint (*see* picture 253), depending for darkness on the number of washes of the lustre-mix applied to the body.

Silver lustre on porcelain was almost entirely used as a trim, edge, or border, not as a total covering, as can occur on earthenware objects. Both silver and gold (pink) lustre could, however, be used in the same way as enamel colours, in order to paint a landscape or other design (*see* picture 254). This type of treatment can be most effective.

Lustre effects on British porcelains mainly falls into the period 1805–30, but unfortunately few specimens were marked. The platinum lustre and the gold-based pink lustre were cheaper to produce, and subsequently to purchase, than finely gilt wares – which needed more gold, talented gilders and burnishers as well as an extra firing.

The bat-printed porcelain teawares that have lustre decoration or trim are still surprisingly plentiful and are generally reasonably priced. All known types of British lustred porcelain and details of the many firms that used this pleasing type of decoration are given in the specialist reference book quoted above.

254

253 An unmarked bone-china London-shape teapot, decorated with a popular and inexpensive form of lustre (and enamel) decoration. Such teawares are normally unmarked, 14cm (5½in) high, *c.*1820, Godden of Worthing.

254 One of a set of three porcelain vases (of Davenport-type). Well decorated in platinum lustre with enamelled landscapes, this is better quality than the majority of lustred porcelain, 14cm (5½in) high, *c.*1810–15, Godden of Worthing.

10
Post-1850 developments and wares

We have already discussed some of the 19th-century porcelains and will now deal with other Victorian and later wares. There were, in the Victorian era, hundreds of manufacturers, many of which were of short duration and very modest concerns, turning out inexpensive useful wares of a quite ordinary kind. We have few records of such makers and in general their products did not bear a mark. Most were situated in the Staffordshire Potteries district and these are listed, and typical productions featured, in *Staffordshire Porcelain*, a multi-author book (edited by G. Godden, Granada, 1983) or in my all-embracing book the *Encyclopaedia of British Porcelain Manufacturers* (Barrie & Jenkins, 1988).

Before we talk of the major later firms I must first mention two typical classes that come within the term porcelain rather than pottery.

Parian

See pictures 53, and 255–7

The parian body superseded the former white biscuit (unglazed) porcelain figures and, in general, is of a creamier tint with a very slight glaze-like sheen. The body was introduced in the early 1840s by Copeland & Garrett*, a partnership that succeeded the Spode firm in 1833. The body was, by them, originally termed "Statuary Porcelain", underlining the intention to reproduce in miniature famous sculptures. In this aim the Art Union of London ably assisted and became the first patron of their work. A contemporary account states that when the editor of the *Art Union* magazine visited the Copeland & Garrett factory at Stoke:

We there witnessed the first efforts to secure popularity for the new art of porcelain sculpture. Two statuettes had been produced in it, one a graceful female bust, and the other "the shepherd boy" after Wyatt, but they had not sold. The public did not show any sign of being prepared to acknowledge the real worthiness of the novelty; and it is by no means improbable that the process would have proceeded no further, had it not

been our good fortune to urge upon Mr Garrett the wisdom of perseverance…a meeting was arranged by us between several sculptors…and Mr T. Battam, the artist of the works. The two honorary secretaries of the Art Union of London were also present. After a careful examination of the new material an opinion was pronounced decidedly in its favour… A commission from the Art Union of London followed, and this new art of parian sculpture was rescued from a peril that might have proved fatal in the first infancy of its career.

The first Art Union commission was for 50 copies of John Gibson's sculpture *The Narcissus*. The total cost was £150 and the copies were available early in 1846. I show an early marked Copeland & Garrett example in picture 255: the fine workmanship and care in the finishing is evident but some later, post-1847, Copeland examples are not quite up to the standard of the first series. These bear a special mark: "Narcissus by Gibson R.A., modelled by E.R. Stephens and executed in *Statuary Porcelain* by Copeland & Garrett for the Art Union of London – 1846".

When I speak of finish, you must remember that this or any other figure or group is assembled from many separately moulded components, each affixed with slip or, in this case, diluted parian. The joints or seams have to be carefully smoothed after assembly and parts of the design sharpened with special tools. Alternatively, sections have to be undercut, or small pieces, flowers, etc have to be added. All this is done by the person known as a "repairer", who also has to make sure that the pieces are assembled in a natural-looking manner so that the figure has "life" and does not look "wooden".

From the mid-1840s the leading firms, particularly Copeland, Minton, Wedgwood, and the Worcester firms produced some fine-quality and most attractive

255 An early "Statuary Porcelain" or parian figure of Narcissus after John Gibson's large original, carved in marble. Printed "Copeland & Garrett" mark, 31cm (12¼in) high, c.1846, formerly in the Godden collection.

---

* Other firms such as Mintons and Boote's produced parian wares at this early date in the 1840s shortly after Copeland & Garrett.

256

257

256 A very well-modelled Minton jug form. One of very many mass produced in the parian body. A design registered in May 1847 and bearing the relevant diamond-shaped registration mark. Minton relief-moulded scroll seal with initial "M" and the model number "320", 23.5cm (9¼in) high, 1847, Godden of Worthing.

257 A Minton parian model of the "New Shepherdess" (one of a pair). This example is rare, being coloured and having gilding – perhaps it was an exhibition piece. It has an incised ermine mark, as is usually found on early Minton parian, 17.75cm (7in) high, c.1850–51, Godden collection.

parian figures, busts, and groups. These are well worth seeking out but I must warn you that by no means all Victorian parian measures up to the best. Much of it, especially that produced by the smaller firms, was of an ordinary nature, with little or no regard to originality or quality, and made to be cheap and affordable to most. At its best parian is very, very good; at its worst it can be extremely bad.

Apart from figures and groups most of the Victorian manufacturers produced in this versatile body a host of semi-ornamental useful objects, and especially relief-moulded jugs (*see* picture 256). Again, the early ones can be extremely fine, particularly those bearing the name marks of the leading firms, but by the 1860s the quality and design had greatly degenerated as the smaller concerns sought to cut costs and to market cheap novelties. These last remarks apply equally to the hundreds of small objects made in parian: butter dishes, trinket dishes, ring stands, etc.

Not all parian was left undecorated. The body could be tinted throughout or the surface only could be coloured in the normal manner and, in some cases, the leading manufacturers added slight gilt enrichments to figures (*see* picture 257) or groups. The leading firms, such as Copeland, Minton, and Royal Worcester, also combined the semi-matt parian figures with glazed and decorated porcelain to produce imposing and often elegant centrepieces (*see* picture 53), clock cases, and similar articles.

The British manufacturers in the table opposite are recorded as having produced parian wares; some like Robinson & Leadbeater specialized in the versatile body. Not all these firms marked their products but this list will enable some name and initial-marked examples to be identified and approximately dated. Further details can be found in the *Encyclopaedia* that has already been mentioned.

The dates that are given, in the case of the larger firms that were active over a long period, relate only to the period in which their parian wares would have been in production, not necessarily the whole duration of that manufactory.

The first standard book on parian wares was Mr and Mrs C. Shinn's *The Illustrated Guide to Victorian Parian China* (Barrie & Jenkins, 1971) but a very detailed multi-authored work edited by P. Atterbury, *The Parian Phenomenon, a Survey of Victorian Parian Porcelain Statuary and Busts*, was published by Richard Dennis in 1989. The books on moulded jugs also feature parian.

Not all white or coloured unglazed figures, groups, or other articles are necessarily of British origin or

Manufacturer	Location	Date
W. Adams (& Sons)	Staffordshire	c.1842–65
S. Alcock & Co.	"	c.1842–59
G. Ash	"	c.1865–82
G. Baguley	"	c.1848–67
J. Bailey	"	c.1860–62
J. Bailey & Co.	"	c.1865–70
Bailey, Beech & Cooke	"	c.1870
Bailey & Bevington	"	c.1867–8
Bailey & Cooke	"	c.1870
Bailey, Murrells & Co.	"	c.1864–6
T. Banks	"	c.1862
Banks & Hodkinson	"	c.1862
Bates, Brown-Westhead & Moore	"	c.1858–61
Mrs J. Beech	"	c.1864–73
J. & M.P. Bell & Co (Ltd)	Glasgow	c.1842–70
Belleek Pottery	Belleek, N.Ireland	c.1863–
N. Bentley	Staffordshire	c.1865–7
W. Berrisford (& Coa.)	"	c.1860
Bevington & Co.	"	c.1867–8
S. Bevington (& Son)	"	c.1853–64
J. & T. Bevington	"	c.1865–78
Bevington & Bradley	"	c.1868–9
Bevington & Worthington	"	c.1862–3
T. & R. Boote (Ltd)	"	c.1849–65
Bourne & Roe	"	c.1856–7
Bradbury, Anderson & Bettany	"	c.1844–54
W. Brammall	"	c.1859–64
Brewer & Bromley	"	c.1861
Bristol Victoria Pottery Co. (Ltd)	"	c.1865–87
Bromley, Turner & Co.	"	c.1862
Bromley, Turner & Hassall	"	c.1862
Brown-Westhead, Moore & Co.	"	c.1861–1904
W. Brownfield (& Son)	"	c.1850–92
Coalport China Works	Coalport, Shropshire	c.1842–65
G. Cocker	Staffordshire	c.1842–60
R. Cooke	"	c.1871–9
W.T. Copeland (& Sons)	"	c.1847–
Copeland & Garrett	"	c.1842–7
T. Daniel	"	c.1851–4
Sir J. Duke & Nephews	"	c.1860–64
Edge & Co.	"	c.1872
Liddle Elliot (& Son)	"	c.1860–69
J. Ellis & Son	"	c.1869
J.B. Evans & Co.	"	c.1877–9
Evans & Buxton	"	c.1863
Foster, Crutchley & Co.	"	c.1862
W.H. Goss	"	c.1858–85
Goss & Peake	"	c.1867–8
G. Grainger & Co.	Worcester	c.1842–65
J. Hackney	Staffordshire	c.1868
Hackney & Co.	"	c.1866–8
Hackney, Warrilow & Co.	"	c.1868
Harrison & Baker	"	c.1870–93
Hassall, Poole & Stanway	"	c.1872–3
Hewitt Bros.	"	c.1919–25
Hewitt & Leadbeater	"	c.1907–19
Leveson Hill, [executors of]	"	c.1859–71
Hill Pottery Co.	"	c.1861–7
E. Hodgkinson	"	c.1864–71
J. Holdcroft	"	c.1868
Holdcroft & Walton	"	c.1868
J. Holmes & Co.	"	c.1859
W. Hopkinson	"	c.1862
Keeling, Walker & Cooper	"	c.1862–6
Kerr & Binns	Worcester	c.1852–62
S. Keys	Staffordshire	c.1853–60
Keys & Briggs	"	c.1860–4
Keys & Mountford	Staffordshire	c.1850–53
J. Lancaster	"	c.1861–5
Livesley, Powell & Co.	"	c.1851–65
N. & T. Massey	"	c.1862–4
Massey & Sons	"	c.1864–5
T.J. & J. Mayer	"	c.1842–55
Mayer Brothers & Elliot	"	c.1855–8
Mayer & Elliot	"	c.1858–60
G. Meli	"	c.1858–62
Meli & Prior	"	c.1861
R. Mellor	"	c.1862–4
Mrs E. Mills	"	c.1852–73
Mills & Swan	"	c.1862
Mills Brothers	"	c.1865–71
Minton(s)	"	c.1842–
Moss & Hobson	"	c.1859–62
J. Mountford	"	c.1853–9
Old Hall Pottery Co. Ltd	"	c.1861–86
J. Oldham (& Co.)	"	c.1860–77
E.Palmer	"	c.1872
Platt & Wild	"	c.1860
J. Poole & Són	"	c.1878–86
Poole & Stanway	"	c.1873–4
Poole, Stanway & Wood	"	c.1875–8
F. & R. Pratt (& Co.)	"	c.1842–70
J. Rickhuss	"	c.1861
Ridgway & Abington	"	c.1842–60
J. Ridgway, Bates & Co.	"	c.1865–8
Robinson & Leadbeater	"	c.1860–1924
H. Roe (& Son)	"	c.1857–64
J. Rose & Co.	Coalport, Shropshire	c.1842–70
Royal Worcester	Worcester	c.1862–
W. Sale	Staffordshire	c.1860s
C. Salt	"	c.1842–64
E. Saul	"	c.1862–4
W. Smith	"	c.1859–60
H. Snow & Co.	"	c.1853–63
South Wales Pottery	Llanelly, S. Wales	c.1842–70
Stanway & Son	Staffordshire	c.1878–9
Stanway & Horne	"	c.1862–4
Stanway, Horne & Adams	"	c.1865–80
E. Steele	"	c.1875–1900
W. Steele	"	c.1850–60s
W. Stubbs	"	c.1847–97
Stubbs, Tompkinson & Billington	"	c.1865–8
D. Sutherland (& Sons)	"	c.1863–77
Taylor & Hopkinson	"	c.1857
H. Timmis	"	c.1850–54
Turner & Co.	"	c.1863–71
Turner, Hassall & Bromley	"	c.1859–62
Turner, Hassall & Peake	"	c.1863–71
Turner, Hassall & Poole	"	c.1871–2
Turner & Wood	"	c.1878–88
Turton & Gregg	"	c.1851–3
C. Twyford	"	c.1859–70
J. Wardle (& Co.)	"	c.1854–84
Wardle & Ash	"	c.1859–65
W. Warrington	"	c.1863–7
Warrington & Co.	"	c.1862–3
Wayte & Ridge	"	c.1864
Wilkinson & Son	"	c.1862–7
Wilkinson & Rickhuss	"	c.1856–62
Wilkinson, Rickhuss & Toft	"	c.1855–6
J. Wilson	"	c.1879–97
G. Wood &	"	c.1864
Wood & Frost	"	c.1864
Worthingon & Green	"	c.1844
Worthington & Harrop	"	c.1856
Worthington & Son	"	c.1863
Yearsley (& Co.)	"	c.1850

indeed made from the parian body, for very many Continental firms produced very similar articles but these are termed "biscuit" or bisque, meaning unglazed porcelain. These can be very decorative but such wares are not seriously collected in Britain, as are the parian wares – see my *Godden's Guide to European Porcelain* (Barrie & Jenkins, 1993, Chapter 8).

While parian may be regarded as an inexpensive body for mass production from moulds of figures, groups, busts, and a host of useful articles, when coloured the body also did service as the ground for the most painstaking and individual method of decoration, the technique known as "pâte-sur-pâte".

Pâte-sur-pâte

| *See* pictures 258–60

As the name (which means paste on paste) will suggest, this technique is of French origin. Experiments were carried out at the French National Sèvres factory in the early 1860s in an effort to copy a Chinese technique. The result was, however, very different from the Oriental prototype, but the experiment was to lead to the adaptation of quite beautiful effects by a process wholly ceramic, in that the design is built up of the body itself. The effect therefore does not depend on added enamel colours.

The result can be likened to a ceramic cameo. Tinted parian normally served as the ground either as a complete vase (or other object) or as a panel let into a plate. On to this coloured ground a figure or other design was built up slowly in white slip, layer by layer, the details of which were sharpened up or otherwise added to, or carved, to accentuate the applied relief design. When complete this opaque mass was fired in the normal manner. The white parts became vitrified and semi-translucent so that in the thinner parts the darker ground showed through, resulting in a pleasing graduation of tint and the appearance of a finished cameo-like design. Until the piece was fired all parts of the design were equally opaque, the skill of the artist being put to the test on vitrification – after which it was too late to correct any error in the depth of slip and colour.

The leading exponent of this painstaking process in England was Marc Louis Solon (1835–1913) who had been trained at the Sèvres factory and who, on arriving in England in 1870, was employed by Minton at Stoke-on-Trent. Here he built up a richly deserved reputation for his masterpieces in the pâte-sur-pâte technique (*see* picture 259). These unique compositions comprised (or prominently included) tall, willowy, rather classical female figures in flimsy drapery. This style gradually gave way to comprise or include children and cupids, somewhat better suited to small objects and to plates bearing small pâte-sur-pâte panels. Some rare pieces include the use of some tinted slip (*see* picture 259), rather than the normal white.

So popular did Solon's work become, and so slow was the process, that he was asked to train apprentices in the same technique to help meet the market for these wares. Many of the apprentice pieces comprise floral compositions but some of the pupils progressed to figurework and, while most collectors seek only pieces from Solon's master hands, some of the apprentice pieces are extremely pleasing and quite inexpensive compared to Solon's work. One of my "specials" happens to be such an apprentice piece: the 1881 vase by Lawrence Birks shown in picture 258. I try not to be too carried away by the fact that it was a bargain purchased on our honeymoon, for surely it serves to typify the charm and quality of Minton's pâte-sur-pâte.

258 A Minton tinted parian vase, decorated in the pâte-sur-pâte technique by one of Solon's apprentices – Lawrence Birks – and signed with an "LB" monogram. Gilt crowned globe "MINTONS" mark, impressed "MINTONS" mark, model number (indistinct), and year cipher for 1881, 31.75cm (12½in) high, 1881, Godden collection.

259 A Minton tinted parian tray that was decorated by M.L. Solon in his pâte-sur-pâte technique. This particular example shows the rare use of slightly tinted slips. Signed "L.Solon 78" and special gilt 1878 Paris Exhibition Minton mark as well as an impressed 1765 (shape number) "MINTONS" and year cipher, 33.75 x 17.75cm (13¼ x 7in), 1878, formerly in the Godden collection.

Solon's pupils at Mintons included Alboine Birks, Lawrence Birks, H. Hollins, T. Mellor, A. Morgan, F. Rhead, T.H. Rice, H. Sanders, and C. Toft. Their work was sometimes initialled and rarely signed in full. Of these Solon trainees the two Birks brothers are generally accepted as having been the most talented. Alboine Birks (*b.*1861) worked at Mintons from 1876 to his retirement in 1937, being mainly employed on pâte-sur-pâte work. He in turn trained Richard Bradbury, who continued the tradition until he was called up in World War II. Although painted designs emulating to some degree the general effect have since been produced, as have some moulded essays in the same manner, it seems unlikely that individual hand-worked pâte-sur-pâte can ever again be produced on a commercial basis, for the cost of such pieces would, in time and money, be prohibitive.

Not all pâte-sur-pâte is Minton. Apart from the fact that several Continental firms, including Dresden and Sèvres, produced very good examples, British manufacturers did not leave Mintons alone to enjoy the market entirely without competition. Several firms produced good work in this field. The Royal Worcester and Grainger-Worcester essays in this style can be most attractive, although they were generally restricted to floral compositions – excluding figure subjects. Moore Brothers of Longton and Brownfield & Sons of Cobridge also produced pâte-sur-pâte in the 1880s.

In terms of quantity George Jones of the Crescent Pottery at Stoke were the leading manufacturers of pâte-sur-pâte, and signed work by the pâte-sur-pâte artist "F. Schenk" often appears in the salerooms (*see* picture 260). However, in comparison with the Minton or Worcester examples these George Jones pieces are but poor relations and most of the Schenk designs seem repetitive as opposed to the one-off designs from Solon's hand. Nevertheless, the George Jones wares can be passed off as Minton and you would do well to note the characteristic forms and designs as illustrated in Plate 328 of my *Illustrated Encyclopaedia of British Pottery and Porcelain* and in Plates 433–4 of my

260

261

British Porcelain, an Illustrated Guide*. Chapter 8 of my *Victorian Porcelain* gives a good general account of English pâte-sur-pâte decoration, including a description of the process quoted from Solon's own 1901 account. However, the specialist book is Bernard Bumpus' *Pâte-sur-Pâte, The Art of Ceramic Relief Decoration, 1849–1992* (Barrie & Jenkins, 1993).

Brown-Westhead, Moore & Co., 1862–1904

I have already mentioned the success of John Ridgway at Cauldon Place, Hanley, and how he was appointed Potter to Queen Victoria. However, in 1856, the old John Ridgway & Co. gave way to Ridgway, Bates & Co., to be followed on John's retirement in 1858 by Bates, Brown-Westhead & Moore and then from December 1861 by Brown-Westhead, Moore & Co., a firm that continued until 1904.

During these 42 years the Cauldon Place factory produced an amazing range of fine and decorative porcelain (as well as most types of earthenware) and although they continued to hold the Royal Warrant, their products are not now generally known, perhaps as so little of their porcelain bears a trademark. In this respect the later partners followed John Ridgway's reluctance to use a name mark.

Brown-Westhead, Moore & Co. exhibited at most of the international exhibitions of the period, winning well-deserved praise. Of their display at the 1878 Paris Exhibition, George Augustus Sala wrote:

260 A George Jones of Stoke circular dish or wall plaque decorated in the pâte-sur-pâte manner, but by a semi-moulded process. Hand-worked by Frederick Schenk, but not a unique design. Impressed "G.J. & Sons" crescent mark, diameter 24.75cm (9¾in), *c.*1875–85, Godden of Worthing.

261 A Brown-Westhead, Moore & Co. bone-china dessert plate. This ribbon border design was registered on 3 November 1869. Impressed diamond-shaped registration mark and painted pattern number, "B4029", diameter 23cm (9in), *c.*1870–72, Godden of Worthing.

Messrs Brown-Westhead, Moore & Co. of Cauldon Place, exhibit decorative porcelain and pottery of a high order in great variety, including elegantly designed vases, well modelled representations of animals, colossal candelabra and brackets of much originality of form, many of these productions being distinguished by great boldness and breadth of design...several of the dessert services are decorated with designs from La Fontaine's fables, hunting subjects, and the like and many of the vases are painted with figures and heads of animals.

The partnership enjoyed the services of a great many talented artists, including Antoine Boullemier (from Sèvres and Mintons), Thomas John Bott, G. Landgraff, and E. Sieffert, but quite apart from these finely decorated porcelains the normal run of shapes are extremely pleasing and display fine potting and finish. Take for example the standard plate shape, the basic form of which was registered on 3 November 1869 (*see* picture 261). Teawares often had attractively moulded rope-like feet. At present a specialist study

---

* For a specialist study of George Jones' varied productions, see Robert Cluett's *George Jones Ceramics, 1861–1951*, (Schiffer, 1998).

262 A typical, richly gilt Coalport dessert plate, with hand-painted Scottish scenic centre. Signed by Percy Simpson, printed crowned Coalport mark, with "England", diameter 21cm (8¼in), *c.*1910, Godden of Worthing.

of the Brown-Westhead & Moore wares (both the earthenwares and fine porcelains) is awaited but in the meantime you could follow the basic outline given in my *Ridgway Porcelain* (revised 1985 edition, Antique Collector's Club) or, of course, the general book *Staffordshire Porcelain*.

Coalport, 1850 to the present day

I have in previous chapters discussed the early John Rose hybrid hard-paste porcelains and the later bone china with the post-1820 lead-free glaze.

In the post-1850 period the old name of John Rose (*d.*1841) fell into disuse and the factory and its products tended to be called "Coalport", although the old official title "John Rose & Co." remained in being for many years, even under William Pugh's ownership.

Some superb richly decorated porcelains were made in the 1850–90 period, but it must be remembered that the standard designs such as the "Indian Tree" pattern represented the bread-and-butter lines and vastly outsold the finer, but more costly, wares. The richer wares often emulated Sèvres shapes and styles of decoration, as these styles were still fashionable.

William Pugh died in 1875 at a period when the works had to some degree lost ground in the market. In 1880 Peter Bruff purchased the concern for £15,000 and put his son Charles Bruff in charge with the task of reorganizing the workforce and production methods,

although he had no ceramic training or background. In general terms he succeeded in this aim, at the time of general difficulties in the industry.

But in 1924 the Coalport company was sold on to the larger Staffordshire firm of Cauldon Potteries Ltd, and in 1926 the Shropshire factory was closed and most of the employees were moved to the Potteries where "Coalport" porcelain has been made ever since. The firm has, over the years, had several changes of ownership and since July 1967 it has been part of the Wedgwood group. The Coalport division, however, continues to produce traditional porcelains under the Coalport name. These include the traditional floral-encrusted "Coalbrookdale" porcelains and the newer attractive figures.

Although Coalport porcelain has been produced entirely in the Staffordshire Potteries since 1926, the local Shropshire association is retained as the original factory is now part of the large Ironbridge Gorge Museum complex. Apart from a shop selling modern Coalport wares, the factory site includes a very good historical museum section, where displays of former wares can be viewed to advantage. On some days you can also see porcelains being made and decorated at the museum on the original site backing on the river Severn, downstream from Ironbridge.

From the 1860s most Coalport porcelains have borne one of the following basic printed marks. It should be noted that from about 1870, the early date "1750" has been incorporated in most Coalport marks. This claimed date of establishment is misleading and does not directly relate to the date of the piece bearing such an unlikely date! Nevertheless, Coalport porcelains have been produced and given pleasure for over 200 years. They represent a rich and varied assortment of fine-quality porcelains. Certainly in the 19th and 20th centuries these Shropshire and, later, Staffordshire porcelains stood with the leading British names.

The printed marks include the following basic types:

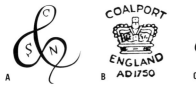

A c.1861–75. B c.1891–1920s, variations occur.
C Sample postwar printed mark.

263 A superb-quality Coalport ornamental vase. The figure panel is signed by Thomas Keeling and the piece shows typical elaborate raised, tooled Coalport gilding. Coalport crown marks printed in gold with "England", gilt pattern number – "V7066", Ironbridge Gorge Museum, 30.5cm (12in) high, c.1905.

For further information and good pictorial coverage of the Coalport porcelains, the reader is referred to my specialist work *Coalport and Coalbrookdale Porcelains* (revised edition, Antique Collectors' Club, 1981) or Michael Messenger's *Coalport 1795–1926* (Antique Collectors' Club, 1995).

Copeland, 1847–1970

The famous Spode firm gave way to the Copeland & Garrett partnership in 1833 and within this 1833–47 period the traditional Spode quality was continued and the new "statuary porcelain" (*see* picture 255) or parian body was introduced. On the retirement of Thomas Garrett in 1847 W.T. Copeland (Alderman and later Lord Mayor of London) continued the Spode works at Stoke under his own name. This title was slightly amended to "W.T. Copeland & Sons" in 1867 to mark the entry of his four sons into the business. The Copeland title remained in use until 1970 when the revised style "Spode Ltd" was adopted to illustrate the continuous link with the Spode works and tradition.

From the late 1840s onwards Copeland's were Minton's great rivals, with each of these nearby Stoke factories producing *tour de force* after *tour de force* in the hope of gaining major medals at the international exhibitions of the period. While I happen to prefer the Minton porcelains, it must be acknowledged that the Copeland wares are also of superb quality. The flower painting is especially noteworthy, and while Copelands were not as preoccupied as Herbert Minton was in the production of sumptuous Sèvres-style porcelains, the reasonably priced, high-quality Copeland parian wares could not be matched by any other manufacturer.

The Copeland marks are refreshingly simple, each including the name, and some of the later wares also incorporate impressed date marks indicating the month and year of manufacture, such as S over 79 for September 1879. Parian wares and most earthenwares bear the Copeland name mark. Standard Copeland printed marks are reproduced below.

A From c.1851. B From c.1875. C From c.1891.

Robert Copeland's chapter (8) in *Staffordshire Porcelain* (Granada, 1983) provides excellent information on the post-1837 porcelains. This author's book *Spode and Copeland Marks* (Studio Vista, 2nd edition 1997) is also helpful and interesting. The latest specialist book is Vega Wilkinson's *Spode – Copeland – Spode. The works and its people* (Antique Collectors' Club, 2002).

Doulton (Burslem), 1882 to present day

While Doulton's of Lambeth had been a household name in the manufacture of stonewares from the first half of the 19th century, the company entered the field of fine porcelain at a comparatively late date, in the 1880s. However, these Doulton porcelains very soon made up for their late arrival and they soon established a very high international reputation.

In 1877 the Doulton company entered into a partnership with Pinder, Bourne & Co. of Nile Street, Burslem in the Staffordshire Potteries. For some five years good earthenware was produced until, in 1882, Doulton took over the old firm and under the new name "Doulton & Co." the production of Doulton fine bone china was added to the existing range of pottery. A number of talented artists were employed, including: Percy Curnock (1885–1919); David Dewsbury, the orchid painter (1889–1919); Edward Raby, the former Worcester flower painter (1892–1919); and George White, the figure painter (1885–1912).

Apart from the finely painted and very richly gilt porcelain decorated in the conventional manner, Doulton's Burslem factory also produced excellent glaze-effect wares and, in more modern times, a series of colourful figures and groups that have found international favour. In December 1959 a pleasing new inexpensive tableware body was introduced under the trade name "English Translucent China". This has been most successfully embellished with simple clean-looking modern designs, and indeed my own family occasional dinner and tea service is of this Doulton body. The revised description "Fine China" has been used since 1979.

Two of the basic Doulton porcelain printed marks are reproduced in the next column but anyone who is interested in the Doulton story and the wide range of the company's products should read Desmond Eyle's *Royal Doulton 1815–1965* (Hutchinson, 1965). More recent works are Desmond Eyles's *The Doulton Burslem Wares* (Barrie & Jenkins, 1980) and the joint work by D. Eyles, R. Dennis, and L. Irvine, *Royal Doulton Figures* (revised edition 1987). In addition there are many price guides and specialist booklets on various aspects of Doulton wares. There is also a Royal

Doulton International Collectors' Club, which itself publishes an informative magazine.

In addition to the standard marks, as shown below, impressed potting dates can occur, for example "1.20" for January 1920. Also a numerical system was employed from 1928. To the number by the mark 27 should be added, so that the number 10 will indicate that the piece was decorated in 1937. The wording "Copyright. Doulton & Co. Ltd" added below a standard printed mark confirms a date after *c.*1960.

A *c.*1902+ **B** *c.*1930+

The output of the Doulton factories was vast and, while some special high-quality pieces painted by leading artists or rare or otherwise highly collectable specimens will command a high price, it does not follow that all Doulton wares are valuable. Some of the standard, mass-produced, or printed tableware, although of above average quality, are not especially costly.

Minton, *c.*1824 to present day

See pictures 19, 39, 53, 210, 256–9, and 264–8

I have already discussed the first period of Minton's porcelains and recorded the early marks that were used before the temporary discontinuation of porcelain manufacture in the approximate period of 1816–24.

When Minton's, that is Thomas Minton and his son Herbert, recommenced the manufacture of fine bone china in 1824, completely new and rich shapes were introduced. Magnificent dessert and tea services were produced, many of which were decorated with ground colours, ornate gilding, and extremely well-painted panels (*see* picture 19). These pre-1850 porcelains are often incorrectly ascribed to other factories, as a trademark was seldom employed. Now, however, collectors can, by reference to *Minton Pottery and Porcelain of the First Period 1793–1850* (Herbert Jenkins, 1968), discover the basic and characteristic Minton shapes and styles of decoration. Collectors will also learn from this book (and from the factory records quoted in it) that Minton produced a superb range of floral-encrusted porcelain of the so-called Coalbrookdale type, as well as some charming Derby-type figures and groups – pieces that are quite unrivalled for quality. The basic

264 265

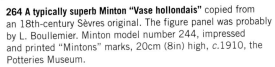

264 A typically superb Minton "Vase hollondais" copied from an 18th-century Sèvres original. The figure panel was probably by L. Boullemier. Minton model number 244, impressed and printed "Mintons" marks, 20cm (8in) high, c.1910, the Potteries Museum.

265 A superb Minton vase in the style of 18th-century Sèvres porcelain. The Minton turquoise colour ground was particularly successful. This was the centre example from a splendid garniture of three. Printed "MINTON" mark, with ermine devices, 31.75cm (12½in) high, c.1850–60, Godden of Worthing.

details and illustrations of typical Minton articles are also covered in my much more recent work the *Encyclopaedia of British Porcelain Manufacturers* (Barrie & Jenkins, 1988).

Progressing on to the post-1850 period, Herbert Minton was rivalling Copeland in the production of tasteful well-finished parian figures (*see* picture 257) and groups and, while we are looking at porcelains in this book, we must not forget that Minton led the world in the production of majolica and in many other types of earthenware – useful and ornamental.

I mentioned the excellence of this company's pâte-sur-pâte at the beginning of this chapter (*see* pictures 258 and 259). To a large degree this high reputation was due to the employment of Lèon Arnoux as Art Director. Arnoux was a practising potter in his native France before joining Minton's Stoke factory in 1848. He went on to win many international awards and it has been stated that Arnoux "will always be remembered… as among the most talented and accomplished French-men who ever honoured our shores and aided us in the development of our art industries".

Apart from the technical improvements introduced by Arnoux in new bodies, colours, and the like, we can on a broader front also attribute to him the Minton pre-eminence in the copies of the rich Sèvres porcelains (*see* pictures 264–6), shapes and styles of decoration that were universally acclaimed, and certainly they suited the richer styles of Victorian furnishing.

The presence of Lèon Arnoux at Minton certainly also attracted many talented Continental artists and designers there, who had left their own countries in the times of unrest in the mid-19th century to practise their art in this country. The French language must have been almost as common as English within the Minton factory! Not all of Minton's artists were, however, of foreign extraction, for there were a great many talented English painters, such as Thomas Allen, Thomas Kirkby, Richard Pilsbury, and Jesse Smith, who could hold their own against all comers.

Nevertheless, it was the wealth of internationally known Continental artists at Minton that set the seal on this factory's success for quality porcelains. While the Continental factories were in decline the bright star of Minton was rising to fill the void. The work of Antonin Boullemier (c.1840–1900), a Sèvres-trained figure painter, deserves special mention for the charm of his composition and for the delicacy of his style. I have experienced great difficulty in selecting one specimen to show the style and quality of Victorian Minton, for hundreds of pieces are contenders for the honour, but the plate shown in picture 268, which is from a magnificent dessert service, serves to illustrate several points.

266

267

Apart from the quite obvious overall quality of this plate there is the wonderful even and mellow, almost liquid turquoise ground colour. Many factories tried to emulate this Sèvres colour but none, I think, with the success achieved by Mintons (as the company was known after 1873). However even the Mintons' colour did, on occasions, fail when it was applied too thickly, resulting in a rather opaque colour and with some crazing or cracking away of the enamel. Note the quality of the gilding and especially the main borders around the rim and the panel. This was applied by the process that is known as "acid-gilding", which was introduced by Mintons in 1863 and later taken up by all the leading porcelain manufacturers. The pleasing contrast between the matt (or dull) and the burnished bright gold (and I do mean gold, not a cheap substitute) is achieved by the use of acid (the rest of the plate being protected by an acid-resisting compound) so that when the gold is applied to the plate, after it has been washed and cleaned, some of it lies on the surface and so is subsequently burnished, while some is in the acid-recessed parts and escapes the action of the burnisher. The effect, as you can see, well repays all the trouble involved in the various processes.

The figure subject panel, painted in monochrome (that is, in shades of one colour), is also noteworthy for the free, light style of painting in the French manner. If

266 One of a pair of Minton vases, in the 18th-century Sèvres style. Note the almost liquid-looking ground colour and the quality of the painting – it is simply superb. Minton marks covered by gilt metal plinths, 24cm (9½in) high, c.1860–70, formerly in the Godden collection.

267 A Minton bone-china plate from an outstanding dessert service. The centres are painted with different Russian scenes and placed within ornately gilt and enamelled border. Note the typical Minton turquoise ground. Impressed and printed "Mintons" name marks, signed "E. Rischgitz", diameter of plate 23cm (9in), c.1878, Godden of Worthing.

the plate is turned the light weight is immediately noticeable, which is due to the thin, workmanlike potting. Also noticeable is the translucency of the pure English bone china, which has a friendly and almost warm glaze.

On the reverse we can see two basic types of factory mark – those that are impressed and consequently were added during the manufacturing process and those that were added overglaze, while, or after, the piece was decorated. The later Minton marks are most helpful and well worth study. First, we find on this particular example the impressed name "MINTONS" (the "S" was added from c.1873, with the singular version "MINTON" appearing between 1862 and 1873). We also have three small ciphers or letters denoting the potter, the month, and year of manufacture; there is an arrow-like device signifying 1874, which was the year of manufacture. The impressed Minton year ciphers were employed from 1842 onwards and they are almost indispensable in determining the date of any example. (The key to this system has been reproduced on p.218; from 1943 the last two digits of the year were impressed.)

The overglaze marks comprise the standard globe mark, with the crown, which was added in 1873 and the plural form of the name "MINTONS". This basic mark was continued up to 1912, when laurel leaves were added each side of the globe. Previously to that, the word "England" had been added in 1891, often giving way to the wording "Made in England" in the 20th century. We also find the painted pattern number "G.1595". Pattern numbers can be a great help, not only for dating an object but also as a guide to the make, and I will explain their purpose further on p.234. Here it is necessary only to state that Mintons "G" series started in 1868 and that some 1,500 such designs had been introduced by 1874. Each stock pattern has a separate number, but this relates only to the main design – for example each piece in this dessert set bears the same pattern number, and yet each of the hand-painted panels is completely different. As a general rule pattern numbers appear only on tablewares, not on Minton vases and such ornamental pieces painted with individual designs.

This one plate has served to make several points, and yet the story of Minton porcelain is a long and complex one, for it started in the 18th century. There is room here only to refer you to printed accounts where you can, if you so choose, look up further details for yourself or feast your eyes on the illustrations of typical specimens. First, you have my *Minton Pottery and Porcelain of the First Period 1793–1850*, secondly we have a recent book *The Directory of Minton* by P. Atterbury and M. Batkin (Antique Collectors' Club,

268 A superb-quality Minton plate from a dessert service. Each finely painted monochrome centre panel in the service is different but in the Sèvres style. Note again the wonderful Minton turquoise ground, as well as the acid-gilding. Impressed and printed "MINTONS" marks, diameter 23cm (9in), *c.*1874, Godden of Worthing.

1990) or *Minton, The First Two Hundred Years of Design and Production* by Joan Jones (Swan-Hill Press, 1993). Do remember that here my résumé has been restricted to the porcelains, but there were also many types of earthenwares produced.

Some of the standard post-1840 Minton marks are given below, with their periods of use. I also provide the key to the year, letters, and signs impressed into many Minton products from 1842 onwards.

A   B   C

A Revised version of standard printed mark no.2707, c.1873 onwards. Note crown added, also "S" added to earlier "Minton". "England" added below from 1891. "Made in England" occurs c.1902–11. The crown was deleted on some earthenwares from c.1901.
B New version of standard Globe mark, c.1912–50.
C Revised standard mark, introduced early in 1951. "BONE CHINA, MADE IN ENGLAND" may occur under this mark.

Minton year cipher marks:

1842	1843	1844	1845	1846	1847	1848	1849
1850	1851	1852	1853	1854	1855	1856	1857
1858	1859	1860	1861	1862	1863	1864	1865
1866	1867	1868	1869	1870	1871	1872	1873
1874	1875	1876	1877	1878	1879	1880	1881
1882	1883	1884	1885	1886	1887	1888	1889
1890	1891	1892	1893	1894	1895	1896	1897
1898	1899	1900	1901	1902	1903	1904	1905
1906	1907	1908	1909	1910	1911	1912	1913
1914	1915	1916	1917	1918	1919	1920	1921
1922	1923	1924	1925	1926	1927	1928	1929
1930	1931	1932	1933	1934	1935	1936	1937
1938	1939	1940	1941	1942			

Royal Crown Derby, 1876 to present day

| *See* pictures 269–70

I have placed this entry for Derby porcelains under "Royal Crown Derby" rather than under "Derby" to underline the point that this company originally had no direct link with the earlier porcelain manufactory in this city (*see* p.88).

The new company, originally titled the Derby Crown Porcelain Co. Ltd, was established in 1876 by Edward Phillips who had been one of the partners in the Royal Worcester Company. The new factory was in Osmaston Road and at first earthenware as well as bone china was produced. The "Royal Crown Derby" period dates from January 1890 when the company was officially appointed manufacturers of porcelain to Queen Victoria and the description "Royal Crown Derby" was added to the trademark.

To a large degree colourful Japan patterns with their red, blue, and gold areas embellished the new wares in the manner of the earlier Derby porcelains and these traditional designs are still produced to this day, finding favour not only in England, but in various overseas markets. Apart from these traditional designs the new Derby company produced a number of ornamental forms, including figures and richly decorated vases and services. The Royal Crown Derby flower painters were supreme, and the signed work of Albert Gregory, Cuthbert Gresley (*see* picture 270), William Mosley, James Rouse, and Désiré Leroy is worth studying.

269 A fine-quality, very delicately painted, Royal Crown Derby plate. The French-style design has been signed by Désiré Leroy. Printed "Royal Crown Derby" "England" mark, with a year cipher that indicates 1898, diameter 21.5cm (8½in), 1898, formerly in the Godden collection.

The piece I have selected to show you is a plate that was decorated by Leroy (*see* picture 269). This French artist worked for Mintons until about 1890, after which his signed work graces some superb Royal Crown Derby Porcelain up to the time of his death in 1908. His compositions tend to reflect his training at the Sèvres factory, often comprising exotic birds in landscapes. This plate is painted in a typical pale mellow palette and, for quality of painting, can hardly be bettered. Some of Leroy's work is in the style of the Limoges enamels, with white or slightly tinted enamels painted over a rich dark-blue ground. Désiré Leroy was also a gilder and he added the gilt embellishments to pieces he had painted. This plate bears, apart from the standard factory mark, the Royal Arms device and the year cipher for 1893. The key to the yearly date ciphers is given in John Twitchett's and Betty Bailey's Royal Crown Derby. It should be noted that these devices, being part of the printed mark, denote the year of decoration. Other impressed ciphers were used to denote the year of potting.

270 A magnificent-quality Royal Crown Derby oval covered bowl of shape 1396. The flower painting is by Cuthbert Gresley. Richly gilt over the popular deep-blue ground. Printed "Royal Crown Derby" crowned mark, with "England" and with a year mark for 1908, 29.5cm (11½in) high, 1908, Godden of Worthing.

A Printed mark, *c.*1876–89.
B Basic post-1890 mark. The words "Made in England" were added from *c.*1921.

In April 1935 the Royal Crown Derby company purchased the small King Street works, which had been established in 1848 by some of the former Derby workpeople, and so acquired an association with the original Derby factory that had been established by William Duesbury in the middle of the 18th century. As I have pointed out, the company still continues to add to the very considerable reputation of Derby in the field of ceramics. Today, in the 21st century the company still produces its tradition-rich Japan patterns and a range of collectable novelties such as fancy paperweights. The factory is open and includes a museum collection.

For further details of the later Derby porcelains there is *Royal Crown Derby China* by F. Brayshaw Gilhespy and D.M. Budd (Charles Skilton, 1964), *Royal Crown Derby* by John Twitchett and Betty Bailey (Barrie & Jenkins Ltd, 1976, third edition Antique Collectors' Club, 1988), or Margaret Sargeant's *Royal Crown Derby* (Shire Publications Ltd, 2000).

Royal Worcester, 1862 to present day

| *See* pictures 271–4

I have already described how Kerr & Binns successfully bridged the ten-year period between the winding up of Chamberlain & Co. in 1852 and the formation of the Worcester Royal Porcelain company in 1862.

At first, in the 1860s, R.W. Binns was content to consolidate the position gained in the previous period. Limoges-style enamelled porcelains continued to win high praise and many fine dessert services were made and tastefully decorated in various styles. Great emphasis was placed on the production of figures not only in unglazed parian but in glazed and decorated finishes, some in the so-called Raphaelesque style. Many later issues were expensively embellished with various tinted gold effects.

Magnificent vases and other ornamental pieces were painted with figure subjects by Thomas Bott, James and Thomas Callowhill (*see* picture 272), Charles Palmere, and Josiah Rushton. The talented flower painters included David Bates, George Hundley, James Sherriff, and William Taylor, but at this pre-1880 period the artists very seldom signed their work. Many pieces were painted with birds; grasses and heather studies seem to have been a Royal Worcester speciality in the Victorian period.

The 1870s saw the production of really magnificent porcelains in the Japanese style, vases enriched with raised gold designs in different tints. Quality oozes from these pieces (*see* picture 271), but you will have to keep a sharp look-out for them as they are now very rare. Many of these Japanese-style Royal Worcester porcelains were modelled by James Hadley (1837–1903), who was, in my judgment, the finest ceramic modeller of the 19th century. After 1875 he worked as a freelance designer but all his work seems to have been

for the Royal Worcester company. In 1896 he went on to establish his own factory at Worcester where quality porcelains were produced under the trade name of "Hadley-ware"*, but soon after Hadley's death in December 1903 the Hadley Works were taken over by the main company, which has continued to market Hadley shapes to this day.

James Hadley modelled for the Royal Worcester company a charming series of children or young persons (*see* picture 273) dressed in Kate Greenaway-style clothes (Kate Greenaway being the popular 19th-century children's book illustrator). Not only were the

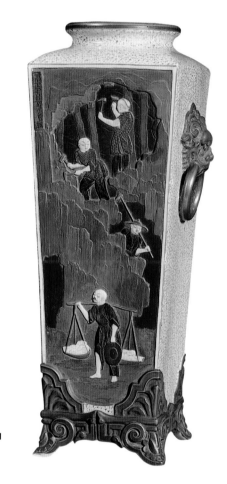

271

271 A Royal Worcester vase (one of a pair) made and decorated in the popular Japanese style of the 1870s. Richly decorated in various tinted golds. This and other Japanese-style vases and figures were shown at the 1872 Exhibition. Printed mark, with year letter for 1872, 28.5cm (11¼in) high, Godden of Worthing.

272 Right, A gold ground "jewelled" Royal Worcester teapot from a cabaret service, with hand-painted portrait panels. Signed by the gilder-jeweller and the artist – the brothers "T. & J. Callowhill" and dated 1867. Crowned Royal Worcester mark with "67" below, 14cm (5½in) high, 1867, formerly in the Godden collection.

---

* See Peter Woodger's specialist book *James Hadley & Sons Artist Patterns Worcester*, (privately published at Dorchester, 2003).

figures and groups purely ornamental; some also served as baskets, dessert centrepieces, condiments, candlesticks, and the like. They were deservedly popular and were produced over many years. Nearly all examples bear Hadley's incised signature but you must appreciate that this appeared on the original master model, from which the moulds were made and the later castings produced. The signature does not mean that Hadley even touched the moulded figure bearing his name, although of course it reflects his flair and original modelling skill.

The very many types of Royal Worcester porcelain and the hundreds of different designs make my choice of a special exhibit extremely difficult; I have so many superbly painted pieces, including the reticulated porcelains by George Owen. So much warrants special mention, but there are excellent specialist books that will give you a great insight into the splendours of Royal Worcester.

I cannot possibly give details of all the 20th-century Royal Worcester productions but I must also briefly mention the intricately modelled bird and flower studies by the late Miss Dorothy Doughty, most of which were issued as strictly limited editions. As a result of the international success of these studies the company has produced a number of superbly modelled masterpieces – equestrian statuettes, animals, figures, groups, and even fish studies. Many of these have been issued in limited editions, with each example being numbered and then the master models destroyed.

To gain some idea of the range and quality of Royal Worcester porcelains you really should visit the museum housed on the factory site at Worcester or, if you cannot manage this, you can refer to the excellent book, *Royal Worcester Porcelain, from 1862 to the Present Day* by Henry Sandon (Barrie & Jenkins Ltd, 1973 and later editions) and the *Dictionary of Worcester Porcelain 1852 to the Present* by Henry Sandon (Antique Collectors' Club, 2001). Also of interest is *The Sandon Guide to Royal Worcester Figures 1900–1970* by Henry Sandon and his sons David and John (Alderman Press, 1987). Turning to earlier books, R.W. Binns's account of the company under his management makes interesting reading for the serious student of Victorian ceramics. This now scarce book is *Worcester China, A record of the work of forty-five years 1852–1897* (Bernard Quaritch, 1897).

Apart from the superb quality Worcester wares, not only porcelains, which I have especially mentioned there is a wealth of more ordinary wares: hundreds of vases and ornamental wares painted with floral subjects, etc or bearing floral printed outline subjects.

273 A pair of Royal Worcester figures, modelled by James Hadley in his popular Kate Greenaway style. This is part of a large range of such figures, table baskets, and other ornaments. Royal Worcester impressed and printed marks. Design registration mark for 23 December 1882 and "J. Hadley" signature at the rear. Model number "893", 22cm (8¾in) high, 1883, Godden of Worthing.

Such objects range from thimbles or miniature items to great vases, oil lamps, jardinières, etc. The range of figures and groups is also vast and these are the subject of the Sandons' 1987 book previously mentioned.

Nearly all Royal Worcester porcelain is clearly marked with one or other of the basic marks that are shown here.

A Last two digits of year can occur, i.e. "73" for 1873. Then from 1867 letters were used – "A" for 1867, "B" for 1868, and so on.
B Redrawn standard mark. Heavier crown settled down on circle. Letter year marks continued – "L" for1876, "M" for 1876. Lower case "a" in 1890.
C Redrawn basic mark with wording. Years denoted by dots each side of crown. 1 dot for 1892. 6 for 1897. Additional dots or other devices then added below.

Up to 1890 year marks were added below printed versions. At first we find the last two numerals of the year, for example 73 for 1873, but from 1867 this system began to give way to single capital letters, starting with "A" in 1867 and progressing in sequence

274 One of a pair of Royal Worcester ewer-shaped vases intricately modelled and gilt. The fruit and flower panels were painted by the foreman-painter W.A. Hawkins. Model number 1309, Royal Worcester crowned, "Royal Worcester, England", mark with 16 year dots, 42cm (16½in) high, 1907, Godden of Worthing.

(omitting F, J, O, and Q) until Z was reached in 1888. In 1889 the letter "O" was belatedly used and in 1890 an italic lowercase letter "*a*". In 1891 the words "Royal Worcester, England" were introduced and in each new year one dot was added – one dot for 1892, until 24 dots appeared to denote 1915. Details of later year marks are provided within Henry Sandon's standard book.

G. Grainger & Co., Worcs., to 1889

The important Grainger Company which had been founded very early in the century (*see* Chapter 9, p.194) continued until 1889 when the firm was taken over by the larger Royal Worcester Company, although production of Grainger wares continued under the old

name until 1902. For long after this the Grainger association was marked by the prefix "G" appearing in front of model or shape reference numbers originally introduced by the Grainger firm.

The Grainger porcelains can be of extremely good quality. The complicated story of the Grainger factory is related clearly in the well-illustrated specialist book *Grainger's Worcester Porcelain* by Henry and John Sandon (Barrie & Jenkins, 1989).

The basic late pointed marks are given here:

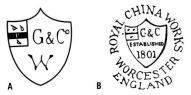

A Printed or impressed mark, *c.*1870–89.
B Printed mark, *c.*1889–1902. "England" added from 1891.

From 1891 onwards a series of letters of the alphabet were added below the then standard shield-shape mark. The letters denote the year of manufacture, or rather of decoration.

Locke & Co. (Ltd), Worcester, 1895–1915

In 1895 Edward Locke, who had been trained at the Royal Worcester factory, established his own small works, which mainly produced inexpensive Worcester-styled trinkets and ornamental objects.

The enterprise lasted for some 20 years, closing in 1915 mainly as a result of the difficult trading conditions of that period. However, in 1902 Locke had lost a legal battle over the right to describe his wares as "Worcester China" or as "Worcester", descriptions claimed by the larger Royal Worcester Company.

Several impressed or painted "Locke & Co." marks were used and the rare printed mark shown here on the left dates from *c.*1895–98, then "Ltd" was added below "Locke & Co." in newly engraved marks from 1898 to 1902. The second mark shown here (on the right) was the standard one that was used between 1902 and 1915.

A helpful booklet by L.H. Harris and T. Willis was published at the time of a local exhibition in 1989. In general it can be said that the Locke-Worcester wares are not as collectable as the Royal Worcester porcelains but, as with all classes, there are devotees who would seek out and worship Locke-Worcester or other porcelains above all others. This is as it should be.

J. Hadley (& Sons) (Ltd), Worcester, c.1896–1905

I have already mentioned James Hadley, who modelled so many superb Royal Worcester figures, groups, and ornamental wares. I must also mention his own wares, made from c.1896, although from 1875 he had worked on a freelance basis supplying designs to the main factory rather than being on its payroll.

The new Hadley factory was situated in Diglis Road. James was assisted by sons Howard, Louis, and Frank, and by several former Royal Worcester people. The Hadley wares are usually of very high quality – perhaps too high for the market at that time and in July 1905 (after the death of James Hadley in 1903) it was amalgamated with the main Royal Worcester company, which for many years continued to use the Hadley models. The Worcester Works Museum contains a good selection of Hadley wares.

Further details are given in Henry Sandon's book *Royal Worcester Porcelain from 1862 to the Present Day*. The basic Hadley printed marks have been reproduced here.

A c.1896–7 B c.1897–1900 C c.1900–1905

Looking forward

I have, in this chapter, taken, in a brief and extremely general way, my coverage of the main British porcelain manufactories into the 21st century. I do not, however, wish to, nor am I able to, give a detailed account of the many changes that took place in the industry between 1900 and 2000. In the post-1950 period these changes were vast, both in style and in production methods. Our tastes or patterns of living also changed – the complete tea service, once the bread-and-butter line of all porcelain factories became a rarity, to be replaced by a host of decorative mugs. I will have to leave the "mug-age" to you and to other ceramic students to study and record.

This is not to say that 20th-century porcelains have not been studied, and there are many excellent books that will awaken your interest. In this regard I asked my ceramic book supplier and good friend Barry Lamb of "Reference Works Ltd." (9 Commercial Road, Swanage, Dorset BH19 1DF, UK, tel: 01929 424423, fax: 01929 422597) to suggest ten books that he considered gave good coverage of 20th-century British ceramics. The following is his choice, in no special order, with his brief comments.

1) Bartlett, J., *British Ceramic Art 1870–1940*, (Schiffer, Atglen, PA, 1993).
   An impressive publication that has many excellent illustrations and a precise and well-researched analysis of each pottery and its wares. Sixty-six potteries are listed alphabetically giving an account of artists, designers, and marks, as well as types of wares and rarity guide. Each entry is between two and four pages in length with an average of six items illustrated from each. The book covers large manufacturers such as Doulton, Moorcroft, and Poole but, more importantly, less well-known firms such as Myott, Ashtead, and Wardle & Co.

2) Bergesen, V., *Encyclopedia of British Art Pottery*, (Barrie & Jenkins, London, 1991).
   Here 220 manufacturers and their artists are covered, many for the first time. The book also includes the complete and updated list of Doulton artists and monograms. This is an essential edition to any library and second only to John Bartlett's book by number of illustrations.

3) Cameron, E., *Encyclopedia of Pottery and Porcelain, the 19th and 20th Centuries*, (Faber, London, 1986).
   An indispensable illustrated encyclopaedia, which covers both English and other European factories, decorating studios, artists, marks, and designers. Any professional ceramic dealer, auction house, or serious collector will find this book more useful than a third hand. With sources and lists for further reading and research for most entries.

4) Casey, A., *20th Century Ceramic Designers*, (Antique Collectors' Club, Woodbridge, 2001).
   The first large-format publication to examine British ceramic design in depth and go beyond the work of Clarice Cliff and Susie Cooper. It covers tableware designs from the 1920s to the end of the 20th century, including the designers Keith Murray, John Clappison, Daisy Makieg-Jones, Eric Slater, Charlotte Rhead, Kathie Winkle, Eve Midwinter, and many more. The increasingly sought-after work of these modern designers has been vividly displayed in over 700 illustrations.

5) Harran, J. and S., *Collectable Cups and Saucers, Identification and Values, Book II*, (Collector Books, Paducah, 2000.)
(Prices in dollars.)
A vast range of coffee- and teawares from the 18th–20th centuries with forwards on the history of tea, decoration, etc. The book has been included here because of the large illustrated English section that includes Addersley, Aynsley, Paragon, Royal Albert, Booths, Hammersley, Foley, Tuscan, Royal Worcester, Royal Crown Derby, etc. It includes reproductions of trade material – including six pages from a 1930 Aynsley catalogue.

6) Godden, G., *Encyclopedia of British Porcelain Manufacturers*, (Barrie & Jenkins, London, 1988).
Covering porcelain from 1740 to 1980, including numerous entries for 20th-century factories and artists and with some illustrations of wares. The depth of research here and new information is quite astonishing and it has been included in this list because it offers information on 20th-century studio and factory porcelain (as opposed to the numerous works on studio and art pottery).

7) Niblett, K., *Dynamic Design, The British Pottery Industry 1940–1990*, (N.C.C. Stoke, 1990).
One of the very few publications that provides information on the 1940–90 period, covering design and designers, modern productions methods and full details of the changes in ownership of these tableware and giftware manufacturers.

8) Watson, O., *British Studio Potter*, (The Victoria and Albert Museum Collection, London, 1998).
In biographical dictionary form and covering some 150 potters in the world's largest collection of studio ceramics. Includes wares purchased by the museum up to 1985.

9) Bunt, C.G.E., *British Potters and Pottery Today*, (F. Lewis, Leigh-on-Sea, 1956).
A unique and scarce publication for 1956 in that it examines 34 firms producing ceramics in the 1950s. Includes firms such as Shelley, Ridgway, Meakin, Midwinter, etc. Appendices include a list of potters working in 1954.

10) Forsyth, G., *20th Century Ceramics. An International Survey of the Best Work Produced by Modern Craftsmen, Artists & Manufacturers*, (The Studio, London, 1936).
In this book Gordon Forsyth, at the time of writing principal of Stoke-on-Trent art schools, surveys numerous potters and factories of the 1930s. Indexed by name, there are 55 entries covering Great Britain.

In addition there are various books on individual, mainly 20th-century, factories or on the Art Deco style and period, Clarice Cliff, etc. Specialist book dealers should be able to offer you advice, as can your local public library.

There is a separate mini-library of books on Studio-type pottery and craftsmen. Such works include:

Fournier, Robert, and Yates-Owen, Eric, *British Studio Potters' Marks*, (A&C Black (Publishers) Ltd., London, 1999).

Lane, Peter, *Contemporary Porcelain, Materials, Techniques & Expressions*, (A&C Black (Publishers) Ltd., 1995).

Peterson, Susan, *Contemporary Ceramics*, (Laurence King Publishing, London, 2000).

There are also several earlier works on modern, individual, potters such as "Potters – The Illustrated Directory of Fellow and Members of the Craft Potters Association", published by Ceramic Review Publishing Ltd in London (this is updated regularly).

11
General advice

The basic facts about the various different types of porcelain bodies, about the manufacturing processes, and the ways in which the completed forms are embellished have now been covered. I have also given an outline history of major British porcelain factories from the 1740s to the 20th century and, in the first chapter, offered some advice on forming your own collection. Now I can pass on some general advice.

There is much to be said for starting a collection in a modest manner, and feeling your way into collecting porcelain without too much expenditure. Even odd cups are well worth attention and they will take up little space. Let me quote briefly from my 1966 book *Antique China and Glass under £5*:

There is probably no better way to know thoroughly the various English (or Continental) porcelain factories and their characteristics than to gather together a representative collection of cups. Once you can tell the difference between a Bow blue and white cup and a Lowestoft one, or between a Bristol hard-paste cup and a Plymouth example, then your ground work is sound and can be enlarged upon. All would-be collectors of eighteenth-century English ceramics should form a collection of typical cups: many costly mistakes could be avoided if they did so...

Mind you, not all odd cups are inexpensive, a good 18th-century specimen might be very cheap at £100 ($150), or even £200 ($300), and a £1,000 ($1,500) cup is not unheard of, or now even a £2,000 ($3,000) odd cup! However, the mass of interesting and decorative 19th-century odd tea or coffee cups can still be picked up relatively cheaply. There are several books on cups and cup or handle shapes, such as Michael Berthoud's *An Anthology of British Cups* (Micawber, 1982) and his *A Compendium of British Cups* (Micawber, 1990). A good range of these everyday objects can also be found in most general books on British ceramics.

Organizing your collection

No matter how modest your collection, you should compile a catalogue, preferably in a loose-leaf book,

allowing one double-sided page to each item. Here you should describe each article, giving the main sizes and a drawing of any factory mark and a note of any unusual feature. Also record any damages or repairs. Include details of the source of the purchase with the date and the cost. From time to time as you come across similar specimens in museums or illustrated in books or collectors' magazines, you should add this cross-reference information to the relevant page in your catalogue. You could also add information on the prices similar pieces have fetched at auction, if you are able to follow closely the London salerooms, or read of the result of the major sales. Remember, however, that some featured high-prices can be one-off freaks!

Once you have done all this you will then have a checklist of your collection, sources, and cost and, in these modern times, such a basic record can be most useful. A written record should always be backed by photographs, or group photographs of several pieces if the cost of individual photographs worries you. These photographs and the catalogue (or a copy of it) should be kept separately from the collection so that if, for example, you do suffer a serious fire you do not lose both the collection and the supporting records! Of course, if your collection grows to be a valuable one you will need to take out separate insurance cover rather than depending on the cover given in a normal householder's comprehensive policy. There will also be a need to have an up-to-date valuation carried out by a specialist.

Filing system

You will, as you read books and magazines, come across interesting facts or references that you may want to keep hold of for further research. This may include information on interesting pieces in museums or private collections. All this information should be carefully filed away where you can find it again at short notice. This means that you will need a filing system.

The easiest method is to write your notes down on separate sheets and to place them in a lever-arch file under the initial letter of the subject, so that, for example, this little note would be filed under "F" for Filing system, perhaps with a cross reference at "R" for

Research. Of course you may prefer to employ the available electronic methods to store and retrieve your useful facts or information. The essential point I am making here is simply to note down the *source* of the information. I have a list of all my reference books, each title having its own initial prefix and number. This number is pencilled inside the relevant book so, when extracting a useful quotation or fact I have only to write at the head of each note the book number and page. For example, "G.72 p.227" identifies for me this book and the relevant page. You can build up your own system as your reading and other studies dictate, and in time you will have a most useful mini-library at your fingertips.

Reference material

I have previously mentioned books and collectors' magazines: today you can easily spend a small fortune on reference books, for they are both numerous and costly and they will inevitably become even more expensive as the cost of raw materials, production, and overheads increases. Yet to get the full benefit of collecting and to keep yourself up-to-date with recent discoveries you must have (or have access to) some of the more reliable sources of information. The specialist collector of one factory's products should have all relevant books on his or her shelves, and this is not excessively expensive, but the general collector has a bewildering assortment of volumes available.

If you were to ask me to choose for you six general books on English porcelain, I would list the following, which are arranged by date of publication:

1) *Old English Porcelains* by W.B. Honey (Faber, 1948, revised edition 1977).
2) *English Blue and White Porcelain of the 18th Century* by Dr Bernard Watney (Faber, 1963, revised edition, 1973).
3) *British Porcelain 1745–1850*, edited by R.J. Charleston (Benn, 1965).
4) *British Pottery and Porcelain for Pleasure and Investment* by Henry Sandon (J. Gifford, 1969).
5) *Encyclopaedia of British Porcelain Manufacturers* by Geoffrey A. Godden (Barrie & Jenkins, 1988).
6) *A Collector's History of British Porcelain* by John and Margaret Cushion (Antique Collector's Club, 1992).

I would like to make a few comments on these books. In choosing W.B. Honey's *Old English Porcelain* I am permitting myself a little nostalgia, for I was brought up on "Honey", as this volume is often affectionately termed, and furthermore I had the good fortune to know and to be advised by this great authority when I was but a novice schoolboy collector. His writings reflect his own personal taste so that some wares are rather hastily dismissed, but you should still have this classic on your shelves, and refer to it often. We now have the benefit of a revised edition, published in July 1977. Now, of course, it needs further revision.

You may have been surprised that I included Dr Watney's specialist book on blue-and-white porcelain in my list of general books. This is because his book gives such a good and detailed history of all English 18th-century porcelain factories, and also due to the fact that it discusses at length the differing bodies and other characteristics. Even if you do not happen to share my love of underglaze blue decoration, do treat yourself to this book. I should, however, mention that since the revised edition was published in 1973, several important discoveries have been made. In particular the Liverpool section is now out of date. The porcelains then attributed to William Ball are now believed to have been made at Vauxhall in London and the wares attributed to William Reid seem now to have been made at Limehouse in London, as I have recorded. I still, however, retain this standard book in my list, although I have now written my own book on English "blue and white".* This type of once inexpensive English porcelain started me on a wonderful, winding road of discovery. I have yet to reach the end of it!

English Porcelain 1745–1850, edited by R.J. Charleston, a former Keeper of the Department of Ceramics, at the Victoria and Albert Museum, is made up of chapters written by specialist contributors. It gives a sound coverage of all the major 18th-century factories but the section on the 19th-century wares is rather inadequate.

Henry Sandon's book *British Pottery and Porcelain for Pleasure and Investment* is a reliable general book covering a wide field of English ceramics and including many interestingly fresh illustrations. I will cheat a little here and also mention Henry's son – John Sandon's book *The Phillips Guide to English Porcelain of the 18th and 19th Centuries* (Merehurst Press, 1989). This is a sound book containing a wealth of knowledge and advice. A later general guide by John Sandon is *Miller's Guide to Collecting Porcelain*, published in 2002.

I have included my own *Encyclopaedia of British Porcelain Manufacturers*, as I genuinely feel that it is a

---

* My specialist book is entitled *Godden's Guide to English Blue & White Porcelain* (Antique Collectors' Club, 2004).

first-rate book containing helpful information (to 1988) on hundreds of British firms, many of which seem not to have used a factory mark. A good range of illustrations is included and the whole period of British porcelains from 1745 to 1988 is covered. Others have kindly shared my enthusiasm. Alas, like other useful works it is now "out of print" but it would be worth trying to hunt around for a copy.

There are several well-illustrated general works of reference available in bookshops or in public libraries. Of these I have chosen, for this personal selection, the late John Cushion's *A Collector's History of British Porcelain* (an Antique Collectors' Club publication) written with the help of his wife, Margaret. I have known John for over 50 years – first meeting him when he was in the Ceramics Department at the Victoria and Albert Museum – and have greatly benefited from his help and advice. He has done more than most of us to encourage new collectors. He formed, I believe, the Morley College Ceramic Circle, and helped to establish the annual Morley College weekend seminar (surely the pioneer ceramic seminar). As an early NADFAS (National Association of the Decorative & Fine Arts Society, see p.230) lecturer, he must have given thousands of instructive lectures on a wide range of ceramic subjects. These will be greatly missed, but he has left us an excellent book to read at our leisure and revel in a wonderful range of (mostly fresh) illustrations. Yes, this book will take some beating in future years.

I have naturally had to confine my choice to those titles published before 2004 and, if you read these pages in later years, there may well by then be excellent new books available. Other, mainly specialist, books are listed in the sections dealing with the different factories or types of decoration in the bibliography.

A fuller general list is also given there, but for the most part you can leave the mass of inexpensive all-embracing books that stock bookshop shelves alone. An author who seeks to cover all European, or even the world's, porcelain factories in 100 pages can hardly be expected to add much to our fund of knowledge. It is far better to save up and buy a worthwhile book written by a knowledgeable authority.

Do, having purchased a book, read it. Understand what has been stated. Even question statements that seem incorrect or are perhaps at variance with other accepted works. If the book is yours and may be considered a working tool, you might even highlight with coloured "text-liners" the points you consider to be the most helpful or relevant. Of course, you would not so mark a book from a public library or a book that you might seek to resell, but it can be a useful pointer to help you find key facts. Naturally, a good reference book should have a pretty comprehensive index, but they are not always exhaustive.

Most readers should have access to a wealth of books, old classics as well as the newer works, through the public libraries. Obviously some libraries hold larger stocks than others, or have different specialities, but each can draw on the national stock and your local library staff should be able to obtain for you any particular reference book that you may desire. (A small, administrative charge may be made.) You may have to consult some early, rare, or expensive volumes within the library, rather than be permitted to read them at home, but this is an understandable condition designed to conserve the book for the benefit of all. It is a small price to pay for the privilege of reading the hundreds of available books.

Many of the articles to be found in the collectors' magazines are of the greatest importance. They often publicize new discoveries or cover subjects that are not found in standard books. They can reflect the specialist knowledge of collectors, museum curators, or others who may not wish to write a full-length book on their subject. You should make it your business to read all the main magazines that may carry articles relating to your subject or to include advertisements of dealers, or others of a like interest. Most town or city libraries will stock these magazines but the monthly outlay is not all that great and you should try to buy at least one yourself. Perhaps you could come to some arrangement with collector friends, by which you each subscribe to one and circulate them all among yourselves.

New discoveries are often first published in the learned papers contained in the *Transactions of the English Ceramic Circle*. Details are available currently from The English Ceramic Circle, c/o 5 The Drive, Beckenham, Kent BR3 1EE, UK.

Price guides

Price guides are extremely popular and several are available on the market. Obviously, as with all sources of reference, you should consult the latest – not one 20 years out of date.

Personally, I have succeeded in forming my own collection over the years without recourse to a price guide. There may well be general, helpful information included in such works, but the value section will, to some degree, be out of date even before the book is published. Most cases cited relate to an object sold at an auction sale. The compiler is unlikely to have been present so we have no knowledge of the circumstances of the sale.

Prices can vary greatly from sale to sale – due to world events, market conditions, the amount of goods on the market, even the weather. An item that failed to reach its reserve in one sale and was "bought in" for, say, £300 ($450), may be offered in the next sale and be bid to £500 ($750)! Any object offered in two sales will be most unlikely to fetch the same price.

Let me cite a recent and extreme case. A sweet Limehouse cream or melted butter boat (like a scaled down sauceboat) of moulded form, which was painted in underglaze blue, was included as Lot 537 in the second sale of Dr Bernard Watney's collection conducted by Phillips on 10 May 2000. It then was sold at the hammer price of £10,000 ($15,000) (the buyer's bill exceeding £11,500/$17,250). The same piece was re-offered by the same auctioneers, being equally well catalogued in "The Pinewood Collection" sale held in October 2001. Then, less than two years later, it sold for just £6,000 ($9,000). The owner obviously received rather less than the hammer price. The piece's price had dropped by approximately 50 per cent.

In this instance the first high price was occasioned by the fact that the piece came from an extremely well-known collection formed over a lifetime by Dr Bernard Watney, the author of standard books and numerous learned papers. Each of the three sales of his collection attracted a large, international gathering of buyers – private, dealers, and museum curators. Each person was seeking to purchase a piece or two from this great collection. The prices reflected this fact and it was also a unique opportunity to purchase "fresh goods", with an almost historic background.

When offered again, the setting was much different. The articles, many of which were purchased at the Watney sale – against the world's top buyers and with the auctioneers' "premium" added – had by now lost their excitement. The same objects were not fresh. Many buyers, myself included, had overspent at the Watney sales. Also the new collection, built up over a relatively short period, was sold under (I assume) a *nom de plume*. None of these factors helped. However, a few items did manage to show an increase – at least when comparing just the hammer prices. If gains are to be made in monetary terms, they will be long term, not over a year or two. But the basic point is not to buy antiques solely as an investment. Buy or collect for the enjoyment or because you like quality items around you.

Researching for yourself

I have already written about existing reference books and the published researches of members of learned societies. Remember – they may not now be fully up-to-date or tell the full story, so treat them as starting points for your own research! We can (or should) never stop learning and one of the best ways to learn about any one type of ceramic is to write a magazine article or paper on the subject. Such an article need not be intended for publication, although if it is, you may well hear from other interested collectors who can add to your knowledge. However, the main object of the exercise is to research the subject – not merely to précis other people's published views but to go back to fundamentals, to recheck all known, or supposed, facts. This can be great fun and is most rewarding and thought-provoking.

My father had an annoying habit, whenever I endeavoured to tell him anything, to respond, "Don't tell me, my boy, I've written books about it." Well, he never actually got around to writing any books but it underlined his oft-told truism, "If you want to learn about a subject write a book about it." Sounds silly doesn't it?

In fact it is so true. To write a worthwhile book you have to have an interest in the subject. It helps to have specimens to live with, to handle, and to understand. Obviously you will have to know what has previously been written about the subject by studying existing books, magazine articles, and learned "Papers". It is also helpful if you have searched out others who collect or have studied the subject, to correspond with them, and hopefully visit them to see their collection.

You can then start to consider if you can improve on or add to previous publications. If not, then there is not much point in progressing! Possibly you may decide that previous authorities got it wrong or did not tell the full story. They may have missed all-important source material – even the long-lost pattern books. Have new excavations of the factory site necessitated a complete re-appraisal?

Research and the writing of a book or article may take years. But they will be exciting times, resulting in a fresh approach or in the awakening of interest in a neglected subject. These are lasting rewards.

Even if the book does not find a publisher, and this is often the most difficult part of the exercise, it is still rewarding – in terms of what you have learned. (If you or your chosen subject does not run to a book, the learning exercise can be restricted to a short article or the preparation of a lecture.) The great thing is not to slavishly repeat what has gone before. Rethink the subject, approach it from a new angle, pose questions, and try to answer them. Yes, "if you want to learn about a subject write a book about it". Strange but true.

Reigns

You may hear references to various periods or reigns when the age of porcelain is being discussed so I've provided a brief list of periods from 1700 onwards – you can see from this that the description "Georgian" is a very loose one, ranging from 1714 to 1830!

William III	1691–1702
Anne	1702–14
George I	1714–27
George II	1727–60
George III	1760–1820
George IV	1820–30
William IV	1830–7
Victoria	1837–1901
Edward VII	1901–10
George V	1910–36
Edward VIII	1936
George VI	1936–52
Elizabeth II	1952–present day

The term Regency is usually considered to embrace the approximate period 1800–1820.

Collecting clubs

There are many local and regional collectors' clubs that hold meetings or discussions with expert speakers or arrange outings to museums. Your local library or museum curator should be able to give you details of any in your locality. Some, such as the very active Northern Ceramic Society, publish an informative newsletter and even a journal, which is free to members. Even if you do not live in the north (so cannot attend the Society's meetings) these publications are well worth the subscription. As I write the Hon. Membership Secretary is S. Cole, Esq., The Old Post Office, Maer, Newcastle-under-Lyme, Staffordshire ST5 5EF, UK, email: oldsamcole@aol.com.*

Courses, seminars, or the like provide other very useful sources of information. These include the Morley College weekend seminar held annually in London, normally in November. You can obtain details by writing to the Morley College Ceramic Circle, Morley College, 61 Westminster Bridge Road, London SE1. The Northern Ceramic Society also organizes seminars that are advertised in its newsletter. My Godden "Ceramic House Parties", which comprise a residential two or three day meeting with lectures, are held at the comfortable Fosse Manor Hotel near Stow-on-the-Wold, in the Cotswolds (tel: 01451 830354). Some dealers also run lectures, such as Mrs L. Richards of Mercury Antique, 1 Ladbroke Grove, London W11 3PA, tel: 0207 727 5106. (Others may be advertised or published in collectors' magazines.)

With all these lecture meetings and seminars there is a real need to book well in advance, for the numbers are restricted and the demand is great.

I would also like to suggest that you can broaden your interests by joining local societies or groups in a wider field of study than simply ceramics. It is best to endeavour to understand the "Fine Arts" as a whole, or at least furniture, fabrics and so on, that, along with the pottery and porcelain, furnish a home, for all arts are related. You might well have a local Arts Appreciation Society, a Collectors' Club, or perhaps a Friends of the Museum group. All will have interesting speakers and your local library should have details of such societies.

There is also a very well-organized and widespread association, NADFAS (or The National Association of Decorative and Fine Arts Societies) – it is actually now international. The head office at NADFAS House, 8 Guilford Street, London WC1N 1DA (tel: 0207 430 0730, fax: 0207 242 0686) will be pleased to give you details of your nearest local group. I, and a host of other lecturers, speak at NADFAS meetings and many educational trips and study days are organized.** When writing to any such body or individual seeking information, a stamped and self-addressed envelope is much appreciated!

Fairs

Fairs come in all sizes, the father of them all, in two senses, being the Grosvenor House Fair, which is held in the great room of the famous Park Lane hotel facing Hyde Park, London. Here you will find a splendid gathering of superb goods of all types, not necessarily ceramics, tastefully set out on elegant stands and presented by very knowledgeable dealers. You may not find a great bargain but you will have little or no cause otherwise to fault your purchase.

At the other extreme there are a multitude of small local fairs or antiques markets, where you may well have a lucky purchase but where you would be well advised to have your wits about you. In between these extremes there are some very worthwhile and well-

---

* In regard to the Northern Ceramics Society the NCS website is currently www.northernceramicsociety.org
** The NADFAS lectures cover a very wide range of subjects. They certainly are not confined to ceramics or to antiques in general.

organized fairs with knowledgeable and reputable exhibitors. I have in mind particularly the Chelsea, Kensington, Solihull, Buxton, and Guildford Fairs, and, of course, the large Antiques Fairs held at the NEC complex near Birmingham. At all of these, and at several others, I have made very good purchases, but it does help if you can join the queue quite early on the opening day. With the Grosvenor House Fair you will need to have an official invitation to the opening or preview, but in the case of the other fairs it would seem that you only need purchase a modestly priced ticket on the day. Speaking of openings, do note that in most cases the official "opening" may be some hours after the public are admitted. If you turn up at the advertised "opening" at, say, 2 or 3pm you will probably find all the bargains have been purchased by the rush of buyers who were there when the doors opened at 11am. This is not true of all fairs, but it is best to check the ticket or advertisement closely.

The fairs that I have mentioned are of a general nature, the dealers exhibiting a variety of antiques, furniture, paintings, silver, and ceramics, to list only the main classes. There are, in addition to these, other organizations that run fairs specializing in ceramics. In a class of its own is the annual International Ceramics Fair and Seminar held in London each June. This is run by Mr and Mrs Brian Haughton of International Ceramics Fair & Seminar Ltd, 3b Burlington Gardens, London W1X 1LE (tel: 020 7734 5491). There are many other antiques fairs organized, the dates and addresses of which are well advertised in the quality press and in collectors' magazines.

The advantage of antiques fairs lies in the fact that a gathering of stock from a wide range of dealers and often from different parts of the country can be seen under one roof at one time. In many cases the dealers will have saved special pieces to grace their stands and, while you may have to pay for the privilege of seeing such a large gathering, it is often well worth the extra cost. If you should wonder why the price may be inflated you can reflect on the cost of the stand and the extra overheads and advertising…

Speaking of advertising, many organizers make great play of the fact that each exhibit has been vetted by an expert committee. Obviously, a vetted fair is better than a non-vetted event but some errors can slip through, so you should still insist on a detailed invoice. I am not suggesting the exhibitors are dishonest, only that they may not have specialist knowledge. I could tell you many stories about strange happenings in fairs, but I will restrict myself to an experience that happened several years ago when these provincial antique fairs were in their infancy. It was the usual crowded opening with a mad rush of dealers and others trying to cover every stand in the minimum of time, and I found myself pushing past a fellow dealer, Bob Williams in fact, who had just picked up a tankard. Seeing me he kindly said, "Isn't this your cup of tea?" It certainly was! A fine unique English Lowestoft crested and initialled tankard in mint state. In rather a dream I purchased this for £11. It turned out later that the selling dealer had previously shown this to a leading expert who pronounced it a fake – no doubt because of its unique nature and superb state, which made it almost "too good to be true"! Having been told that it was not "right", this dealer proceeded to offer it cheaply on his stand – to my joy! (It has now been passed on to grace a specialist museum collection.)

It is obviously advantageous, therefore, to really know your subject so that you can reap the rewards offered by the less specialist dealers, who perhaps have not recognized the rarity or importance of a piece.

Dealers

I have written at some length in Chapter 1 about the traditional dealer, but do remember that an active dealer cannot always be readily available when you deem to pay a visit. Dealers have to travel to find individual pieces, to view and attend auctions. They may be spending days carrying out a large valuation or may be away exhibiting at a fair. If you really wish to speak with a dealer, to obtain advice or to sell a piece, do make an appointment – as you might with your accountant or doctor.

Descriptive invoices or receipts

Do obtain a full written invoice or receipt whenever you make a purchase and retain this document in a safe place. It not only serves as a record of the price and date of purchase and can be very useful if the article should be the subject of an insurance claim, it is also your form of guarantee that the piece you purchased is as it was verbally described.

If, for example, you were told that the figure or vase was "Chelsea", about 1760, and perfect, then see that these basic facts are included within the written invoice. An unheaded scrap of paper simply stating "To a decorative china figure £100" is useless. It is much better in the long run to pay a fair market price and receive a formal receipt, on headed paper, which reads something like:

To:
An antique Chelsea porcelain figure of a Shepherdess,
in unrestored condition and perfect except for a chip to
the hat, as pointed out at time of purchase. Unmarked.
English (Chelsea) c.1760–5.
£1,200
Paid by cheque, with thanks, 22/11/2003.

I (and some other dealers) have sometimes rather rashly offered to take the piece back if it does not fit in with the buyer's scheme or live happily in the cabinet with other pieces. We want satisfied customers who will return to our premises. If such an offer is made it should be added to the invoice and a time limit stated. (It is unreasonable for a buyer to expect, as of right, to be able to return a piece for no good reason years after the purchase.) The following phrase could easily be added to the above invoice, "Subject to return, with a full refund, if found not suitable within three months of purchase".

Damage

We can now turn to some outstanding points. I shall start with damaged pieces. You will probably find that about half the available specimens of old porcelains have suffered some damage over the years. Some say that all faulty examples, no matter how minor the injury, should be rejected. This is good advice if your purse is long and you are collecting purely as an investment. If, however, you aim to be a true collector you will find that this is bad advice. I shudder to think of the interesting documentary pieces I would have missed had I been interested only in mint specimens!

When I started collecting in my early teens I begged from my father damaged pieces that he was throwing out because they were (then) unwanted. I acquired a triangle-marked Chelsea crayfish salt in this way and many other interesting objects that served, at very little cost, to familiarize me with the different pastes and potting characteristics of these wares. I do not know how I could have gained this vital groundwork had it not been for these badly damaged examples. I could certainly not have afforded to buy perfect pieces even at the then ruling low prices, and there were few other opportunities for an eager schoolboy to handle antique porcelains. The late Dr Bernard Watney, later to be President of the English Ceramic Circle, shared my interest, even love of, interesting damaged specimens.

Of course, there are degrees of damage. A large, discoloured crack across the face of a plate or dish is not to be recommended, but I see little to complain about in minor cracks or small edge chips, especially on wares for everyday use. I call such damage "honourable" or "honest" and I marvel that so much has remained free of faults for over 200 years. How long can you expect your present-day teapot to remain mint?

For my money I prefer examples that are not ashamed to show their little blemishes to those painted-up articles that have become the curse of salerooms, antique fairs, and some dealers' stocks in recent years. Such pieces are all too often sold as perfect, or at least the repairs are not explained to the buyer, with the result that a badly damaged article is acquired at a fancy price, as the purchase has paid unwittingly for the restorer's art or craft.

This practice is one of the main reasons why you must ask for a detailed invoice or receipt when buying and, if no damage is pointed out, see that the article is described on the invoice as perfect or in unrestored state. If such statements are not forthcoming you can draw your own conclusion! Of course, the dealer may well have purchased the piece in good faith as perfect, so good can be the modern repair. I have refunded over £1,000 ($1,500) to the buyer of a piece that I had purchased from another dealer and sold on as perfect. Over six months later it was returned as being repaired. I naturally refunded the full price but there must surely, in fairness, be a reasonable time limit in returning objects. I would jibe at a refund after, say, five years, for after all it could easily have been damaged and repaired after I had correctly sold the piece as perfect!

Repairers

The restorer can do an extremely useful job and I have nothing against a modest amount of overpainting or respraying when you are aware that such work has been carried out. Yet, to my mind, it is much better to buy damaged pieces in their unrestored state, being fully aware of all the faults, and then, if you so wish, have the repairs carried out yourself. If you cannot trace a good china restorer in a telephone directory or in a collectors' magazine, a dealer should be able to put you in touch with one, or you can turn yourself into a do-it-yourself repairer. There are books that seek to teach you the craft but, as always, a practised specialist will be able to do a better professional repair than a new amateur repairer. Remember if you seek a skilled hand then your piece will take some considerable time to come to the front of the queue. Do also obtain a quotation before you leave your treasure, as the cost of restoration can sometimes exceed the value of the piece! After all, however good the repair it will not make the piece perfect!

If you should seek to take up the craft of china repairing on a professional basis then there are various courses available. One lengthy, full-time residential course is run by the British Antique Dealers Association at West Dean in West Sussex. Much helpful advice and a great many repairers' addresses are given in *The Bonhams Directory: The Collector's Guide to Care, Restoration and Repair* (Kyle Cathie, 1991) or later, more up-to-date, books may become available. Your local bookseller or library may be able to guide you in the right direction.

Baking cracks

It is correct to distinguish between damage inflicted in use and the faults that can occur during manufacture, (*see*, for example, pictures 158 and 160). It must always be remembered that the 18th-century potters were pioneers, working under great difficulties with materials that were not absolutely pure or constant, and that the temperature of the kiln could not be controlled as the heat in modern kilns can, with their oil or electricity firing. It is small wonder that some old pieces show tears, open cracks, or other firing or baking faults then. A baking crack is simply, in effect, a contraction of the body and the crack will be slightly open at the edge with perhaps the glaze having flowed slightly into the openings. Such characteristic features are almost standard on some early porcelains, such as Chelsea, and it is nearly (but not quite) true to say that an early Chelsea piece without a slight baking fault or without a partly ground-flat foot should be rejected as a fake.

Seconds

It is often forgotten that many pieces of now antique pottery and porcelain were originally sold at a low price as "seconds" or even as "thirds". In recent times we may call such faulty pieces "export rejects" and the reject shops that sell nothing but slightly faulty wares do a roaring trade at discounted prices. This is no new idea; at any period a manufacturer is loathe to smash up articles that can be sold to redress some, or all, of the costs occurred in production.

If today's manufacturers produce faulty wares, with all their up-to-date equipment and refined raw materials, it is small wonder that we find so much 18th-century porcelain that is a little short of perfection. Perhaps an article was slightly overtired so the underglaze blue has somewhat blurred or run with the glaze, or perhaps a handle has slightly warped out of true. To a hard-up housewife such minor defects were almost welcomed if the price of her porcelain was reduced.

Amateur decoration

I have previously mentioned the main independent decorators who, working in London and at other centres, used to embellish blank or white pottery and porcelain. Even today there are many commercial firms who decorate, by contract or for their own subsequent sale, blank pieces made by other firms.

However, not all these "outside decorated" wares were professionally painted, for it was fashionable in the 19th century for amateurs to paint on pottery or porcelain. One of my earliest magazine articles dealt with such Victorian attempts at china painting (*Country Life*, 2 October 1958) but the fashion goes back further than the Victorian era. From the early 1800s the Coalport firm supplied thousands of blanks to amateur and professional painters and the records of the Chamberlain company of Worcester show that it too supplied not only white porcelains but also complete sets of ceramic colours, and also on occasions the company's artists gave lessons in china painting. One entry in June 1806 shows these expenses charged to a Prince Bariatinksky at Cheltenham:

A complete set of colours	£1/1/0d
Pencils, oils, knives, etc.	8/0d
A batch of bronzes	10/0d
Regilding a plate and three candlesticks	19/0d
Eight lessons in painting	£6/16/6d
Expenses to Cheltenham	£5/16/0d

Sometimes such amateur home decoration bore gilding, which was fired and burnished at the factory as numerous charges show, but as a general rule amateur work did not include gilding and the colours tended to be muddy with the painting being rather wooden or laboured. Notwithstanding all these faults, the painters tended to sign their work fully and often a date was added. For this reason alone the amateur painting can be of great interest. Normally, however, it is not commercially as desirable as decoration carried out by a professional painter.

Limited editions

Within recent years many manufacturers have produced pieces in "limited editions" of, say, 500 examples. Many of these pieces bear explanatory marks and, in some cases, each item is numbered, for example "Number

100 of a limited edition of 300". Such pieces cater for the collector or investor who seeks built-in rarity but, while there are merits in some of the finer productions, such as the Royal Worcester figures or groups, I can see little merit in mass-produced commemorative plates and the like. You can all too easily glut the market even with a limited edition of 200, if, say, only 100 persons wish to own that particular item.

Some modern wares are advertised as being a limited edition in that the number made will be limited to, say, 100 firing days. This is meaningless unless an indication is given as to the number included in each firing – it may be several thousands!

Limited editions will always have their devotees, and by all means join them if you wish, but do judge each piece on its quality and design, not on the fact that only 500 were made. It is most unlikely that the finished objects, even when signed, will have been hand-painted, as they are mass produced from one original design or painting.

Most antique objects exist in very small numbers. They are very much rarer than these modern limited issues and in some instances only one or two antique examples are known, or at least can be expected to come on the market.

Unique pieces

I have often been shown porcelains that the owner fondly claims to be unique or "nearly unique". There are no degrees of uniqueness – an article is either unique or it is not! In most cases this claim is nonsense for ceramic articles were originally made in commercial quantities. Printed designs were always mass produced: if a company was only making one it would not go to the considerable expense of having copper plates engraved. Moulded articles will likewise have been mass produced and articles bearing pattern numbers are likely to be stock designs.

Some decorative effects such as lustres may be unique, in that no two pieces will come out of the kiln with exactly the same effect but many examples of that shape and general design will have been made. Some hand-thrown "Studio Pottery" may be unique but this is hardly ever the case with antique, factory-made, commercial productions.

Other fallacies

I could fill this book with fallacies, ranging from the fond belief that because the cracked saucer belonged to a person's grandmother it must be valuable, to the idea that Americans are queuing up to pay hundreds of dollars for a stained and rightly discarded Willow pattern plate or lidless teapot. Owners who are bent on selling their unwanted knick-knacks tend to make unwarranted claims as to their age, playing family arithmetic to make an Edwardian tea set Queen Anne (who reigned before the secret of making porcelain was discovered in Britain) in the mistaken belief that age in itself is a virtue!

Family arithmetic runs something like this, "Oh but it must be 200 years old because it belonged to my grandfather and he died aged 90 and my mother lived to be 70 and I'm over 50, so you see, it is really well over 200 years old." There is an overlap of generations: the 70-year-old mother was not born as grandad passed on at 90! It is also rather unlikely that dear grandad purchased the dinner service on his first birthday! If your grandfather should be rash enough to buy a copy of this book that will not make it an antique, or especially desirable just because your grandfather made the purchase!

Pattern names

Many marks incorporate or feature only the name of a particular pattern, for example "Willow", "Rose", "Abbey", "Pekin", or "Asiatic Pheasants". These names in themselves do not give an indication of the maker, nor were they intended to as the designs cited, and many other standard designs, were mass produced by several firms, large and small.

Perhaps the only reason in making this point about pattern names is to try to stem the flood of letters I receive from owners wishing to know the age and make of their plate bearing only the name of the pattern. I'm sorry, it can't be done! What I can say, however, is that any piece bearing the name of a pattern, design, or shape will not be 18th century.

Pattern numbers

Painted pattern numbers are to be found on a large range of British porcelains from about 1790 onward and while few, if any, numbers are unique to one factory, they can be a positive method of identification when the factory pattern books are available – in other instances they can very often be of great help in tracing the manufacturer or in dating an object.

The purpose of a pattern number was to enable the retailer and the customer to identify or reorder a given pattern; it also enabled the manufacturers to price, invoice, and identify their wares. Each factory had a set of pattern books in which the numbered designs were reproduced in colour. The various painters copied the master designs from the pattern books and painted the appropriate pattern number under the article. As a very general rule pattern numbers are found only on British porcelains and then mainly on useful wares – tea sets, dessert and dinner services (and parts thereof) – rather than on ornamental objects such as vases, although when decorated with a stock design these could also be numbered.

The patterns were numbered consecutively as new designs were introduced. This was straightforward until an unwieldy four-figure number was reached; in some cases the numbering was then restarted under the numeral "2", showing that the number was from the second series. (Such a number I have described as a fractional pattern number.)

In some instances the new series of patterns was distinguished by a letter prefix, so that pattern 999 might be followed by A1 to commence a new series. Some other factories continued their numbering consecutively so that their patterns climbed into several thousands. Therefore there are three possible pattern numbering systems; the fractional, the prefixed, and the consecutive – once the number 999 or 1000 had been reached the various factories used one of these three options.

A study of factory pattern books, accounts, and other records – or the pieces themselves – enables the system followed by each major factory to be classified and in some cases the date of introduction of various patterns to be gauged. The subject is, however, a large and complicated one and our knowledge is continually being updated. It is therefore quite impossible to give details of the numbering systems followed by even the major porcelain factories. But the reader is referred to my *Encyclopaedia of British Porcelain Manufacturers* (Barrie & Jenkins, 1988), pp.35–50 for further information on this subject.

Impressed or moulded numbers relate to the shape (or size) of the object. Numbers such as "9876/2" identify the teapot or vase shape and that it is of the second size. (Many standard objects were made in various sizes.) The sizes commanded different prices so the individual size needed to be known for pricing, invoicing, etc. Within the factories such markings identified the moulds. In general terms such model numbers indicate a period after about 1860. This leads me on to other basic Godden rules of thumb…

Maker's marks

The maker's marks that are to be found on so many examples of British ceramics can be of the greatest help to collectors, but they can also be most misleading. Indeed, if you were to set out to reproduce a valuable article the easiest part of the exercise is to fake the mark. Ceramic marks were applied in three basic ways:

(1) They were incised (cut into the body) or impressed into the unfired clay during the first manufacturing process. It will be apparent that such marks cannot be added later by a faker, although they can be employed by anyone who is setting out to make an outright fake. Indeed the standard impressed "Wedgwood"* name mark has been employed with slight variations by other firms hoping to pass their own products as those of the famous firm, but here I am straying from our subject, porcelain, into the field of pottery.

(2) Marks can be applied under the glaze in a painted or printed form. These were applied early in the manufacturing process before the piece was glazed, and again these are not often faked except when there is a definite attempt to palm something off on the unsuspecting collector. Some Continental hard-paste reproductions of costly Worcester porcelain will, for example, bear the underglaze blue square-mark of the original, or even the Worcester blue crescent, as is the case of the piece shown in picture 277.

(3) Most marks, however, were added over the glaze as the decorating process was drawing to a close and most marks were printed to save time (as literally hundreds or thousands of pieces would bear the same standard factory mark).

These three classes represent only the very basic methods. To the incised and impressed types we could add the seal marks (impressed from a metal or fired clay seal) or the relief-moulded marks where the device stands up above the surface. All these marks, which were added before the object was fired, could be called "clay marks".

These marks, however they were applied, could also include one or more identifying points. The most helpful is, of course, the full name mark, for example, "R.W. Martin & Bros, London & Southall", but most marks incorporate initials only. Single initials such as

---

* Do note that the true Wedgwood marks do not have a second extra "e". Marks reading "Wedgewood" do not relate to the main firm founded by Josiah Wedgwood. Nor do the true marks have additions such as "& Co.".

"B" or "M" are not that helpful as they fit many potters, but three or more initials together can normally be linked to a definite person or firm, especially when a town is added to the initials. Often one of the towns making up the Staffordshire Potteries was shown by its initial, so that the mark "H & G" with "B" underneath can correctly be related to Heath & Greatbatch of Burslem. The main Staffordshire Pottery towns were Burslem, Cobridge, Fenton, Hanley, Longton, and Tunstall; luckily each has a different initial.

Some marks have only a trade name or a device such as an anchor or crown. These are, of course, unhelpful to the novice but in most cases each mark can be identified and dated by reference to modern standard mark books, such as my *Encyclopaedia of British Pottery and Porcelain Marks*, but because of their very nature do not expect one of the shorter and more inexpensive handbooks to answer all your queries.

The following general Godden rules will help in determining the earliest period of many objects.

(1) Marks incorporating the Royal Arms date from the 19th or 20th centuries.
(2) Marks incorporating the name of the pattern are subsequent to 1810 and often much later.
(3) The word "Limited" or the standard abbreviations denote a date after 1861.
(4) The words "Trade Mark" indicate a date that is subsequent to the Act of 1862.
(5) The word "Royal" in a firm's title or trade name indicates a late date, probably after 1860.
(6) The word "England" usually denotes a date that is post-1891.
(7) The words "Made in England" evidence a 20th-century date, normally one after 1910.
(8) The words "Bone China" or "English Bone China" also indicate a 20th-century date.
(9) It is also best to disregard any date incorporated in a printed mark: these so often relate to the real, or claimed, date of the firm's establishment or of the period when the design was introduced.

However, many of the large firms employed semi-secret forms of dating their wares (this was done so that the firms could sell the oldest stock first without risking putting customers off buying wares that they might consider out of date if the pieces had a date a few years old on them). Most pieces produced by Mintons from the 1840s, by Wedgwood from 1860, by the Royal Worcester Company from the 1860s, and by the Royal Crown Derby Company from 1882 bear such devices, the keys to which are given in my large encyclopaedia of marks and in my *Encyclopaedia of British Porcelain Manufacturers*, which is now, unfortunately, out of print.

In some instances month and year numbers were impressed into the plates or dishes as they were made. Such potting marks usually take the form "J.01" or "1.01" for January 1901. Such impressed date marks were not employed before about 1870. (Markings impressed into thin porcelain can be more easily seen if the piece is held against a strong light.)

I have mentioned that the words "England" or "Made in England" usually denote a date after 1891 or after 1910 respectively. It must not be assumed, however, that if such words do not occur the piece was made before these dates. These additions were only required by other countries on imported goods. Many small firms supplying only a home market, as for example the Goss local trinkets, do not bear the word "England". The same point applies to many other types of ceramic and to all the general guides that are cited above.

You should also not assume that because a piece is unmarked it must be old as you will almost certainly find unmarked wares in a modern china shop. These are, however, unlikely to be the product of a leading manufacturer having a long reputation to trade on!

Retailer's marks

Some wares bear not only the maker's mark but also that of the ordering retailer or shipper, showing the district or country for which such pieces were made. A large quantity of porcelain from about 1810 onwards may bear only the name of the retailer, be it a large London firm such as Goode or Mortlock or a more humble retailer in a country town selling perhaps local view wares to holiday makers. No book can list all such retailers but the periods of the more important London firms are given in my encyclopaedia of marks (*see* Bibliography, p.262). Local directors or local libraries will assist in other cases. English retailer's marks can occur on non-British items, imported by that firm.

Various markings

Many pieces you will come across will bear several types of marks. Let us look at the reverse side of a Minton plate, (*see* the black and white picture 275). First you may just see at "A" the rather indistinctly impressed name mark "MINTONS" with the plate marker's personal tally mark, and at "B" the quartered square device that is the year cipher for 1881. At "C" is

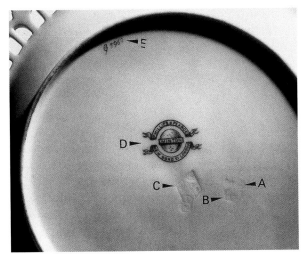

275 The reverse of a Minton bone-china dessert plate showing various types of marks. "A" – impressed "MINTON" name mark applied before firing. "B" – Minton's impressed year cipher. "C" – the impressed registration of shape device. "D" – Minton's printed trademark, in this case with the name and address of the supplying London retailer. "E" – the painted factory pattern number, with the series prefix "G", 23cm (9in), Godden of Worthing.

the diamond-shape design registration device (here applied upside down), which will indicate the day, the month, and the year that the shape, in this case the pierced border motif, was first registered (*see* p.260). This purely British system of marking commenced in 1842 and continued until 1883, after which the registrations became numbered in sequence. All these Minton marks were clay marks applied before this plate was fired.

Turning to the overglaze markings applied after or during the decorating processes, we have at "D" the standard printed Minton globe mark surrounded by the London retailer's name and address. In this an old engraving of the mark has been used, for the firm added "S" to their name mark in 1872, nine years before this plate was potted. Lastly, at "E" we find the hand-painted pattern number with the prefix "G". This series ran from 1868 to *c.*1900 and this number was introduced in 1879.

From this one plate we can therefore tell which factory produced it, the year, and also the fact that the pierced border was a registered design. We can also learn the name of the retailer who stocked this piece or service and sold it to the first user. The pattern number also enables us to check with factory records and, in some cases, to trace the artist and the original cost of the article. Indeed, the back of a plate can often be more interesting than the front! Remember, however, when dating to take the latest indicator, not the earliest!

Unmarked wares

An unmarked piece is not necessarily early. It may be so, but more likely the piece was made by a person or firm without a well-known name. In general, the products of a large, established company will bear a clear trademark advertising the origin of the piece, for in part the buyer is expected to prefer goods produced by a nationally known firm, and the purchaser is often happy to pay extra for the guarantee of quality, but Bill Muggins working in a Burslem backstreet pot bank can hardly be expected to have wasted precious seconds marking his wares, if his name was unknown outside his home town.

Fakes

By now you will know how to distinguish most blatant fakes. You will know that most English porcelains are of the soft-paste variety and that fakes of Chelsea, Bow, Derby, or Worcester porcelains are nearly always of a cold, glittery, hard-paste body.

You will know that the easiest part of the faker's craft is to reproduce the mark of the original and that in the cheaper mass-produced fakes the mark is prominently placed. Look at the little pair of hard-paste 20th-century Continental figures illustrated in picture 276, for example, They are quite attractive in their way, but look at that outsized gold-anchor mark on the reversed figure. Note also the little blow hole above the mark, and keep well away from supposedly 18th-century English figures or groups displaying this feature. Further information on Continental fakes and reproductions of English porcelains is given in Chapter 2 of my *Godden's Guide to European Porcelain* (Barrie & Jenkins, 1993).

Brash fakes of this type should not fool even novice collectors but some early Samson (*see* below) and other reproductions are of very good quality (*see* picture 277) and being themselves now "antique" they have acquired a certain respectability and pedigree of their own, although they are still hard-paste, not soft-paste English porcelain. The best Samson reproductions can also be most decorative. At one Godden study meeting I had put out on a table just such a French copy of a Chelsea figure as an example of what not to buy, only to find a group of ladies going into raptures over it. To them it was the most desirable of objects and from a decorative point of view they were quite right! Did you notice that my decorative frontispiece (title page, p.2) was a 19th-century reproduction of an 18th-century Derby figure, made in a hard glittery body? It has

Derby-fashion model numbers "189", and even a size indicator "2". Note, however, that these are impressed (in small-size type), not incised by hand. The model number will not link correctly with the published lists of Derby figure numbers – a boy riding on a seahorse in this case. The French hard-paste example also has the small regular, late-style, vent hole at the back, similar to that shown in picture 276, left. It also bears an unlikely gold-anchor mark.

Nowadays any Continental reproduction or fake tends to be proudly described as "Samson", which underlines the high reputation of the Paris firm that prospered on producing high-quality reproductions for over 100 years. Unfortunately, it was only the leader of a mini-industry producing decorative fakes of old collectable ceramics. There is now a French language book dealing with the wide range of Samson wares – *Samson Genie de l'Imitation*, by F. Slitine (Editions Charles Massin 2003).

Not all fakes are hard-paste. Some are even made of an earthenware body and are therefore opaque. The copies of Worcester porcelain made by Booths of Tunstall still fool some people. Their copies of standard Worcester blue-and-white objects are quite good and, when marked, bear the crescent and "B" device that is shown below.

I illustrate some Booth reproduction Worcester blue-and-white porcelains in my *Godden's Guide to English Blue and White Porcelain of the 18th Century* (Antique Collectors' Club, 2004), Appendix 1.

Even Chelsea porcelain was copied in earthenware, on the Continent. Recently I received a series of letters from a most excited American who thought he had discovered a key piece that was to upset all previous writings on the Chelsea factory, for his piece was dated 1740! He went into great detail in describing this piece but neglected to state that it was pottery not porcelain! The blatant mark should have given warning for, apart from the large size, the mark was just too good to be true. It comprised not only the anchor device but the word "Chelsea" and the date 1740! Do note that the word "Chelsea" does not occur on genuine anchor-marked specimens. Indeed the place name will not occur on porcelain in painted form at all, except on later, non-Chelsea, wares where the name has been used only to distinguish the pattern, which the maker may fancy has a Chelsea flavour to it.

I have in previous books pointed out that the Swansea and Nantgarw marks were widely copied, and some fake Derby and Rockingham marks are to be found, but the great mass of post-1800 marks are above suspicion, for it only pays fakers to produce commercially valuable and highly collectable wares. However, as certain classes of later, even 20th-century wares command high prices, fakers have turned their attention to such articles. Sometimes the mark is changed, replacing a minor name with the mark of a fashionable manufacturer. When such works first come on the market they are often passed as genuine because the collectors are not expecting reproductions but, as fakers put more and more specimens on the market, normally by way of the auction sales, so the experts are alerted by the sudden flood of new, unrecorded types.

The Wedgwood Portland-vase trademark has been added to certain types of the fashionable "Fairyland Lustre" wares of the 1920s and 1930s. I am not a lawyer but as this Wedgwood mark is a registered trademark fakers must be running a real risk, quite apart from the protection that is offered by the Trade Description and the Misrepresentation of Goods Acts. The Royal Worcester and the Doulton marks also seem to have been copied in recent times and, as is generally known, the "WEDGWOOD" name mark has been misapplied since the 18th century. It can even appear on the reverse of modern plaster copies of old jasper wares! You will therefore no doubt see the advantage of dealing with a reputable firm, where knowledge will be backed by a written descriptive invoice.

Redecoration

You should be warned of another dangerous form of fake that can crop up in collections. I refer not to the pieces that were entirely made at a later period, but to genuine old porcelain that has been re-dressed in an expensive, desirable manner – such pieces are known as redecorated specimens.

276 A pair of Continental hard-paste figures made to emulate Chelsea-style models, but too brightly coloured and with thin gilding. Note also the over-large fake gold-anchor mark and the small vent hole, above the mark, 17cm (6¾in) high, 20th century, Godden Reference collection.

277 A good-quality, hard-paste reproduction of an 18th-century Worcester plate, probably by Samson of Paris. A quality production now antique in its own right and collectable. Blue open crescent mark, diameter 21.5cm (8½in), c.1860–70, Godden Reference collection.

276

277

278 A grouping of genuine 18th-century Worcester porcelain, but redecorated in the 19th century in expensive, desirable, styles. There was a mini-industry in such enhancement. The right-hand example is typically fussy and cramped being painted over a simple underglaze blue design that is now hidden by the opaque enamels. Genuine marks can occur on such pieces. Spoon tray 15.5 x 9.5cm (6⅛ x 3¾in), porcelains 1770–80 but decoration 19th century, Godden Reference collection.

Here the porcelain base is perfectly genuine but it has been "enhanced" with more desirable styles of decoration, so increasing its saleability. The three pieces shown in picture 278 are of 18th-century Worcester porcelain. The cup on the left shows traces of a simple original gilt pattern. This has been removed and very well-painted flowers and fruit with coloured and richly gilt floral design added. This redecoration is of such high quality that it could have been added at an 18th-century professional studio such as that owned by James Giles (*see* p.93). Giles and other decorators obviously required blanks to work upon, but many inexpensive, simple designs were available when the main factories would not supply white blanks.

The Worcester spoon tray in the centre of picture 278 is also a convincing, high-quality production. Here it is the heavy, opaque, ground colour that gives the game away. It almost certainly hides the original, simple Worcester pattern.

The cup and saucer on the right represent a rather more common type of redecoration. The turquoise borders and the other colours are more opaque than they should be and the composition is cramped. If you put these pieces to a strong light you will see the reason. The heavy enamels cover a simple blue-printed floral design. Here a Victorian decorator has purchased a standard blue-and-white Worcester cup and saucer for a few shillings and overpainted it in a more expensive manner to sell on as a rare Worcester cup and saucer. In this case there are signs of refiring – black speckling on the underside and a dark mark around the foot. These are tell-tale signs of redecoration but they do not always show up.

Obviously the later redecorated porcelains were painted in rare, expensive styles. Often rather heavy ground colours have been applied, such as the famed Worcester apple-green ground. Again, buy from a reputable source and obtain a full descriptive invoice!

Washing

It is surprising how wonderful porcelain and real gilding can become once it has been cleared of the grime that accumulates over the years. But once clean you should submit your porcelains to a minimum of washing and take elementary precautions – the water should be warm rather than hot, and rinse each piece well in clean water before putting it on one side to drain. Use a plastic bowl rather than a metal or stone sink to wash it in, and if you can cap your taps with those rubber nozzles so much the better – as this will avoid the piece being knocked against a hard object. Do not use abrasives and do not use bleach if the article has any gilding. Once washed, dry the object well with a soft, not harsh, cloth. Make sure you watch out for damage, as the water may melt the old glue and the object may come apart.

I find a shaving brush an ideal tool for washing china, as it is soft but the long hairs will get in all the crevices. It is almost indispensable when washing floral-encrusted porcelains and you can dry these intricate pieces with a hairdryer. Do note, I have been referring to old-fashioned washing by hand. Never take a short-cut and trust your treasures to a machine.

Sticky tape

Sticky tape of "Sellotape" or "Scotch tape" type should not be used on ceramics, certainly not where the piece has been gilded. Auctioneers, some dealers, and private owners think they are being clever in applying sticky tape to perhaps fix a cover in place on a teapot or other object. When taking this off it will almost certainly also remove some of the gilding, so detracting from the visual appearance of the piece and from its value.

If you have a gilt object with sticky tape already on it, do remove it with the greatest of care. I find soaking the piece in warm water will, in most cases, break the bond between the tape and the gold. Remember, sticky tape and ceramics do not mix. As an aside, I do not like the practice of gluing on covers or lids. All is well until you want to unfix them. In repairs, never do anything that you can't undo!

A closing note

Do remember to follow your own taste, but always try to respect quality and also try to buy the best you can reasonably afford. Such well-chosen subjects will give you the greatest pleasure and reward.

One last little snippet of advice: I have, in the main, been discussing old or antique porcelains, but do remember that these were once new and that they were purchased originally both for use and for pleasure. You too can follow this example yourself by keeping an eye open for pleasing examples of contemporary porcelain.

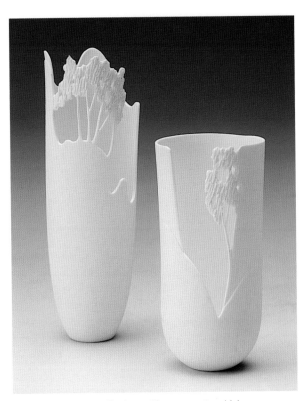

279 Two hand-carved slim, bone-china ornaments, which have been slip-cast. These pieces are not antique (yet!) but are quite beautiful. Impressed "I S" seal as used by the potter Irene Simes of Market Drayton, who trained at Stoke-on-Trent, Portsmouth, and at the Royal College of Art in London, 14cm (5½in) and 10.75cm (4¼in) high, 1977, in the Godden collection.

These need not be costly limited issues, which can run into three figures. Some of the modern studio potters now produce some really delightful individual porcelains and the last illustration (picture 279) clearly demonstrates the appeal of such productions. These articles can be far superior to some of the avidly collected earlier factory-produced porcelains.

I hope you have enjoyed this book and that you have gained some help from my experiences. I trust too that you will enjoy some "good hunting" and, having been bitten by the collecting bug, will go on to build a satisfying collection. Indeed the study of English ceramics is not an exact science. It is more like a complicated jigsaw or crossword puzzle. But it is certainly fun and rewarding.

Postscript
The author, writing this book as a grandfather in his 70s, regrets that he is no longer able to offer an identification or valuation service. To carry out such an exercise the specialist must see and handle the object – whatever it may be. It is unfair to both parties and to the piece to expect otherwise.

12
Values and comments

I have tried to make this book as helpful as possible and have, in this case, broken new ground in using only colour illustrations. I am about to go a stage further and offer some general advice on values and will even suggest some values for the pieces that have been illustrated in this book.

As I have previously stated, I am against "Price Guides", certainly when they are used as a Bible, with commandments not to be broken – Thou shalt not give over £100 for this or that! Most of my most treasured possessions, even some of my greatest bargains, were obtained by paying "over-the-odds"! (That is, more than the accepted market price.) I did so because I "fell" for the pieces – they stopped me in my tracks. Perhaps I felt we were meant for each other, or that the chance to purchase such pieces might never come again. I have often said to myself on entering an auction room or a dealer's shop – "that's mine". You may think that is greed, but what I really meant was that the price was of secondary importance.

In collecting it is a truism that people seldom regret what they did buy – they usually regret what they did NOT buy. Chances seldom come a second time.

Admittedly I have enjoyed a great advantage, in that my collections have been built up over a long period, starting in a tentative way back in the mid- or late 1940s, over 50 years ago. As things have turned out, all my early purchases of the 1950s or even of the 1960s now seem ridiculously cheap – as does your first house – mine cost well under £10,000! But neither my porcelains nor the house seemed cheap at the time because I was earning under £10 a week. The expenditure of £5 on a Lowestoft cup and saucer or on a little Worcester blue-and-white leaf-shaped dish needed serious thought. But what lasting pleasures such purchases have given me.

All the collectors of my period purchased pottery or porcelain purely for pleasure or research and interest. We certainly did not regard it as an investment. We really had no idea that prices would soar in value. We had not heard of or thought about inflation as wages and the cost of living was then reasonably steady.

I cannot tell what will happen in the future. Will inflation and the lowering of the value of currency, in whatever form, continue? Will the value of antiques in general continue to increase? Not necessarily. I have always advised people not to buy as an investment but purely for pleasure. Start a collection because the subject or the objects interest you or the articles give you pleasure. If, over a period, there is an increase in value that is an added bonus, but it should not be the sole objective. Tastes change, different types or styles come in or out of favour and fashion – even in antiques. If you collect for pleasure such changes need not trouble you.

Having made these basic points, I will endeavour to put a price or value on the pieces that are illustrated in this book. But how should I value the articles?

There are two obvious bases – a buying price or a selling price. They are obviously not the same – as with selling anything. Even at auction the seller has to pay the auctioneer commission and extras such as insurance or the cost of illustrations plus VAT* (currently at 17.5 per cent). That is obviously assuming the piece finds a buyer. The picture may not be all that rosy with direct sales or a sale to a dealer. First you must find the right buyer, or the dealer who specializes in your type of article. The dealer obviously has to make a profit on the buying price, having many overheads. It is therefore not that easy selling at the very top of the market.

The television programme *Antiques Roadshow* tends to take the easy way out and quote a figure said to represent the insurance value. This is very convenient because it cannot be disproved – it is an opinion. Insurance values are traditionally high because they represent the replacement value. An insurance value certainly does not represent a selling price.

My prices will represent my idea of current realistic insurance value, but not overly high. No two valuers, however experienced they may be, will place exactly the same value on a range of objects, but they should come up with a total that is within, say, ten per cent of each other. But how to set a realistic value? Firstly you must know what you are looking at. Is, for example, the figure on the title page 18th-century Derby or Bow?

---

* "Value Added Tax" – as applied to most services and many goods. A real tax, to be taken into account.

Is it a rare model that collectors will covet? Or is it a common subject that collectors will already have in their collection? Is it perfect? Is it damaged and well repaired? Or not repaired? Without such information or knowledge you cannot begin to place a value. As it happens the piece is a 19th-century reproduction and has little more than a decorative (furnishing) value.

If you can correctly identify and date an object, can you value it? Not necessarily. For example, museum curators, although knowledgeable, are not trained to value. In most cases they are not permitted to value. Many specialist dealers and I have, however, had much experience in buying and selling. Such dealers should know the market – its strength or weakness. They may have access to the ultimate buyer of that object*. They should also have a good library of reference books, subscribe to trade papers and magazines, and, of course, auction sale catalogues and price lists. Much of the same applies to the specialist departments of the leading auction houses. They, like the dealers, are professionals.

So what follows are the values I have placed on the illustrations. Don't be carried away if you see a high value. A £10,000 ($15,000) rarity may well be less pleasing than a £50 ($75) odd cup or £100 ($150) milk jug. When buying, always go your own way, choosing something because you like it.

I have assumed, unless otherwise stated, that the pieces are perfect. Remember, however, that the values are my own personal idea and that in five or ten years time they may appear quaint rather than accurate!

Suggested values

Title page £300 ($450)
A 19th-century French hard-paste copy of a Derby figure. Good quality but really only of decorative or research interest.
Picture 1 £80-200 ($120–300) each
Typical 19th-century bone-china cups and saucers. The value depends on the quality of the decoration.
Picture 2 £120 ($180)
A superb example of its kind, made for the English market. Many 18th-century Chinese odd teabowls may be found for £30 ($45) or so.
Picture 3 £500 and £300 ($750 and $450)
A Worcester soft-paste salad bowl (left) and a Chinese hard-paste copy. The Worcester example is the more expensive as it is more collectable, although the Chinese copy is rarer – but not so saleable!

Picture 4 £5,000 ($7,500)
A sweet and rare early Worcester milk jug, which is highly collectable.
Picture 5 £200 ($300)
Caughley leaf dish, printed "Fisherman" pattern. A standard example of a fairly common print.
Picture 6 £800 ($1,200)
A Lowestoft tea canister, with its cover, shown with part of the mould.
Picture 7 £2,500 ($3,750)
A desirable early Worcester milk jug with average, rather than superb or rare, painting.
Picture 8
Sagger only – of interest but of little commercial value.
Picture 9 £4,000 ($6,000)
Pair of Derby basket figures. These are a good pair of table ornaments, and you should remember that slight damages are to be expected with such pieces.
Picture 10
Reverse of Chelsea plate, educational illustration only.
Picture 11
Part Lowestoft "Redgrave"-style tea and coffee service.
Coffee pot and cover £3,600 ($5,400)
Spoon tray £1,200 ($1,800)
Milk jug £650 ($975)
Waste bowl £450 ($675)
Teapot stand £1,600 ($2,400)
Teapot and cover £1,800 ($3,600)
Teabowls and saucers (each) £150 ($225)
Coffee cups and saucers (each) £250 ($375)
The coffee pot, spoon tray, and the teapot stand are the rarest and most desirable items.
Picture 12 £1,000 ($1,500)
A very rare form of Rockingham teapot.
Picture 13 £2,500 ($3,750)
A rare, large size, early Worcester teapot.
Picture 14 £900 ($1,350) (without cover)
A rare early Worcester teapot. With its original cover the value would probably exceed £5,000 ($7,500).
Picture 15 £1,800 ($2,700)
This is a good, even if standard, Worcester blue-scale ground teapot.
Picture 16 £900 ($1,350)
A good Worcester teapot, at c.1775–80, slightly late in period for a high value. Stand, £400 ($600) on its own.
Picture 17 £1,200 ($1,800)
A rare dated (1796) Chamberlain-Worcester teapot, clean and pleasing, but a standard example would only command around £400 ($600).

* Simon Spero, the London dealer, often contributes interesting articles or résumés of major ceramic auction sales to the magazine *Antique Collecting* (published monthly by the Antique Collectors' Club).

Picture 18 *£1,250 (£1,875)*
An early New Hall silver-shape teapot with rosette feet.

Picture 19 *£1,000 ($1,500)*
A decorative, fine-quality Minton teapot, richly gilt. This is about as good as they come.

Picture 20 *£350 ($525)*
A good early Victorian teapot with bat-printed Royal subject. A standard but not common pot.

Picture 21 *£5,000+ ($7,500+)*
A unique Lowestoft presentation tea canister, which is dated 1797. It is difficult to value such one-off, highly desirable objects.

Picture 22 *(left to right) £650 ($975), £1,000 ($1,500), £600 ($900)*
Rare Caughley tea canisters with their covers.

Picture 23 *(left to right) £650 ($975), £750 ($1,125), £650 ($975)*
Three jugs: a rare Bristol, attractive Worcester with its cover, and a problem blue-printed milk jug – of Bow or Isleworth. If the latter is deemed to be Isleworth the price would be increased.

Picture 24 *£2,000 ($3,000), £450 ($675)*
A rare and highly desirable early New Hall "high Chelsea ewer" and a "low Chelsea ewer" of a more ordinary type – Worcester.

Picture 25 *£4,000 ($6,000)*
A sweet and rare Neale porcelain covered milk jug, painted by Fidelle Duvivier. Such a delight could command almost any price up to £10,000 ($15,00)

Picture 26 *£3,500 ($5,250)*
A rare and superbly decorated gold-anchor marked Chelsea milk or cream jug, with its ornate cover.

Picture 27 *£450 ($675)*
A 19th-century Minton waste bowl with hand-painted views and neat gilding. Waste bowls are not the most desirable of articles.

Picture 28 *£2,500 ($3,750)*
This rare example commanded the hammer price of £2,300 ($3,450) in the September 1999 sale of the first portion of the Watney sale. I sold this example to Dr Watney in 1948 for, I believe, £9!

Picture 29 *£850+ ($1,275+)*
A very rare colour outline printed Vauxhall spoon tray. Sold (damaged) in the first Watney sale for £750 ($1,125). I later gave a rather higher price for this now re-repaired piece.

Picture 30 *£4,000 ($6,000)*
A good, typical raised-anchor marked Chelsea teabowl and saucer c.1750. From Uppark in West Sussex.

Picture 31 *£2,500 ($3,750)*
A good early Worcester coffee cup and saucer. This is a popular pattern but not the rarest.

Picture 32 *£350 ($525)*
A good Flight period Worcester "trio" of saucer, tea bowl, and handled coffee cup. Blue and gilt decoration with owner's crest.

Picture 33 *£90 ($135), £65 ($100)*
A good bat-printed New Hall coffee can and also an attractive (perhaps factory "Z") hand-painted can. The latter is nice, but there are more collectors of New Hall.

Picture 34 *£12,000 ($18,000)*
A superb and rare early Worcester blue-and-white small coffee pot. These items are so desirable that it is difficult to value a piece. If offered in a Watney sale it may have commanded £20,000 ($30,000) or even more!

Picture 35 *£2,500 ($3,750)*
An equally rare, good-looking marked Neale porcelain coffee pot. To many people it seems rather better than the previous item, but is a later example – c.1790.

Picture 36 *(left to right) £150 ($225), £200 ($300), £350 ($525), £350 ($525)*
Decorative and superb-quality Chamberlain-Worcester breakfast wares. The egg cup is particularly rare and collectable. The large cup is a typical breakfast size.

Picture 37 *£5,000 ($7,500)*
A rare and collectable set but not in the same league as the Derby example. However, it would still be highly desirable to a Caughley collector.

Picture 38 *£14,000 ($21,000) for a complete set*
Such sets are difficult to value as complete sets very seldom come on the market. This Derby example is particularly trim and desirable. The pieces are also highly collectable as individual pieces: tray £4,500 ($6,750); covered sugar £1,200 ($1,800); small jug £2,000 ($3,000); cup and saucer £900 ($1,350) (there are normally two – his and hers!); and the teapot £2,500 ($3,750).

Picture 39 *£3,000 ($4,500)*
A rare and attractive Minton set, neatly gilt. Again this is desirable, but as it is from c.1851 it is not in the 18th-century price range.

Picture 40 *£1,800 ($2,700)*
A very good-quality marked Chamberlain-Worcester cabinet cup and saucer, painted with named views.

Picture 41 *£3,500 ($5,250)*
A superb-quality Derby cup and saucer rather in the Continental manner. The panels were probably painted by Fidelle Duvivier – an artist much in demand.

Picture 42 *£1,200 ($1,800)*
An early Worcester sauceboat. These were made in various sizes but they are not usually highly priced.

Picture 43 *£2,000 ($3,000)*
A decorative marked Chamberlain-Worcester "Japan" tureen and cover from a dinner service.

Picture 44 *£3,000 ($4,500)*

A "Flight" period Worcester plate from a single Royal order, *c*.1789.

Picture 45 *£3,000 ($4,500)*

A later, (*c*.1813), Worcester crested plate of really superb quality – the best of the best!

Picture 46 *£1,500 ($2,250)*

A rare Chelsea candlestick. Again a pair would be worth more than two singles.

Picture 47 *£1,800 ($2,700)*

A single early Derby basket figure for use on the table. A pair in good condition would command £5,000 ($7,500) or so – which is more than double the value of a single figure.

Picture 48 *£2,500 ($3,750)*

A good Derby ice pail (or fruit cooler). Well gilt, with attractive hand-painted scenic views. These were issued in pairs with the more expensive dessert services.

Picture 49 *£2,500 ($3,750)*

A splendid four-piece Coalport ice pail decorated in a costly style – more decorative than the Derby example.

Picture 50 *£500 ($750) (as damaged)*

This Derby centrepiece from the Watney collection is badly damaged – hence the modest price. A perfect example would fetch around £1,800 ($2,700). They were made in various sizes and versions – at several different factories.

Picture 51 *£880 ($1,320)*

Minton dessert wares of the mid-1840s of fine quality. Tureens £500 ($750) the pair with stands, plates £140 ($210) each, comports in various sizes about £250 ($375) each.

Picture 52 *£650 ($975)*

Decorative dessert wares of the 1840s. Dishes about £140 ($210) each, plates £80 ($120), and the sugar and cream tureens about £350 ($525) for the pair.

Picture 53 *£2,500 ($3,750)*

A high-quality Minton parian and decorated porcelain centrepiece. This is an imposing example.

Picture 54 *£5,000 ($7,500)*

A pair of pale yellow-ground Worcester open-work baskets of the 1760s. Perfect pairs are scarce.

Picture 55 *£2,500 ($3,750)*

A superb Ridgway basket with Royal marks. The finest Ridgway piece I have owned.

Picture 56 *£4,800 ($7,200) (a single)*

The finest Dr Wall Worcester bulb pot I have seen, and typical of this rich type of Worcester. A single, rather than part of a desirable pair.

Picture 57 *£2,500 ($3,750) (a single)*

A fine Derby bulb pot. Such items should have pierced covers (often damaged) and be part of a matching pair.

Picture 58 *right £1,800 ($2,700)*

A good early Worcester milk jug of a popular but not rare pattern.

Picture 59 *£1,200 ($1,800)*

A very good specimen of the later (*c*.1775) style of Worcester printing. Scarce, but most collectors prefer earlier types.

Picture 60 *£1,000 ($1,500)*

A good, but not very rare, blue-painted Worcester mask-head jug. These come in various sizes, makes and added designs.

Picture 61 *£4,000 ($6,000)*

A very rare Chinese large saucer or plate, printed in England from a signed and dated (1757) Hancock copper plate. It is coloured over and slightly gilt. The only example of this size – known to me.

Picture 62 *£2,500 ($3,750)*

A superb and rare early Worcester cream boat with over-glaze prints. A most collectable item.

Picture 63 *£1,000 ($1,500)*

A large and cleanly printed Worcester King of Prussia mug. These occur in various sizes and with variations of print. This example is about as good as they come!

Picture 64 *£300 ($450)*

An unusual gold-printed Spode ewer.

Picture 65 *£120 ($180)*

An attractive gold-printed New Hall saucer, which has a gilt border.

Picture 66 *£600 ($900)*

A very finely decorated Chamberlain-Worcester plate, well painted and gilt.

Picture 67 *£400 ($600)*

A superbly painted display plate with raised gold-work border. Magnificent but a late example.

Picture 68 *£2,000 ($3,000) (damaged)*

A magnificent Daniel porcelain ice pail from a Royal service showing gilding at its best. It is difficult to value examples in a perfect state. Other parts of the service are still in the British Royal Palaces.

Picture 69 *£1,650 ($2,475)*

A very rich gilt Cauldon dessert set. Plates £350 ($525) each, dishes £450 ($675) each, and the footed comport £400 ($600).

Picture 70 *£350 ($525)*

An attractive, rare, well-gilt Caughley dessert dish.

Picture 71 *£2,000 ($3,000)*

A rare, superb-quality Chamberlain-Worcester dessert dish. Feather and shell subjects are very collectable.

Picture 72 *£1,100 ($1,650)*

Rare Daniel porcelain miniature teawares, part of a set on tray. Sugar bowl £300 ($450), teapot £500 ($750), jug £300 ($450).

Picture 73 *(left to right)* £1,500 ($2,250) and £700 ($1,050)

These are splendid and rare Baddeley-Littler pieces. Although rare, the market is limited.

Picture 74 £1,200 ($1,800)

A rare, printed Baddeley-Littler teapot and cover in a clean state – interesting and collectable.

Picture 75 £700 ($1,050)

A standard pattern Baddeley-Littler teapot that is in a damaged state.

Picture 76 *(left to right)* £150 ($225) and £400 ($600)

The larger jug is damaged and of a standard Baddeley-Littler pattern. The milk jug is perfect and of an attractive, well-painted pattern.

Picture 77 £450 ($675)

A Bow "sparrow-beak" small milk jug. Decorated in the "Famille Rose" style of decoration.

Picture 78 £600 ($900)

A good, quite large Bow shell-shape dish. The quail design is reasonably common – rather than rare.

Picture 79 £500 ($750)

A moulded Bow milk jug with ornate handle. This probably originally had a cover, which would increase the value by at least £100 ($150).

Picture 80 £1,500 ($2,250)

A good late Bow figure with an ornate bocage. One of a pair.

Picture 81 £12,000 ($18,000) (cracked)

A rare, *marked* "Bristol" moulded sauceboat of c.1750. No such example was included in the Watney sales. A perfect example might command £20,000 ($30,000) if it was bearing the rare name mark.

Picture 82 *(left to right)* £1,000 ($1,500), £1,500 ($2,250), £1,000 ($1,500)

The Caughley tureen is a particularly rare form with its bud knob. The mask-head jug is a rare, early example. The small teapot is from the set shown in picture 37.

Picture 83 £10,000 ($15,000)

A magnificent and rare, marked "Turner Gallimore Salopian" moulded jug. Ex-Watney collection, lot 425, September 1999. The hammer price was £8,800 ($13,200), and the total price that was paid was £10,351 ($15,530). Few Caughley specimens would be valued so highly.

Picture 84 £700 ($1,050)

An above-average quality, neatly decorated, early Caughley creamer. Willingly purchased for £700 ($1,050) in June 2001, but most later examples would be less expensive.

Picture 85 £400 ($600)

A better than average Caughley enamelled small creamer. Always desirable objects.

Picture 86 *(left to right)* £450 ($675), £400 ($600), £350 ($525)

Three good, early, Caughley sparrow-beak jugs all of popular types. The differing values reflect the rarity of the patterns.

Picture 87 *(left to right)* £500 ($750), £300 ($450), £800 ($1,200) (square dish), £400 ($600), £800 ($1,200), and £300 ($450)

The dessert dish, which is painted with the Weir pattern, is an important piece, as is the earlier large square dish. The smaller items are very collectable, especially the ladle.

Picture 88 £400 ($600)

A good Caughley globular teapot bearing one of the less common underglaze blue-printed patterns.

Picture 89 £600 ($900)

A large meat dish well covered with blue-printed pattern, emulating the hand-painted importations from China. Smaller examples will be less costly.

Picture 90 £300 ($450)

A quite rare Caughley plate – one of two in a tea set, bearing the popular Fisherman pattern. This design is found on a very wide range of articles, some common, others rare.

Picture 91 £320 ($480)

A good French-style Caughley dessert dish. This item was purchased from a London exhibition in June 2001 for £320 ($480).

Picture 92 £500 ($750)

An attractive, neatly gilt, Caughley personalized mask-head jug with cursive monogram. Purchased privately in January 1998 for £450 ($675).

Picture 93 £200 ($300)

A particularly rare and desirable Caughley teabowl from a service that is now housed in the Victoria and Albert Museum. Printed odd teabowls of standard patterns will be less expensive.

Picture 94 £2,500 ($3,750)

A really splendid, one-off, armorial Caughley cabbage-leaf jug. Probably decorated in the Chamberlain studio in Worcester.

Picture 95 £1,200 ($1,800)

A magnificent, well-gilt, Caughley mug decorated at Chamberlain's Worcester studio to a special order. What quality!

Picture 96 *(left to right)* £5,000 ($7,500), £6,000 ($9,00), £40,000 ($60,000)

Early, undecorated Chelsea porcelains of the 1740s. All very rare and desirable objects. The sleeping boy sold at auction (at Phillips) in March 2000 for a hammer price of £43,000 ($64,500). A second example might not command such a price.

Picture 97 *£1,500 ($2,250)*

A good, marked, Chelsea waste bowl. Well painted in an attractive manner.

Picture 98 *£900 ($1,350) (damaged), £2,000 ($3,000)*

Two early but unmarked Chelsea creamers that have typical mock-Japanese designs. Rare and desirable even when damaged.

Picture 99 *£350 ($525)*

A good but not spectacular red-anchor marked plate. A standard product. Purchased for lecturing purposes in July 2001 for £320 ($480).

Picture 100 *£800 ($1,200)*

A colourful Chelsea dessert dish with typical exotic birds in landscapes.

Picture 101 *£500 ($750)*

A gold-anchor period Chelsea tall cup, possibly a chocolate cup with typical rich blue ground and rare figure subjects.

Picture 102 *£6,000 ($9,000) (some damage)*

A very rare and early pair of Derby figures, enamelled in a typically pale early style. Originally from a set of four.

Picture 103 *£2,000 ($3,000)*

A decorative early Derby jug with pale yellow ground.

Picture 104 *£1,800 ($2,700)*

A good early (*c.*1760) Derby teapot, painted with floral sprays in a typical manner.

Picture 105 *£1,600 ($2,400)*

A reasonably typical Derby figure of the early 1770s. It was produced in various models and sizes.

Picture 106 *£450 ($675) (repaired)*

An attractive and typically finely modelled Derby biscuit (unglazed) figure. Purchased in London for £450 ($675) in February 2002.

Picture 107 *£700 ($1,050)*

A particularly attractive Derby group from around the early 1790s.

Picture 108 *£1,000 ($15,000)*

A well-painted, neatly gilt Derby odd coffee can. A rightly collectable and rather costly specimen, this is typical of Derby at, or near, its best.

Picture 109 *(left to right) £1,000 ($1,500), £500 ($750) (damaged), £250 ($375)*

A Giles-decorated Worcester milk jug, a splendid but badly damaged Giles-decorated armorial, Worcester plate (worth over £2,000/$3,000 if perfect), and a Giles-decorated Chinese porcelain teabowl.

Picture 110 *£3,500 ($5,250) (some damage)*

A very rare, highly collectable St James's bird model. Formerly termed the "Girl in a Swing" class of porcelain.

Picture 111 *£6,000 ($9,000)*

It is difficult to value such a St James's porcelain covered container, small as it is, as no others are recorded. In a good sale it could well be bid to over £10,000 ($15,000).

Picture 112 *£6,000 ($9,000)*

A superb Isleworth mug. One of the finest known pieces currently attributed to Isleworth. Formerly in the Watney collection – attributed to Derby.

Picture 113 *£2,500 (£3,750)*

A rare relief-moulded and blue-painted Isleworth sauceboat. Purchased in June 1998 (before the Watney sales) for £2,000 ($3,000).

Picture 114 *£800 ($1,200)*

A seemingly rare Isleworth waste (or sugar) bowl printed with this factory's version of the Fisherman pattern. Common in other factories but very rare in Isleworth porcelain.

Picture 115 *(left to right) £4,000 ($6,000), £1,500 ($2,250), £800 (£1,200)*

Very rare, formerly Derby-type blue-printed porcelains now attributed to Isleworth. The above prices were paid by me in June 1998 – not cheap, but I could not find other specimens.

Picture 116 *£500 ($750) (cracked)*

Again, a rare Isleworth fluted plate from a tea service. Ordinary in Worcester or Caughley but not in Isleworth.

Picture 117 *£400 ($600) (stand cracked)*

A rare Isleworth tall bowl and recessed saucer or stand. A few of these have been recorded. This rather Continental form was made in at least two sizes.

Picture 118 *£1,000 ($1,500) (teapot without cover), £5,000 ($7,500) (cracked)*

It is extremey difficult to value such rarities, especially in Limehouse porcelain of the 1740s, and after the Watney sales.

Picture 119 *(left to right) £3,000 ($4,500) (chipped), £2,000 ($3,000), £10,000 ($15,000) (slightly damaged)*

Limehouse joys. How do you value such items? The cup is the only example known, as is the teapot.

Picture 120 *£5,200 ($7,800) (some damage)*

A good and typical Limehouse sauceboat. Purchased from the second Watney sale in May 2000 for £5,200 ($7,800), plus the auctioneer's "premium". A perfect example might command more than double this reasonably modest, "damaged", price.

Picture 121 *£22,000 ($33,000)*

A sweet early teapot, sold in 2003 for this price. Only in recent years has English blue and white fetched such high prices. A rare and early delight.

Picture 122 *£1,800 ($2,700) (cracked)*

A very good quality, relief-moulded Liverpool large-size sauceboat. Now attributed to William Reid. Sold by Phillips in the second portion of the Watney sale in November 2000, for £1,700 ($2,550). It has a crack and slight chips.

Picture 123 *£950 ($1,425)*

A brightly enamelled Liverpool waste bowl of a rather large size. This splendid example has been attributed to Samuel Gilbody.

Picture 124 *£220 ($330)*

A Liverpool Seth Pennington "high Chelsea" ewer. Painted in underglaze blue with overglaze enamelling. A typical but not that popular class of decoration.

Picture 125 *£1,000 ($1,500)*

A good-quality Philip Christian Liverpool moulded mug – one of a pair. These are found in various sizes.

Picture 126 *£1,500 ($2,250)*

A good and typical Philip Christian Liverpool coffee pot – painted overglaze with floral sprays.

Picture 127 *£2,000 ($3,000)*

A very typical, relief-moulded, Longton Hall dish. Plates are more plentiful than such dishes. Various subjects occur in the middle of these pieces.

Picture 128 *£6,000 ($9,000) for the pair*

A rare pair of early Lowestoft large tea canisters (that are missing their covers). Purchased at a London Antiques Fair in June 1953, for £45 ($70)!

Picture 129 *£1,200 ($1,800)*

A good and typical Lowestoft mug. These occur in various sizes and with many different designs.

Picture 130 *£4,000 ($6,000)*

A perhaps unique Lowestoft jug painted with these shipping panels. Unfortunately stolen from the author's collection.

Picture 131 *£3,000 ($4,500)*

A very rare form of late Lowestoft teapot but painted with a popular Redgrave-style pattern.

Picture 132 *£3,500 ($5,250)*

A large size Lowestoft tea- or punch pot enamelled in the Chinese style. It was purchased in 1991 for £3,420 ($5,130)– a steepish price.

Picture 133 *£2,500 ($3,750) and £3,000 ($4,500)*

Of these two inscribed "Trifle" mugs, the one that has an inscription relating to Bungay is the rarer. Later fakes of these popular "Trifles"' exist.

Picture 134 *£50 ($75) each (cups), £900 ($1,350) ("Trifle" mug)*

These are late examples of the 1790s but they are rare, especially the "Trifle from Lowestoft" mug purchased from the Colman collection.

Picture 135 *£6,000 ($9,000) (damaged)*

A rare, perhaps unique, pair of Lowestoft standing figures. Much damaged but very desirable. Stolen from the author's collection.

Picture 136 *£350 ($525)*

An odd cup but Neale porcelain and almost certainly painted by Fidelle Duvivier. If anything I have under-valued this cup.

Picture 137 *£2,000 ($3,000) (cover missing)*

A rare and typical Pinxton product. The floral panel was almost certainly painted by William Billingsley.

Picture 138 *£1,200 ($1,800)*

A rare Pinxton coffee can and saucer, with pale yellow ground and landscape panels.

Picture 139 *£1,500 ($2,250)*

A typical Pinxton teapot, with landscape panels each side and neat gilding.

Picture 140 *£600 ($900)*

A good Vauxhall sauceboat. Typically painted in a free manner, in a light underglaze blue.

Picture 141 *£400 ($600) (teabowl and saucer), £450 ($675) (cream boat)*

A standard Vauxhall design, combining underglaze blue with overglaze enamels and slight gilding.

Picture 142 *£4,000 ($6,000) (my original valuation but see below)*

A very rare Vauxhall teapot and cover, with outline prints in various colours. Enamelled over to enhance the printed design. This teapot in fact was sold at Christie's South Kensington in October 2002, to a specialist London dealer, for a hammer price of £15,000 ($22,500).

Picture 143 *(left to right) £400 ($600), £500 ($750), £850 ($1,275)*

Typical West Pans porcelains – note the handle form. The large dish may have been enhanced with unfired gilding or enamels.

Picture 144 *£3,500 ($5,250)*

A very rare, early Worcester cream or butter boat. The reliefs picked out in underglaze blue.

Picture 145 *(left to right) £7,000 ($1,050), £2,500 ($3,750), £3,000 ($4,500)*

Rare and highly collectable early Worcester. The dinner plate is particularly desirable and therefore is difficult to value!

Picture 146 *(left to right) £2,000 ($3,000), £900 ($1,350), £3,000 ($4,500), £900 ($1,350), £1,500 ($2,250), £1,000 (£1,500)*

Six rare and desirable examples of early Worcester blue and white. The leaf-moulded dish is particularly rare.

Picture 147 *£4,000 ($6,000)*

A beautifully moulded, oval, open, butter dish. It is attractively painted in the Chinese manner and is also very collectable.

Picture 148 *(left to right) £1,500 ($2,250), £2,500 ($3,750), £2,000 ($3,000)*

Three very attractive examples of enamelled early Worcester porcelain.

Picture 149 *£2,500 ($3,750)*

A sweet and rare earlyish Worcester teapot.

Picture 150 *£750 ($1,125)*

An attractive Worcester printed small milk or cream jug. Purchased in America.

Picture 151 *£850 ($1,275) (badly cracked)*

A large and most attractive Worcester mask-head, cabbage leaf moulded jug. Rare pale yellow ground with its panels painted in puce. In perfect condition the value would be about £4,000 ($6,000).

Picture 152 *£1,000 ($1,500)*

A Flight-period Worcester mug. Not spectacular but it is dated, 1784.

Picture 153 *£5,000 ($7,500)*

A splendid blue-ground Worcester mask-head, cabbage leaf moulded jug, well painted with exotic birds in landscape. This is a top-quality piece.

Picture 154 *£200 ($300) (badly damaged)*

A good Worcester dessert dish of *c*.1780. In perfect condition the valuation would rise to £800 ($1,200).

Picture 155 *£600 ($900) (teapot)*

A Worcester fan-pattern (Japanese style) teapot that has its cover.

Picture 156 *£10,000 ($15,000) (teapot), £1,500 ($2,250) (cup)*

This is part of a superb English decorated Chinese tea service. The cup was my first £1,000 ($1,500) cup – some years ago.

Picture 157 *£2,000 ($3,000) (cracked)*

A very rare and fine deep dish. This is an example of Chinese porcelain that was decorated in England, *c*.1750–55.

Picture 158 *£2,500 ($3,750) (firing faults)*

A rare but typical Plymouth jug, showing characteristic firing faults.

Picture 159 *£2,000 ($3,000) (candle holder is missing)*

A good and rare Plymouth group.

Picture 160 *£600 ($900)*

A typical Bristol hard-paste fluted waste bowl. The main floral decoration is on the other side.

Picture 161 *£2,200 ($3,300) (teapot), £500 ($750) (plate), £480 ($720) (teabowl and saucer, cracked)*

Bristol porcelains sold by Phillips in September 2001, for the quoted hammer prices.

Picture 162 *£3,500 ($5,250)*

A good Bristol standing figure, one of a set of four.

Picture 163 *£2,100 ($3,150) (pair dishes), £7,200 ($10,800) (single dish), £300 ($450) (pair plates, cracked)*

Typical Bristol floral-painted dessert wares.

Picture 164 *£2,500 ($3,750)*

A very rare early New Hall mug. A slightly faulty example in the first Watney sale of September 1999 sold for £2,000 ($3,000).

Picture 165 *£2,000 ($3,000)*

A very rare, and seemingly unique, early New Hall jug shape. Accordingly it fetched a total of £2,234.88 ($3,355) at Phillips in December 1999.

Picture 166 *£800 ($1,200) each*

Three rare New Hall creamers of differing patterns.

Picture 167 *£10,000 ($15,000)*

A rare New Hall jug complete with cover. Painted by Fidelle Duvivier.

Picture 168 *£3,000 ($4,500) (repaired)*

A rare New Hall tureen stand, which was painted by Fidelle Duvivier.

Picture 169 *£1,200 ($1,800)*

A rare large size blue-printed New Hall bowl.

Picture 170 *£150 ($225) (creamer) and £600 ($900) (teapot)*

Two rare early "Factory Z" pieces, both desirable.

Picture 171 *(left to right) £200 ($300), £500 ($750), £250 ($375)*

Three very rare and early Chamberlain-Worcester jugs.

Picture 172 *(left to right) £1,500 ($2,250), £3,000 ($4,500), £1,000 ($1,500)*

Three very rare early Chamberlain articles, all hard to duplicate and value.

Picture 173 *£2,000 ($3,000)*

A very rare or unique, dated (1794), Chamberlain teabowl and saucer.

Picture 174 *£7,000 ($1,050)*

A very good and perfect Chamberlain vase and cover.

Picture 175

Representative parts of a superb-quality Chamberlain-Worcester harlequin dessert service.

Top dish £2,000 ($3,000);

Plates £1,000–1,500 ($1,500–2,250) each, depending on decoration;

Tureen and cover £6,000 ($9,000) (this has desirable shell decoration on it);

Square dish £2,000 ($3,000);

Shaped dish £4,000 ($6,000) (this has desirable feather decoration on it);

Centrepiece £7,000 ($10,500) (with view of Worcester and the factory);

A very similar, but more complete set of 43 pieces was sold in 2002, to a London dealer, for £72,000 ($108,000).

Picture 176 *£10,000 ($15,000)*

This is the major item from a superb one-off armorial tea service.

Picture 177 *£600 ($900)*

A very rare, marked example but modestly decorated. Without the Royal Arms mark, such a piece might be valued at little more than £100 ($150).

Picture 178 *(left to right) £1,000 ($1,500), £2,500 ($3,750), £1,500 ($2,250)*

Three very rare and early Coalport jugs. The centre example is inscribed and dated.

Picture 179 *£1,500 ($2,250)*

A very rare early Coalport jug.

Picture 180 *£60 ($90) (cup)*

The Coalport/Caughley factory wasters have nominal, research value. Odd cups of such simple ungilt designs should be in the £40–80 ($60–120) range.

Picture 181 *£600 ($900)*

A good Coalport teapot, decorated with a colourful and typical "Japan" pattern.

Picture 182 *(left to right, top to bottom) £400 ($600), £300 ($450), £2,000 ($3,000), £800 ($1,200), £900 ($1,350), £80 ($120)*

Six well-decorated early Coalport plates. The values largely depend on the type or quality of decoration.

Picture 183 *£400 ($600) each (dishes), £250 ($375) (plate), £600 ($900) (centrepiece), £500 ($750) (oval tureen)*

These are representative components of a "Japan" pattern Coalport dessert service.

Picture 184 *£200 ($300) (trio), £450 ($675) (teapot), £150 ($225) (bowl), £300 ($450) (covered dish), £250 ($375) (decorative plate), £200 ($300) (teapot stand)*

These are representative components of a "Japan" pattern Coalport tea service, c.1812–14.

Picture 185 *£900 ($1,350)*

A very decorative and large Coalport (punch) bowl.

Picture 186 *£20,000 ($30,000)*

A large and highly important covered vase, featuring the Coalport factory. A true museum piece.

Picture 187 *£4,000 ($6,000)*

A Coalport vase decorated in Thomas Baxter's London Studio, c.1805.

Picture 188 *£10,000 ($15,000)*

A set of four Coalport vases, painted by Thomas Baxter, 1801. Missing from the Godden collection.

Picture 189 *£3,000 ($4,500)*

A Coalport bulb pot decorated in Thomas Baxter's Studio.

Picture 190 *£800 ($1,200)*

A rare form of a Miles Mason jug.

Picture 191 *£400 ($600) (coffee can and saucer), £600 ($900) (sugar bowl and cover), £100 ($150) (teabowl), £350 ($525) (milk jug), £180 ($270) (teapot stand), £650 ($975) (teapot).*

These are representative components of a Miles Mason tea service. A standard printed outline pattern, c.1805.

Picture 192 *(left to right) £500 ($750), £800 ($1,200), £600 ($900)*

Very rare specimens of Turner porcelain.

Picture 193 *No commercial value*

Highly important Wolfe-Mason wasters from the Liverpool factory site, but they are really of no commercial value.

Picture 194 *(left to right) £450 ($675), £300 ($450), £400 ($600)*

Rare examples of Wolfe-Mason, Liverpool porcelains, c.1797–9.

Picture 195 *(left to right) £800 ($1,200), £400 ($600), £900 ($1,350)*

Very rare Wolfe-Mason, Liverpool porcelains, c.1798.

Picture 196 *(left to right) £750 ($1,125) , £100 ($150), £1,200 ($1,800)*

Very rare and attractive tewares of the 1790s.

Picture 197 *£1,000 ($1,500), £1,500 ($2,250)*

Two rare, and early, "Factory X" (Keeling) covered sugar bowls. The price depends on the quality and style of decoration.

Picture 198 *(left to right) £300 ($450), £1,500 ($2,250), £1,000 ($1,500)*

Three early "Factory X" (Keeling) specimens, which are tastefully decorated in gold.

Picture 199 *£100 ($150) (jug) and £1,000 ($1,500) (coffee pot)*

Two typical examples from the "Factory Z" group.

Picture 200 *£800 ($1,200) (some damage)*

A rare Keeling porcelain teapot from a marked tea service – a key piece.

Picture 201

A group of "Factory Z" teawares of pattern 25. The typical prices might be:

Teapot, cover, and stand *£600 ($900)*;

Covered sugar bowls *£350 ($525)*;

Milk jugs (various shapes occur) *£250 ($375)*;

Cups (and saucers) *£120 ($180)*.

Picture 202 *£250 each ($375)*

Three rare and desirable jugs of the 1790s/early 1800s.

Picture 203 *£3,000 ($4,500)*

A rare marked "W (***)" class vase.

Picture 204 *£1,000 ($1,500) (bulb pot) and £700 ($1,050) (figure)*

Scarce marked "W (***)" class porcelains.

Picture 205 *£400 ($600) (teapot), £250 ($375) (creamers)*

Scarce "Pattern Book" class porcelains, but with rather limited appeal.

Picture 206 *£1,000 ($1,500)*

A splendid, hand-painted Spode jug. Above average.

Picture 207 *£400 ($600) (sugar box), £250 ($375) (jug)*

Rare examples of a simple early Minton pattern.

Picture 208

Early c.1805 Minton teawares of a tasteful design, possible values are:

Teapot £450 ($675);

Sugar box £400 ($600);

Jug £250 ($375);

Oval stand £120 ($180);

Trio of cups and saucers at £140 ($210).

Picture 209 £500 ($750)

A rare form of fluted, early Minton sugar box.

Picture 210 £1,200 ($1,800)

A rare form of Minton teapot, cover, and stand, with good-quality decoration.

Picture 211 £700 ($1,050)

A well-decorated Ridgway dessert dish.

Picture 212 £650 ($975)

A good Ridgway dessert dish.

Picture 213 £450 ($675)

Although this looks like a dish, it is a two-handled Ridgway dessert plate.

Picture 214

Rare "CB" marked Charles Bourne porcelains.

Milk jug £400 ($600);

Cat model £1,200 ($1,800);

Spill vases at £750 ($1,125);

Plates at £650 ($975);

Pen tray £850 ($1,275);

Punchbowl £1,500 ($2,250).

Picture 215

Representative pieces of the Daniel services made for the Earl of Shrewsbury, c.1827. A sumptuous one-off service. Valued as perfect, but most examples have body cracks.

Tureen and cover £4,000 ($6,000;)

Plate £1,250 ($1,875);

Comport £6,000 ($9,000);

Covered dish £5,000 ($7,500);

Two tier cake stand £6,000 ($9,000).

Picture 216 £2,500 ($3,750)

A very decorative, high-quality, Daniel jug.

Picture 217

Representative examples of a Daniel dessert service. Well decorated with shell centres.

Tureen and cover £1,000 ($1,500);

Dessert dishes at £800 ($1,200);

Plate £600 ($900);

Comport £1,500 ($2,250).

Picture 218 £400 ($600)

A good-quality Herculaneum (Liverpool) trio of teacup, coffee can, and saucer.

Picture 219 £2,000 ($3,000)

A good and rare (French-style) Herculaneum vase.

Picture 220

Representative parts of a Wedgwood porcelain tea service. An attractive printed outline pattern.

Teapot, cover, and stand £1,200 ($1,800);

Covered sugar box £800 ($1,200);

Plate £250 ($375);

Waste bowl £400 ($600);

Milk jug £500) ($750);

Teacup and saucer £250 ($375);

Coffee can £120 ($180).

Picture 221 £350 ($525) each

Three printed outline patterned New Hall bone-china milk jugs. All attractive and very collectable.

Picture 222 £500 ($750) (cracked)

A rare New Hall bone-china dessert dish c.1825.

Picture 223 £250–450 ($375–675) each

Four typical Coalport plates of the 1820s. Values largely depend on the quality and type of decoration.

Picture 224 £450 ($675) (left), £350 ($475) (right)

Both are rare, early examples of Alcock's porcelain, but the plate on the left is a more expensive pattern.

Picture 225 £350 ($525)

A pleasing, early Alcock dessert dish.

Picture 226 £900 ($1,350)

A good-quality Alcock dog model. One of a pair and larger than most examples.

Picture 227 £1,500 ($2,250)

A superb-quality, large Alcock jug painted with landscapes and flowers. These were made in various sizes.

Picture 228 £400 ($600) (repaired)

One of a pair of large (French-style) floral-encrusted Alcock vases.

Picture 229 £500 ($750)

A superb-quality Alcock dessert plate.

Picture 230 £1,200 ($1,800)

A good, decorative, Chamberlain-Worcester, "Japan" pattern teapot, cover, and stand.

Picture 231 £2,500 ($3,750)

A superb-quality, marked, Chamberlain-Worcester vase with Shakespeare subject.

Picture 232 £1,600 ($2,400)

A superb-quality, Chamberlain-Worcester spill vase, with mock jewelling.

Picture 233 £1,200 ($1,800)

A good, marked, Chamberlain dog model.

Picture 234 £850 ($1,275)

A floral-encrusted Coalport covered bowl.

Picture 235 £950 ($1,425)

A good, well-decorated, Coalport rococo-style teapot and cover.

Picture 236

Representative pieces from a Coalport dessert service

of the 1830s. Centrepiece £600 ($900), dessert dishes at £350 ($525), plates at £150 ($225).

Picture 237 £300 ($450)

A good-quality Davenport trio. The coffee cans have now given way to shaped cups.

Picture 238 £250 ($375)

A rare and decorative Davenport trio.

Picture 239 £500 ($750)

An above-average quality Derby plate that is of the Bloor period.

Picture 240 £600 ($900)

A typical Derby dessert dish, which has a hand-painted, scenic centre.

Picture 241 £600 ($900)

A King Street, Derby reissue of Dr Syntax.

Picture 242

A page from the King Street, Derby catalogue, which is decorated with the popular "Japan" patterns.

Picture 243 £1,600 ($2,400)

A very good, inscribed, Grainger-Worcester, floral-painted jug.

Picture 244 £500 ($750) (repaired)

A rare, Grainger-Worcester letter rack. Well painted with flowers.

Picture 245 £3,000 ($4,500)

A rare and decorative, marked Rockingham mug.

Picture 246 £750 ($1,125)

A typical fancy-shaped Rockingham teapot and cover.

Picture 247 £6,000 ($9,000)

A typically fine-quality pair of Worcester jardinières or cachepots. Panels painted with desirable shell painting.

Picture 248 £2,000 ($3,000)

A Flight, Barr & Barr period Worcester dessert dish, with ground-laid border and quality gilding.

Picture 249 £750 ($1,125)

A decorative Kerr & Binns Worcester dessert plate.

Picture 250 £1,200 ($1,800)

A superb-quality Kerr & Binns Worcester, Limoges enamel-style covered cup by Thomas Bott.

Picture 251 £1,250 ($1,875)

A well-painted Swansea moulded dessert plate.

Picture 252 £400 ($600) (damaged)

A decorative, high-quality, Nantgarw dessert plate. If perfect the price would be around £2,000 ($3,000).

Picture 253 £350 ($525)

A good but standard, lustred London-shape teapot/cover.

Picture 254 £800 ($1,200)

A decorative, lustred porcelain vase. All such vases were originally issued in pairs or sets.

Picture 255 £900 ($1,350)

A rare, early, marked, Copeland & Garrett, parian "Art Union" figure.

Picture 256 £600 ($900)

A well-moulded, parian jug with cover. This is a typical Minton product with an above average price.

Picture 257 £500 ($750) (one of a pair)

A Minton, coloured, parian figure, which was in fact an 1851 Exhibition model. The pair would fetch about £1,200 ($1,800).

Picture 258 £1,200 ($1,800) (cover not shown)

A Minton pâte-sur-pâte vase. An apprentice piece, hence the lowish price.

Picture 259 £4,500 ($6,750)

A rare, Minton, pâte-sur-pâte tray. An exhibition piece with coloured reliefs, by Solon.

Picture 260 £800 ($1,200)

A typical George Jones dish, decorated in the pâte-sur-pâte style but not as highly regarded as Minton examples.

Picture 261 £150 ($225)

A hand-painted, Brown-Westhead, Moore & Co. dessert plate, c.1870.

Picture 262 £1,000 ($1,500)

A splendid Coalport dessert (or cabinet) plate signed by Percy Simpson c.1910.

Picture 263 £2,500 ($3,750)

A superb-quality Coalport vase, painted by Keeling. A late example, but the quality makes it worth more.

Picture 264 £5,000 ($7,500) (one of a pair)

A magnificent Minton Sèvres-style two-piece mantle vase. A pair would fetch around £12,000 ($18,000).

Picture 265 £6,000 ($9,000) (one of a set of three)

A magnificent Minton Sèvres-style covered vase. About as good as they come. A complete set of three would fetch around £20,000 ($30,000).

Picture 266 £4,500 ($6,750) (one of a pair)

A graceful, Minton Sèvres-style covered vase mounted on a gilt-metal base. The pair would fetch £10,000 ($15,000) or so.

Picture 267 £1,000 ($1,500)

This is a superb-quality Minton hand-painted plate. Each example from the dessert service has a different Russian view on it.

Picture 268 £1,250 ($1,875)

A splendid Minton plate from a dessert service, hand-painted and with acid-gilding.

Picture 269 £2,500 ($3,750)

A tastefully decorated Royal Crown Derby plate by Désiré Leroy – a talented artist.

Picture 270 £4,500 ($6,750)

A magnificent Royal Crown Derby covered bowl, hand-painted by Gresley.

Picture 271 £1,500 ($2,250) (one of a pair)

A richly gilt Royal Worcester vase that was emulating the fashionable Japanese style.

Picture 272 *£4,000 ($6,000)*
A richly decorated Royal Worcester teapot with gold, jewelled ground. This is a signed and dated example.

Picture 273 *£1,000 ($1,500)*
A typical, attractive, pair of Royal Worcester figures by James Hadley.

Picture 274 *£1,800 ($2,700)*
A superb-quality Royal Worcester ewer-shaped vase (one of a pair), painted by W.A. Hawkins.

Picture 275
Detail of marks on reverse of plate.

Picture 276 *£300 ($450)*
A decorative but reproduction pair of mock Chelsea figures of Continental origin and late date.

Picture 277 *£350 ($525)*
This is a very decorative and good-quality Continental (Samson) copy of an 18th-century Worcester plate. Antique in its own right but still a copy.

Picture 278 *£1,100 ($1,650) for the group*
These are difficult to value. The porcelain is original 18th-century Worcester, but the decoration is 19th century. Left to right: £400 ($600) (this is very good quality), £400 ($600) (a rare object that has quality decoration), and £300 ($450) (overdecorated but still attractive and interesting). However, most specialist collectors would steer clear of such redecorated items.

Picture 279 *£120 ($180) each*
A selection of modern, but individual, hand-carved slim, bone-china ornaments.

My total for the objects illustrated in this slim book comes to over £750,000 ($1,125,000). But this was merely a personal valuation exercise. You can gain great enjoyment from just a few well-chosen pieces rather than spending a huge amount of money.

Looking back

I have added this very personal section to help my younger readers in the hopes that it will, perhaps, put some matters in perspective. I think these personal observations are in keeping with the overall aim of this book and they help to place our porcelains in the context of their time. Some points reflect on the values placed on the objects illustrated in this book, which is why I have included them in this chapter.

I obviously have no idea what monumental changes are going to be experienced during the 21st century. However, it might be interesting if I gave a résumé of some aspects of life in England during the 18th century, which is when most of the great British porcelain manufactories were established.

This need (of putting young readers in the picture), was underlined the other day when my son (born as the first man landed on the moon in 1969) phoned me to ask how many inches there are in a foot. Yes, our units of measurement and our currency – as well as our communication systems, indeed our whole way of life – have changed in just one generation. Just think how much has changed in over 250 years, since Chelsea, Bow, Worcester, and Derby commenced producing translucent porcelain.

In my school days (during 1939–45's World War II), and for centuries before, we measured in inches, feet, and yards. There were, and still are, 12 inches to the foot and three feet to the yard. This traditional system was originally based on convenient body parts – the width of a finger, the length of an average foot, and the length of an outstretched arm. Now, in my 70s, I have no (little) idea of the current units of measurement – millimetres, metres, and so on are truly foreign to me. Yet they are simple and basic to the younger people brought up with this system – as all other modern modes of life are.

Even our calendar has been amended. England belatedly adopted the Gregorian calendar in 1752. The 3 September became the 14 September (we "lost" ten days) but more importantly the new year number then came into being on 1 January of any year, rather than within April. There can, therefore, be confusion with documents or letters dated, for example, 3 January or 3 February 1750 – were they written early in 1751 or late in 1750? This change only affected England (and perhaps Wales) – Scotland saw the light much earlier, in January 1600, as had much of Europe.

Of great interest to the English manufacturers and other traders was the heavily rising population figures. Accurate figures are difficult to trace, but the following *approximate* figures show the rapid rise.

1751	6,500,000
1801	9,000,000
1851	18,000,000
1901	32,500,000
1951	44,000,000
2001	58,000,000

The great growth in the population, particularly during the 19th century, gave rise to the need to import more food, mainly from British Colonies, but also from the Americas. It also increased the market for table china – the "bread-and-butter" of the ceramic industry.

I have earlier explained in this book that the British porcelain industry – if it could initially be called an "industry" – was founded in the mid- to late 1740s. These early porcelain makers were almost certainly born in the reign of George I (1714–27). King George was a Hanoverian German (the present Germany was then a series of separate states: Saxony, Prussia, etc) by birth. He could hardly speak English and only indulged in one provincial tour outside London. However, he returned to Hanover almost yearly and died and was buried on the Continent. He and his successor, George II, were only really known to their subjects from their image on coinage. Newspapers were few and costly, and photography didn't appear until much later.

The Hanoverian King George I was succeeded by his son, George II, in June 1727. He lived until October 1760 and so witnessed the birth of the main porcelain factories and the failure of some early ventures, such as that at Limehouse. His reign of more than 30 years was to see not only the birth of British porcelain and the vast improvements in the pottery industry, but other vital improvements in manufacture of various types – materials and machinery. These have been conveniently classed together under one heading, "The Industrial Revolution", which was prompted by the great goal of wealth – or at least by advancement.

The period was also one of conflict between nations, as well as between classes. These hostilities ranged from local rebellions, such as that with Scotland in the 1745–6 period, to the great Seven Years' War waged on the Continent of Europe between 1756 and 1763, and, of course, also fought at sea between the maritime powers. The same period saw the conquest of India in 1757 and, two years later, the victory over the French outside Quebec, leading to British possession of Canada in 1760.

What is now known as the United States of America was then (until 1776) considered as British, generally referred to as "our North American Colony" or colonies.

Much of North America had not been explored or populated by immigrants from England, or other parts of Europe. The white population was relatively small and mainly confined to the eastern side and the north rather than the deep south. Most of the country was still occupied and worked by native North American Indian tribes. Still the white influence was spreading rapidly and the "New World" – as it was to be called – became a vital part of the British export trade – in goods as well as people. I will refrain from mentioning the large trade in slaves, but it was part of the generally accepted way of the (white) world in the 18th century (indeed it was not officially abolished in the British Empire until 1833).

While wars are always costly, the British Navy and the Army (helped by various allies) was generally victorious. Britain gained countries, and therefore markets for its goods and the foundation was being laid for the "Empire on which the sun never sets". The apt title "Great Britain" and the description "British" were used after The Act of Union in 1707, which united England and Scotland. London was becoming one of the major capitals of the world.

All this and more you, Hannah, may learn at school, or be able to read about in books, or gather from other new methods of learning. What may be more important in our understanding of the early British porcelains is the situation within the British Isles itself.

Leaving aside the almost continuous conflicts – it is important to remember that England was largely an agricultural country, as more men were employed on the land than in towns or cities. As far as basic food was concerned Britain was then a self-sufficient land. From time to time there may have been bad harvests and shortages, but the modest population did not need to import basic foods. Certainly some special foods or spices were imported from the East by the English East India Company and other goodies such as sugar from the West Indies, but Britain was not dependent on imports. Fuel to drive the growing industries was right under English feet – coal. Other sources of power were water and wind – water wheels and windmills to grind flour and other materials. Petrol and oil and such fuels were yet to be in demand. The chief industries were not so "heavy", as coal had only recently lent its weight to assist manufacturing industries. Wool and woollen goods were a major industry. Tin was mined within Cornwall, lead in Derbyshire. Roads were poor, and transport depended on the horse. The canal system, therefore, was to become important. Slow as it was, water transport was relatively cheap and the barges or ships carried far more bulk and weight than had been possible on wagons drawn over poor roads by horses.

While everyone depended on candles (or animal fat tallow) for light, the country was very much divided by the class system, depending largely on people's wealth. For the working classes, the labourers, working hours were long, conditions hard, and wages low. Education, if available, was rudimentary. A very high proportion would need to sign their wills or other documents with a cross, as they were unable to write their own names. Their homes and table would be humble.

The important, ever-expanding middle, or merchant, class, which included the professions, obviously fared very much better. They enjoyed a family life, a fair education perhaps at a grammar school. Such people, as they progressed, employed servants and lived in substantially built houses. Their furniture was well made and suitable to their station or style of living. For most of the 18th century mahogany replaced the earlier walnut furniture. In county districts much was still made from native woods such as oak but the local craftsman would endeavour to emulate city styles, helped by the publication of books of new fashion designs. The merchant classes would rejoice in attractive glassware, pottery, even porcelains, and some silver objects. Still, sanitation was very basic and modes of transport depended on the horse.

Then, of course, there was the landed gentry and nobility that enjoyed an independent income. Such people probably had a "Town House" in London as well as one or more country estates. They were great employers of labour and might well have been patrons of the Arts. It was this upperclass market that the leading porcelain manufacturers – particularly Chelsea – catered for. In high-class pottery Josiah Wedgwood aimed at this restricted but prestigious market. One difficulty was, however, that the Lords were slow to pay. Bills might be settled once a year!

These were the educated classes, the young sons being sent off on "The Grand Tour" as they came of age. Many of Britain's great houses still display the "high art" that was brought back from Italy from these trips. The homes would also include a library. Serious books would line the walls, not only relating to British culture but also French and Italian. Later studies, such as Adam Smith's *The Wealth of Nations* of 1776, would be included. This book, which has been described as a "turning point in economic history", is still a required read. The monthly *The Gentleman's Magazine* containing a digest of information, letters, and articles might be on subscription.

Even among the staff employed in the great houses there was a very real class system. The "below-stairs" servants, including kitchen hands and cleaning staff, were considered inferior to the above-stairs staff – who had less need to dirty their hands or knees. It was very much a case of be seen but not heard; you did not speak unless spoken to.

Obviously with an overall population of just a small fraction of that living in the British Isles today, the cities and towns were extremely compact by today's standards. Every town has spread greatly over the years – taking in and joining up once outlying villages. The Chelsea factory, for example, is now considered to have been in London, but in the 18th century it was a separate village surrounded by fields and farms!

While most commodities and services were cheaper in the 18th century than today, there were several exceptions. Transport, that is coach travel, was costly – as was the postal service. Letters were charged (to the receiver) according to distance travelled as well as by weight. Uniform postal rates and pre-payment in the form of postage stamps was far off in the 19th century. Great Britain, you will learn, led the world in this regard with the introduction of postage stamps in 1840, the famous "Penny Black" being sold in such vast numbers that examples are still not that scarce or costly today.

Tea was also relatively expensive, the sole source then being China and its direct importation into England being the monopoly of the English East India Company. The high cost was increased by government tax, which led to wholesale smuggling.

The tea leaf is a good example of the difficulty in quoting prices for commodities in the 18th century. The basic prices varied from year to year depending on how much arrived safely in England from China on the East Indiamen – the sailing vessels that brought their mixed cargoes from the East, either direct from China or via India. The number of vessels varied each year – many were lost on voyage, or taken by the enemy – French or sometimes Dutch vessels.

Apart from the quantity available dictating the basic price, the type or quality of the tea also varied. Another consideration was where, or by whom, it was sold. Transport costs and middlemen complicate the equation. Let me briefly quote the various types of tea that were advertised in Peter Paul of Bath and Bristol in December 1787:

The present prices of *new Teas* are as follows:-

	s.	d.
Good common Bohea	1	10
the best imported	2	0
Good Congou or Souchong	3	8
Fine	4	0
Very fine	5	0
Superfine	6	0
Best imported	8	0
Good Green Tea	3	8
Speckled-leaf fine	4	0
Fine Bloom	5	0
Good Hyson Tea	6	0
Very good	7	0
Superfine	8	0
and the best imported, at	10	0

Fresh Roasted Coffee of a superior quality and flavour, Patent Chocolate and Cocoa, with refined Sugars, at the very lowest prices.

That is Chinese tea from under two shillings (10p) to ten shillings (50p), I assume per pound weight. The almost equally popular coffee and chocolate was rather less expensive than the teas, but they again varied according to market conditions.

Tea, or the fashion for tea drinking in family groups, was, of course, vital to the porcelain manufacturers. In Society the taking of tea required delicate porcelains. At first, from about 1690, the porcelain tea equipment – the teapot, the sugar and waste bowl, the milk or cream pot, and the handleless teabowls – were imported via the East India Company, along with the tea itself, from China. From the mid-1740s the newly established English porcelain makers joined in the commercial race to equip the "tea table". This book and any other on my subject will feature more teawares than any other type or class of porcelain. As early as 1717 Thomas Twining opened the first tea shop within London, in Aldwych, catering specifically for Ladies. The cities, particularly the central City of London, had more "Coffee Houses" than this generation has "McDonalds"! At these Coffee Houses great trade was carried on – one, Lloyds, was to become the centre (the world centre) of insurance. They were great meeting and trading places, with national newspapers being available. We have no such centres today – except perhaps, in its unique way, the Internet.

Yet the home was the most important centre for the porcelain industry, as a home for the increasing middle and professional classes was not complete without porcelain. This included porcelain tea sets as well as separate dessert and dinner services – and even ornamental vases and figures, perhaps.

The currency to purchase such goods was gold. The standard gold coin was the guinea, representing (from 1717) one pound one shilling (the half guinea being ten shillings and six pence). There were smaller silver and copper coins being divisions of the pound – sterling. There were 20 shillings to the pound and 12 pence (or pennies) to the shilling. But the gentlemanly unit was the guinea. In some circles this pricing remains even today, but it is not convenient with modern notes or pound coinage.

As to the present-day value of the old guinea, various explanations are banded about and the results differ widely. The basic point to remember, is that in the 18th century a weekly wage of a guinea or a guinea and a half was a fair wage, enough for a family to live on and enjoy at least the basic comforts of life.

As I write these notes, in January 2003, a new Sovereign (a gold coin with a 19th-century face value of £1) costs £57.50 ($87). An ounce of gold is quoted at £218.49 ($328). Today the pound sterling is approximately worth at least 1.5 US dollars (in my youth there were four dollars to the pound). We have a new European currency, the Euro, which is roughly the same value as a US dollar. Other benchmarks are the FTSE 100 (which indicates the cost of the 100 leading shares in the London Stock Exchange), and in the United States, the Dow Jones index. Such figures change daily, as shares are affected by world events, confidence or lack of confidence in the market, in individual shares, or by supply and demand – to name only the major influences that can govern such indexes on the strength of the stock market or of a nation and its economy.

Today, in the 21st century, Britain has a "National Minimum Wage". As from October 2003, this was set at £4.50 ($7) an hour (for an adult that is aged 22 or over). Therefore, for a modest eight hour day the minimum permitted wage is £36 ($54), and for a basic five-day week this equates to £180 ($270). Yet, with present-day value added tax on goods and services and the high cost of living, a person on this minimum wage would, I fancy, be worse off than the 18th-century worker earning a guinea, for a much longer working week.

This is not to say that life was easy during the 18th century. It certainly was not – at least not by modern standards. Try reading a few 18th-century newspapers to give you a flavour of life at that time. Here are quotes from a few that I have acquired:

The Chester Weekly Journal – 23 February 1731
Last night the Sessions ended at the Old Bailey when the eight following malefactors received Sentence of Death, Thomas...and Thomas...for Street Robbery, Thomas...and Thomas...for Felony and Burglary, Edward...for breaking open a shop and stealing a silk Handkerchief, George...for returning from Transportation, and Jane...for stealing £14-10-0 and two Gold Rings.

On Thursday next there will be preached at the Parish Church of St. Mary le Bow, Cheapside, a Sermon...for relieving the Poor, by establishing a new Colony on the uncultivated part of Carolina of such necessitous families from hence as are in great Distress here at home thro' want of Employment, and therefore desirous of being settled there, where they may live comfortably by their labour and industry; and also for instructing the Negroes of the British Plantations in the Christian Religion and other good Purposes.

This emigration was long before Britain sent felons to Australia – indeed long before Captain Cook landed at Botany Bay in 1770*. However, emigration of mainly working classes to North America – "The New World" – had been popular over a very long period. In the 1840s the Potters set up an Emigration Society to buy land in America to set up a new town, "Pottersville".

Back in Britain, crime seemingly abounded – even when the death penalty was given for what we would consider trivial matters. Here are a few quotes from *The London Evening Post* of 10 August 1797.

Surrey assizes held at Croydon…the following criminals received judgment of death – Mary Cooper for stealing in the shop of John Cook five yards of calico, William Harland for stealing 39 sheep; George Walts for robbing George May of two guineas and a half and some silver; Rebecca Dunn and her daughter for coining shillings…

On Tuesday, at Worcester, William Price and Joseph Tucker, for stealing a quarter of malt, received sentence of Death.

George Hartland for stealing a hen, to be publicly whipped. Richard Clements for stealing coals, to be privately whipped and kept to hard labour in the house of correction for three calendar months.

What punishment awaited a house-clearing gang at work in London in January 1798 one can only guess. But the report clearly shows that large-scale crime is no new thing…

On Saturday night last a house in Brook Street, Grosvenor Square, was robbed of the whole of the furniture, by some persons who came prepared with a cart and horses for the purpose.

Britain was at war in the mid- to late 1790s, a fact men out a'walking or a'drinking in London would have been made well aware of by the dreaded activities of the Press Gangs – taking and kidnapping unfortunate men to serve in the Navy. Two reports in *The London Evening Post* from 24 November 1796 report such activities in a routine manner:

Yesterday the Press on the River (Thames) was greater than at any former period. The men who had protections were indiscriminately impressed, and sent on board the receiving ships. One man endeavouring to make his escape, jumped over a ship at Deptford and was drowned…

Yesterday noon a number of imprest men were put

on board two tenders from the receiving ship at the Tower, to be put on board the Sandwich guardship at the Nore, from whence they will be distributed to ships whose crews are not complete.

At sea the British Navy itself was hard pressed, the same issue reported great loss of shipping to the French, even of coastal traders. The *Brighton* was lost to the French on voyage from London to the local south coast port of Littlehampton; she was "carried into Boulogne".

I recall similar losses to German submarines and mines in the early 1940s. On land many military groups or regiments were formed, under local landowners, to protect their locality. This in turn was mirrored in World War II (1939–45) with the "Home Guard" or "Dad's Army".

Still the daily or weekly papers abound with more cheerful snippets of information reflecting life at that time. The spread of information was slow. Letters travelled by ship or horse, the postboys often being robbed on their journey. There was none of today's wireless, television, or mobile phone. Yet *The London Evening Post* of 24 November 1796 carried a report of some advancement:

On Saturday night a curious piece of mechanism was displayed in Hyde Park: it is constructed so as to convey four different letters the space of a mile in one minute, and return an answer in the space of one minute and a half.

This, I assume, depended on reflecting mirrors and a light source. Each relay was restricted in length of passage by the curvature of the earth. In time electricity was to take over and lead to "signalling through space without wires" in the 1890s (improved by Marconi). Edison's electric lights and power machinery dates from 1878 – an American improvement over many earlier experiments and trials.

Today we live in an age when the kitchen is filled with convenience foods – tins of this or that, packets of dried or frozen commodities, semi-prepared meals can be purchased for future consumption. This has always been the ideal, especially for the traveller or seafarer. I noticed in *The London Gazette* (an offical government publication):

Portable Soup is found a very useful commodity among Gentlemen and Ladies, both on Journey and at Home,

---

* Men, women, and families were sent to Botany Bay for a period of years. Some stayed there, preferring life in Australia to the hard times in England.

by being always handy so that a mess of broth may be made in two minutes at any time, as strong and rich as you please, only with boiling water. As it never spoils if kept dry, therefore it is of vast use at sea...

There are books on every subject, works to widen your knowledge. Old cookery books can help us to understand life and table customs before our time. There are even books on preserved foods – one work I found most interesting was Sue Shephard's *Pickled, Potted and Canned. The Story of Food Preserving* (Headline Book Publishing, 2000). The National Trust has published an informative book by Sara Pastor-Williams, entitled *The Art of Dining. A History of Cooking & Eating* (National Trust Enterprises Ltd., 1993). The various National Trust properties around Great Britain help to show life as it was, and in most cases they will display our ceramics in their correct, mainly 18th-century, setting. Visit these wonderful old homes, or rather great houses, they are an education and a delight.

Well, I have digressed from the specific subject of porcelain. Yet you should know something of the times and customs of the people for whom early British porcelains were made. I have mainly confined my quotations to the 18th century, but in terms of money values and the cost of living, they remained remarkably static – no raging inflation – until the early post-war period, say the 1950s or 1960s.

In 1929, the year of my birth, the authoress Virginia Wolfe wrote in her *A Room of One's Own* – "No force in the World can take from me my £500. Food, house and clothing are mine forever..." Alas if she had lived into the 1970s, the £10 or so a week would not have provided much in the way of a house (with its upkeep – heating, lighting, rates, and perhaps a mortgage), a decent wardrobe, and food. The buying value of the pound had fallen and was to fall further. This state of affairs has not been confined to Britain – it is worldwide, to varying degrees. One of the prime duties of any government is to preserve the value of its currency, to preserve the value of its citizens' savings. It can be a difficult task.

I leave you with a few dates; each event can be researched in depth by visits to your local library.

1768	The Royal Academy established in London.
1773	The Boston Tea Party (still celebrated twice a day in Boston). The start of the American Revolution and the British loss of that important Colony.
1776	The American Declaration of Independence.
1777	The Grand Trunk Canal (later the Trent and Mersey Canal) completed. This linked the Staffordshire Potteries (and other places) with the great port of Liverpool.
1778	The completion of the first iron bridge in the world across the river Severn, near the Caughley porcelain factory and just upstream from the later Coalport works. It is still in existence today.
1786	Anglo-French Trade treaty. Reducing taxes on the importation and exportation of English and French goods. Taxes were always of concern to British porcelain manufacturers.
1791	The Directors of the English East India Company resolved that they would cease their *bulk* importation of Chinese porcelain. The resulting dearth of Chinese porcelain greatly helped British manufacturers.
1798	Nelson's great (night-time) victory over the French Fleet, at the Battle of the Nile.
1805	British naval victory at Trafalgar and the death of Admiral Lord Nelson.
1815	More war. The Battle of Waterloo – a near-run thing, but again ending in British victory over the French army.
1825	The first public passenger carrying steam railway, the Stockton-Darlington railway, opened. The Liverpool-Manchester line commenced in 1830.
1829	The British Police Force was founded by Robert Peel.
1833	Slavery abolished in the British Empire.
1833	The English East India Company's State Monopoly in trade to the East terminated. The trade was open to private enterprise.
1840	Uniform inland postage rate appears in Britain, along with the introduction of the pre-paid stamp – the "Penny Black" and the increase in letters, postal advertising, etc.
1851	The Great Exhibition held in England, which was the first International Exhibition. It attracted goods – of almost every class and make – to "The Crystal Palace" within Hyde Park, London.
1886	Karl Benz, German, held the patent for a petrol-engined motor vehicle. In England the Emancipation Act of 1896 led the way to rapid progress in "horseless carriages", although the speed limit was 12mph (19kmph), until 1903.
1903	The first, short, flight of the Wright brothers in America, which was the birth of air travel.

What changes have been witnessed in a 100 years – the world has, in effect, shrunk.

1914–18 World War I, fought mainly in France. The war to end all wars.

1929 The Wall Street Crash. An American-led financial bombshell that marked my birth that same year.

1939-45 World War II. I will refrain from personal comment. There are libraries of books on all aspects of this conflict.

1968 The first British hovercraft cross-channel service, between Dover and Boulogne.

1969 Man's first landing on the moon, via an American rocket-propelled craft.

1970 Introduction of decimal currency in the United Kingdom, which led to a general marking up of prices!

1973 United Kingdom, or Great Britain (as I prefer), entered the "Common Market".

2002 Twelve European countries all adopted a common currency, the Euro, from 1 January.

Appendix

Registered designs

In 1842* a form of design copyright was introduced to give protection to new shapes or printed decoration on ceramics and other materials. Such shapes or designs needed to be registered at the Design Registry in London, and so consequently they became known as "Registered Shapes" or "Registered Designs". The diamond-shaped device was called the "Registration Mark". The letters or numerals within the four inner angles can be decoded to show the day, the month, and the year of registration, with the "parcel number" – this is, in effect, the entry number in the official file for that date. Pottery and porcelain designs comprised "Class IV", and this is stated above the main diamond shape. The basic arrangement took two forms. From 1842 to 1867, the year letter was shown within the top segment. From 1868 to 1883, the day of the month appeared in this segment and the year was placed on the right. Below are examples of the two versions of the registration device.

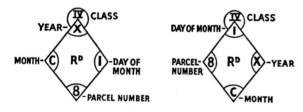

When decoded, such a device shows the earliest possible date of registration – not the precise date of manufacture. Officially the coverage of a registration mark was for a three-year-period, but in practice the registration was often not renewed and the mark remained in use for a much longer period than it should have done. The point to remember is that this device (when clear and correctly decoded!) will only show the earliest possible date of manufacture.

The original entry of each mark used will show the name (and basic address) of the person who registered the shape or pattern. In most (but not all) cases this will be the British manufacturer that produced the object.

The original files that provide this information are held in the Public Record Office at Kew, Surrey (see opposite). They are heavy, dirty, and many in number. I spent years copying the basic facts, and these are tabulated on pp.171–245 of my *New Handbook of British Pottery & Porcelain Marks* (Barrie & Jenkins, London. 1999). This long, unique (copyrighted) list also gives basic information on the subject of the registered entry.

Below I provide the basic decoding information that will enable you to discover the date and parcel (entry) number of a registration.

Table of Registration Marks 1842–83

1842–67 Year = letter at top		1868–83 Year = letter at right	
A = 1845	N = 1864	A =1871	L = 1882
B = 1858	O = 1862	C = 1870	P = 1877
C = 1844	P = 1851	D = 1878	S = 1875
D = 1852	Q = 1866	E = 1881	U = 1874
E = 1855	R = 1861	F = 1873	V = 1876
F = 1847	S = 1849	H = 1869	W = 1878
G = 1863	T = 1867	I = 1872	(1–6 March)
H = 1843	U = 1848	J = 1880	X = 1868
I = 1846	V = 1850	K =1883	Y = 1879
J = 1854	W = 1865		
K = 1857	X = 1842		
L = 1856	Y = 1853		
M = 1859	Z = 1860		

Month letters for both periods are as follows:

A = December	H = April
B = October	I = July
C or O = January	K = November (and December 1860)
D = September	M = June
E = May	R = August (and 1–19 September 1857)
G = February	W = March

* General information on earlier systems is given in *Staffordshire Porcelain* under my editorship (Granada, 1983), appendix III.

Registered numbers

From 1 January 1884 a new system came into being for registering all new products, which meant that the entries were numbered from 1 progressively (we are now in excess of 3 million). These numbers appear on the article, usually prefixed with the abbreviation R^{D}N^O. The number allocated on 1 January of each year from 1884 is given below.

The original records are housed at the Public Record Office, Kew, Richmond, Surrey, TW9 4DU (Tel: 020 8876 3444). Post-1989 records are available on the Patent Office website (www.patent.gov.uk). Click on "designs", then "search our records" for more information.

Table of Registration Numbers 1884–2003

1 = 1884	841040 = 1944	630190 = 1914	965185 = 1974
19754 = 1885	842670 = 1945	644395 = 1915	969249 = 1975
40480 = 1886	845550 = 1946	653521 = 1916	973838 = 1976
64520 = 1887	849730 = 1947	658988 = 1917	978426 = 1977
90483 = 1888	853260 = 1948	662872 = 1918	982815 = 1978
116648 = 1889	856999 = 1949	666128 = 1919	987910 = 1979
141273 = 1890	860854 = 1950	673750 = 1920	993012 = 1980
163767 = 1891	863970 = 1951	680147 = 1921	998302 = 1981
185713 = 1892	866280 = 1952	687144 = 1922	1004456 = 1982
205240 = 1893	869300 = 1953	694999 = 1923	1010583 = 1983
224720 = 1894	872531 = 1954	702671 = 1924	1017131 = 1984
246975 = 1895	876067 = 1955	710165 = 1925	1024174 = 1985
268392 = 1896	879282 = 1956	718057 = 1926	1031358 = 1986
291241 = 1897	882949 = 1957	726330 = 1927	1039055 = 1987
311658 = 1898	887079 = 1958	734370 = 1928	1047799 = 1988
331707 = 1899	891665 = 1959	742725 = 1929	1056078 = 1989
351202 = 1900	895000 = 1960	751160 = 1930	2003720 = 1990
368154 = 1901	899914 = 1961	760583 = 1931	2012047 = 1991
385180 = 1902	904638 = 1962	769670 = 1932	2019933 = 1992
403200 = 1903	909364 = 1963	779292 = 1933	2028115 = 1993
424400 = 1904	914536 = 1964	789019 = 1934	2036116 = 1994
447800 = 1905	919607 = 1965	799097 = 1935	2044227 = 1995
471860 = 1906	924510 = 1966	808794 = 1936	2053121 = 1996
493900 = 1907	929335 = 1967	817293 = 1937	2062149 = 1997
518640 = 1908	934515 = 1968	825231 = 1938	2071520 = 1998
535170 = 1909	939875 = 1969	832610 = 1939	2080158 = 1999
552000 = 1910	944932 = 1970	837520 = 1940	2089210 = 2000
574817 = 1911	950046 = 1971	838590 = 1941	2098500 = 2001
594195 = 1912	955342 = 1972	839230 = 1942	3000500 = 2002
612431 = 1913	960708 = 1973	839980 = 1943	3009770 = 2003

A European Directive was implemented in the UK in December 2001. The new system then recommenced at 3,000,000.

Bibliography

The following reference books are those that I have found particularly helpful, and they have been arranged under different headings, such as those for general reference books, marks, the various factories, and particular shapes.

These selected titles do not include any works on earthenwares, nor do they include price guides (for values, see p.242). Several other specialist "Papers" or important articles are listed in the text, within the relevant chapters.

Many of these standard reference books are now out-of-print, difficult to trace, or costly to purchase. Fortunately libraries are a reliable source. Obviously not every specialist work will be stocked by provincial libraries but they will (for a small administrative fee) seek to obtain a scarce book on short loan for you to consult. The libraries should also be able to produce a list of works by any given author or on most subjects.

The bibliography is then followed by a short list of magazine titles, collectors' associations, and the current, popular, educational seminars and meetings on ceramic subjects. In the latter, specialists present lectures on advertised subjects, questions may be asked of them, and problem pieces may be identified and discussed – but not commercially valued.

General books

Battie, D. (ed.), *Sotheby's Concise Encyclopaedia of Porcelain*, (Conran Octopus, London, 1990).

Bradshaw, P., *18th Century English Porcelain Figures 1745–1795*, (Antique Collectors' Club, Woodbridge, 1981).

Burton, William, *A History and Description of English Porcelain*, (Cassell & Co., London, 1902).

Charleston, R.J. (ed.), *English Porcelain 1745–1850*, (Benn, London, 1965).

Charleston, R.J. and Towner, D. (eds), *English Ceramics, 1580–1830*, (Sotheby Parke Bernet, London, 1977).

Cushion, J. and M., *A Collector's History of British Porcelain*, (Antique Collectors' Club, Woodbridge, 1992).

Eccles, H. and Rackham, B., *Analysed Specimens of English Porcelain*, (Victoria and Albert Museum, London, 1922).

Field, R., *MacDonald Guide to Buying Antique Pottery & Porcelain*, (Wallace-Homestead, Radnor, PA, 1987).

Godden, G.A., *An Illustrated Encyclopaedia of British Pottery and Porcelain*, (Herbert Jenkins [Barrie & Jenkins], London, 1966).

Godden, G.A., *British Porcelain, an Illustrated Guide*, (Barrie & Jenkins, London, 1974, revised edition 1991).

Godden, G., *Eighteenth-Century English Porcelain* (Granada, London, 1985).

Godden, G.A., *Encyclopaedia of British Porcelain Manufacturers*, (Barrie & Jenkins, London, 1988).

Godden, G.A., *Godden's Guide to European Porcelain*, (Barrie & Jenkins, London, 1993). This book is particularly helpful on fakes, Paris porcelain – styles, etc.

Godden, G.A., *Victorian Porcelain*, (Herbert Jenkins, London, 1961).

Godden, G. (ed.), *Staffordshire Porcelain*, (Granada, London, 1983).

Haggar, R.G. and Mankowitz, W., *The Concise Encyclopaedia of English Pottery and Porcelain*, (A. Deutsch, London, 1957).

Honey, W.B., *English Pottery and Porcelain*, (A & C Black, London, 1933, 5th edition 1962).

Honey, W.B., *Old English Porcelain*, (Faber, London, 1928, revised 1977).

Jewitt, L., *The Ceramic Art of Great Britain*, (Virtue & Co., London, 1878, revised edition 1883). A revised and re-illustrated edition covering only the period from 1800 onwards was published by Barrie & Jenkins in 1972. Reprint, Sterling Publishing Co., New York (distributor), 1985.

Lane, A., *English Porcelain Figures of the Eighteenth Century*, (Faber, London, 1961).

Peirce, Donald C., *English Ceramics: The Frances and Emory Cooke Collection*, (High Museum of Art, Atlanta, GA, 1988).

Sandon, H., *British Pottery and Porcelain for Pleasure and Investment*, (J. Gifford, London, 1969).

Sandon, J., *Miller's Guide to Collecting Porcelain*, (Millers, London, 2002).

Sandon, J., *Starting to Collect Antique Porcelain* (Antique Collectors' Club, Woodbridge, 2003 edition)

Savage, G. and Newman, H., *An Illustrated Dictionary of Ceramics*, (Thames & Hudson, London, 1974).

Watney, B., *English Blue and White Porcelain of the 18th Century*, (Faber, London, 1963, revised edition 1973).

Young, H., *English Porcelain 1745–95. Its Makers, Design, Marketing and Consumption*, (V&A Publications, London, 1999).

Mark books

Cushion, J. and Honey, W.B., *Handbook of Pottery and Porcelain Marks*, (Faber, London, 1956 and later editions).

Godden, G.A., *Encyclopaedia of British Porcelain Manufacturers (see General books).

Godden, G.A., *Encyclopaedia of British Pottery and Porcelain Marks*, (Herbert Jenkins (Barrie & Jenkins), London, 1964, revised edition 1991).

Godden, G.A., *New Handbook of British Pottery & Porcelain Marks*, (Barrie & Jenkins, London, 1999).

Haslam, M., *Marks and Monograms of the Modern Movement 1870–1930*, (Lutterworth Press, Guildford and London, 1977).

Henrywood, R.K., *Staffordshire Potters 1781–1900*, (Antique

Collectors' Club, Woodbridge, 2002).

Kowalsky, A. and D., *Encyclopaedia of Marks 1780–1980*, (Schiffer, USA, 1999).

Perrott, E. George, *Pottery & Porcelain Marks, European, Oriental and U.S.A. in Chronological Order*, (Gemini Publications, Bath, 1997).

Yates-Owen, E. and Fournier, R., *British Studio Potters' Marks*, (A. & C. Black, London, 1999).

Blue and white

Fisher, S.W., *English Blue and White Porcelain of the 18th Century*, (Batsford, London, 1947).

Godden, G.A., *Godden's Guide to English Blue and White Porcelain*, (Antique Collectors' Club, Woodbridge, 2004).

Spero, Simon, *The Simpson Collection of 18th Century Blue and White Miniature Porcelain* (not published at time of print).

Watney, B., *English Blue and White Porcelain of the 18th Century*, (Faber, London, 1963, revised edition 1973).

Bow

Adams, E. and Redstone, D., *Bow Porcelain*, (Faber, London, 1981, revised edition 1991).

Begg, Chris, ed., *A Treasure of Bow*, (the Ceramics and Glass Circle of Australia, Hawksburn, 2000).

Bradshaw, P., *Bow Porcelain Figures circa 1748–1774*, (Barrie & Jenkins, London, 1992).

Gabszewicz, A., *Made at New Canton: Bow porcelain from the collection of the London Borough of Newham*, (English Ceramic Circle, London, 2000).

Gabszewicz, A. and Freeman, G., *Bow Porcelain – The Collection Formed by Geoffrey Freeman*, (Lund Humphries, London, 1982).

Tait, H., *British Museum Catalogue of the 1959 Bow Exhibition*, (British Museum, London, 1959).

Bristol

Severne Mackenna, F., *Champion's Bristol Porcelain*, (F. Lewis, Leigh-on-Sea, 1947).

Caughley

Godden, G.A., *Caughley and Worcester Porcelain, 1775–1800*, (Herbert Jenkins, London, 1969, revised edition Antique Collectors' Club, Woodbridge, 1981).

Godden, G.A., *Godden's Guide to English Blue and White Porcelain*, (Chapter XIII), (*see* Blue and white).

Holloway, C. and Marno, F., *Caughley Toy Wares*, exhibition catalogue, (Stockspring Antiques, London, 2001).

Messenger, M., *Caughley Porcelains – A Bi-Centenary Exhibition*, exhibition catalogue, (Shrewsbury Art Gallery, 1972).

Chamberlain-Worcester

Godden, G.A., *Chamberlain-Worcester Porcelain, 1788–1852*, (Barrie & Jenkins, London, 1982).

Chelsea

Adams, E., *Chelsea Porcelain*, (Barrie & Jenkins, London, 1987, revised and enlarged edition British Museum Press, London, 2001).

Austin, John C., *Chelsea Porcelain at Williamsburg,* (Colonial Williamsburg Foundation, Williamsburg, 1977).

Bryant, G.E., *Chelsea Porcelain Toys,* (Medici Society, London, 1925).

Severne Mackenna, F., *Chelsea Porcelain. The Gold Anchor Period*, (F. Lewis, Leigh-on-Sea, 1952).

Severne Mackenna, F., *Chelsea Porcelain. The Red Anchor Wares*, F. Severne Mackenna (F. Lewis, Leigh-on-Sea, 1951).

Severne Mackenna, F., *Chelsea Porcelain. The Triangle and Raised Anchor Wares*, (F. Lewis, Leigh-on-Sea, 1948).

Coalport

Berthoud, M., *The Lost Patterns of John Rose*, (Micawber Publications, Bridgnorth, 2002).

Godden, G.A., *Coalport and Coalbrookdale Porcelains*, (Herbert Jenkins, London, 1970, revised edition Antique Collectors' Club, Woodbridge, 1981).

Godden, G.A., *Godden's Guide to English Blue and White Porcelain*, (Chapter XIV), (*see* Blue and white).

Messenger, M., *Coalport 1795–1926*, (Antique Collectors' Club, Woodbridge, 1995).

Cups

Berthoud, M., *A Compendium of British Cups*, (Micawber Publications, Bridgnorth, 1990).

Berthoud, M., *An Anthology of British Cups*, (Micawber Publications, Bridgnorth, 1982).

Berthoud, M. and Maskell, R., *Cups in Colour*, (Micawber Publications, Bridgnorth, 2003).

Goss, S., *British Tea and Coffee Cups 1745–1940*, (Shire Books, Princes Risborough, 2000)

Daniel

Berthoud, M., *H & R Daniel 1822–1846* (Micawber Publications, Bridgnorth, 1980).

Berthoud, M. and Price, L., *Daniel Patterns on Porcelain*, (Micawber Publications, Bridgnorth, 1997).

Davenport

Lockett, T.A., *Davenport Pottery and Porcelain 1794–1887*, (David & Charles, Newton Abbot, 1972).

Lockett, T.A. and Godden, G.A., *Davenport China, Earthenware and Glass 1794–1887*, (Barrie & Jenkins, London, 1989).

Derby

Barrett, F.A. and Thorpe, A.L., *Derby Porcelain*, (Faber, London, 1971).

Blackwood, R. and Head, C., *Old Crown Derby China Works. The King Street Factory*, 1849–1935, (Landmark Publishing Ltd, Ashbourne, 2003).

Bradley, G., *Derby Porcelain 1750 – 1798*, (T. Heneage & Co., London, 1990).

Bradshaw, P., *Derby Porcelain Figures 1750– 1848*, (Faber, London, 1990).

Gilhespy, F.B., *Crown Derby Porcelain* (F. Lewis, Leigh-on-Sea, 1951)

Gilhespy, F.B., *Derby Porcelain*, (Spring Books, London, 1961).

Gilhespy F.B. and Budd, D.M., *Royal Crown Derby China*, (Charles Skilton, London, 1964).

Godden, G.A., *Godden's Guide to English Blue and White Porcelain*, (Chapter VII), (*see* Blue and white).

Haslem, J., *The Old Derby China Factory, the Workmen and their Productions*, (G. Bell & Sons, London, 1876).

Ledger, A.P., (compiled by), *Derby Porcelain Archive Research. Vol. 2 – The Bedford Street Warehouse and the London China Trade, 1773–1796*, (Derby Museum & Art Gallery, Derby, 2002).

Rice, D.G., *Derby Porcelain, The Golden Years 1750–1770*, (David & Charles, Newton Abbot, 1983).

Sargeant, Margaret, *Royal Crown Derby*, (Shire Publications Ltd, Princes Risborough, 2000).

Twitchett, J., *Derby Porcelain*, (Barrie & Jenkins, London, 1980).

Twitchett, J., *Derby Porcelain, 1748–1848, an Illustrated Guide* (Antique Collectors' Club, Woodbridge, 2002).

Twitchett, J. and Bailey, B., *Royal Crown Derby*, (Antique Collectors' Club, Woodbridge, 1988).

The Derby Porcelain International Society also publishes journals and reports of recent research. Meetings are also held at various venues and visits to museums and collections are organized*.

Doulton

Dale, J., *The Charlton Standard Catalogue of Royal Doulton Figures*, (Charlton Press, Birmingham, second edition 1991).

Eyles, D., *The Doulton Burslem Wares*, (Barrie & Jenkins/Royal Doulton, London, 1980).

Eyles, D., *Royal Doulton 1815–1965*, (Hutchinson, London, 1965).

Eyles, D., Dennis, R., and Irvine, L., *Royal Doulton Figures*, (Royal Doulton/R. Dennis, London 1987 and later editions).

Kovel, R. and T., *The Kovel's Illustrated Price Guide to Royal Doulton*, (Crown, New York, second edition 1984).

Pearson, K., *The Doulton Figures Collectors Handbook*, (Kevin Francis Publishing, London, 1988).

Pollard, R.M., *The Official Price Guide to Royal Doulton*, (House of Collectibles, New York, sixth edition 1988).

Many other works cover both Doulton earthenwares and the porcelains – your local bookseller or library can provide a listing, as can the Royal Doulton International Collectors Club.

Isleworth

Gabszewicz, A. and Jellicoe, R., *Isleworth Porcelain*, exhibition catalogue, (R. Jellicoe, London, 1998).

Godden, G.A., *Godden's Guide to English Blue and White Porcelain*, (Chapter VII), (*see* Blue and white).

Massey, R., Pearce, J., and Howard, R., *Isleworth Pottery and Porcelain, Recent Discoveries*, exhibition catalogue, (Museum of London and E.C.C., London, 2003).

Limehouse

Godden, G.A., *Godden's Guide to English Blue and White Porcelain*, (Chapter IV), (*see* Blue and white).

Various contributors: Kieron Tyler and Roy Stephenson with J. Victor Owen and Christopher Phillpotts, *The Limehouse Porcelain Manufactory. Excavations at 108–116 Narrow Street, London, 1990*, (MoLAS monograph 6, Museum of London, London, 2000).

Limehouse Ware Revealed, a multi-author work edited by David Drakard and published by the English Ceramic Circle in 1993. (ISBN 0.951.6384.3.2)

Liverpool

Berthoud, M., *Patterns on Herculaneum Porcelain*, (Micawber Publications, Bridgnorth, 2002).

Hillis, Dr M., *The Liverpool Porcelains*, (Northern Ceramic Society, 1985).

Jellicoe, R. and Hillis, Dr M., *Liverpool Porcelain of William Reid. A catalogue of porcelain and excavated shards*, (R. Jellicoe, London, 2000).

Smith, A., *The Illustrated Guide to Liverpool Herculaneum Pottery*, (Barrie & Jenkins, London, 1970).

Watney, B., *English Blue and White Porcelain of the 18th Century*, (Faber, London, 1963, revised edition 1973).

Watney, B., *Liverpool Porcelain of the Eighteenth Century*, (Richard Dennis, London, 1997).

Longton Hall

Watney, B., *Excavations at the Longton Hall Porcelain Manufactory*, (Post-medieval archaeology, Vol.27, 1993).

Watney, B., *Longton Hall Porcelain*, (Faber, London, 1957).

Lowestoft

Godden, G.A., *Godden's Guide to English Blue and White Porcelain*, (Chapter IX), (*see* Blue and white).

Godden, G.A., *The Illustrated Guide to Lowestoft Porcelain*, (Herbert Jenkins, London, 1969).

Godden, G.A., *Lowestoft Porcelain*, (Antique Collectors' Club, Woodbridge, 1985).

Smith, S., *Lowestoft Porcelain in Norwich Castle Museum*, Vol.1 "Blue & White", (Norfolk Museum Service, Norwich, 1975).

Smith, S., *Lowestoft Porcelain in Norwich Castle Museum*. Vol.2: "Polychrome Wares", (Norwich Museum Service, Norwich, 1985).

Spelman, W., *Lowestoft China*, (Jarrold & Sons, London, 1905)

Spencer, C., *Early Lowestoft*, (Ainsworth & Nelson, London, 1981).

Lustre

Godden, G.A. and Gibson, M., *Collecting Lustreware*, (Barrie & Jenkins, London, 1991).

Other books on lustrewares are mainly concerned with pottery.

Mason

Godden, G.A., *Godden's Guide to Mason's China and the Ironstone Wares*, (Antique Collectors' Club, Woodbridge, 1980, revised edition 1991).

Godden, G.A., *Godden's Guide to Ironstone, Stone & Granite Wares* (Antique Collectors' Club, Woodbridge, 1999)

Godden, G.A., *The Illustrated Guide to Mason's Patent Ironstone China*, (Barrie & Jenkins, London, 1971).

Haggar, R.G., *The Masons of Lane Delph*, (Lund Humphries, London, 1952).

Haggar, R.G., "Miles Mason", *Transactions of the English Ceramic Circle*, Vol.8, Part 2 (E.C.C., 1972).

Haggar, R.G. and Adams, E., *Mason Porcelain and Ironstone 1796–1853*, (Faber, London, 1977).

Roberts, G.B., *Masons The First Two Hundred Years*, (Merrell Holberton Publishers, London, 1996).

---

* The current (2004) contact address is The Hon. Sec., DPIS, PO Box 6997, Coleshill, Birmingham B46 2LF. Alternatively the Derby City Museum may be able to provide a contact address.

Roberts, G.B. and Twitchett, J., *The Raven Mason Collection. The Catalogue of the Collection at Keele University*, (Keele University Press, Edinburgh, 1997).

Skinner, D. and Young, V., *Miles Mason Porcelain. A Guide to Patterns and Shapes*, (City Museum, Hanley, 1992).

Minton

Atterbury, P. and Batkin, M., *The Dictionary of Minton*, (Antique Collectors' Club, Woodbridge, 1990).

Cumming, N. Robert, *Minton Bone China in the Early Years 1800–1816*, (privately published, Canada, 1988).

Cumming, R. and Berthoud, M., *Minton Patterns of the 1ˢᵗ Period*, (Micawber Publications, Bridgnorth, 1997).

Godden, G., *Minton Pottery and Porcelain of the First Period 1793–1850*, (Herbert Jenkins, London, 1968).

Godden, G., *Victorian Porcelain*, (Herbert Jenkins, London, 1961).

Holt, G., *A Cup of Tea. Treasures for Teatime*, (Pavilion Books, London, 1991).

Jones, J., *Minton, The First Two Hundred Years of Design and Production*, (Swan-Hill Press, Shrewsbury, 1993).

Langford, D., *Regency Minton Porcelain 1800–1815*, (Langford & Clarke, Canterbury, 1997).

Nantgarw

John, W.D., *Nantgarw Porcelain*, (Ceramic Book Co., Newport, 1948, supplement 1956).

Nance, E.M., *The Pottery and Porcelain of Swansea and Nantgarw*, (Batsford, London, 1942).

Williams, R., *Nantgarw Porcelain 1813–1822*, (Friends of Nantgarw China Works Museum, c.1993).

Neale

Edwards, Diana, *Neale Pottery and Porcelain, Its Predecessors and Successors 1763–1820*, (Barrie & Jenkins, 1987).

New Hall

Godden, G.A., *New Hall Porcelains*, (Antique Collectors' Club, Woodbridge, 2004).

Holgate, D., *New Hall*, (Faber, London, 1987).

Holgate, D., *New Hall and its Imitators*, (Faber, London, 1971).

Preller, P., *A Partial Reconstruction of the New Hall Pattern Book*, (P. Preller, Bude, 2003).

de Saye Hutton, A., *A Guide to New Hall Porcelain Patterns*, (Barrie & Jenkins, London, 1990).

Stringer, G.E., *New Hall Porcelain*, (Art Trade Press, London, 1949).

Parian

Atterbury, P. (ed.), *The Parian Phenomenon, a Survey of Victorian Parian Porcelain Statuary and Busts*, (R. Dennis, Shepton Beauchamp, 1989).

Barker, D., *Parian Ware*, (Shire Books, Princes Risborough, 1998).

Godden, G.A., *Victorian Porcelain*, (Herbert Jenkins, London, 1961).

Shinn, C. and D., *The Illustrated Guide to Victorian Parian China*, (Barrie & Jenkins, London, 1971).

Pâte-sur-pâte

Bumpus, Bernard, *Pâte-sur-Pâte, The Art of Ceramic Relief Decoration, 1849–1992*, (Barrie & Jenkins, London, 1993).

Pinxton

Exley, C.L., *The Pinxton China Factory*, (Mr and Mrs Coke-Steel, Sutton-on-the-Hill, 1963).

Gent, N.D., *The Patterns and Shapes of the Pinxton China Factory 1796–1813*, (privately published, Pinxton, 1996).

Sheppard, C.B., *Pinxton Porcelain 1795–1813*, (C.B. Sheppard, Tibshelf, 1996).

Plymouth

Mackenna, F.S., *Cookworthy's Plymouth and Bristol Porcelain*, (F. Lewis, Leigh-on-Sea, 1947).

Watney, B., *English Blue and White Porcelain of the 18th Century*, (Faber, London, 1963, revised edition 1973).

Ridgway

Godden, G.A., *Ridgway Porcelains*, (Antique Collectors' Club, Woodbridge, 1985).

Rockingham

Cox, A. and A., *Rockingham Pottery and Porcelain 1745–1842*, (Faber, London, 1983).

Cox, A. and A., *Rockingham 1745–184*, (Antique Collectors' Club, Woodbridge, 2001).

Cox, A. and A., *The Rockingham Works*, (Sheffield City Museum, Sheffield, 1974).

Eaglestone, A.A. and Lockett, T.A., *The Rockingham Pottery*, (Rotherham Library and Museum, Rotherham, 1964. Revised edition 1973, David & Charles, Newton Abbot).

Rice, D.G., *The Illustrated Guide to Rockingham Pottery and Porcelain*, (Barrie & Jenkins, London, 1971).

Rice, D.G., *Rockingham Ornamental Porcelains*, (Adam Publishing Co., London, 1965).

Spode

Copeland, R., *Spode and Copeland Marks*, (Studio Vista, 1993).

Copeland, R., *Spode's Willow Pattern and Other Designs After the Chinese*, (Studio Vista, London, 1980, reprinted 1990).

Drakard, D. and Holdway, P., *Spode Printed Ware*, (Longman, London, 1983).

Hayden, A., *Spode and His Successors*, (Cassell, London, 1924).

Whiter, L., *Spode. A History of the Family and Wares from 1733 to 1833*, (Barrie & Jenkins, London, 1970 and later editions).

Wilkinson, Vega, *Spode – Copeland – Spode. The Works and Its People*, (Antique Collectors' Club, Woodbridge, 2002).

Swansea

John, W.D., *Swansea Porcelain*, (Ceramic Book Co., Newport, 1957).

Jones, A.E. and Joseph, Sir L., *Swansea Porcelain, Shapes and Decoration*, (D. Brown & Sons, Cowbridge, 1988).

Nance, E.M., *The Pottery and Porcelain of Swansea and Nantgarw*, (Batsford, London, 1942).

Teapots

Emmerson, R., *British Teapots and Tea Drinking 1700–1850*, (HMSO, London, 1992).

Miller, P. and Berthoud, M., *An Anthology of British Teapots*, (Micawber Publications, 1985).

Sandon, Henry, *Coffee Pots and Teapots for the Collector*, (John Bartholomew & Son, Edinburgh, 1973).

Vauxhall

Godden, G.A., *Godden's Guide to English Blue and White Porcelain*, (Chapter VI), (*see* Blue and white).

Worcester

Banyan, L., French, N., and Sandon, J., *Worcester Blue & White Porcelain 1751–1790*, (Barrie & Jenkins, London, 1981 and later editions).

Barrett, F.A., *Worcester Porcelain and Lund's Bristol*, (Faber, London, 1953, revised edition 1966).

Binns, R.W., *A Century of Potting in the City of Worcester*, (Quaritch, London, 1865, second edition 1877).

Binns, R.W., *Worcester China, A record of the work of forty-five years, 1852–1897*, (Quaritch, London, 1897).

Godden, G.A., *Godden's Guide to English Blue and White Porcelain*, (Chapters V and XII), (*see* Blue and white).

Marshall, H. Rissik, *Coloured Worcester Porcelain of the First Period*, (Ceramic Book Co., Newport, 1954).

Reynolds, D., *Worcester Porcelain 1751–1783, The Marshall Collection*, (Phaidon/Christie's, London, 1989).

Sandon, H., *The Dictionary of Worcester Porcelain 1852 to the Present Day*, (Antique Collectors' Club, Woodbridge, 2001).

Sandon, H., *Flight & Barr Worcester Porcelains 1783–1840*, (Antique Collectors' Club, Woodbridge, 1978).

Sandon, H., *The Illustrated Guide to Worcester Porcelain*, (Herbert Jenkins, London, 1969).

Sandon, H., *Royal Worcester Porcelain from 1862 to the Present Day*, (Barrie & Jenkins, London, 1973).

Sandon, H. and J., *The Sandon Guide to Royal Worcester Figures 1900–1970*, (Alderman Press, London, 1987).

Sandon, J., *The Dictionary of Worcester Porcelain: Vol. 1. 1751–1851*, (Antique Collectors' Club, Woodbridge, 1993).

Shirley, D., *A Guide to the Dating of Royal Worcester Porcelain Marks from 1862*, (Privately published, 1999).

Spero, S., *Worcester Porcelain – The Klepser Collection*, (Lund Humphries, Aldershot, 1984).

Spero, S. and Sandon, J., *Worcester Porcelain 1751–1790. The Zorensky Collection*. (Antique Collectors' Club, Woodbridge, 1997).

Collectors' seminars etc

In recent years several organizations have arranged courses, study weekends, and seminars. These can be most instructive and interesting, as leading authorities are available to share their knowledge and be questioned. Information on these events can be obtained from the following places (other, similar courses may be advertised in collectors' magazines):

The Secretary, Morley College Ceramic Circle, Morley College, 61 Westminster Bridge Road, London SE1.

Northern Ceramic Society Seminars (various locations, as advertised).

Geoffrey Godden's "House Parties" held in the Cotswolds. Information from Geoffrey Godden, 3 The Square, Findon, West Sussex BN14 0TE.

Some dealers, such as Mrs Richards of Mercury Antiques in London, also hold exhibitions and lecture meetings (*see* p.230). Such events are normally advertised in the main collectors' magazines, such as *Collectors Guide*.

Antique trade associations

There are two main British associations that the majority (but not all) of leading dealers belong to. These associations impose strict conditions on the quality of stock, knowledge, and codes of practice, and they are:

The British Antique Dealers Association (BADA), established in 1918: 20 Rutland Gate, London SW7 1BD; www.bada.org

The London and Provincial Antique Dealers Association (LAPADA), established in 1974: 535 Kings Road, London SW10 0SZ; www.lapada.co.uk

American and Canadian associations include:

The Art and Antique Dealers League of America: 1040 Madison Avenue, New York, NY 10021; www.artandantiquedealersleague.com

The National Antique & Art Dealers Association of America, Inc.: 220 East 57th Street, New York, NY 10022; www.naadaa.org

Art Dealers Association of Canada: 55 St Clair Avenue West, Suite 255, Toronto, Ontario, M4V 2Y7; www.ad-ac.ca

The secretaries of each association should be able to supply lists of members, but remember that not all members will be ceramic specialists, or even stock any pottery or porcelain.

A book that may help in any searches for porcelain on the Internet is:

Edwards, S., Ellis, P., and Hanes, J. (contributors), *Miller's Antiques, Art & Collectables on the Web*, (Miller's, London, 2002).

Collectors' magazines etc

The main magazines that may be expected to include (on a reasonably regular basis) articles of interest to collectors of English porcelain include:

Antique Dealer and Collectors Guide, Statuscourt Ltd., PO Box 805, Greenwich, London SE10 8TD.

The *Antiques Trade Gazette,* a weekly mainly angled at the Trade, can be of interest as it contains reports on the major auction sales, giving prices realized for the main lots. In addition to such reports on past sales, the major auctioneers advertise their forthcoming sales.

The *Antiques Magazine* (HP Publishing, 2 Hampton Court Road, Harborne, Birmingham, B17 9AE) fulfils a similar function but of course both cover the whole field of antiques, not only ceramics. I should also mention *Antique Collecting*, which is the journal of the Antique Collectors' Club, the address of which is Sandy Lane, Old Martlesham, Woodbridge, Suffolk IP12 4SD, and *Art Ceramics*, Wedgwood Society of New York, 5 Dogwood Court, Glen Head, NY 11545, USA.

Transactions of the English Ceramic Circle are also highly informative, as are the newsletters and journals of the Northern Ceramic Society. The Membership Secretary of the latter is currently M.S. Cole, The Old Post Office, Maer, Staffordshire ST5 5EF[**]. These, and other, societies organize interesting lectures and exhibitions (*see*, for example, under "Derby").

Several other general collectors' magazines are published – titles and details should be available from public libraries or copies obtainable from major newsagents.

[**] The Potteries Museum at Hanley, Stoke-on-Trent, Staffordshire ST1 3DW, should be able to provide updated details of the Society's officers.

Index

Acknowledgements

Many of the questions that I have tried to answer in this book were first posed to me by collectors, when they visited my former showrooms or attended my study weekends and lectures, and so I am greatly indebted to numerous collectors who have pointed out to me various aspects of collecting that are not covered in the so-called standard reference books. I am regretfully unable to acknowledge each collector's assistance, indeed I do not know all their names, but many readers may well recognize their own questions as they read this book and, if this is the case, please accept my thanks.

To a great degree the many illustrations in this book have been drawn from objects in my own collection or from examples formerly in the stock of "Geoffrey Godden, chinaman" or from the stock of the parent firm "Godden of Worthing Ltd", which was founded by my grandfather in 1900.

I am most grateful to the following individuals, firms, and museums for their generous assistance in supplying photographs and to the many photographers who produced such excellent reproductions. (Articles credited to business firms or auction houses will probably not still be in their ownership.)

Mrs Elizabeth Adams, Paul Atterbury, Norman Bayliss, Michael Berthoud, Miss A. Blist, Bonhams, W.A. Bowler, Gilbert Bradley, P.A. Britain, The British Museum, Mrs M. Browne, Miss Vera Browne, Mrs Margaret Cadman, Castle Museum, Norwich, E.H. Chandler, Christies, Robert Copeland, J.A. Davidson, Mr and Mrs Roger Edmundson, Harry Frost, Mr and Mrs J. Godden, Godden of Worthing Ltd, Miranda Goodby, Jonathan Gray, Guildhall Library, Mr and Mrs Reg Haggar, Mrs S. Halls, Mr and Mrs Rodney Hampson, Miss J. Hepworth, Dr and Mrs M. Hillis, David Holgate, Dr P. Homefield, Ray Howard, Ironbridge Gorge Museum Trust and Staff, Roderick Jellicoe, Keele University Library and Staff, Barry Lamb, Liverpool City Museum, Terence A. Lockett, Barry Lomax, John V.G. Mallet, Mintons, Museum of London, Nicholas G. Panes, E.H. Parker, H. Peat, Phillips (now Bonhams), Jackie Pierce, Roger Pomfret, The Potteries Museum, The Public Record Office, Mrs L. Richards, Miss Gaye Blake Roberts, Bill Saks, Henry Sandon, John Sandon, Sothebys, Simon Spero, Victoria and Albert Museum, Mrs Sadia Walsh, Dr Bernard Watney, Mrs D. Williams, Frank Wilson, Worcester Works Museum, Worthing Public Library, Revd Maurice Wright, Hilary Young.

The majority of the colour photographs included in this work have been posed and taken by various directors and staff of my local, long-established, professional firm – Walter Gardiner Photography. Their work includes all groups credited to Godden of Worthing or to other Godden ownerships. I am most grateful for their expertise.

I also record my gratitude to a team of typists who have translated my hand-written manuscript into a tidy typescript acceptable, I trust, to my publishers. These patient ladies are Mrs Barbara Keenan, Jackie Tulett, and Mrs Jan Welch.

To my wife Jean, my gratitude for bearing so well her solitude while I have been all but locked away preparing this work when I should have been helping her in so many ways, and to our son Jonathan, his wife Sally (and young Hannah) for their interest in my porcelains. This interest has prompted me to pass on my experiences, gained over more than 50 years of collecting, dealing in, and lecturing on British porcelains. It has been a team effort, which I trust will help future generations of collectors.

Geoffrey Godden
Findon, West Sussex

Additional note

It should be noted in reference to the captions that the dates given can only be approximate, but they should be correct to plus or minus five years. The sizes given, while they relate to the example illustrated, may well not relate to similar examples – as most objects were made in various stock sizes. Yet the sizes given against my illustrations are correct to a quarter of an inch. Unless otherwise stated the examples are unmarked, as the majority of 18th- and early 19th-century English porcelains do not bear a helpful trademark.